FAMILY–SCHOOL LINKS
How Do They Affect
Educational Outcomes?

FAMILY–SCHOOL LINKS
How Do They Affect
Educational Outcomes?

Edited by
Alan Booth
Judith F. Dunn
Pennsylvania State University

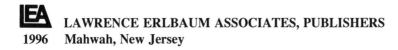
LAWRENCE ERLBAUM ASSOCIATES, PUBLISHERS
1996   Mahwah, New Jersey

Lawrence Erlbaum Associates, Inc., Publishers
10 Industrial Avenue
Mahwah, New Jersey 07430

Library of Congress Cataloging-in-Publication Data

Family–school links : how do they affect educational outcomes? /
   edited by Alan Booth, Judith F. Dunn.
      p.   cm.
   Includes bibliographical references and index.
   ISBN 0-8058-1840-5
   1. Home and school—United States. 2. Academic achievement—
United States. 3. Family—United States. I. Booth, Alan, 1935–
II. Dunn, Judith F., 1939–
LC225.3.F387 1995
371.19′312—dc20   95-20987
                                       CIP

Printed in the United States of America
10 9 8 7 6 5 4 3 2 1

Contents

Preface

The topic of the links between families and schools and how these affect children's educational achievement encompasses a host of questions, each of key social and educational significance. How far does parental involvement in schools affect children's experiences and achievement at school? What explains the great differences between schools, families, and communities in the extent of such involvement? Are these differences a matter of school practices, or do they reflect much broader social and cultural divisions? What is the nature of the impact of schools on children and their families? And, most importantly, how can family–school partnerships be fostered in a way that helps children?

The chapters in this book address these questions and related issues. The authors take very different perspectives, highlight different aspects of the issues, and suggest widely differing answers to the questions. The chapters are based on the presentations and discussions from a national symposium on family–school links held at the Pennsylvania State University October 31–November 1, 1994, as the second in a series of annual symposia focused on family issues. The symposium was organized around four overarching questions; for each of these four themes, there was a lead paper, followed by three discussants' papers. These themes form the four sections of the book, and they are followed by a final overview chapter.

In the first section of the book, the chapters focus on how families and schools can work together to promote children's education and school success. In the lead chapter, Eccles and Harold review the evidence on the extent and the sequelae of parental involvement, and present findings from two important large scale studies, conducted in Chicago and in Maryland. Their data show that parents and teachers can play a critical role if they work together, but note that although both teachers and parents think collaborative links are important, they are not as involved as either group would like to be, and that there is a drop in such collaboration as children move from elementary to middle school. Eccles and Harold provide recommendations for ways to increase parental involvement—especially at home, the place where parents chiefly participate in their children's education. Practical recommendations are prominent, too, in the chapter by Haynes and Ben-Avie discussing Eccles and Harold's contribution. Haynes and Ben-Avie draw on Comer's program to provide a guide for how a framework for collaboration might be developed. They argue that parent participation in school programs can be sustained—and is not a transitory fad of educationalists.

A more cautious, pessimistic note is struck in the next two chapters. First, Dornbusch and Glasgow emphasize the key importance of structural factors that either promote or impede family involvement in children's and adolescent's school experiences and success. Specifically, they argue that forms of school organization, tracking, social networks, bilingual education, and ethnic-specific parenting practices are all key to the nature of family–school collaboration. They note, for instance, that ethnic differences in parental behavior and values *must* be taken into consideration in framing strategies. They agree with Eccles and Harold that parents *do* continue to have an impact on their children's educational success through adolescence, even though parents, teachers, and students do not share this belief.

Annette Lareau takes a perspective on parental involvement that differs very much from that of Eccles and her colleagues. She draws on her study of Caucasian and African-American children and their families to argue that the impact of class differences in social networks is crucially important; she shows that there was little agreement between parents and educators in her study about child rearing, or about responsibility for education. There are also key differences in power between teachers and parents: Teachers may feel powerless and frustrated, but they can in fact prevent children from passing a grade, and can suspend them from school. Working class parents, she argues, often perceive educators as threats to their families. Better communication, she comments, cannot always resolve deeply felt conflicting worldviews.

The second section considers the question "How do school processes affect children and their families?" In their lead chapter, Alexander and Entwisle consider three possibilities: (a) that schools may compensate for initial inequalities that students bring to school, (b) that schools reinforce initial differences, to increase those inequalities during students' school careers, and (c) that schools are neutral in this regard—that they preserve but do not magnify initial inequalities. The authors draw on their Beginning School Study data to show that "family disadvantage translates into educational disadvantage right at the start of children's formal schooling, and that the gap between lower and upper SES children's test scores widens over the years." However, they argue that their data do not imply that schools do little to compensate for family disadvantage. Rather, their data indicate that it is during the summer months that the upper SES children move ahead of the lower SES children. So, although the authors argue for early interventions, improved tracking procedures, and a "better school climate," they emphasize that such school-based solutions can only be expected to make a relatively small impact in the face of the powerful forces outside the school in the lives of disadvantaged children.

The three chapters that discuss Alexander and Entwisle's chapter acknowledge the significance of Alexander and Entwisle's data, though they take issue with some of the interpretations of the findings. Cook argues that the data in fact show that although there are likely to be summer learning differentials, these operate increasingly less strongly with each passing school year. Summer and year-round programs in communally organized schools are recommended by Gamoran—referring to the significance of social networks stressed by Lareau. Gamoran points out that the significance of SES inequality may be different at elementary and at secondary school levels, and that tracking leads to an increase in inequality by social background within the school. At the secondary level, inequality grows in the school year as well as during the summer.

The theme that schools by themselves cannot make up for the lack of material resources and intellectual opportunities that many disadvantaged students face outside school is taken up again by Goldenberg. He urges those working in schools to focus on educational productivity, rather than on the hugely intractable challenge of eliminating the SES inequalities. To illustrate his case he draws on his own programs for improving the academic achievement of Latino immigrant children, which show encouraging improvements in literacy.

The third section asks whether and how family and household structure are related to variations in parental involvement in children's education. In his lead chapter, Zill examines a range of outcomes—not only scholastic achievement but problems such as suspensions, grade repeats, and drop-outs. Summarizing the data from several large-scale surveys, he shows that there are indeed differences in these outcomes for children growing up in mother-father families, divorced, single-parent, and remarried families, even when differences in economic and demographic factors are controlled. Zill criticizes the view that these patterns are attributable largely to the economic disadvantage experienced by those in single-parent families, pointing out that children in stepfamilies—with less economic disadvantage than those from single-parent families—have achievement and misconduct problems that are almost as frequent as those of children from single-parent families. Rather, he argues that, for behavior problems, higher levels of parental involvement were associated with better outcomes in all family types.

How the association between income and educational achievement should be interpreted, and what its policy implications might be, is a controversial issue that runs throughout the three chapters discussing Zill's chapter. Mare reminds us that although the findings linking family structure to school achievement are relatively consistent across the data sets, they do not overshadow the key impact of SES on educational success. He points out that income redistribution is indeed an effective, feasible policy instrument. In her discussion, Menaghan sets out the problems in attributing *causal* status to current family structure, highlighting the variables that may lead to early pregnancy, dropout from school, and subsequent work or marital problems. Drawing on her own research, she argues that the changes in employment opportunities and in labor force participation need to be taken into account *as well as* changes in family arrangements, and that families' interactions and involvement with children are dependent not only (or even chiefly) on family structure variations; rather, they are affected by a wide array of resources and vulnerabilities, which are importantly linked to employment quality and to culturally shaped gender roles. Her conclusion is that we need to focus on the social factors that influence family composition and interaction as much as on the effects on children.

Scott-Jones' discussion of Zill's chapter centers on three concerns: (a) the size of differences in children's outcome between the family structure groups (which she views as small), (b) the lack of information from these large-scale surveys about family ecology, and (c) the lack of precision in the outcome measures. She then considers the role of ethnicity, pointing out the evidence from McLanahan and Sandefur's data cited by Zill, that the proportionate increase in dropout rates for children from single-parent families (compared with those from mother-father families) is greatest for Caucasian students, followed by Hispanic students, and least for African-American students. Citing this and other evidence—such as the fact that historical changes in educational attainment have not paralleled the changes in family structure—she argues that it is important to examine variables such as ethnicity and parental educational level as well as family make-up. She concurs with Mare that although an adequate family income will not guarantee educational success, it will greatly increase the likelihood of children's success at school.

The implications of what has been learned from research into family–school links for policy and for intervention, raised and discussed in each of the chapters in the first three sections of the book, take center stage in the final section. In her lead chapter, Epstein reviews the history of this field of study of connections between families and schools, and documents how the questions asked have changed—for example, from "Are families important for success at school?" to "How can schools help all families?" She provides an overview to her approach to intervention, and "unpacks" her general emphasis on communication, with a discussion of the six types of involvement that her programs stress: assistance in parenting, communication with families about school programs and student progress, improvement in volunteering programs, learning activities at home, including families in decision making at schools, and coordinating the community resources to strengthen both schools and families. She looks to the future by highlighting five topics that will benefit from the collaborative attention of researchers, policymakers, and educators: partnerships at transition points in school careers; partnerships at the high school level; connections between communities and schools; the role of students themselves in family–school partnerships; and different forms of collaborative research by those involved in policy, research, and teaching.

Two of the discussions of her chapter consider policy makers' involvement in fostering family–school links, the first at the federal and the second at the state level. Moles discusses the new Federal education initiatives—new laws such as the Goals 2000: Educate America Act, 1994, which includes a new National Education Goal for parent participation. A second new law, the Elementary and Secondary Education Act of 1994, reorganizes the aid to low-income and low-achieving students, and for many programs requires consultation with parents in reviewing school plans. He reviews research and policy links currently being explored by the U.S. Department of Education, and the white paper called *Strong Families, Strong Schools.*

Lloyd's chapter describes a series of programs presently being conducted in Utah—a model framework based on Epstein's work, in which the programs specifically attempt to implement the six types of involvement. In contrast, Lichter takes a very different view from that of Epstein and several of the earlier chapters, arguing that the responsibility—and the blame—for school problems and children's academic failures lie not with the schools but with the family. He criticizes the implicit premise of Epstein's approach—that schools can compensate for what he sees as deficits in disadvantaged families. It is a controversial stance; however, he comments that his point is not to endorse a "Bell Curve" conclusion but to urge education researchers to be explicit about their goals: Are these to achieve academic productivity for all or to reduce academic inequality across different groups?

In the final chapter, Bierman draws together common threads running through the book, and highlights the diversity of perspectives. Her discussion focuses especially on intervention issues; she points out the complexity of addressing the causal issues, as well as the factors contributing to patterns of parenting children in disadvantaged groups, and she highlights some useful research strategies and the relatively neglected developmental issues.

Our goal in organizing the conference and the book was to provide the reader with current information on what is known about family–school–community links, and to provoke new ways of thinking about these links and their implications for children's education and well-being. The lively debate and the vigor with which diverse viewpoints are expressed in what follows reflect the sense of urgency among all of our contributors about these issues, and their concern that we should make progress toward ensuring a better future for all of our children. Educational opportunities—at present notably unequal for children from different backgrounds—play a key role in those futures.

ACKNOWLEDGMENTS

There are many to thank for assistance with the symposium. We are indebted to the Pennsylvania State University Population Research Institute, the Center for the Study of Child and Adolescent Development, Department of Psychology, Department of Sociology, Intercollege Research Programs, and the College of Liberal Arts for funding the symposium. We appreciate the advice and encouragement, throughout the process of planning and conducting the symposium, of members of the Population Research Institute and the Center for the Study of Child and Adolescent Development. The contributions of Joy Barger, Michelle Gingery, Cassie Johnstonebaugh, Sondra Morrison, Sherry Yocum, and Chuck Herd in assisting with the administration of the symposium were invaluable. Special thanks to Professors Nan Crouter, David Eggebeen, Dennis Hogan, and Susan McHale for their excellent work in presiding over the four sessions, and for their contributions to the flow of ideas during each session.

FAMILIES AND SCHOOLS: HOW CAN THEY WORK TOGETHER TO PROMOTE CHILDREN'S SCHOOL SUCCESS?

1

▼▼▼▼▼▼▼

Family Involvement in Children's and Adolescents' Schooling

Jacquelynne S. Eccles
University of Michigan

Rena D. Harold
Michigan State University

We have known for some time that parents play a critical role in both their children's academic achievement and their children's socioemotional development (e.g., Clark, 1983; Comer, 1980, 1988; Eccles, Arbreton, et al., 1993; Eccles-Parsons, Adler, & Kaczala, 1982; Epstein, 1983, 1984; Marjoribanks, 1979). It is only recently, however, that researchers have studied the role schools play in encouraging and facilitating parents' roles in children's academic achievement. Critical to this role is the relationship that develops between parents and teachers and between communities and schools. Although a relatively new research area, there is increasing evidence that the quality of these links influences children's and adolescents' school success (e.g., Comer, 1980; Comer & Haynes, 1991; Epstein, 1982, 1987; 1990; Stevenson & Baker, 1987; Zigler, 1979), in part because high quality linkages make it easier for parents and teachers to work together in facilitating children's intellectual development (e.g., Bronfenbrenner, 1974, 1979; Epstein, 1983, 1986; Epstein & Dauber, 1988; Jacobs, 1983; Stevenson & Baker, 1987). Yet, mounting evidence suggests that parents and teachers are not as involved with each other as they would like to be. Several studies find that parents want to be more involved with their children's education and would like more information and help from the schools in order to meet this goal (Baker & Stevenson, 1986; Comer, 1980, 1988; Dauber & Epstein, 1989; Dornbusch & Ritter, 1988; Leitch & Tangri, 1988; Rich, 1985). Teachers also want more contact with parents (Carnegie Foundation, 1988; Epstein & Becker, 1982). Furthermore, the situation gets worse as children move from elementary school into secondary school, when parents' active involvement at the school declines dramatically (Carnegie Corporation, 1989; Epstein, 1986).

The message, then, seems clear: Both teachers and parents think collaborative involvement in children's education is important. So why are parents and teachers not more involved with each other? This question usually takes the form of "why aren't parents more involved at school?" and we discuss a variety of reasons why this is true (e.g., time, energy and/or economic resources; familiarity with the curriculum and confidence in one's ability to help; attitudes regarding the appropriate role for parents to play at various ages; and prior experiences with the schools that have left some parents disaffected). But, even more importantly, the extent of family–school collaboration is affected by various school and teacher practices, characteristics related to reporting practices, attitudes regarding the families of the children in the school, and both interest in and understanding of how to effectively involve parents. There is mounting evidence that specific school and teacher practices are a major factor influencing parent involvement (Dauber & Epstein, 1989; Epstein, 1986; Epstein & Dauber, 1991). Furthermore, the power of schools and teachers to influence parent involvement and to improve parent–school links has been demonstrated even with hard-to-reach parents (e.g., Comer, 1980, 1988; Epstein, 1990). According to Epstein (1990): "Status variables are not the most important measures for understanding parent involvement. At all grade levels, the evidence suggests that school policies and teacher practices and family practices are more important than race, parent education, family size, marital status, and even grade level in determining whether parents continue to be part of their children's education" (p. 109). So why aren't parents more involved at school? Why is it so difficult for schools and families to work together more effectively in educating children?

To fully understand what is limiting parent involvement, a general model of parent involvement is needed. Presenting such a model is a primary goal of this chapter. Another goal is to summarize the results of two studies designed to investigate this model. The first study—The Michigan Childhood and Beyond Study (MCABS)—focuses on the elementary school years. The second study—The Maryland Adolescent Growth in Context Study (MAGICS)—focuses on the junior high school years. For each of these studies we present findings regarding the amount and type of parent involvement in their children's intellectual education. When possible, we compare these findings with parents' more general levels of involvement in other aspects of their children's lives, particularly in the development of their children's athletic abilities. We then summarize preliminary analyses of the predictors of parent involvement outlined in Fig. 1.1. In these summaries, we focus on the proximal influences on parent involvement both at home and school. Finally, we make recommendations regarding better strategies for more effective collaboration between schools and parents in the service of children's education.

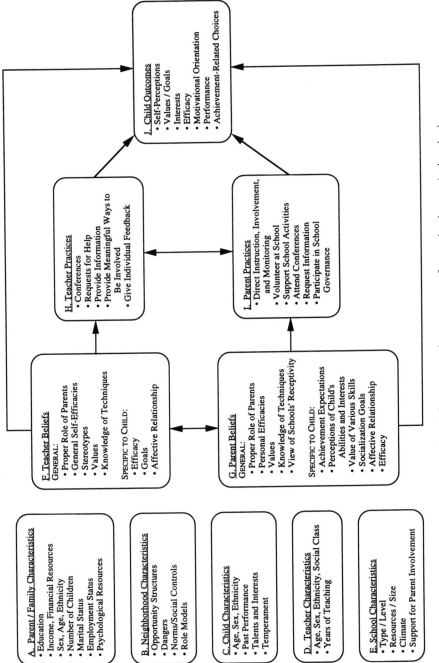

FIG. 1.1. A model of the influences on and consequences of parent involvement in the schools.

INFLUENCES ON PARENT INVOLVEMENT

As noted previously, a theoretical framework or model is needed to guide an analysis of effective parent involvement. One such model is presented in Fig. 1.1. This model provides a framework for thinking about the dynamic processes that underlie parents' involvement in their children's education (Eccles & Harold, 1993). It treats parent involvement as both an outcome of parent, teacher, and child influences, and as a predictor of child outcomes. It also suggests a framework for thinking more generally about the ways in which both schools and parents influence children's school performance.

In Fig. 1.1, we hypothesize that there are a variety of influences on parent involvement. The first set of influences (commonly referred to as *exogenous variables*—variables that have indirect or more global and removed effects on parent involvement) are summarized in the left column of Fig. 1.1. They include various family/parent characteristics, neighborhood/community influences, child characteristics, general teacher characteristics, and school-structural and general-climate characteristics. We have included no arrows connecting these five boxes with the others in the model because these variables have both direct and indirect effects on all of the other boxes. The second column (boxes F and G) includes teacher and parent beliefs and attitudes. This model assumes these beliefs and attitudes affect each other and have a direct effect on the two boxes in the third column, namely, specific teacher practices (box H) and specific parent practices (box I). Finally, the variables listed in boxes F, G, H, and I are assumed to affect directly the child outcomes listed in the last column (box J). This model summarizes a wide range of possible relations among the many listed influences. For example, the impact of the exogenous variables listed in boxes A, B, C, D, and E on teachers' practices of involving parents (box H) are proposed to be mediated by teachers' beliefs systems (box F) including their stereotypes about various parents' ability and willingness to help their children in different academic subjects. Some of the child outcome variables listed in box I are identical (or very similar) to the child characteristics in box C. This overlap is intentional and captures the cyclical nature of the relations outlined in the model. Today's child outcomes become tomorrow's child characteristics; so the cycle continues over time. A more detailed discussion of the most important of these many influences follows.

Parent/Family Characteristics

Numerous studies document the relation between parent involvement and such characteristics as family income, parents' education level, ethnic background, marital status, parents' age and sex, number of children, and parents' working status (e.g., Baker & Stevenson, 1986; Bradley, Caldwell, & Elardo, 1977; Bradley, Caldwell, & Rock, 1988; Clark, 1983; Coleman & Hoffer, 1987; Coleman et al., 1966; Corno, 1980; Eccles-Parsons, 1983; Epstein, 1990; Harold-Goldsmith,

Radin, & Eccles, 1988; Marjoribanks, 1979). For example, better educated parents are more involved both in school and at home than other parents; parents with fewer children are more involved at home; but family size does not affect the amount of involvement at the school; and employed parents are less likely to be involved at school but are equally involved at home (Dauber & Epstein, 1989). The following parent/family characteristics are also likely to be important:

1. Social and psychological resources available to the parent (e.g., social networks, social demands on one's time, parents' general mental and physical health, neighborhood resources, and parents' general coping strategies).

2. Parents' efficacy beliefs (e.g., parents' confidence that they can help their child with schoolwork, parents' view of how their competence to help their children with schoolwork changes as the children enter higher school grades and encounter more specialized subject areas, and parents' confidence that they can have an impact on the school by participating in school governance).

3. Parents' perceptions of their child (e.g., parents' confidence in their child's academic abilities, parents' perceptions of the child's receptivity to help from their parents, parents' educational and occupation expectations and aspirations for the child, and parents' view of the options actually available for their child in the present and the future).

4. Parents' assumptions about both their role in their children's education and the role of educational achievement for their child (e.g., what role the parents would like to play in their children's education, how they think this role should change as the children get older, how important they believe participation in school governance is, and what they believe are the benefits to their children of doing well in school and having parents who are highly involved at their children's school).

5. Parents' attitude toward the school (e.g., what role they believe the school wants them to play, how receptive they think the school is to their involvement both at home and at school, the extent to which they think the school is sympathetic to their child and to their situation, their previous history of negative and positive experiences at school, their belief that teachers only call them in to give them bad news about their child or to blame them for problems their children are having at school versus a belief that the teachers and other school personnel want to work with them to help their child).

6. Parents' ethnic, religious, and/or cultural identities (e.g., the extent to which ethnicity, religious, and/or cultural heritage are critical aspects of the parents' identity and socialization goals, the relationship between the parents' conceptualization of their ethnic, religious, and/or cultural identities and their attitudes toward parent involvement and school achievement, and the extent to which they think the school supports them in helping their children learn about their ethnic, religious, and/or cultural heritage).

7. Parents' general socialization practices (e.g., how does the parent usually handle discipline and issues of control versus autonomy, and how does the parent usually manage the experiences of their children).

8. Parents' history of involvement in their children's education (e.g., parents begin accumulating experiences with the school as soon as their children begin their formal education. Parents have also had their own experiences with schools as they as grow up. These experiences undoubtedly affect parents' attitudes toward and interest in involvement with their children's schools and teachers).

Community Characteristics

Evidence also suggests that neighborhood characteristics such as cohesion, social disorganization, social networking, resources and opportunities, and the presence of undesirable and dangerous opportunities affect family involvement (e.g., Coleman et al., 1966; Eccles, McCarthy, et al., 1993; Furstenberg, 1993; Laosa, 1984; Marjoribanks, 1979). These factors are associated with variations in both parents' beliefs and practices, and opportunity structures in the child's environment. For example, Eccles, Furstenberg, Cook, Elder, and Sameroff are studying the relation of family management strategies to neighborhood characteristics as part of their involvement with the MacArthur Network on Successful Adolescent Development of Youth in High-Risk Settings. These investigators are especially interested in how families try to provide both good experiences and protection for their children when they live in high-risk neighborhoods—neighborhoods with few resources and many potential risks and hazards. To study this issue, they are conducting two survey interview studies (one of approximately 500 families living in high- to moderate-risk neighborhoods in inner-city Philadelphia and the other of approximately 1,400 families living in a wide range of neighborhoods in a large county in Maryland). Initial results suggest that families who are actively involved with their children's development and in their children's schooling use different strategies depending on the resources available in their neighborhoods. Families living in high-risk, low-resource neighborhoods rely more on in-home management strategies to both help their children develop talents and skills and to protect their children from the dangers in the neighborhood; families in these neighborhoods also focus more attention on protecting their children from danger than on helping their children develop specific talents. In contrast, families in less risky neighborhoods focus more on helping their children develop specific talents and are more likely to use neighborhood resources, such as organized youth programs, to accomplish this goal. Equally interesting, there are families in all types of neighborhoods who are highly involved in their children's education and schooling (e.g., Eccles, McCarthy, et al., 1993; Furstenberg, 1993).

Such neighborhood characteristics have been shown to influence the extent to which parents can successfully translate their general beliefs, goals, and values into effective specific practices and perceptions. Evidence from several studies suggests that it is harder to do a good job of parenting if one lives in a high-risk neighborhood or if one is financially stressed (e.g., Elder, 1974; Elder & Caspi, 1989; Flanagan, 1990a, 1990b; Furstenberg, 1993; McLoyd, 1990). Not only do such parents have limited resources available to implement whatever strategies they think might be effective, they also have to cope with more external stressors than White middle-class families living in stable, resource-rich neighborhoods. Being confronted with these stressors may lead parents to adopt a less effective parenting style because they do not have the energy or the time to use a more demanding but more effective strategy. For example, several investigators find that economic stress in the family (e.g., loss of one's job or major financial change) has a negative affect on the quality of parenting (e.g., Elder, 1974; Elder, Conger, Foster, & Ardelt, 1992; Flanagan, 1990a; Harold-Goldsmith et al., 1988). Schools could help to relieve some of this stress if they could facilitate more effective parent involvement.

Far less work has investigated the dynamic processes by which these global social factors actually affect parent involvement and children's school outcomes. In addition, it is clear that there is substantial variation in parental involvement within any of these social categories, and that teachers can successfully involve even the hardest-to-reach parents (e.g., Becker & Epstein, 1982; Clark, 1983; Dauber & Epstein, 1989; Epstein & Dauber, 1991; Scott-Jones, 1987). More research is needed to identify the characteristics of parents that are associated with effective parent involvement, especially in underrepresented ethnic groups and high-risk neighborhoods and especially for adolescent children.

Child Characteristics

Numerous studies indicate that parents vary their involvement in their children's school achievement depending on the characteristics of the child. We know, for example, that the child's sex and age influence the extent of parent involvement (e.g., Baker & Stevenson, 1986; Dornbusch & Ritter, 1988; Eccles-Parsons et al., 1982; Epstein & Dauber, 1988; Stevenson & Baker, 1987). Age is especially relevant for this discussion. As noted earlier, parent involvement drops off rather dramatically as children move into junior high or middle school. Why? It is likely that some of this decrease reflects a belief held by many parents that they should begin to disengage from their adolescents (Carnegie Corporation, 1989). Parents may feel that young adolescents both desire and need independence, and thus feel that involvement in their children's education is not as important. They may also feel that the children do not want them to be as visible, as evidenced by a common adolescent plea to not have their parents chaperone school activities. Although there may be an element of truth in this belief, it is too extreme. Adolescents may want greater autonomy, but they still need to know that their parents support their educational endeavors. They need a safe haven in which to explore their independence, a safe haven in which both parents and schools are actively involved.

The decrease in parent involvement as their children move into secondary school may also result from a decrease in parents' feelings of efficacy as their children grow older. Parents may feel less able to help their children with school work as it becomes more advanced and technical; children are no longer working on basic reading and spelling skills or drilling on math facts. Parents may feel the method of teaching math, for instance, is very different from the one they learned and if they try to help their children, they will mislead them. Finally, research (Freedman-Doan, Arbreton, Harold, & Eccles, 1993) shows that parents believe they will have more influence over their children when they are in the elementary grades than they will when their children reach adolescence.

At a more general level, it seems likely that the child's previous academic experiences and personality can also affect parent involvement (i.e., parents may be more likely to try to help a child who is having trouble than a child who is doing very well, especially if that child has done well in the past; alternatively, parents of high-achieving children may be more likely to participate in school governance and school activities than parents of lower achieving children. Parents should also be more likely to continue trying to help a child with whom they get along than a child with whom they have many conflicts). Finally, it seems likely that the parents' experiences with helping the other children in the family will impact the parents' involvement with the seventh-grade targeted child in this study.

School and Teacher Characteristics and Practices

It is also important to think about the school and teacher characteristics that influence parent involvement. As noted earlier, work by Epstein and her colleagues (e.g., Epstein & Dauber, 1991) suggests that school factors are a primary influence on parent involvement. In fact, the strongest predictors in several studies are the specific school programs and teacher practices being used (or not used) to encourage parent involvement: When parents feel schools are doing things to involve them, they are more involved in their children's education (Dauber & Epstein, 1989).

Two aspects of school characteristics are especially important for this chapter: the physical and organizational structure of schools, and the beliefs and attitudes of school personnel. Variations in the physical and organizational structure of the school building itself are likely to either facilitate or hinder parent–teacher collaboration. For example, change in the physical and organizational structure is one of the primary differences parents and students confront as children move from elementary into secondary school. Junior high and middle schools are much bigger, they serve a wider range of communities and social/ethnic groups, they are typically more bureaucratic in the governance and management systems, and are more likely to be departmentalized resulting in less personal contact between specific teachers and either students or families. Changes such as these can result in an increase in parents' feelings of alienation from the school. These changes are associated with greater feelings of alienation on the part of the adolescents themselves (Eccles & Midgley, 1989; Simmons & Blyth, 1987). Parents who are involved in neighborhood elementary schools may see this involvement as a connection with their community and friends. The home elementary school may seem like an extension of the family, particularly in neighborhoods where the population is relatively stable. Parents and teachers get to know each other well over the years their children are in the school. As children leave their home schools and several elementary schools merge into one middle school, there may be a decrease in the extent to which the families feel connected to the school. Junior high and middle schools expand the physical community but may not expand the emotional sense of community. The sense of belonging and investment may decrease and, as a result, parents may feel less able and less inclined to be involved and/or try to affect change in the educational experiences of their children. Additionally, children typically spend 6 or 7 years in an elementary school and only 2 or 3 in a middle school. The attachments, which often form over the elementary years when parent help seems more essential, have less time to form and may feel less necessary in the middle and upper grades.

Alternatively, school personnel may either facilitate or inhibit parent involvement by their own beliefs and attitudes about parent involvement. Like parents, teachers and school personnel at this level may think it is better for the adolescent to have less parental involvement. They may also think it is too much trouble to involve parents at this level because parents are busy, disinterested, or unknowledgeable. As a result, school personnel at this level have been found to actively discourage parent involvement in the classroom and the school (Epstein & Dauber, 1991; Hoover-Dempsey, Basslet, & Brissie, 1987; Carnegie Corporation, 1989). This appears to be especially true in low-income and minority neighborhoods where parents are seen as part of the problem in educating their children, rather than as a resource (Comer, 1980). The negative interactions, which these parents are likely to have with the schools, combined with potentially negative recollections of their own educational experiences, can serve as a major barrier to parent involvement in ethnic communities and high-risk inner-city school districts. The following teacher and school characteristics are likely to be important predictors of the school's response to parent involvement and collaboration: (a) beliefs about what is the appropriate amount and type of parent involvement; (b) beliefs about influences on parents' levels of participation, particularly their beliefs regarding why parents are not more involved; (c) sense of efficacy about their ability to affect the parents' level of participation; (d) knowledge of specific strategies for getting parents more involved; (e) their plans for implementing these strategies; and (f) support for implementing specific plans.

In the next section, we summarize two on-going studies designed to assess some of the relations described thus far. These studies focus primarily on the parent and school characteristics that influence parent participation.

EMPIRICAL STUDIES OF THE INFLUENCES
ON PARENT INVOLVEMENT

The Michigan Childhood and Beyond Study

Eccles and her colleagues (Eccles & Blumenfeld, 1984; Eccles, Blumenfeld, Harold, & Wigfield, 1990) are conducting a large-scale, longitudinal study of development in four primarily White, lower middle to middle-class school districts in Midwestern urban/suburban communities. The study began with groups of children in kindergarten, first, and third grade, and initially followed them for 4 consecutive years (at which time the cohorts were in third, fourth, and sixth grades). The study examined many issues including children's achievement self-perceptions in various domains and the roles that parents and teachers play in socializing these beliefs. Parent involvement in their children's education was also explored and the results are summarized in this section.

During the third wave of the study, 354 children were in the second grade, 375 in the third, and 518 in the fifth grade. Because of variations between the school districts in school structure, 247 fifth graders were in an elementary school setting and 262 fifth graders were in a Grade 5–6 middle school setting. This structural difference allows for exploring differences across the three grades, and within the two types of fifth grade. Questionnaire data were gathered from the children, approximately two thirds of their parents, and from their teachers. Teachers supplied information on their classroom practices including those regarding parent involvement, and completed an individual assessment questionnaire on each child who participated in the study.

Involvement With Teachers and at School. Parent data on parent–school involvement are presented in Tables 1.1 and 1.2. Three scales were formed based on the parent data in Table 1.1. The first (Monitor) deals with the parent's response to teacher requests for helping their child with school work; the second (Volunteer) is made up of items that ask about parent participation in volunteer activities at school; and the third (Involvement) is a report of parent involvement with the child's daily activities. In addition, two single items were asked: Do you contact the school about your child's progress? and Do you contact the school about how to give extra help?

Similar to other studies (e.g., Dauber & Epstein, 1989), the parents of fifth graders did significantly less monitoring of their children's work than the parents of second and third graders. In addition, parents of fifth graders housed in the middle school did less monitoring than parents of fifth graders housed in the elementary school. Although there is also a downward trend in the percentage of time parents report volunteering in school across the grades, the significant decrease is only found between the elementary and middle school fifth grades, as shown in Table 1.2. As discussed earlier, the grade-level difference may reflect

TABLE 1.1
Parent Scales and Items: Variable Descriptions
and Reliability Estimates of Scales

Scales/Items	Variable Descriptions	Reliability[a]
Monitor	Parent response to teacher requests and information (1 = *never* . . . 4 = *about once a month* . . . 7 = *daily*) Listen to child read Listen to or discuss a story that child writes Practice spelling or other skills before a test Check to see that homework is complete Check to see that homework is done correctly Do arithmetic problems with child	.88
Volunteer	The rate of parent participation in volunteer activities at school (0 = *no*, 1 = *yes*) PTO/PTA participation Leader in PTO/PTA General volunteer work at school	.65
Involvement	Parent report of frequency of involvement with child's daily activities (1 = *never* . . . 4 = *weekly* . . . 7 = *almost every day for a long while*) Help child do his or her homework Check homework after completion Help child prepare for tests	.83
Progress	Do you contact the school about child's progress? (0 = *no*, 1 = *yes*)	
Extra help	Do you contact the school about how to give extra help? (0 = *no*, 1 = *yes*)	

Note. [a]Cronbach's α coefficients as reliability estimates were computed on scales consisting of multiple items.

parents' assumption that their children need and desire less direct supervision as they enter early adolescence. Although a decrease was expected, the difference within the fifth grade suggests that school structure is also a factor. Perhaps parents feel less connected with the middle school outside of their neighborhood and therefore volunteer less often; or perhaps middle schools make less of an effort to connect with parents. The new environment of the middle school may also heighten the awareness of adolescent changes for parents, leading to the difference between the two types of fifth grades. Alternatively, a decrease in feelings of parental efficacy could account for some of the decrease in parental monitoring of school work. As the material children are taught gets more technical, parents may feel that they do not have adequate background to help their children, particularly in math and science.

The amount of reported parent involvement and the extent of contact with the school did not differ significantly by grade. However, the frequency with which

TABLE 1.2
Means, Standard Deviations, and F Statistics of Parent Scales and Items by Grade Level and School Type

Scales/Items	Grade							School Type[a]				
	2 (n = 216)		3 (n = 229)		5 (n = 340)			elementary (n = 140)		middle (n = 193)		
	M	(SD)	M	(SD)	M	(SD)	F	M	(SD)	M	(SD)	F
Monitor	3.50	(1.78)	3.02	(1.80)	2.67	(1.53)	14.20***	2.93	(1.60)	2.50	(1.46)	6.17*
Volunteer	.30	(.34)	.28	(.34)	.26	(.32)	1.18 ns	.33	(.34)	.21	(.29)	12.79***
Involvement	3.90	(1.30)	3.88	(1.22)	3.72	(1.21)	1.83 ns	3.59	(1.16)	3.71	(1.22)	2.76 ns
Progress	.52	(.50)	.52	(.50)	.46	(.50)	1.23 ns	.46	(.50)	.46	(.50)	.00 ns
Extra help	.40	(.49)	.38	(.49)	.46	(.50)	.80 ns	.27	(.44)	.40	(.49)	6.13*

Note. [a]Among the fifth graders; ns not significant; *p < .05; **p < .01; ***p < .001.

parents contact the school to learn how to give their children extra help increases significantly among the parents of fifth graders who are in the middle school setting. It may be that the heightened awareness of approaching adolescence also arouses a heightened sense of the seriousness of school and achievement, leading parents to seek new ways to help their children. Alternatively, these parents may feel they are not getting as much information from the schools as they need to help their children and are, therefore, asking for more to bring them back up to the level they had been accustomed to during the elementary school years.

Tables 1.3 and 1.4 present teacher data. The first scale (Help tips) encompasses ideas or tips that teachers send home regarding how parents can help their children with school work; the next scale (Goals) relates to teachers' sharing of information with parents about classroom goals; and the final scale (Requests) assesses the number of requests that teachers make of parents to monitor their children's work. Two single items are also included in the analyses: How often do you encourage parents to get involved? and Did you provide feedback other than regular conferences or report cards for this child?

Consistent with the findings of Epstein and Dauber (1991), there were no significant differences across grades or within the fifth grade in the extent of most types of communications from teachers to parents. The only significant grade-level effect occurred for the extent of evaluative feedback—the fifth-grade teachers, particularly if they worked in a middle school context, provided less supplemental feedback than second- or third-grade teachers. What is especially striking about the communication findings is the absolute low levels of several types of communication: On the average, these teachers provided helpful hints about how to work with one's child less than once a month; furthermore, between 50% and 70% of the teachers provided no supplementary evaluation to parents about how their children were doing in school beyond the information provided at conferences and on report cards.

There are also two interesting school type effects: both the extent to which fifth-grade teachers encouraged parents to get involved in classroom activities and the extent to which fifth-grade teachers provided supplementary feedback on the children's performance were lower for fifth-grade teachers in a middle school than for fifth-grade teachers in an elementary school context. The first finding is consistent with the notion that the school–home connection is not as strong in the middle school as in the elementary school. With regard to the second finding, providing supplementary evaluative feedback, perhaps fifth-grade teachers, particularly those in the middle school, subscribe to the notions that the children should be more independent by this time, and that parents need less child-specific feedback because they are already accustomed to their children being in school and understand the ways that school systems and teachers function. The teachers may not understand that the link between parents and teachers is particularly important during this early adolescent period. This difference may account for the heightened levels in the fifth-grade middle school

TABLE 1.3
Teacher Scales and Items: Variable Descriptions and Reliability Estimates

Scales/Items	Variable Descriptions	Reliability[a]
Help tips	Ideas or tips for how parent can help child (1 = never . . . 4 = a few times a month . . . 7 = daily) Ideas to help parent talk with child about school work Ideas on how to monitor homework Ways to practice spelling or other skills at home before a test	.87
Goals	Sharing information about goals or orientation (1 = never . . . 4 = a few times a month . . . 7 = daily) Learning objectives for the school year Expectations about completion of assignments How report card grades are earned	.72
Requests	Requests of parent to monitor work (1 = never . . . 4 = a few times a month . . . 7 = daily) Listen to or discuss a report or story child has written Practice skills before a test Check to see that homework is done Check to see that homework is done correctly Review materials with child	.87
Encourage	How often to you encourage parents to get involved in classroom activities? (1 = very infrequently . . . 7 = very frequently)	
Feedback	Did you provide feedback other than regular conferences or report cards for this child? (0 = no, 1 = yes)	

Note. [a]Cronbach's α coefficients as reliability estimates were computed on scales consisting of multiple items.

parents' contacts with the school seeking information on how to give extra help to their children discussed earlier. Although the teachers may feel these parents need fewer individual contacts or feedback, the parents are responding to the decline with an increased desire for information concerning how to help their early adolescent children.

Involvement at Home. At each wave, the parents were asked to indicate how often they do various activities with their children at home using a scale anchored with specified frequencies (e.g., 1 = never, 4 = once a week, and 7 = almost everyday for a long while). We focus on the data for families with two parents in the home because we want to present and discuss some of the sex of parent effects. Findings from both Wave 1 (when the children were in kindergarten, first, and third grade) and Wave 3 (when the same children were in second, third, and fifth grade) are summarized to provide a full picture of

TABLE 1.4

Means, Standard Deviations, and F Statistics of Parent Scales and Items by Grade Level and School Type

| | Grade | | | | | School Type[a] | | |
| | 2 (n = 23) | 3 (n = 23) | 5 (n = 31) | | | elementary (n = 19) | middle (n = 12) | |
Scales/Items	M (SD)	M (SD)	M (SD)	F		M (SD)	M (SD)	F
Help tips	2.79 (1.60)	3.54 (2.51)	2.76 (1.62)	1.28 ns		2.98 (1.89)	2.36 (.96)	1.02 ns
Goals	3.31 (1.93)	4.22 (2.02)	2.95 (1.66)	3.11 ns		3.13 (1.64)	2.64 (1.72)	.61 ns
Requests	4.02 (1.97)	4.57 (2.11)	4.03 (1.81)	.56 ns		4.15 (2.05)	3.82 (1.35)	.20 ns
Encourage	5.17 (1.56)	5.48 (1.44)	4.60 (2.19)	1.63 ns		5.50 (1.58)	3.25 (2.34)	9.93**
Feedback[b]	.49 (.50)	.50 (.50)	.37 (.48)	6.86**		.44 (.50)	.30 (.46)	8.06**

Note. [a]Among the fifth graders; ns not significant; *p < .05; **p < .01; ***p < .001. [b]This item is based on the Teacher's Individual Assessment Questionnaire. The sample size of each group is 237, 245, and 358 for the second, third, and fifth grade, respectively. Within the fifth grade, n = 174 in the elementary schools and n = 184 in the middle school.

developmental changes during the elementary school years. Table 1.5 summarizes the MANOVA results for the time use data from the first and third waves. Table 1.6 summarizes the means and standard deviations associated with each of these sets of MANOVAs.

At each wave, there were substantial sex of parent effects. Mothers were much more involved with their children's intellectual and school-related development than fathers, even for math and science-related activities in the early grades. In contrast, fathers were more involved in their children's athletic development. There were also consistent and stereotypic sex of child effects: Girls did more reading with their parents (primarily their mothers) than boys, and boys did more athletics activities with their parents (primarily their fathers) than girls.

There were also interesting grade-level effects that suggest a curvilinear pattern during the elementary school period. Parents appeared to become more involved in monitoring their children's school work as the children moved from kindergarten to third grade and then became less involved in this type of activity from the third to the fifth grade. This pattern is evident in both the cross-sectional and the longitudinal results.

A different pattern emerged for parents' involvement in less formal activities related to their children's intellectual development. As one might expect, the frequency with which parents read to their children declined steadily over the elementary school years. In contrast, the frequency of parents helping their children prepare for tests, teaching their children general knowledge, and discussing both news events and their children's experiences at school remained stable and fairly high over these years. Finally, the frequency of parents helping their children with homework increased during the early grades and stabilized at a relatively high level from third to fifth grade.

It is interesting to compare these changes to the results for parents' involvement with their children in recreational domains. The frequency of these parents active involvement with their children in both indoor and outdoor play activities declined steadily over the elementary school years. In addition, at virtually all grade levels, parents (mothers in particular) reported interacting directly with their children in school-related activities more frequently than in recreational activities, suggesting that these parents were very involved on a regular basis with their children's intellectual education even though they are not very involved at their children's schools.

Predictors of Parent Involvement. To investigate the model presented in Fig. 1.1, we correlated indicators of several of the parent/family and child characteristics with a composite indicator of parent involvement comprised of both the encouragement and the time-use measures within a specific domain (e.g., reading, math, and sports). Because the results are very similar for the two waves, we only summarize the findings for the Wave 3 data. And because the results do not vary in any meaningful way across grade levels, the findings are

TABLE 1.5
Repeated Measures MANOVA F Statistics of Parent Time Spent With Child

| | Between-Subject Effects | | | Within-Subject Effects—Parents | | | |
Question	Grade	Sex	Grade by Sex	Parent	Grade by Parent	Sex by Parent	Grade by Sex by Parent
Wave 1							
Do math or science activities with child	1.53	—	—	12.73***	—	3.80*	—
Read to child	43.81***	—	—	98.92***	—	—	—
Help child with his or her homework	6.03**	—	—	74.26***	—	—	—
Check child's homework after completed	2.24	—	—	26.19***	—	—	—
Play sports with child	2.71	23.96***	—	32.69***	—	6.52**	—
Play indoor games with child	15.54***	—	—	6.58**	—	2.34	3.13*
Wave 3							
Do math or science activities with child	2.01	—	3.35*	1.67	—	—	—
Read to child	55.68***	—	3.26*	67.57***	3.51*	—	—
Have child read to you	53.08***	4.51*	—	58.45***	3.59*	—	2.4
Help child with his or her homework	—	—	2.81	33.32***	—	—	—
Check child's homework after completed	7.15***	—	—	53.25***	—	—	—
Help child prepare for test	1.13	—	—	55.31***	4.41*	—	—
Discuss important news with child	—	—	—	55.60***	2.14	—	—
Play sports with child	—	31.07	2.33	86.21***	—	3.93*	3.10*
Play indoor games with child	12.76***	—	—	—	2.18	—	—

Notes. N = 272; sample size may vary slightly due to list-wise deletion. $*p < .05$; $**p < .01$; $***p < .001$. F value is less than 2.00.

TABLE 1.6
Means for Time Parents Spend With Child

Wave 1

Question	Grade			Sex of Child		Parent	
	Kindergarten X̄	First X̄	Third X̄	Girls X̄	Boys X̄	Mother X̄	Father X̄
Do math or science activities with child	3.45	3.17	3.24	3.30	3.27	3.48	3.07
Read to child	4.68	4.00	3.06	4.07	3.97	4.61	3.43
Help child with his/her homework	3.71	3.52	4.12	3.84	3.64	4.26	3.20
Check child's homework after completed	3.85	3.86	4.32	4.00	3.94	4.42	3.63
Play sports with child	3.33	3.18	2.90	2.82	3.50	2.82	3.53
Play indoor games with child	4.16	3.57	3.21	3.66	3.73	3.83	3.56
Do active, outdoor activities with child	4.23	3.65	3.61	3.73	3.95	3.70	3.98

Wave 3

Question	Grade			Sex of Child		Parent	
	Second X̄	Third X̄	Fifth X̄	Girls X̄	Boys X̄	Mother X̄	Father X̄
Do math or science activities with child	3.41	3.35	3.17	3.31	3.28	3.34	3.24
Read to child	3.97	3.41	2.22	3.06	3.11	3.48	2.69
Have child read to you	3.78	3.09	2.38	3.10	2.90	3.15	2.66
Help child with his/her homework	4.03	4.01	4.00	4.01	4.02	4.29	3.71
Check child's homework after completed	4.03	4.11	3.56	3.74	3.98	4.23	3.47
Help child prepare for tests	3.52	3.65	3.42	3.51	3.53	3.81	3.16
Discuss important news with child	4.11	4.13	4.14	4.12	4.13	4.45	3.69
Play sports with child	3.13	2.97	2.95	2.63	3.36	2.48	3.48
Play indoor games with child	3.60	3.33	2.93	3.17	3.30	3.27	3.20

collapsed across grade level. Finally, because the fathers' data essentially repli-
cates the findings for mothers, the results for mothers for math and reading and
the results for fathers for sports (focusing in each domain on the parent most
frequently involved with that area of the child's education) are summarized.

At the general level, two parent-psychological characteristics were significantly correlated with parent involvement in both reading and math education:
intellectual confidence ($r = .21$, $p < .01$; $r = .26$, $p < .01$) and achievement
motivation ($r = .16$, $p < .05$; $r = .31$, $p < .01$). The more confident a mother was
of her intellectual abilities and the more she expressed high achievement motivation (liking intellectual challenges and sticking with hard problems rather than
giving up), the more actively she was involved in her child's education in math
and reading. We also looked at two family-level characteristics: valuing mastery
(importance of learning, sticking with problems, and using time productively)
and valuing competition (importance of winning, doing better than others, and
the enjoyment of beating each other at games). There was a significant positive
association between mothers' perception of the family's valuing of mastery and
her involvement in her children's education in math ($r = .37$, $p < .01$) and reading
($r = .27$, $p < .01$). The valuing of competition was not related in either subject
area. Contrary to what was expected, neither a mother's education level nor a
family's income was related to the mother's involvement in her children's
education for either math or reading, perhaps because the sample of two-parent
families was composed of largely middle-class families.

At the more specific level, the extent of mothers' involvement in their children's math education was positively related to their evaluation of their children's
math interest ($r = .13$, $p < .05$) and to their confidence in their ability to help
their child with math work (efficacy, $r = .28$, $p < .01$). Similarly, mothers'
involvement in their children's reading education was positively related to their
evaluation of their children's reading interest ($r = .13$, $p < .05$) and to their
confidence in their ability to help their child with language arts work (efficacy,
$r = .31$, $p < .01$). In both intellectual domains, however, these relations largely
disappeared when one controlled for the general parent- and family-level characteristics discussed in the previous paragraph. Apparently, mothers' involvement
in their children's math and reading education are linked more strongly to general
beliefs about the importance of mastery and achievement than to more specific
beliefs about either one's child or the specific subject matter itself during the
elementary school years.

A somewhat different picture emerges for fathers' (and mothers') involvement
in their children's athletic development. As was true for math and reading, fathers'
education was not related to involvement. In contrast, family income was weakly
and negatively related to fathers' (but not mothers') involvement in their child's
athletic development ($r = -.17$, $p < .05$, for fathers). Of the general parent- and
family-level characteristics, fathers' view of the importance of competition within
the family was most strongly related to their involvement in their child's sports

activities ($r = .23$, $p < .01$): Higher ratings of competitiveness were associated with higher levels of involvement. Fathers' rating of family mastery orientation was also related ($r = .17$, $p < .01$). The biggest contrast of this domain with the results for the math and reading domains occurred for the correlations between the sport-specific predictors and fathers' involvement with their children's sports: Fathers were more involved if they rated their child's sport ability and interest high ($r = .42$, $p < .05$ and $r = .46$, $p < .01$, respectively), rated the general importance of sports skills high ($r = .51$, $p < .01$), and were confident of their ability to influence their child's ability and interest in this domain ($r = .45$, $p < .01$). These effects continued to be quite strong even after controlling for the children's gross motor skills and the father's rating of the family's competitiveness. Apparently, involvement in one's children's sports education is much more idiosyncratic than involvement in one's children's intellectual education among these middle-class families.

We correlated these parent characteristics with the parent–school involvement variables outlined in Tables 1.1 and 1.2. These correlations were quite weak and usually not significant. Only parents' intellectual confidence related to the parents' volunteering at school (more confident parents were more likely to volunteer at school), but this association was quite weak ($r = .13$, $p < .01$). The strongest associations occurred between mother's and father's education and parents' requests for information from the school about their children's progress: Both mother's and father's education were positively associated with these requests ($r = .21$, $p < .01$ and $r = .17$, $p < .01$, respectively). Finally, contrary to what one might expect, both mother's and father's education were negatively related to the extent to which parents' monitored their children's school work ($r = -.14$, $p < .01$, and $r = -.12$, $p < .01$, respectively). This latter effect, however, makes sense if teachers make more requests for parental monitoring when a child is having difficulty with his or her schoolwork. Such requests for additional monitoring are probably needed less if a child is performing satisfactorily. In support of this explanation, there is a positive correlation between teachers' reports of making requests for parents to monitor their children's schoolwork and parents' reports of the extent to which they monitor their children's schoolwork ($r = .15$, $p < .01$). Again, however, this association is quite weak.

The Maryland Adolescent Growth in Context Study

The second study was conducted in Maryland with a population of approximately 1,400 African-American and European-American early adolescents and their parents. All children were enrolled in a 2-year middle school comprised of Grades 7 and 8. The population included a wide socioeconomic range in both the African-American and European-American samples. Data were gathered from the primary caregiver and the target adolescent in their home using both a face-to-face interview and a self-administered questionnaire, and by telephone. The data reported here were collected either during the adolescent's seventh grade school year or in the summer immediately following the seventh grade year.

Investigating parents' involvement in their adolescents' education was one of the primary goals of this study. We gathered extensive information regarding parents' involvement both at home and at school. First, we describe the results regarding involvement at school; next we summarize the results regarding involvement at home; and finally, we summarize the results regarding the predictors of parent involvement both at school and at home.

Frequency of Involvement at School. As has been found in other studies, the parents in this study were not very involved at their children's school. Although 61% were members on the Parent Teacher Student Association (PTSA), only 5% to 6% reported playing a leadership role either in the PTSA or other school advisory groups. On the average, all parents reported attending between three and four activities and between two and three teacher conferences per year at school; they also reported doing volunteer work at the school one to two times during the seventh-grade school year. A much higher percentage indicated that they would like to be involved at school and 86% agreed with the statement that schools are more effective when parents are involved. The vast majority (65%) also agreed that teachers should do more to get parents involved.

The parents were asked why they were not more involved at school. The most frequently checked reasons related to work commitments (62% indicated this was an important limiting factor). In contrast, parents rarely rated the following reasons as important: feeling they could not be of help, child not wanting them to come to school, and teachers making them feel unwelcomed.

Our data also suggest that the schools were making relatively little attempt to involve the parents more in educational activities, either at home or in school; the one exception being requests for parents to monitor the completion of homework. For example, the parents reported that teachers had provided information regarding specific homework assignments only one to two times over the year, and regarding meetings and other school activities only two to three times. In response to a question regarding how often teachers gave their children assignments that required getting information from the family, 36% of the parents said this had never happened and another 38% said it had happened only once. Finally, we asked how often the parents thought their children's teachers wanted parents to visit class in order to see what their children were doing; 44% said never and another 43% said once a month or less.

Frequency of Involvement at Home. In contrast, parents were much more involved with their children's education at home. On the average, these parents reported helping their children with homework one to three times each week, more often than they reported doing any other single activity with their children except discussing current news events. They also reported checking their children's homework an average of four times per week. Clearly, these parents were reporting relatively high levels of involvement in their children's school-related academic activities at home even though they were not very involved with activities at the school itself.

We asked the youth similar types of questions and received similar responses. When asked about their teachers' efforts to involve their parents in their school work they, like their parents, reported relatively infrequent attempts. For example, they reported that their teachers asked them to get someone at home to help them study for tests, to check their homework, and to help them with school projects an average of one to two times per month. In contrast, they reported that they get help from their parents on their schoolwork an average of one to three times a week. Like their parents, they reported that they work with their parents on their schoolwork as much or more than any other single activity. They also reported that their parents actively monitored their school progress fairly often (averaging between 3.3 to 3.8 on a 5-point scale with 1 = *almost never*, 3 = *sometimes*, and 5 = *almost always*).

Predictors of Parent Involvement in Their Adolescents' Education. We have just begun our analyses of the predictors of parent involvement in this study. As a first step, we have correlated both the parents' reports of their involvement at school and home and the adolescents' reports of their parents' involvement at home with indicators of the following constructs drawn from the model illustrated in Fig. 1.1: (a) family demographic characteristics, (b) demands on parents' time, (c) parents' sense of efficacy to help their children with their schoolwork, (e) parents' perceptions of their children's characteristics, (f) parents' valuing of education in general and of parent involvement in particular, (g) parents' perception of the school, and (h) parents' more general involvement in their children's activities.

The significant relations were all in the predicted direction; but the effects are generally quite weak; the correlations were typically in the range of .12 to .25. In addition, because these data are correlational and represent only one point in time, it would be unwise to speculate about the causal nature of these relations until the subsequent waves of longitudinal are available for analysis. Consequently, at present, one should take these results as food for thought.

In general, higher income, more education, and being married rather than single predicted greater parent involvement at school but not at home. In addition, African-American parents were somewhat more involved at home than European-American parents, whereas European-American parents were somewhat more involved at school than the African-American parents. Both of these effects, however, were very small although highly reliable given the sample size.

As expected, having other demands, like work and family responsibilities, on one's time was related negatively to involvement both at school and at home. In contrast, and again as one would expect, both parents' confidence in their ability to influence their child's academic performance and school experiences and the importance they attached to being involved in their children's schooling were correlated positively with involvement both at home and at school. These associations were among the strongest predictors of involvement at school—ranging from .15 to .35 with most between .22 to .26.

There was also fairly consistent support for the significance of the parents' perception of the school context as a correlate of involvement at school. Parents who had a positive view of the school in terms of its concern about the families and adolescents in the school, the accessibility of school personnel to parents, and the teachers' desire to actively involve parents were more involved at the school. And, as one would expect, parents who reported more frequent requests from their child's teachers for parent involvement also reported greater involvement in their children's education both at school and at home. Their children also reported greater parental involvement at home.

Finally, parents with a more positive view of their child and higher educational expectations for their child were more involved in their children's education both at home and at school. Furthermore, there was evidence of consistency in parents' involvement in their children's lives more generally. Parents who were actively involved in several different aspects of their children's lives and who engaged in the most proactive encouragement of skill acquisition in other domains were also the parents most likely to be actively involved in their children's academic education.

INCREASING PARENT AND SCHOOL COLLABORATION

Specific suggestions about the ways to improve parent–teacher collaboration on behalf of children's education are now discussed. Epstein and her colleagues (e.g., Epstein, 1987; Epstein & Dauber, 1991) suggested the following six areas of parent–school involvement:

1. Basic obligations of families to provide for the safety and health of their children.
2. Basic obligations of schools to communicate with families about school programs and the individual progress of their children.
3. Parental involvement at school.
4. Parental involvement in learning activities at home.
5. Parental involvement in decision making at school.
6. Collaboration and exchange with community organizations.

In a study of parental involvement in education in Ireland, Morgan, Fraser, Dunn, and Cairns (1992) suggested that involvement can be divided into three levels.

Low level involvement is the traditional parent–school link (referred to in Point 2, just cited), which tends to be of a formal nature and consists of such activities as parent–teacher conferences regarding their individual child and open houses that discuss curriculum. At this level of involvement, parents are primarily interested in their students' progress, and the school's focus is on how parents can support the institutional goals to maximize that progress. The second level of involvement parallels Epstein's third and fifth points: parents extending their relationship with the school beyond their focus on their own children and volunteering in the classroom, helping on field trips, and participating in parent–teacher organizations. This type of involvement, the authors suggest, is more difficult to maintain because the relevance is more limited. Morgan et al. (1992) suggest a final level of "formal, structural involvement" that is more political in nature, such as a school board. Few parents ever become involved at this level.

We focus our recommendations on two areas: communication with parents and involvement in learning activities at home, because these areas are particularly relevant to the concerns raised in this chapter regarding both grade-level differences in parent participation at school, and capitalizing on the ways parents are already participating in their children's education.

Communicating With Parents.   Schools and teachers communicate with parents about school programs and the individual progress of their children in several ways: Parent–teacher conferences, curriculum nights, open houses, phone contacts, report cards, and summaries of standardized test results are typical examples of this type of parent–school connection. In order to develop an effective system of communication between the school and the family, however, it is critical that old stereotypes of family be rethought to welcome the variety of persons who now make up students' families (Pennekamp & Freeman, 1988). Who should be invited to school functions? Should schools change father–daughter or mother–son events to parent–child or even significant adult–child events? Who should receive copies of report cards and test scores? Making the definition of family more inclusive in the school's communications home may result in more children having adult parent-type figures participate on their behalf. In addition, schools must be cognizant of working with families from diverse cultural and linguistic backgrounds and may need to find new methods of forming the family–school connection (Delgaldo-Gaitan, 1991; Salend & Taylor, 1993).

School–family communication begins in the earliest grades and usually continues through high school, although the nature and frequency of the contacts may change as the child goes through the school system. As students move to the middle grades and have more than one core teacher, *capsule* nights are sometimes used to provide parents with both information about each class and an opportunity to meet each teacher. Such programs involve attending a miniaturized version of the child's daily schedule, (e.g., 15 minutes in each classroom) and are generally held in the evening to accommodate working parents. Many school districts also have special programs for parents and students at transitional points like the transition into junior or senior high school. Such an opportunity was provided by the district in the MAGIC study and it was highly successful from the perspective of the parents: 72% of the parents in this sample reported attending this program; of these, 64% reported that it was very useful and another 28% reported that it was mildly useful.

Providing extensive and accurate information regarding curricular choices to parents becomes increasingly critical as their children move into and through secondary school. As children move into junior high or middle school, they begin to make course choices that have short- and long-term implications for the future options open to adolescents. Often, neither the full range of choices nor the implications of various choices are made clear to parents. For example, in one of the school districts we have studied, school administrators explained that parents make the decision regarding which math class their child is to be placed into in the seventh grade at the end of the sixth-grade school year. It was clear from interviews with parents in this school district, however, that they did not know they had this choice. Instead, what actually happens is that the sixth grade teachers send home the course selection form with the seventh grade math course already filled in with the teacher's recommendation regarding the child's math placement. The teachers do not explicitly indicate that this is only a recommendation. In addition, the parents did not know the consequences of being placed in the various seventh grade math courses. Clearly, the school had not communicated their policy clearly enough to the parents for the parents to really play a role in this important decision. Early course choices in subjects like math and science often play a major role in shaping a high school student's curricular track. If parents do not fully understand this connection, they cannot play their role as advocates for their children.

Recent findings reported by Dornbusch (1994) confirms our speculations about the likely consequences of poor curricular choices, making the negative consequences of this lack of communication to parents even more apparent. In a survey of students in four northern California high schools, Dornbusch found that 55% of the students did not know even one entrance requirement of the University of California system and that lack of knowledge was not related to their achievement level. He also summarized the findings that teachers are also uninformed about the entrance requirements of the university system, particularly teachers with a high proportion of students of color in their classrooms. As a consequence, Dornbusch (1994) also found that many students who intend to go to college and have the requisite ability according to eighth-grade achievement tests have not taken the courses required for entrance into the college or university of their choice.

One way to avoid these enrollment mistakes is for schools to make sure parents understand the requirements as well as the implications of not taking particular courses. We asked the parents in the MAGIC study whether the school had provided them with curricular information. The results contain both good and bad news. With regard to making course selections for their child in the seventh grade, the vast majority (70%) of the parents indicated that the school had provided them with adequate information on the available options. The results for information on college requirements were less encouraging: Only 40% of the parents indicated they thought they knew most of the courses in the college preparatory sequences and 60% the parents indicated they had not received any information from the schools about these issues. These results suggest that the schools in this county, at least, are not doing an adequate job of providing parents with the information they need to help their adolescent children select the courses they will need to get into the colleges they want to attend.

There is growing evidence of the importance of personalized communication with the families, especially during the secondary school years. Two kinds of such communication are needed. First, there is a need for coordination among teachers at this grade level to insure effective monitoring of the child's socioemotional development so that parents and other relevant support persons can be alerted to any danger signs. The ability to provide this type of information is particularly important in early adolescence following the transition into junior high. We have found that junior high teachers are not very good at identifying students who are having difficulty with this transition (Lord, Eccles, & McCarthy, 1994). Yet, they are the adults who spend the most time with these youth and thus are uniquely situated to identify danger signs at school early enough to get at-risk students the help they need. Working more closely together with each other and with the parents of their students could help them play this critical role in the lives of early adolescents and their families. Middle schools in some districts handle this issue by organizing each of their student cohorts into *houses*. Each house often has a counselor and secretary who travels with their group of students from sixth through eighth grade. In addition, the students can be assigned to an advisory teacher with whom they meet as a group on a regular basis to discuss a variety of issues. Often this person is also their teacher for one of their core subjects. These advisory teachers can function as liaisons between the parent and the school, and between other teachers and each of their own advisory students.

Teachers are in a unique position to help parents provide appropriate educational and occupational counseling for their children. Because teachers see many adolescents and interact with each student more directly in terms of intellectual skills, teachers are well positioned to help students and parents think about the adolescent's talents and aptitudes in terms of future occupational choices. Parents often do not know very much about the relation of specific academic skills to various future job possibilities, particularly if they themselves do not excel in the same domains. For example, we know that girls are less likely to pursue careers in the fields of applied mathematics (e.g., engineering) and physical science than boys. We also know girls are less likely to take these courses in secondary school than boys. Girls appear to be selecting themselves out of these intellectual domains; they do so at great cost to themselves. By not taking these courses in high school, they are not eligible to take many college courses, including courses and majors they might be interested in like nursing, economics, or ecological sciences. They also significantly decrease the possibility of deciding in college to major in engineering or the physical sciences. Parents often do not understand these implications. And, parents may not notice that their daughter is exceptionally good in math and science (see Eccles, 1989). Bright girls often do quite well in all of their courses and may not give their parents any reason to think they are unusually good in math and science. In addition, parents may not understand that there are many good jobs in these fields and females are more likely to be paid an equitable salary in these areas. Teachers can provide parents with this type of specific information relevant to their child's future. They can also let parents know about special programs for which their child is eligible. Ample evidence documenting the power of such information to increase the odds that girls and minority students will take advanced courses in math and science in high school, and will consider occupations requiring these courses and requiring a college education now exists (see Eccles, 1989). For example, in a study of the 20 best programs in terms of placement of high numbers of females in advanced placement math and science courses, Casserly (1980) found that direct and frequent encouragement to the parents of talented females was one of the distinguishing characteristics of the most effective teachers. Information such as this is especially important for families who live in high-risk neighborhoods and for families who have recently immigrated to this country or to the state or city in which they are currently living.

Involvement in Learning Activities at Home. The findings reported earlier indicate that parents are very actively involved with their children's education at home, even in middle school. Numerous studies document the importance of this type of involvement for school achievement. Participation, however, does seem to decline with age, according to the reports of the parents in MCABS and the adolescents in MAGICS. Given the importance of this involvement and the fact that this is the type of involvement parents are most likely to do on their own, teachers and other school personnel ought to be doing as much as they can to encourage and support this type of collaboration with parents, particularly during the middle grades.

Schools and teachers try to foster this type of involvement in a variety of ways. For example, in our samples the teachers sometimes asked family members to work with their children on particular learning tasks that might facilitate and promote the child's class work. Parents being requested to monitor their children's homework is another example of this type of collaboration, which was done with some regularity in both samples. Some of the teachers in the studies also provided information on learning goals and ways in which parents may be helpful to their children in achieving these goals, but they did this less frequently than the previously mentioned strategies.

Work by Epstein and her colleagues (e.g., 1987) suggests that these kinds of practices begin in early elementary school and continue through secondary school, although the kind of information provided and the tasks that are targeted for help usually change across grade levels. As children get older, teachers often send home *contracts* at the beginning of a term (i.e., letters that detail their expectations, their grading system, and/or assignments), which both students and parents are asked to sign. Teachers are also less likely to ask for parent help with specific skills such as reading or learning math facts. This may be due to perceptions held by both teachers and parents that (a) students should have mastered basic skills by this point, and (b) parents are less able to help now than they were before. Although neither of these perceptions is necessarily true, teachers seem more likely to describe a larger task, such as a science project, where parents might choose to be involved with a given part of the project. But, given the concerns that many teachers raise about parents' expertise and ability to help their children with homework as the subject matters being taught become more technical, it would be helpful for schools to consider some ways in which they could provide parents with some supplementary educational training so the parents could both be more helpful and could feel more confident in their ability to help. Family Math and Family Computers are two exemplar programs with this goal. Both seek to provide supplementary educational experiences for both students and parents. Both are run at school by teachers in the evenings and on weekends. Both have generated great enthusiasm among both parent and teacher groups. And both are relatively inexpensive to introduce and sustain in a school system.

Teachers could also increase parent involvement in learning activities at home by developing assignments that provide a meaningful role for parents to play. Adolescence, for example, is a time when children are increasingly interested in things like their cultural heritage, their parents' experience while growing up, and their community's history. They are also interested in how people make important life decisions and how people learn from their mistakes. Teachers could take advantage of these interests by giving assignments that involve interviewing one's parents and other community members, or involve accompanying one's parents on important activities like work or volunteer activities. Assignments such as these might accentuate the areas in which parents have special expertise and information rather than highlighting the areas in which the parents' knowledge may be dated or limited. Similar activities can be designed for younger children. For example, teachers can have children bring in stories about the kinds of toys their parents played with and activities they did while they were growing up.

SUMMARY

In this chapter, we have accomplished three goals: first, we documented the importance of parent involvement in their children's schooling; second, we discussed the various influences on parental involvement and the many barriers to parent involvement; and third, we provided some concrete recommendations for ways to increase parent involvement in their children's educational development, particularly at home, because this is the place that most parents participate in their children's education. The chapter began by noting the critical role parents and teachers can play if they work together to support healthy development. Unfortunately, the collaborative relationship between parents and schools seems to decrease as children move into their adolescent years and into secondary schools. Ways in which this downward trend might be reversed were discussed. There are effective ways to involve parents in a collaborative relationship with the schools even during the secondary school years. Furthermore, there is every reason to believe that parent involvement is just as important, if not more important, than a collaborative relationship with the schools during these years.

ACKNOWLEDGMENTS

The work reported in this chapter was supported by grants to the first author from the MacArthur Research Network on Successful Adolescent Development among Youth in High-Risk Settings and the MacArthur Foundation Education Program and by grants to both authors by the NICHD. We thank the following people for their help in conducting these studies: Amy Arbreton, Elaine Belansky, Phyllis Blumenfeld, Nick Butler, Diane Early, Kari Fraser, Carol Freedman-Doan, Ariel Kahl, Linda Kuhn, Karen McCarthy, Allan Wigfield, and Kwang Suk Yoon.

REFERENCES

Baker, D. P., & Stevenson, D. L. (1986). Mothers' strategies for children's school achievement: Managing the transition to high school. *Sociology of Education, 59,* 156–166.

Becker, H. J., & Epstein, J. L. (1982). Parent involvement: A study of teacher practices. *Elementary School Journal, 83,* 85–102.

Bradley, R., Caldwell, B. M., & Elardo, R. (1977). Home environment, social status, and mental test performance. *Journal of Educational Psychology, 69,* 697–701.

Bradley, R. H., Caldwell, B. M., & Rock, S. L. (1988). Home environment and school performance: A ten-year follow-up and examination of three models of environmental action. *Child Development, 59,* 852–867.

Bronfenbrenner, U. (1974). *Is early intervention effective? A report on longitudinal evaluations of preschool programs* (Vol. 2). Washington, DC: Department of Health, Education, and Welfare.

Bronfenbrenner, U. (1979). *The ecology of human development: Experiments by nature and design.* Cambridge, MA: Harvard University Press.

The Carnegie Corporation (1989). *Turning points: Preparing American youth for the 21st century* (Report on the task force on education of young adolescents). New York: Author.

The Carnegie Foundation (1988). *The condition of teaching: A state by state analysis.* Princeton, NJ: Author.

Casserly, P. (1980). An assessment of factors affecting female participation in advanced placement programs in mathematics, chemistry, and physics. In L. H. Fox, L. Brady, & D. Tobin (Eds.), *Women and the mathematical mystique* (pp. 138–163). Baltimore: Johns Hopkins University Press.

Clark, R. M. (1983). *Family life and school achievement: Why poor Black children succeed or fail.* Chicago: University of Chicago Press.

Coleman, J., Campbell, E., Hobson, C., McPartland, J., Mood, A., Weinfeld, F., & York, R. (1966). *Equality of educational opportunity report.* Washington DC: U.S. Government Printing Office.

Coleman, J. S., & Hoffer, T. (1987). *Public and private high schools: The impact of communities.* New York: Basic Books.

Comer, J. P. (1980). *School power: Implications of an intervention project.* New York: The Free Press.

Comer, J. (1988). Educating poor minority children. *Scientific American, 259*(5), 42–48.

Comer, J. P., & Haynes, N. M. (1991). Parent involvement in schools: An ecological approach. *The Elementary School Journal, 91,* 271–277.

Corno, L. (1980). Individual and class level effects of parent-assisted instruction in classroom memory support strategies. *Journal of Educational Psychology, 72,* 278–292.

Dauber, S. L., & Epstein, J. L. (1989). *Parents' attitudes and practices of involvement in inner-city elementary and middle schools* (CREMS Report 33). Baltimore: Johns Hopkins University, Center for Research on Elementary and Middle Schools.

Delgado-Gaitan, C. (1991). Involving parents in the schools: A process of empowerment. *American Journal of Education, 100,* 20–46.

Dornbusch, S. M. (1994, February). *Off the track.* Presidential address to the Society for Research on Adolescence, San Diego, CA.

Dornbusch, S. M., & Ritter, P. L. (1988). Parents of high school students: A neglected resource. *Educational Horizons, 66,* 75–77.

Eccles, J. S. (1989). Bringing young women to math and science. In M. Crawford & M. Gentry (Eds.), *Gender and thought: Psychological perspectives* (pp. 36–57). New York: Springer-Verlag.

Eccles, J. S., Arbreton, A., Buchanan, C. M., Jacobs, J., Flanagan, C., Harold, R., MacIver, D., Midgley, C., Reuman, D., & Wigfield, A. (1993). School and family effects on the ontongeny of children's interests, self-perceptions, and activity choices. In J. Jacobs (Ed.), *Developmental perspectives on motivation: Vol. 40 of the Nebraska Symposium on Motivation* (pp. 145–208). Lincoln: University of Nebraska Press.

Eccles, J. S., & Blumenfeld, P. C. (1984). *Psychological predictors of competence development* (Grant No. 2 R01 HD17553-01). Bethesda, MD: National Institute of Child Health and Human Development.

Eccles, J. S., Blumenfeld, P. C., Harold, R. D., & Wigfield, A. L. (1990). *Ontogeny of self and task concepts and activity choice* (Grant No. 2 R01 HD17553-06). Bethesda, MD: National Institute of Child Health and Human Development.

Eccles, J. S., & Harold, R. D. (1993). Parent–school involvement during the early adolescent years. *Teachers College Record, 94,* 560–587.

Eccles, J. S., McCarthy, K., Lord, S. E., Furstenberg, F., Geitz, L., & Teitler, J. (1993, March). *How parents respond to risk and opportunity in moderate to high risk neighborhoods.* Paper presented at the biennial meeting of the Society for Research in Child Development, New Orleans, LA.

Eccles, J. S., & Midgley, C. (1989). Stage/environment fit: Developmentally appropriate classrooms for early adolescents. In R. E. Ames & C. Ames (Eds.), *Research on motivation in education* (Vol. 3, pp. 139–186). New York: Academic Press.

Eccles-Parsons, J., Adler, T. F., Kaczala, C. M. (1982). Socialization of achievement attitudes and beliefs: Parental influences. *Child Development, 53,* 310–321.

Eccles-Parsons, J. (1983). Expectancies, values, and academic behaviors. In J. T. Spence (Ed.), *Achievement and achievement motives* (pp. 75–146). San Francisco: Freeman.

Elder, G. H., Jr. (1974). *Children of the great depression.* Chicago: University of Chicago Press.

Elder, G. H, Jr., & Caspi, A. (1989). Economic stress in lives: Developmental perspectives. *Child Development, 56,* 361–375.

Elder G. H., Jr., Conger, R. D., Foster, E. M., & Ardelt, M. (1992). Families under economic pressure. *Journal of Family Issues, 13,* 5–37.

Epstein, J. L. (1982). *Student reactions to teacher practices of parent involvement* (Parent Involvement Report Series P–12). Baltimore, MD: The Johns Hopkins University Center for Research on Elementary and Middle Schools.

Epstein, J. L. (1983). *Effects on parents of teacher practices of parent involvement.* Baltimore, MD: Center for Social Organization of School, The Johns Hopkins University.

Epstein, J. L. (1986). Parents' reactions to teacher practices of parent involvement. *The Elementary School Journal, 86,* 277–294.

Epstein, J. L. (1987). What principals should know about parent involvement. *Principal, 66*(3), 6–9.

Epstein, J. L. (1990). School and family connections: Theory, research, and implication for integrating sociologies of education and family. In D. G. Unger & M. B. Sussman (Eds.), *Families in community settings: Interdisciplinary perspectives.* New York: Haworth Press.

Epstein, J. L., & Becker, H. J. (1982). Teachers' reported practices of parent involvement: Problems and possibilities. *The Elementary School Journal, 83,* 104–113.

Epstein, J. L., & Dauber, S. L. (1988, August). *Teacher attitudes and practices of parent involvement in inner-city elementary and middle schools.* Paper presented at the American Sociological Association meeting, Atlanta.

Epstein, J. L., & Dauber, S. L. (1991). School programs and teacher practices of parent involvement in inner-city elementary and middle schools. *The Elementary School Journal, 91,* 289–305.

Flanagan, C. A. (1990a). Families and schools in hard times. In V. C. McLoyd & C. A. Flanagan (Eds.), *New directions for child development* (Vol. 46, pp. 7–26). San Francisco: Jossey-Bass.

Flanagan, C. A. (1990b). Change in family work status: Effects on parent–adolescent decision-making. *Child Development, 61,* 163–177.

Freedman-Doan, C., Arbreton, A. J., Harold, R. D., & Eccles, J. S. (1993). Looking forward to adolescence: Mothers' and fathers' expectations for affective and behavioral change. *Journal of Early Adolescence, 13,* 472–502.

Furstenberg, F. (1993). How families manage risk and opportunities in dangerous neighborhoods. In W. J. Wilson (Ed.), *Sociology and the public agenda* (pp. 231–257). Newbury Park, CA: Sage.

Harold-Goldsmith, R., Radin, N., & Eccles, J. S. (1988). Objective and subjective reality: The effects of job loss and financial stress on fathering behaviors. *Family Perspective, 22,* 309–326.

Hoover-Dempsey, K. V., Basslet, O. C., & Brissie, J. S. (1987). Parent involvement: Contributions of teacher efficacy, school socioeconomic status, and other school characteristics. *American Educational Research Journal, 24,* 417–435.

Jacobs, J. H. (1983). *Parent involvement. Remarks.* (ERIC Document Reproduction Service No. ED 241 175).

Laosa, L. M. (1984). Social policies toward children of diverse ethnic, racial and language groups in the United States. In H. W. Stevenson & A. E. Siegel (Eds.), *Child developmental research and social policy* (pp. 1–109). Chicago: University of Chicago Press.

Leitch, M. L., & Tangri, S. S. (1988). Barriers to home–school collaboration. *Educational Horizons, 66,* 70–74.

Lord, S. E., Eccles, J. S., & McCarthy, K. (1994). Surviving the junior high school transition: Family processes and self-perceptions as protective and risk factors. *Journal of Early Adolescence, 14,* 162–199.

Marjoribanks, K. (1979). *Families and their learning environments: An empirical analysis.* London: Routledge & Kegan Paul.

McLoyd, V. C. (1990). The impact of economic hardship on black families and children: Psychological distress, parenting, and socioemotional development. *Child Development, 61,* 311–346.

Morgan, V., Fraser, G., Dunn, S., & Cairns, E. (1992). Parental involvement in education: How do parents want to become involved? *Educational Studies, 18,* 11–20.

Pennekamp, M., & Freeman, E. M. (1988). Toward a partnership perspective: Schools, families, and school social workers. *Social Work in Education, Summer,* 246–259.

Rich, D. (1985). *The forgotten factor in school success—The family.* Washington, DC: The Home and School Institute.

Salend, S. J., & Taylor, L. (1993). Working with families: A cross-cultural perspective. *Remedial and Special Education, 14,* 25–32, 39.

Scott-Jones, D. (1987). Mother-as-teacher in the families of high- and low-achieving low-income Black first-graders. *Journal of Negro Education, 56,* 21–34.

Simmons, R., & Blyth, D. (1987). *Moving into adolescence: The impact of pubertal change and school context.* Hawthorn, NY: Aldine de Gruyter.

Stevenson, D. L., & Baker, D. P. (1987). The family–school relation and the child's school performance. *Child Development, 58,* 1348–1357.

Zigler, E. (1979). Project Head Start: Success or failure? In E. Zigler & J. Valentine (Eds.), *Project Head Start: A legacy of the war on poverty* (pp. 495–507). New York: The Free Press.

2

▼▼▼▼▼▼▼

The Structural Context of Family–School Relations

Sanford M. Dornbusch
Kristan L. Glasgow
Stanford University

Eccles and Harold (1994) focused, in their words, on the proximal influences of parent involvement at home and at school. We applaud the central aim of their chapter, which is to examine attitudinal and behavioral processes within families and schools that differ by grade level and form of school organization. The chapter is both informative and provocative.

Let us, in turn, attempt to be provocative by providing somewhat different interpretations of their findings. As sociologists, we bring a slightly different perspective to this conference on family–school links. We place more emphasis on the influence of home and school contexts, focusing on the importance of structural factors within these settings. Our discussion therefore considers a number of different structural factors and their implications for the relations between students, parents, teachers, and schools. In particular, we attempt to show that types of school organization, curriculum tracking, social networks, bilingual education, and ethnic-specific parenting practices each affect the strength and nature of the family–school link. Our emphasis on structural factors will, we believe, assist Eccles and Harold to adapt their analyses so that the recommendations drawn from their excellent study will apply more closely to specific targeted groups.

We start with Eccles and Harold's finding that school organization (elementary school or middle school) was associated with more significant differences in the parent involvement scales than was grade level (Eccles & Harold, 1994, Table 2). What's going on? We agree with the authors that the gradual decline in parental involvement across grade levels probably reflects the widespread belief that children need and desire increased autonomy as they enter adolescence. We want to stress another reason for this decline, however, one that is built into the form of school organization. The instructional arrangements in elementary schools differ from those in middle schools, and these structural differences may be contributing to their findings on parental involvement.

In the elementary school context, for example, a single teacher instructs the same group of students for the entire day. In the middle school context, each class period brings a different group of students to each teacher. The middle school teacher, unlike the elementary school teacher, typically has a hundred or more students each day. This structural difference is likely to generate corresponding changes in the nature of teacher–student relations, as well as in the opportunities for parental contacts. Middle schools teachers have neither the time nor the resources to closely monitor the performance of each student *and* keep parents informed of ways in which they can assist their children. Such parental contact would become an overwhelming task for each teacher in the middle school, and there are seldom built-in structural arrangements that bring teachers together to generate coherent feedback for individual students. Thus, the attitudes of teachers, and the reports of students and parents as to existing contact, can be seen in part as arising from the structural arrangements within middle schools and elementary schools.

Curriculum tracking is a second structural factor affecting the family–school link. Although Eccles and Harold are primarily concerned with the proximal influences of parental involvement in schooling, we believe that they will gain much from analyzing their data both within and across tracks. Tracking is a pedagogical organizational practice that further alters the structural arrangements within and between classrooms.

Stratification through systems of curriculum tracking and ability grouping is widespread in the United States and abroad (Kerckhoff, 1986; Oakes, Gamoran, & Page, 1992). Curriculum tracking is premised on an ideology of individual differences. Because students differ in their levels of academic ability and instructional need, school practitioners generally assume that reducing this heterogeneity better enables students to progress at a speed and level commensurate with their capacities (Hallinan, 1994; Oakes, 1987; Slavin, 1990). Curriculum tracks and ability groups attempt to minimize heterogeneity by grouping students with similar capacities and interests into separate programs of instruction, which ostensibly facilitate learning for all students.

Research on the effects of curriculum tracking portrays a contrasting image, however. Channeling students into objectively distinct instructional groups creates a within-school status hierarchy, which formally recognizes some students as better and more capable than others (Oakes, 1987; Persell, 1977). Curriculum tracking produces inequalities in educational experiences and opportunities for students who are placed at different tiers of this hierarchy. Large-scale survey analyses and ethnographic studies show marked differences between ability groups and curriculum tracks in both academic and social domains (for reviews, see Gamoran & Berends, 1987; Oakes et al., 1992). The practice of selecting and sorting students into instructional groups has important consequences for teachers, parents, students, and their relationships to each other.

For example, the ways in which teachers of classes at the highest track levels relate to parents are notably different than the ways used by teachers of lower-track classes, as evident in a paper we published 8 years ago, "Teacher Perceptions of Parent–School Communication" (Prescott, Pelton, & Dornbusch, 1986). That paper shared one characteristic with the current research by Eccles and Harold: Many items were borrowed from the previous work of Joyce Epstein. Because we were instructed to relate the Eccles and Harold's chapter to our own work on family and schools in preparing this discussion, we describe relevant aspects of that study on teacher perceptions, as well as other studies by us, as follows.

In May 1985, we surveyed 252 teachers at five diverse San Francisco Bay Area high schools. We adapted a questionnaire initially developed for elementary schools to survey the opinions of high school teachers. The survey asked for teacher opinions and judgments about a number of topics relating to teacher–parent relations. High school teachers were specifically asked what they did and what they wanted to do to encourage parental involvement. We were shocked by their responses. Teachers overwhelmingly said they did not want more par-ent-initiated contact. Indeed, teachers were often resentful of parent-initiated contact. They welcomed contact when there was a problem and when *they* asked the parent to come in for a conference. Such contacts operated in a context of teacher control, with parents asked to assist the teacher. Although more than 80% of high school parents wanted to continue to be involved in the education of their children, the majority of teachers reported little contact with parents of average students and, in fact, did not prefer more contact with these parents (Dornbusch & Ritter, 1988).

This surprising finding does not support the widespread view that teachers want more parent contact and greater parental involvement. It is possible that our finding that teachers do not desire more parental involvement is an unintended consequence of our method of data collection. We had the teachers fill out their anonymous questionnaires during a school-wide faculty meeting. There was no way that individuals could be linked to their responses. Under conditions of anonymity, people feel more free to state that they do not desire that which is socially desirable.

On a similar note, Eccles and Harold observed that the absolute levels of several types of teacher communication were surprisingly low. They reported that, on the average, helpful hints were provided to parents less than once a month, and 50% to 70% of teachers in their study provided no supplementary student evaluations to parents beyond the information communicated in report cards and at conferences (Eccles & Harold, 1994, p. 12). What teachers report and what they actually do in practice are not necessarily perfectly aligned. In view of this possibility, Eccles and Harold should include in future analyses some measure of the teacher's perception of the desirability of increased parent involvement, particularly parent-initiated involvement. Sadly, Eccles and Harold cannot assume that teachers and schools are eagerly waiting for advice on how to increase family–school cooperation. The inertia of current structural arrangements will often overcome platitudinous exhortations to bring parents into the institution of schooling. Determining which factors increase school receptiveness to school–family contacts is as important as learning ways to increase parental participation in schooling.

We found in our study that, when contacts were made with parents, teachers often had bad news to convey about the student's progress, regardless of track level. Teachers of classes at all levels were more likely to contact parents when students were exerting little effort or were having discipline problems. Not surprisingly, then, teachers of lower-track classes initiated significantly more contact with parents than did teachers of higher-track classes.

In addition, there was also a slight tendency, though not significant, for more parent-initiated contact with teachers in high-track classes than with teachers in lower-track classes. Among students whose parents contacted teachers in the high tracks, parents of outstanding students initiated the most contact and showed a prior interest in helping their children in school. On the other hand, parents whose children were making little effort, having difficulty learning, or having discipline problems more frequently contacted the teachers who taught the lower-track classes. Except for the parents of outstanding students in the highest tracks, both parent-initiated and teacher-initiated contacts were a function of academic or behavioral problems at school.

Only a select population of parents was told what could be done at home to facilitate student performance in high school. At the high school level, parental aid was no longer considered an appropriate discussion topic with each parent. This is different from the earlier findings of Becker and Epstein (1982), in which 65% of elementary teachers reported discussing "with each parent" what assistance parents could provide their children in regard to school work. In secondary schools, it was the parents of students in the highest level courses who are singled out for such discussions. When students in the highest tracks exert little effort or have disciplinary problems, the teacher is more likely to contact the parent for assistance in resolving the difficulty. Teachers of lower-track students tend to see the parental role in education as a passive one.

Thus, the frequency of teacher and parent initiatives, as well as the kinds of issues discussed in teacher–parent conferences, vary across tracks levels and appear to be directly related to students' academic performance and classroom conduct. Therefore, when considering alternative mechanisms for increasing or facilitating parents' participation in schooling, recommendations should take into account the track level, performance, and disciplinary history of specific groups of students.

Eccles and Harold have the data to do further analyses in terms of teacher and parent initiation. Their teacher scales of *encourage* and *feedback,* and their parent scales of *progress* and *extra help* are directly responsive to the issues we are raising. In addition, *requests* represent one form of teacher-initiated parental involvement in the learning process. They already noted some major structural differences for some of these measures when middle schools were compared to elementary schools. Adding information on the types and levels of initiated contact taking place within tracks to their analyses would be feasible and instructive.

Our emphasis on tracking is also based on a recent collaborative study in which the senior author was aided by Kenneth D. Wood, Laurence D. Steinberg, B. Bradford Brown, and P. Herbert Leiderman. We found considerable evidence of the importance of tracking as a structural feature of schools (Dornbusch, 1994). This study examined cumulative school files and self-reported survey responses of 1,245 students from freshman, sophomore, junior, and senior classes in six San Francisco Bay Area high schools. Students were selected to provide variability in school performance within four ethnic groups: African American, Hispanic American, Asian American, and non-Hispanic White. To the extent possible, an equal number of high-, mid-, and low-performing students within each gender-ethnic group were selected. The result is a most unusual sample, with no appreciable difference in school performance across ethnic groups in the level of school performance.

In reference to this work, Eccles and Harold correctly noted that curricular choices, in the form of track assignments, determine many of the immediate and future learning opportunities available to adolescents. Indeed, we found substantial effects of curriculum tracking on student outcomes. For example, high-ability students (indicated by a high eighth grade math test score) placed in the lower tracks did not earn high grades in their last math and science courses. Students in these tracks did less work and "sank" to the level of their course-mates. It appears that high-ability students in lower tracks were not challenged to do good work. They reported that their courses were easy, and they did less homework in those courses.

Teachers of lower-track classes are themselves lower in ability and experience and set lower academic standards for their students compared with teachers of higher-track classes (Oakes, 1985, 1987). Rosenbaum (1976, p. 179) concluded some years ago, based on interviews with 50 high school seniors in the Boston area, that "even when noncollege-track students get the same teachers as college-track students, they do not get as much attention, concern, or effort from their teachers." Research by Carrasco (1988) showed that teachers of classes with a high proportion of minority students know less about college entrance requirements and correspondingly have less information to communicate about that important issue. The nature of teacher–parent contacts examined by Eccles and Harold is likely to be influenced by teachers' knowledge, expectations, and standards, which appear to vary with track level.

Schools overestimate their ability to assess ability, and numerous students, particularly those in the middle level of ability, are misassigned. We examined information from students who satisfied three criteria: They wanted to graduate from a four-year college or university; they expected to graduate; and they believed they were in the college-prep track. Within this restricted group, we found that almost half of the disadvantaged minorities (African Americans and Hispanic Americans) were not in the right courses in math and science, compared to about 20% among non-Hispanic Whites and Asians. We then added a fourth criterion: Students had demonstrated the ability to go to a four-year college by scoring among the top half of students in the United States on their eighth grade math achievement test. With this additional criterion, the proportion misassigned dropped to about a third among disadvantaged minorities and to 13% among non-Hispanic Whites and Asian Americans. If these proportions of misassigned students are even close to the national proportions, millions of talented students in every ethnic group are being shortchanged.

We also examined the impact of parenting practices on track assignment, net of eighth grade math tests scores. Because earlier grades and eighth grade test scores are to some extent the product of parenting practices, one would not expect that parenting practices would necessarily show significant relations to track once test scores were controlled. Yet, a number of family processes had significant relations to track placement. All of these relations were in the direction foretold by previous research on family processes. The most powerful parenting practice associated with track placement was parental use of encouragement, praise, and offers to help. This finding supports our earlier research on the development of internal motivation for academic achievement. These findings on family processes suggest that Eccles and Harold, who detailed information on parenting as well as parent–school relations, will get a rich return from interweaving parenting practices, track, and parent–school contacts.

Schools are often not eager to spread information to students and parents about the implications of particular curricular choices within the tracking structure, as Eccles and Harold noted in their chapter. Research by Useem (1991, 1992) shows that parents are often unaware of their child's track placement. Schools do not advertise the extent to which they are tracking students, nor do they go out of their way to point out that many students are taking courses that will not count for college admission. A finding from Eccles and Harold's MAGIC study illustrates this point. In their sample, only 40% of the parents thought they knew what courses were college preparatory, and 60% of the parents indicated that they did not get their information from the school.

What produces this collective ignorance among students and parents? Combining our studies with those of Oakes (1985, 1987) leads to a general theme: School officials and teachers gain from the ignorance of students and their parents (Meyer & Rowan, 1977). Parents and students cannot see problems when they are left in the dark. Ignorance can be functional for the personnel at individual schools, even as it leads to disaster on a national scale.

Given this widespread ignorance of track assignment, it would be instructive to observe the role of social networks in diffusing school-related information. Eccles and Harold may be able to move beyond their discussion of direct contacts between school and family to examine a third structural factor: the social networks of both parents and children. To some extent, critical information may be flowing from schools to homes indirectly through informal social networks.

Useem (1991, 1992), for example, showed that middle-class parents learn from informal networks of friends and acquaintances about what is happening in the course assignments of their children. Whereas Useem noted the role of such middle-class institutions as the bridge club in diffusing information about schools, a doctoral dissertation by Stanton-Salazar 1990) focused on a very different population for his network analysis. He limited himself to Mexican-American high school students and their families and friends. He was concerned about the flow of academic information to these students. The role of school personnel in information networks was also supportive of existing structures of inequality. One third of the Mexican-American adolescents reported never getting information from school personnel, and only 19% of all information networks included school personnel. Mexican-American adolescents used their parents and extended kin for information. Sadly, only the students with middle-class kin were aided by their information networks. Those whose kinship network was lower class were not helped by the information they tried to obtain. Those who know little have little to convey.

Lareau's (1987) work on social class differences in family–school relations also points to the importance of social networks as informational sources. In her study, parents from a middle-class community had more extensive information about their children's classroom and school activities than did working-class parents. Lareau attributed much of the difference in parents' information about schooling to compositional differences in parents' social networks. The networks of middle-class parents consisted of other parents from the school community. The social contacts of working-class parents, by contrast, were limited to relatives in the area. These parents seldom socialized with other parents from their children's school and, consequently, did not obtain information that could be used to build a strong family–school link.

In addition, children's leisure time activities also affect the amount of information flowing to parents about school. Lareau (1987) found that the activities of the working-class children tended to be informal (e.g., bike riding, watching television, playing with neighborhood children). Middle-class children, on the other hand, were more likely to be enrolled in formal after-school activities (e.g., swim lessons, arts and crafts lessons, soccer). Parents would often stay to watch these activities, providing an opportunity to interact with other school parents. Discussions usually centered on teachers' reputations and the children's academic progress (Lareau, 1987). Thus, the characteristics of social networks may either block or assist the flow of school-related information, thereby influencing the nature and frequency of parent–teacher contacts.

The structure of ethnic communities and the location of students and their families on a continuum of acculturation also influence contacts between parents, teachers, and schools. The level of academic performance, with corresponding position in the tracking structure, is affected by acculturation. Using various measures of cultural identity, Stanton-Salazar (1990) found that Mexican Americans who were bicultural were higher in their academic performance than were Mexican Americans who either rejected their Mexican heritage or who were exclusively Mexican in their cultural orientation.

The issue of biculturalism relates to the fourth structural factor in schools that may affect the family–school link—bilingual education. As U.S. schools have increased the proportion of foreign-born children, there has been a movement towards bilingual education. Students who are supposedly weak in English are taught all subjects in their native language. In theory, bilingual classes are intended to be a short-term expedient, but the reality is different. Schools and teachers, for reasons of inertia and self-interest, are often slow to mainstream students in bilingual classes after they have achieved reasonable proficiency in English. In one state, active attempts by parents to move their child out of bilingual education can be legally ignored. Assignment to bilingual education in New Jersey is mandated for all students lacking fluency in English, regardless of the wishes of the parents (Nappi, 1994).

A recent study (Dillon, 1994) examined ethnic differences in the probability of students getting out of bilingual education classes in New York City within 3 years. The differences were striking, with 90% of Korean children leaving bilingual education classes in 3 years compared with only 50% of Hispanic children. The explanation given was parental attitudes and behavior. Korean parents wanted their children to learn English swiftly and become bicultural, whereas Hispanic parents exerted less pressure toward biculturalism. This is just one instance of ethnic differences in what is considered appropriate parental behavior with relation to schooling.

Such ethnic differences in parental behavior and values will necessarily be relevant to the parent–school link studied by Eccles and Harold. Ethnic-specific parenting practices is the fifth, and final, structural factor warranting consideration. For example, Asian parents generally tend to have low levels of participation in school activities designed for parents, such as open-school nights. They seldom visit classrooms or develop relations with teachers. Instead, they emphasize effort at home. Their tactics range from insisting on additional homework time to insistence that their children not take part-time jobs. The point is that different ethnic groups exhibit high involvement in schooling in different ways. Therefore, analyses should be done within and across specific ethnic groups. The MAGIC study had a heterogeneous sample in terms of ethnicity and social class, and we believe that analyses within subgroups will be instructive. In addition, because the eventual conclusions will include suggestions about ways of involving hard-to-reach families, strategies that are based on ethnic-specific data are more likely to be successful.

Finally, we have not intended to argue that Eccles and Harold were wrong in seeing a significant decline in parental involvement by grade. Parents, teachers, and students unfortunately all agree on the greater role of parental influence for younger children when compared with preadolescents and adolescents. Dornbusch's work with Larry Steinberg, B. Bradford Brown, and P. Herbert Leiderman suggests that the impact of parents continues through adolescence and is not attenuated by age. But things that people believe, even when they are wrong, are real in their consequences, as Thomas and Thomas (1928) once said. Within the structural constraints of schools, such an attitude toward parenting has real consequences.

In conclusion, we have considered five structural factors that operate to promote or impede family involvement in children's and adolescents' schooling: forms of school organization, tracking, social networks, bilingual education, and ethnic-specific parenting practices. Eccles and Harold already indicated their intention to do careful analyses of neighborhood and community influences, which we applaud. Their excellent study holds considerable promise in contributing to remedial actions that are based on knowledge rather than good intentions.

REFERENCES

Becker, H. J., & Epstein, J. L. (1982). Parent involvement: A survey of teacher practices. *Elementary School Journal, 83*, 85–102.

Carrasco, J. A. (1988). *The flow of college-related information for students in high school settings: An organizational perspective.* Unpublished doctoral dissertation, Stanford University, Stanford, CA.

Dillon, S. (1994, October 20). Report faults bilingual education in New York. *The New York Times,* pp. 1, 4.

Dornbusch, S. M. (1994). *Off the track.* Presidential address presented at the biennial meeting of the Society for Research on Adolescence, San Diego, CA.

Dornbusch, S. M., & Ritter, P. L. (1988). Parents of high school students: A neglected resource. *Educational Horizons, 66,* 75–77.

Eccles, J. S., & Harold, R. (1994, October). *Family involvement in children's and adolescents' schooling.* Paper presented for the National Symposium on Family–School Links: How Do They Affect Educational Outcomes? Pennsylvania State University, University Park, PA.

Gamoran, A., & Berends, M. (1987). The effects of stratification in secondary schools: Synthesis of survey and ethnographic research. *Review of Educational Research, 57,* 415–435.

Hallinan, M. T. (1994). Tracking: From theory to practice. *Sociology of Education, 67*(2), 79–84.

Kerckhoff, A. (1986). Effects of ability grouping in British secondary schools. *American Sociological Review, 51,* 842–858.

Lareau, A. (1987). Social class differences in family–school relationships: The importance of cultural capital. *Sociology of Education, 60,* 73–85.

Meyer, J. W., & Rowan, B. (1977). Institutionalized organizations: Formal structure as myth and ceremony. *American Journal of Sociology, 83,* 340–363.

Nappi, C. (1994, October 27). Jersey needs an alternative to its bilingual education program. *The New York Times,* p. 1.

Oakes, J. (1985). *Keeping track: How schools structure inequality.* New Haven, CT: Yale University Press.

Oakes, J. (1987). Tracking in secondary schools: A contextual perspective. *Educational Psychologist, 22,* 129–153.

Oakes, J., Gamoran, A., & Page, R. N. (1992). Curriculum differentiation: Opportunities, outcomes, and meanings. In P. W. Jackson (Ed.), *Handbook of research on curriculum* (pp. 570–608). New York: MacMillan.

Persell, C. (1977). *Education and inequality.* London: Collier MacMillan.

Prescott, B. L., Pelton, C. L., & Dornbusch, S. M. (1986). Teacher perceptions of parent–school communication: A collaborative analysis. *Teacher Education Quarterly, 13*(2), 67–83.

Rosenbaum, J. E. (1976). *Making inequality: The hidden curriculum of high school tracking.* New York: Wiley.

Slavin, R. E. (1990). Achievement effects of ability grouping in secondary schools: A best-evidence synthesis. *Review of Educational Research, 60,* 471–499.

Stanton-Salazar, R. (1990). *The role of social and information networks in the formation of educational and occupational expectations among Mexican-origin high school youth.* Unpublished doctoral dissertation, Stanford University, Stanford, CA.

Thomas, W. I., and Thomas, D. S. (1928). *The child in America: Behavioral problems and programs.* New York: Knopf.

Useem, E. L. (1991). Student selection into course sequences in mathematics: The impact of parental involvement and school policies. *Journal of Research on Adolescence, 1*(3), 231–250.

Useem, E. L. (1992). Middle schools and math groups: Parents' involvement in children's placement. *Sociology of Education, 65,* 263–279.

3

$\blacktriangledown\blacktriangledown\blacktriangledown\blacktriangledown\blacktriangledown\blacktriangledown\blacktriangledown$

Parents as Full Partners in Education

Norris M. Haynes
Michael Ben-Avie
Yale University

THE CASE FOR PARENTAL INVOLVEMENT: MULTIPLE OUTCOMES

The case for parental involvement in schools includes, but is not limited to, promoting children's academic and socioemotional development. Eccles and Harold (chap. 1, this volume) deal well with student outcomes that stem from parental involvement in schools. To complete the model that they present in their chapter, it is of worth to consider other outcomes that are not so readily discernible:

1. Teacher outcomes: Through increased parental involvement in the schools, school staff increase their knowledge base of the sociocultural context of the communities served by the school. This knowledge base enables staff to gain a greater understanding of the students ranging from idiosyncratic speech and language patterns to the stresses that children encounter in their daily lives outside of school and that have an impact on their learning. This knowledge base is likely to lead to an increased sense of efficacy among teachers and more effective and improved classroom climate and thus the teacher's sense of efficacy among teachers and more effective classroom management strategies and pedagogy.

2. Parent outcomes: Parents who become involved in the school learn ways to help their children and become motivated to further their own education, and those parents who are alienated from mainstream culture or have had negative school experiences could come to perceive the school as a bastion of hope for their children and for themselves.

3. School outcomes: The key to sustaining educational change, when the new initiatives are no longer "new," is through empowering parents to be advocates of their children; the stake parents have in their children's school success is a powerful change force when parent involvement is an integral and significant aspect of school changes processes that mobilize parents.

4. Community outcomes: When these two primary societal institutions (the family and the school) team up, the school becomes a potent force in the community, in promoting healthy holistic development among all children. Instead of taking upon themselves the tasks of families or relegating parental involvement to narrow areas of activity such as monitoring homework completion and supplementing teacher assigned lessons, schools need to encourage parents to broaden their spheres of activities so that parents become catalysts for change in the school and the community and informed advocates for their children. In order to do so, schools "must become more flexible, responsive, child-centered, culturally sensitive, community linked and family connected" Haynes, Gebreyesus, & Comer, 1993, p. 165).

A distinction may be made at the outset between schoolwide programs that promote parental involvement as an integral aspect of schoolwide planning management and operational processes and that which is dependent on the personal initiative of either the individual teacher or the individual parents as described by Eccles and Harold. As Comer (1986) noted, most teachers and administrators are not taught "how to work with parents or to use them as allies in promoting the growth and development of students" (p. 443). Schools should have a well-thought-out mechanism in place to harness the energy and talents of the parents. A Comer parent (cited in Haynes et al., 1993) described well the situation when a mechanism exists in the school for promoting parental involvement:

> I feel that the school's climate is wonderful; it's a nice secure place for the children here; and, it's a lot different than it was before. The Comer Process came into the school, not only pertaining to the children, but also to the parents and the way the parents feel when they come in because at first, before the Comer Process was here, there was hesitance on the part of some of the parents to come in, and there was a difference in the reception you got here, too, as compared to now, and it's a big difference. You feel comfortable coming to the school. You feel that the school is not a separate place anymore where it's them and us. It's no longer them and us. Now we are we. (p. 37)

The teachers described by Eccles and Harold did not have an incentive to include parents. Given our knowledge of human ecology systems theory (Comer, 1991), the teachers described by Eccles and Harold could have viewed involving the students' parents as risky, a task beyond their professional duties, and conflict ridden. As we have noted in the past, "the area of parent participation that produces the least anxiety for teachers is that of homework assignments" (Bruno, Joyner, Haynes, Comer, & Maholmes, 1994, p. 7).

KINDS OF PARENT INVOLVEMENT

It is worthwhile to consider the difference between Eccles and Harold's approach to parental involvement and what the School Development Program (SDP) considers parental involvement. Eccles and Harold have developed five variables that constitute in their opinion parental involvement: Monitor (parent response to teacher requests and information), Volunteer (the rate of parent participation in volunteer activities at school), Involvement (parent report of frequency of involvement with child's daily activities), Progress (do you contact the school about child's progress?), and Extra Help (do you contact the school about how to give extra help?). In contrast, in the SDP's model, we have created a three-tier model of what constitutes parental involvement: (3) General Participation, (2) Helping in classrooms or sponsoring and supporting school programs, and (1) Parent participation on the School Planning and Management Team (SPMT). Thus the SDP's parental involvement approach focuses on permitting parents "to play meaningful roles with staff approval and support in school and with clear direction and purpose" (Comer & Haynes, 1991, p. 277). Thus a distinction may be made between Eccles and Harold's understanding of parental involvement, which focuses on specific types of activities, and our parent involvement paradigm, which includes significant participation in decision making in order to enhance the educational process and improve the overall climate of schools (Comer & Haynes, 1991, p. 271).

The distinction between the two approaches becomes clear when considering what Eccles and Harold (chap. 1, this volume) call "limiting factors" to frequency of involvement at school (see p. 23). Frequency of involvement at school, according to the items, is understood as PTO/PTA participation, leader in PTO/PTA, and general volunteer work at school. Parents were asked to check reasons why they were not more involved at school and, not surprisingly, 62% indicated work commitments. However, in SDP schools in which parents having meaningful roles pertinent to the functioning of the school, even work commitments are not seen as obstacles but rather as logistical problems in need of solving. As Comer and Haynes (1991) relate:

> It is sometimes difficult to get parents involved at this [the School Planning and Management] level because many work during the school day when meetings might take place. This problem was solved in one school when the principal contacted employers, explained the importance of the team's work, and requested that parent members be given time off to attend such meetings. The employers agreed, and all five parents were able to be active members of the SPMT. In other schools, team members have agreed to meet before or after school or in the evenings. (p. 274)

Eccles and Harold talk about parental involvement at school in terms of parents visiting their child's classroom to see what their child is doing or attending school activities and teacher conferences (p. 23). This approach minimizes the meaningful role parents can have in the life of the school; Comer (1986) noted, for example, that "many Parent/Teacher Organizations function superficially, under the principal's control, and don't do much to improve the climate of the school" (p. 444). Parents who encounter this attitude in their children's school will, of course, be inclined to limit the frequency of their involvement at school. Consider the situation of parents who are told that parents are, of course, welcome in the school but encounter a sign that reads "Visitors are welcome. Please report to the principal's office" (Winters & Schraft, 1977, cited in Bruno et al., 1994, p. 6).

SELECTED COMPONENTS OF ECCLES AND HAROLD'S MODEL

Among the exogenous variables that Eccles and Harold note is *Parents' attitude toward the school* which includes as part of its explanation, "the extent to which they [the parents] think the school is sympathetic to their child and to their situation, their previous history of negative and positive experiences at school" (p. 7). Given the SDP's extensive experience on this issue in particular, Comer's (1994) analysis of a "Culture of Failure" is especially relevant. He wrote:

> The response of school people, without adequate preparation, is to punish what they understand as bad behavior and to hold low expectations for underdeveloped or differently developed children. This leads to difficult interactions between students and staff, and intern staff and parents, and eventually a Culture of Failure in school. Distrust, anger and alienation often develop between home and school. This makes it difficult for parents and staff to relate in ways needed to support the level of overall development needed for children to function well in the cognitive area necessary for school success. (p. iv)

In Comer's analysis, either a cultural dissonance between the parents and the school or negative experiences with schooling (either parents' own schooling or their child's) is at the very heart of the issue of what factors influence parental involvement. Schools may be differentiated between those schools that understand that involving parents sometimes requires a *political socialization process* that does not manipulate parents but rather works with them in understanding how parent participation in program and policy decisions can result in benefits to themselves, their children, and the community and it teaches parents the *savior-faire* needed to have an impact on the school *and those* schools that keep parent involvement at low levels of participation, expect the parents to already have the savvy to organize school-wide activities, do not acknowledge the anger and distrust that some parents might have towards the school, or assume that there exists a natural cultural continuity among all the parents and the school. Our experience suggests that this political socialization process can be tedious and sometimes painful (Joyner, Haynes, & Comer, 1994, p. 28). Comer (1980) noted, "It is of no particular surprise that parents who have had negative experiences with schooling or perceive their child's school promoting parental involvement in name only will limit their involvement at the school. This, of course, only provides reinforcement to the school staff who, perhaps genuinely, believe they tried to involve parents, but they weren't interested" (p. 330).

Another component of Eccles and Harold's model worth highlighting is the organizational structure of the school (p. 10), an issue that especially pertains to the nature of the middle school, as they so rightly discerned. We observed that "far too many teachers in the middle school have become subject oriented and neglect to build the kinds of relationships with students that aid their growth and development" (Joyner et al., 1994, p. 12). Integral to the relationship that teachers build with students is a cooperative relationship with the child's parents. In middle schools that have taken upon themselves the characteristics of a preparatory for high school program, both the students and the parents encounter a multitude of teachers responsible for educating the students thus leading to the parents' perception that they are not sure to whom to speak in the school regarding their child's education. Coupled with the intensification of peer group influences and the relative decline of parental and family social network influences on young people at this age group (Joyner et al., 1994, p. 11), middle schools, perhaps even more than elementary schools, need to reach out to parents as co-partners. The SDP's experiences with middle schools that have successfully involved parents in enhancing the educational process indicate the content of the SPMT and MHT (Mental Health Team) meetings are more complex than that of the elementary school (Joyner et al., 1994, p. 10), as befitting the more complex developmental and environmental situation that the young adolescents face. Eccles and Harold's model would perhaps benefit from clearly indicating that parental involvement at the elementary school level and at the middle school level needs to be qualitatively different and not, as it stands now, an extension of the same types of activities that characterize parental involvement during the elementary school years.

A third component of Eccles and Harold's model worth highlighting also relates to school and teacher characteristics and practices (p. 10). In addition to the aspect of the organizational structure of the school, Eccles and Harold discussed school personnel's beliefs and attitudes; the discussion is limited, however, to beliefs and practices that are directly related to parental involvement (e.g., "beliefs about what is the appropriate amount and type of parent involvement," p. 11). School personnel's beliefs and practices relating to parental involvement are an integral part of the school's ethos and it is importand that their beliefs and practices should be considered. First, it is of worth to note that schools are intentional cultural communities deliberately designed by educators in order to engender a school ethos that they consider to be most beneficial to the schools' mission. Secondly, schools may be differentiated by whether they see the school as an integral part of the community in which they reside or whether they deliberately try to foster a distance between themselves and the communities. For example, a school's ethos that is characterized by the conscious sentiment that the students need to be removed from the negative influences in their home and neighborhood environment and raised by professionals within a decontextualized setting is a mediating variable when the school personnel reflect on beliefs and practices relating to parental involvement. Another way to understand this point is to consider a school's ethos that is characterized by what Comer (1986) termed the *medical model* (p. 444). Comer wrote in regards to professionals influenced by the medical model, who are untrained or inadequately trained in child development:

> They respond to even normal developmental crises and to problems caused by the organization and management of schools as if students were "sick" or "bad." Teachers, ill-prepared to understand and respond to anything but complaint behavior, often dispatch the "bad" child to an administrator for correction. When this doesn't work, the youngsters are passed on to the professional "behavior fixers" . . . Parents of the children they "treat" are put on the defensive, and so the parent/school relationship is further complicated. (p. 444)

A school's ethos noted for this medical model approach will be a negative mediating variable when the school personnel consider ways to involve parents: If kids are "sick" because of their home environment, then, the school personnel reason, the best course of action is to isolate as much as possible the school from the parents.

Along the same train of thought, the next component of Eccles and Harold's model relates to the application of the "bell-shaped curve" paradigm to education. This paradigm by definition assumes that some children will do well in school, most children will be in the middle, and some children will inevitably fail. In Eccles and Harold's discussion of child characteristics (p. 9), they noted that "parents of high achieving children may be more likely to participate in school governance and school activities than parents of lower achieving children" (p. 10). Their discussion, however, does not fully capture the complexity of this issue; Parents of low achieving children may be responding to the fact that the school has labeled their children low achieving and has nurtured this perception by regulating them to lower ability groups or has instituted retention policies for them. The SDP has found that through shared decision making and shared responsibility, "even very troubled parents whose children are experiencing serious difficulty with the school have become more cooperative. Less time is wasted on broken appointments, blaming and recriminations, crises, and failure to follow through" (Schraft & Comer, 1979, p. 323).

The last component of Eccles and Harold's model that we would like to highlight is in reference to the variable labeled Community Characteristics (p.

8). Although their discussion details community characteristics such as high-risk and low resources, they do not discuss the role the school itself can play in the community. Comer (1989) noted:

> While there are many social and political problems that we must address at this point in time, one of the things that we can do in our schools is to pay attention to child development and relationship issues so that more children can get the kind of education that will allow them to make this society different. We can make a change to meet their needs, to meet our needs, and to make it possible for this society to continue to thrive. (p. 139)

Schools that go beyond a narrow definition as to their mission and consider themselves "human resource development centers," (Presseisen, Smey-Richman, & Beyer, in press) not only for the students in their charge but for the entire community, can play a role in revitalizing depressed neighborhoods, in gathering under one roof all the social services essential to families in need of them, in spearheading community action, and in community education. The SDP observed, for example, that "although in actuality, only a very few parents were intimately involved [as members of the school governing board and in workshops with staff in a school described as unstable], *the results were visible to the entire community [italics added]*" (Comer, 1980, p. 334). In addition, Schraft and Comer (1979) noted that through the implementation of parent programs in schools that successfully lead to increased parental involvement, a healthy environment is engendered that provides a viable foundation for problem solving and clinical intervention with troubled families. Thus, Eccles and Harold would perhaps benefit from including in their variable of Community Characteristics (as well as in the variable of parent/family characteristics under the heading of social and psychological resources available to the parent) the role the school itself plays in the community.

THE HEART OF THE ISSUE

In an extraordinarily frank dialogue between Comer and Ronald Edmonds, shortly before the latter's untimely death, the topic of parental involvement came up. Edmonds said to Comer:

> See, Jim, I don't dispute what you are saying. I just am unwilling to put forth a design for school improvement that depends on parents, because the scenario I envision is one in which the school people say, "We tried to get parent cooperation but we didn't get it, therefore. . ." I stick with what is inside the school because there is no way to avoid that. (O'Neill & Shoemaker, 1989, p. 62)

Comer responded:

I argue that you don't have to accept that when they say that. I back up to your position. You can do without parents. It will be easier for you. But it will be better for the parents and better for the children in the long run with parents. (p. 62)

Comer's response was based, in part, on his understanding that "the self-affirmation of the child comes more from home than from school. Without parental support for school staff and programs, children who sense any degree of rejection or being outside the mainstream of society will pull away from the attitudes, values, and ways that could lead to sustained school and related life success" (Comer, 1991, p. 186). When parents and school staff join forces together though collaborative work on meaningful projects, "a sense of community is established and adult authority is available to aid the development and behavior of students" (Comer, 1991, p. 187).

WHAT THE SDP LEARNED ABOUT PARENT INVOLVEMENT

Eccles and Harold asked parents if they agreed or disagreed with the statement that teachers should do more to get parents involved; 65% responded in the affirmative (p. 23). The SDP has learned the value of having an external change agent in the field to help deal with issues such as parental involvement by helping to institutionalize it. The Comer Facilitator orchestrates the initiation of a well-conceived parent involvement program rather than leaving the issue up to the initiative of the teacher acting by himself or herself or the initiative of individual parents working by themselves. Working with the SPMT, the teachers, and the parents, the Comer Facilitator nurtures the school–family interaction and helps the school community (which includes the parents) to design parent programs that are meaningful and make sense to the whole community. The Comer Facilitator prods the school community to take ownership of initiatives and to be accountable for the success of programs. Thus, with the assistance of a trained change agent, staff and parents, with endorsement of the school community, develop a parent program that is integrated into the fabric of the school.

A few examples suffice. For example, Comer (1989) narrated that in the first year of the intervention in one school district:

As few as 15–30 parents turned out for the most important school programs, but this gradually changed. Parents serving on a governance and management team helped develop the school plan. Parent group activities were integrated into the school plan, and their involvement gave parents a sense of ownership and a stake in the outcome of all school activities. By the third project year, more than 400 parents turned out for the Christmas Program, and an average of 250 parents for each major activities. (p. 5)

In another school district:

> We promoted three levels of parent participation—the general turnout as just described [500 parents of a school with only 400 students showed up for a school activity], the parent group planning and carrying out various activities as the second, and the parent representatives working in governance and management as the third. At the point of the greatest elaboration of our project, one parent served in each classroom as an assistant to the teacher [helping to carry out the academic program of the classroom, assisting on field trips, and supporting desirable behavior of students within the school]. They were paid the minimum wage for ten hours and most volunteered 20–30 more hours per week. (p. 5)

These examples illustrate the organic and dynamic nature of the SDP's parent involvement programs. Parents are involved in both instructional and noninstructional activities. Parents work directly in the classrooms; parents have meaningful roles in the schools that are directly related to educational activities and the curriculum; parents are involved in changing the climate of the school so that authentic learning and teaching can occur; and parents are an integral part of the schools' governance and management teams. Through their involvement, parents not only grow to have a sense of ownership of the school's program but they also effectively involve other parents, including the "hard-to-reach" parents; additionally, their own sense of efficacy and self-confidence increases. The fact that parents are volunteering 20–30 more hours per week than they are paid for because they support the mission of the school and the need for education does not go unnoticed by the students.

Researchers have documented the links between parent involvement and children's school achievement. For example, Henderson (cited in Swap, 1993) concluded after reviewing 36 studies in 1981 and 49 in 1987 that "the evidence is now beyond dispute; parent involvement improves student achievement. When parents are involved, children do better in school" (p. 3). In addition, Henderson observed that in order for parental involvement to have an impact on student achievement, less important is the form of the involvement but crucial is that it is reasonably well-planned, comprehensive, and long-lasting (Swap, 1993, p. 3). In another review of research, Sattes (cited in Swap, 1993) concluded after reviewing 40 studies that "parent involvement impacts student achievement when that involvement is meaningful to parents" (p. 3).

By involving themselves in the schools, parents support the development of their own children, serving, as Comer (1989) noted, as important role models and guides. He wrote: "The children observed and identified with their parents ad active learners and contributors to the school program, and they internalized the attitudes, values and ways of the school" (p. 26). In contrast to the attitude expressed by Eccles and Harold in regard to parents' efficacy beliefs (p. 7), the parents' efficacy need not be related to their ability to help their children complete their homework in specialized subject areas, but involved parents' efficacy stems from their demonstrating to their children that learning is a life-long process that is valued.

A final note on what the SDP has learned about parent involvement is best illustrated recalling the mistakes we made. When the SDP model was first implemented, we did not expect that the parents who had been members of the teams would want to continue in their roles even after their children graduated from the schools. Thus, policies such as "No parent could serve for more than 2 consecutive years on the SPMT" and "only parents who have children in the school can serve" needed to be instituted. In addition, the SDP's earliest parent program efforts floundered because it was not anticipated that parents would need a liaison from the school staff to help them learn how to navigate in the school setting, to help them develop the skills necessary to run an effective parent program, and to facilitate parent–staff relations (Comer, 1991, p. 188). Of special importance, the SDP learned that a parent program needs to be part of a comprehensive school change initiative and that the other key players in the school community, such as the central office, the principal, teachers, and other staff, need to be oriented to the program. Timing is essential. The implementation of the governance and management structure should be in place before the parent program is established (Comer & Haynes, 1991, p. 275). Also, we learned that in order to avoid confusion and conflict, clearly defined roles and activities for parents need to be generated.

CONCLUSIONS

Having considered Eccles and Harold's model, the framework is laid for understanding the variables relating to family–school collaboration. The SDP's strength in this area may serve as a guide to how the framework might be developed. In regards to the empirical studies, more clarity is needed to understand how the instruments assess the model. It is recommended that the instruments' development would be in the direction of assessing the manifold facets of family–school collaboration in all its forms. In closing, we recall the title of one of Dr. Comer's articles on the subject entitled *Parent Participation: Fad or Function?* In explaining the title, he wrote, "If parents are involved in supporting the staff and the program of a school in a way that promotes the attachment and bonding of their children to the program, parental involvement can be sustained as a critical function rather than declining in a few years as one more unsuccessful fad in education" (Comer, 1991, p. 188).

REFERENCES

Bruno, K., Joyner, E., Haynes, N. M., Comer, J. P., & Maholmes, V. (1994). Parent involvement and school improvement. *School Development Program Research Monograph*. New Haven, CT: Yale Child Study Center.

Comer, J. P. (1980). Working with Black parents. In R. Abidin (Ed.), *Parent education and intervention handbook*. Springfield, IL: Thomas.

Comer, J. P. (1986). Parent participation in the schools. *Phi Delta Kappa, 67*(6), 442–446.

Comer, J. P. (1989). Parent participation in schools: The School Development Program as a model. *Family Resource Coalition Report, 8*(4–5), 26.

Comer, J. P. (1991). Parent participation: Fad or function? *Educational Horizons, 69*(4), 182–188.

Comer, J. P. (1994). Introduction and problem analysis. *School Development Program Research Monograph*. New Haven, CT: Yale Child Study Center.

Comer, J. P., & Haynes, N. M. (1991). Parent involvement in schools: An ecological approach. *The Elementary School Journal, 91*(3), 271–277.

Haynes, N. M., Gebreyesus, S., & Comer, J. P. (1993). *Selected case studies of national Implementation of the School Development Program*. New Haven, CT: Yale Child Study Center.

Joyner, E., Haynes, N. M., & Comer, J. P. (1994). Implementation of the Yale School Development Program in two middle schools: An ethnographic study (School Development Program Research Monograph). New Haven, CT: Yale Child Study Center. (ERIC Document Reproduction Service No. ED 371 091).

O'Neill, K., & Shoemaker, J. (1989). *A conversation between James Comer and Ronald Edmonds: Fundamentals of effective school improvement*. Washington, DC: National Center for Effective Schools Research and Development.

Presseisen, B., Smey-Richman, B. B., & Beyer, F. (in press). Cognitive development through radical change: Restructuring classroom environments for students at risk. In J. N. Mangieri & C. C. Block (Eds.), *Creating powerful thinking in teachers and students: Diverse perspectives*. Fort Worth, TX: Harcourt, Brace & Jovanovich.

Schraft, C., & Comer, J. P. (1979). Parent participation and urban schools. *School Social work Quarterly, 1*(4), 309–325.

Swap, S. A. (1993). *Developing home–school partnerships*. New York: Teachers College Press.

4

▼▼▼▼▼▼▼

Assessing Parent Involvement
in Schooling: A Critical Analysis

Annette Lareau
Temple University

Proponents of family–school relationships, including Professors Eccles and Harold (chap. 1, this volume) have been very positive about family involvement in schooling. Eccles and Harold, for example, report that parents—virtually all parents—share their desire for increased family–school contact. Teachers also seek more involvement with parents. Dismayed by uneven compliance with these educational goals, they frame their research question in the following way: "Why are parents and teachers not more involved with each other?" A key part of their answer focuses on teacher and school practices.

At the risk of being contrary, I must say that I find their position on parent involvement to be seriously flawed. My goal is to share my concerns and to sketch out an alternative perspective. My concerns do *not* center on the relationship between parent involvement and children's achievement noted by so many. Nor do I contest their emphasis on altering school and teacher practices. I do, however, argue that we need to evaluate critically prevailing professional standards of childrearing. Thirty years ago, most cars did not have seat belts or child seats. Today, parents are severely criticized—in rare cases, such as car accidents, even arrested—for not belting children in a car. Other fashions in childrearing are embraced strongly by professionals and often infused with a sense of moral righteousness. Social scientists, however, have a special obligation to retain a more distant perspective. They need to evaluate the nature of the standards as well as the factors facilitating or impeding compliance with them.

In my view, the emphasis on family involvement in education is one such historically contingent standard, newly evolved and shrouded in sentimental enthusiasm. I argue that many working-class and lower-class parents do not accept, nor comply, with crucial aspects of the model of family–school involvement presented by the authors. Middle-class parents are much more likely to see themselves as having shared responsibility for the schooling process. Working- and lower-class parents, however, appear to turn over responsibility for education to the school. Thus, to preview my argument, I first suggest that the authors do not take seriously social class differences in what *parents* mean when they report that they want to be helpful. Second, I argue that they overemphasize a consensus between parents and educators and fail to acknowledge deep conflicts over childrearing, for example, in encouraging children to hit other children to solve a problem. Third, I maintain that they need to take more seriously the impact of the class differences in social networks on family–school relationships.

To be sure, social class is not the only feature shaping family–school relationships. Within a single family, mothers take a more active role in one child's schooling than another. In addition, parents of similar social class positions often approach teachers differently. Nevertheless, in their work, researchers have at times lost sight of the broader social context, the constant shifts in the advice of professionals, and the fact that some parents comply with this advice more than others. The broader conceptual model of Bourdieu (1984; Bourdieu & Passeron, 1977) provides a framework for analysis of these issues. Briefly, Bourdieu's concept of cultural capital highlights the point that the more parents share the same standards of institutions, the easier it is for them to facilitate the success of their children. In other words, cultural preferences have the potential to produce social profits when displayed in particular social fields.[1]

My comments draw on a research project that is still in progress. Seventy-two children have been observed in their third grade classroom followed by separate 2-hour interviews with their mother, father, or guardian. In addition, we are in the process of doing intensive observations on 12 of these families by visiting their home about 20 times for 2 or 3 hours each often within the space of 1 month. The design includes White and African-American children who are middle class, working class, and lower class in a Midwestern small city and a metropolis in the Northeast.[2] The purpose of the study is to understand the meaning of these

---

[1]Of course, the concept of cultural capital is only one small part of Bourdieu's framework, which includes other forms of capital (i.e., social, economic, and educational), life dispositions (i.e., habitus), and life trajectories of individuals and the social space (i.e., fields) individuals negotiate (Bourdieu, 1984). This chapter, however, focuses on only two of Bourdieu's points: First, cultural standards are selectively validated by schools, and second, these cultural standards are historically specific. Although admittedly taken out of theoretical context, the concept of cultural capital suffices for the purposes of this discussion. It should be noted that the parents' disciplinary techniques and childrearing methods, while compatible with Bourdieu's formulation of cultural capital, are not explicitly included in his original discussion.

[2]Middle class is defined as a household where one person has a college degree and a job involving a significant degree of autonomy; working class is a household where one adult has a high school education (or some college) and a job with limited autonomy; lower class is a household on public assistance. Usually, the adults have a high school education and are not in the labor force.

events in daily life; it falls within the rubric of "ethnographic" research and shares the normal limitations of intensive case studies.

It is precisely in following families around in their daily life that I have come to question the findings noted by the authors that parents want to be more involved in their children's education and would like more information and help from the schools. I have no doubt that parents do check off these answers in survey research. The meaning, however, differs radically. The same phrase "contacting the school, checking homework, helping with homework, and talking to teachers," appears to have a different meaning to the parents in our current study (see also Lareau, 1989). For example, in the middle-class school, mothers often initiate calls to educators. They define it as well within their right to raise questions and criticize teachers, including making demands that a Christian song using the word *God* be removed from the holiday program to complaining that their child was unable to perform a play to classmates the previous day. By contrast, the working-class and lower-class parents did not presume similar rights or responsibilities.

A White working-class girl in our study, for example, Wendy, is currently in the fifth grade. Although she is on grade level in math, she is a nonreader and is on a pre-primer. She has never been retained, but she has been in a pull-out special education program since the first grade. Her mother is aware of her school difficulties. She sees herself as a concerned parent. She went to school for back-to-school night and complained to me that there were only two parents there out of the 13 children in the class. She sees herself as a helpful and involved parent. She says, "They know they can always call me." Yet her notion of involvement involves carefully watching educator activities but not criticizing, initiating, or intervening. In short, she does not and, I believe, will not comply with the standard of "collaborating" with the school. For example, last spring when she was at school for the parent–teacher conference, she saw the school counselor briefly, who told her that they were going to send home a paper to get her approval and to attempt to test her daughter in the spring before the end of school. For 3 weeks, every day, she waited for the paper to arrive. It did not. She was frustrated; she told me many times about how they were supposed to send the paper. She thought about it every day. In one of our many conversations about it, I asked her, "Did you think of calling?" She said, "No, I'll wait. If it doesn't come by the end of next week (a full 4 weeks after the initial proposal), then I'll call the school." It is noteworthy, in this context, that working-class and lower-class parents virtually always described individual educators as "the school"—even when they were describing a meeting with only one person— whereas middle-class parents almost always referred to the specific name of the teacher or the administrator and sometimes by their first name. The paper came at the end of the third week. The patience exhibited by Wendy's mother was not characteristic of her interactions with other institutions, including the cable company, her landlord, and retail stores. For example, faced with a landlord who was slow fixing a broken kitchen faucet, she called him and told him, "If you don't get it fixed by Monday, I'm going to call a plumber and deduct it from my rent." Similarly, when the cable company—despite having been paid fully in cash—did not hook up their cable when promised, she called several times and complained, even asking to speak to a supervisor. By contrast, in the arena of school, Wendy's mother did not define it as within her right to call. Similarly, when she got the report on the testing a few weeks later and found it completely incomprehensible, she also did not call the school. Other working-class and lower-class parents (although certainly not all) also followed this pattern of careful monitoring without intervention. By contrast, the middle-class parents, especially mothers, were strikingly more outspoken in their interactions; mothers complained that the math projects sent home were too time consuming, took their children for private IQ testing to gain entrance in the gifted program, complained about teachers reading grades aloud in the classroom (on the grounds that it humiliated some students), and complained about the wording of a request by the choir teacher that parents remain quiet during the spring concert.

Family–school researchers, including Professors Eccles and Harold, suggest that there is strong evidence of a desire on the part of parents to be actively involved in schooling. My research seeks to alter that formulation. There is a fundamental disparity in the definitions of what parents mean by being involved, especially in the division of responsibility. When Wendy's mother did not call the school, it was not because of a lack of interest or concern but because she did not define it as her proper responsibility or right to call. Informing parents that they should be active is ineffectual because many parents, including Wendy's mother, already believe that they are active—indeed more active than other parents in the school or in their neighborhood. As with visions of medical care in the 1950s, parents hold a notion of professional expertise. Just as parents took their children to the doctor and the doctor "cured" them, parents take their children to school where they are educated. They believe it is not up to them. So, my first point is that many working-class and lower-class parents had a very different standard of the meaning of what parents should do to help their children. Compared to middle-class parents, they had a powerful sense of professional expertise and of their own limited ability to intervene.

Secondly, although other researchers acknowledge variations in parents' socialization practices, they generally presume a consensus between parents and teachers in matters of education. They do not sufficiently emphasize the serious conflicts between families and schools. For example, school officials were universally opposed to children hitting one another. They also objected to parents telling children to hit one another; they complained "it was sending the wrong message." This standard of childrearing clashed with the deeply felt beliefs and behaviors of some working-class and lower-class parents. An African-American lower-class boy, for example, observed his mother engaging in "play fighting" with his older sister; a White working-class boy was explicitly trained by his father and uncle to go to school and "beat up" another boy in the class; they were proud when he "got the job done" and did not mind that he was suspended for it. Wendy's mother and her fiancé encouraged their daughter to strike a boy who persisted in pulling her ponytail in class. Wendy's mother said she told her, "Punch him." Her fiancé said, "Hit him when the teacher isn't looking."

Thus, there are strong differences of opinion about how children should be treated. As in marital relationships, better communication cannot always resolve deeply felt conflicting worldviews. Unlike marital relationships, however, parents and teachers do not have the potential to have equal status and power. Teachers have more power at school; they can and will suspend children from school or the bus for hitting. They also can prevent children from passing a grade because of behavior problems. Of course, in their day-to-day life, most teachers experience feelings of powerlessness, not power, constrained as they are by endless school and district regulations and often hampered by parents in their efforts to teach. Nonetheless, teachers' subjective experiences of frustration—which are considerable—should not overshadow the legal and social prerogative teachers have to confront parents when they are concerned about children's welfare.

This greater power of teachers over parents is not simply in their decisions about children at school but also in their potential authority to turn them in to the Department of Human Services (DHS). This anxiety that parents will do something wrong with school and "they will come take my kids away" spontaneously was mentioned by working-class and lower-class parents many times in different contexts. For example, one night after working, a White working-class mother came home and found that her child had been in the nurse's office complaining that her wrist hurt. The mother was tired and was certain it was nothing, but she arranged for her mother-in-law to watch her baby, arranged a ride, and took her daughter to the emergency room anyway:

> Every time the school sends something home, I am worried if I don't do something about it that they'll report it to DHS. . . . So even though I knew it was nothing, I took her to the hospital to have them tell me it was nothing. . . . They send you this big card and even though I'm her mother, I feel that the school if you don't do something that they will report you, and they'll come and take your kids away.

The concern about DHS did not seem to preoccupy middle-class parents. In fact, in all of the fieldwork, it came up only once in a middle-class family and then in a much more lighthearted manner.

Moreover, the anxiety of working-class and lower-class parents appeared to have foundation. For example, one Sunday night a young boy had welts on his arm where his mother had hit him with a belt; she was correctly worried about sending him to school in this condition. Fashions in childrearing have shifted; belts, a popular method of disciplining children for many decades, have fallen out of fashion, especially among professionals in the middle class. Verbal negotiation has taken its place. In moments of frustration, parents sometimes say to their children statements they regret, including, for example, a statement a middle-class mother made to her 4-year-old child, "I don't want to be your mother anymore" because of her child's behavior. Setting aside the desirability, or effectiveness, of various strategies of discipline, the point is that parents are generally not at risk for being turned in to child protective services on the basis of a verbal comment. By contrast, beating a child with a belt does place a parent at risk for consideration by child protective services.

The collaborative family–school model presumes similar concepts of childrearing and, especially, equal power. Indeed, the very term *family–school* **partnership**, raises the prospect of equal power. This concept is inaccurate. It does not correctly describe the relations between parents and teachers. Nor does it acknowledge that in the diversity of childrearing practices in this country, social class has an important, although not determinative, impact on parents following the standards of childrearing espoused by dominant institutions. Working-class and lower-class parents perceive educators as ambassadors for dominant institutions and, in many instances, as a possible threat to their family. This looming and possible threat of educators to family stability creates a context within which family–school relations are created. My second point is twofold: that family–school proponents minimize the deep conflicts that exist in the area of childrearing, particularly around the issue of physical force, and that they fail to note the imbalance of power that teachers have, in certain respects, over parents.

Third, to their credit, Eccles and Harold have a vision of families being embedded in different neighborhoods, but they do not take sufficient account of the role of the broader social context in facilitating or impeding parents' ties to school. The working-class and lower-class children in my study spent extensive periods of time with their cousins in heterogenous age groups, usually in unstructured activities. By contrast, middle-class children's lives were not tied to kinship but to a relentless schedule of structured activities including soccer, traveling soccer, music lessons, basketball, and scouts. These age-based activities drew parents into contact with other parents of children in the same grade and, at times, the same school. Thus, middle-class children's social lives facilitated parent involvement in education, because parents built networks with other parents of classmates at these activities, whereas heavily kinship relations reduced the need and interest for networks with other parents. Thus, my third point is that teachers are building school involvement in very different social contexts.

To summarize, then, many family–school proponents have a flawed analysis. They do not consider systematic variations in families' approaches to school, especially the meaning attributed to being helpful, the number of serious conflicts in childrearing strategies, the perceived power and threat of teachers in their lives, and the social networks connecting parents to one another.

In closing, I turn briefly to the theoretical and policy methodological implications of this discussion. On the theoretical side, many students of family–school relations pose an endless line of educational opportunities and emphasize the way in which children's educational performance can be improved. This approach misses the fact that there are finite openings at the top, for example, at Harvard. Nor do they note the modest but steady shifts in how schools operate as well as the criteria for getting into elite institutions. We live in a socially stratified society. Many parents, including middle-class parents, have considerable anxiety about their children's futures. Some parents have closer connections to institutions and are able, more easily, to keep abreast of the steady shifts in professional advice. As Bourdieu (1984) pointed out, the content of a cultural norm is arbitrary. Once defined as legitimate and desirable, however, compliance with this norm can facilitate success in the social selection process.

The policy issues are complex. On the one hand, I am not optimistic about the possibility of eliminating the influence of social class on parent involvement in schooling. On the other hand, in my many hours in schools, I have never met a teacher who did not want more parent involvement. As we seek to develop policies to help educators, I believe we would all be well advised to follow the old journalistic guideline of immediately stating "who, what, when, where, and how." Too often the policies are vague and even vacuous. In my limited space, I shall focus on: "who" and "what."

On the question of "who," Professors Eccles and Harold focus primarily on parents, but I personally believe educators need to consider other sources than parents. Parents' educational skills are often quite weak. For example, we observed a White working-class father subtract 8 from 13 by counting on his fingers; an African-American mother, a high school graduate, unable to convert 59 inches into 4 feet 11 inches; and a mother stumble over the word *heredity* when she was reading a birthday card to her 3-year-old niece. Thus, parents, especially parents of working-class and lower-class children, are not always an educational resource. A better approach is to draw on children (such as older cousins) who are still in school or other educated adults in their lives. Students could be required to appoint three designated homework helpers at the beginning of the year to help monitor their progress at school. These designated homework helpers could sign a contract promising to monitor homework completion.

On the issue of "what" family–school policies should do, I believe that educators should adopt lessons from commercial advertising. In particular, teachers should focus on a relatively small number of points and repeat them endlessly. Educators might follow a pattern of 5, 10, 50: five types of requests for educational experiences in the home, each repeated 10 times a year, expecting a 50% response rate. In a somewhat different vein, for policymakers at the state or federal level, there needs to be a financial investment to develop a better infrastructure at school sites to promote family involvement. Schools are amazingly antiquated; the only place to make a phone call is the main office, which is often hectic and loud; similarly, requests to parents are made on poorly duplicated paper flyers. Policies should seek to upgrade technological resources, including the purchase of voice mail systems for teachers, construction of a small quiet room where teachers could make phone calls, and the development of glossy, attractive brochures soliciting parent involvement in school. Teachers are already asked to do too many things; a useful policy would be funding a graphic artist or desktop publishers who would go from school to school and develop individualized requests for each teacher soliciting parent involvement on a variety of subjects that teachers could use for a few years.

Increasing family–school contact is a complex topic. Most of the solutions, I regret to say, involve an increase in teachers' labor and parents' labor, at the same time that labor force participation rates, poverty, school safety, and other factors make it more difficult for parents and teachers to devote time and energy to the issue. Nevertheless, by pursuing a more critical analysis of family–school relationships, we stand to develop policies that are more effective and better suited to variations in family life in this country.

ACKNOWLEDGMENTS

This research was generously supported by funds from the Spencer Foundation as well as the National Science Foundation. The author is grateful to Kevin Delaney, Gretchen Condran, Robert Kidder, Craig Watkins, and Patricia Houck for comments on this chapter. The views expressed in this chapter, of course, are solely those of the author and do not reflect those of the funding agencies.

REFERENCES

Bourdieu, P. (1984). *Distinction*. Cambridge, MA: Harvard University Press.
Bourdieu, P., & Passeron, J. P. (1977). *Reproduction*. Newbury Park, CA: Sage.
Lareau, A. (1989). *Home advantage*. London: Falmer Press.

II

HOW DO SCHOOL
PROCESSES AFFECT CHILDREN
AND THEIR FAMILIES?

5

Schools and Children At Risk

Karl L. Alexander
Doris R. Entwisle
The Johns Hopkins University

A life course perspective has led to some major breakthroughs in those aspects of human development covered by the term *schooling*, especially in our understanding of the adolescent transition and its longer term consequences (Feldman & Elliott, 1990). This paradigmatic shift has also prompted a more interdisciplinary approach. Sociologists of the family, for example, have linked children's progress in school to their mothers' life histories (Furstenberg, Brooks-Gunn, & Morgan, 1987), and sociologists of education have progressed beyond thinking of the child's family only as a kind of repository for college plans (Ensminger & Slusarcick, 1992). The social contexts in which children's development occurs intersect, and that intersection is no longer being ignored.

Still, development in middle childhood, particularly the earliest years of formal schooling, has received relatively little attention in research from a life course perspective. When children start formal schooling, they acquire a new definition of self—the academic self—and add a new role to their role set, that of student. Children are no longer wholly dependent on the family, and their work is evaluated by teachers, classmates, and ultimately by society as a whole (for overview of our perspective on early schooling as a "critical period" in children's life course, see Entwisle & Alexander, 1989; see also Higgins & Parsons, 1982).

Convinced that the period of *early* schooling was key to better understanding the entire schooling process, because it encompassed an important life transition that in many ways was different from other transitions, we initiated the Beginning School Study (BSS) in 1982. It is now in its 13th year. The idea was to observe children who had a relatively "clear slate" in terms of formal schooling and then to watch over time how their initial settling in experiences at school affected their later academic and personal development. We were also convinced that to understand schooling required continuous observation of a broad sample of *all* children that the schools enroll. This way we could be alert for what enabled students to do well, rather than to focus just on "problem" students.

Selection of schools and pupils for participation in the BSS involved a two-stage process. First, 20 public elementary schools throughout Baltimore were selected at random from within strata defined by racial composition (segregated White, segregated African American, integrated) and community socioeconomic status (SES) level (white collar, blue collar); pupils then were sampled randomly from 1981–1982 kindergarten rosters and fall 1982 first-grade rosters. All regular first-grade classrooms in the 20 schools were included in the sampling and only 3% of parents declined to have their children participate in the project.

The resulting sample of 790 beginning first graders was 55% African American, 45% White; 47% were in single parent households; 67% of the children's families qualified for reduced price meals at school, indicating low income; and 38% of the study children's mothers did not finish high school. Those who remained in Baltimore's public schools through the end of middle school (about 60% of the group) were more disadvantaged still: 52% in single-parent households; 76% receiving meal subsidies, 42% high school dropout mothers, and 71% African American. The families of BSS children thus reflect high levels of socioeconomic disadvantage even though schools in upper income and predominantly White communities were oversampled to enable comparisons across SES and racial/ethnic lines.

The fact that children from low SES family circumstances are at severe risk of academic failure is well established (Natriello, McDill, & Pallas, 1990). Less clear is how schools fit into the picture. Do they function to offset the out-of-school circumstances that put such children at risk academically, as most of us would want; do they magnify children's difficulties by reinforcing outside patterns of advantage/disadvantage, as many critics of schooling suppose; or are they essentially irrelevant, a view widely held in the wake of the early school effects literature (Coleman et al., 1966; Hodgson, 1973)?

This longstanding debate still is unsettled, although the weight of sentiment is probably that schools help little or perhaps even contribute to disadvantaged children's academic difficulties through practices like tracking that sometimes allocate school resources unfairly. Kind words for the public schools in large urban centers are rare (see Bracey, 1991), and it is easy to understand why. Schooling is often seen as the chief remedy for inequalities in social and economic opportunity, but schools do not compensate fully for inequalities in other spheres of life. Certainly in urban areas like Baltimore, where dropout rates still hover in the vicinity of 50% despite improvement nationally (e.g., Hammack, 1986), the sense of educational crisis is palpable.

In our view, though, despite surface indications that seem to suggest the opposite, the public schools in places like Baltimore are a more powerful, positive force in children's lives than is generally realized. In the first part of this chapter, data from the BSS show how Baltimore City's public schools function so as to offset differences across SES lines in out-of-school learning opportunities and so foster greater educational equality. At the same time, daunting problems remain, and the second part of the chapter outlines some potential leads for how schools might do more to help students whose out-of-school resources in support of their learning put them at risk academically.

TRENDS IN SES DISPARITIES OVER TIME

Do schools help or hinder low SES children's cognitive development relative to that of children from more advantaged family circumstances? The correct answer, as we see shortly, is that they help such youngsters keep pace, although the way yearly achievement patterns track over time would seem to indicate the opposite.

Table 5.1 displays achievement test averages and comparisons by SES level year by year for the first 8 years of BSS children's schooling. The testing data come from Baltimore City Public School (BCPS) system records. SES distinctions are derived from a composite scale that combines survey and school record data. The SES composite is an average of five indicators: mother's and father's educational level (coded as years of school completed); mother's and father's occupational status (coded in the Featherman–Stevens 1982 SEI metric); and whether or not the child participated in the federal school lunch program, a rough measure of family income level (eligibility is determined by family income relative to family size).[1]

The *high, middle, low* distinctions used in Table 5.1 lead to half the sample being classified as low SES, about a fourth middle and another fourth high.[2] The mother's education averages for the three groups are 10.4, 12.0, and 14.6 (pooled $SD = 2.6$); father's education, 10.4, 12.1, 15.1 (pooled $SD = 2.7$); mother's occupation, 26.5, 40.5, and 60.1 (pooled $SD = 19.7$); father's occupation, 22.6, 31.1, and 60.4 (pooled $SD = 22.4$); and the percentages receiving free or reduced price meals are 95.1, 53.7, and 13.0, respectively (pooled $SD = 47.4$). Fifty-four

[1]The SES scale is the average of the five separate indicators after converting them to Z scores. Just under half the sample (46.9%) had data on all five indicators, 18.1% were covered by four indicators, 19.5% by three indicators, 9.7% by two indicators, and 5.4%, or 43 youngsters, by one indicator (for 30 of these, the one was mother's education; for 10 others, it was the meal subsidy measure). Only 3 of the 790 children were missing data on all five indicators.

[2]SES scale scores .5 SDs or more above the sample wide mean comprise the high group. The lower bound for the middle group is the lowest scale value that yields educational averages above 12 (i.e., high school graduate) for both parents.

TABLE 5.1
CAT Averages and Differences in CAT Averages by SES Level, from the Fall of First Grade Through the Spring of Year 8

	Fall Year 1	Spring Year 1	Spring Year 2	Spring Year 3	Spring Year 4	Spring Year 5	Spring Year 6	Spring Year 7	Spring Year 8
CAT-R									
Full Sample Avg	281.1	340.2	390.2	417.7	455.3	481.9	504.1	517.9	552.9
(N)	(675)	(732)	(644)	(556)	(539)	(566)	(496)	(446)	(405)
Low SES Avg	272.6	327.9	378.0	400.2	434.3	462.3	485.4	494.1	527.4
(N)	(342)	(369)	(334)	(310)	(299)	(321)	(290)	(261)	(234)
High SES Avg	300.3	359.6	416.8	456.4	504.6	530.0	553.1	582.2	618.1
(N)	(164)	(178)	(152)	(119)	(110)	(102)	(92)	(76)	(71)
High–Low SES Diff	27.7	31.7	38.8	56.2	70.3	67.7	67.6	88.1	90.7
Diff as % SD	.68	.70	.82	.98	1.00	.92	.92	1.13	1.14
CAT-M									
Full Sample Avg	292.1	341.0	384.2	413.6	446.7	476.0	498.5	515.8	542.7
(N)	(693)	(722)	(639)	(556)	(538)	(560)	(490)	(437)	(399)
Low SES Avg	282.1	330.6	373.2	399.0	429.2	458.5	481.7	493.5	516.3
(N)	(357)	(365)	(330)	(310)	(299)	(315)	(284)	(255)	(226)
High SES Avg	312.3	355.8	406.0	446.6	484.9	511.3	533.0	574.4	598.8
(N)	(164)	(174)	(151)	(119)	(109)	(102)	(92)	(76)	(73)
High–Low SES Diff	30.2	25.2	32.8	47.6	55.7	52.8	51.3	80.9	82.5
Diff as % SD	.95	.69	.87	.98	1.01	.86	.80	1.15	1.16

percent of the low SES youngsters were in single-parent households at the start of first grade, versus 40% of middle SES youngsters and 28% of high SES youngsters. Two-parent households include stepparents, biological parents, and families with other adults in residence along with two parents.

Achievement trends are monitored via two subtests from the California Achievement Test (CAT) battery Form C: reading comprehension in the verbal domain (CAT-R) and math concepts and reasoning in the quantitative domain (CAT-M). These subtests tap competencies central to the elementary school curriculum, they are free of ceiling constraints in the first two grades (which is not the case for some of the other CAT subtests),[3] and they are included in all versions of the CAT battery from first grade into high school, so changes over time in the same skill areas can be monitored. The averages reported are *scale scores*, vertically calibrated across levels of the CAT battery (Level 11, Level 12, etc.) designed for administration at different grade levels.

The first entries in Table 5.1, from the fall of first grade, indicate where children stood at the beginning of their formal schooling. The averages favor high SES youngsters by a wide margin. The CAT-R and CAT-M differences between high and low SES youngsters are 27.7 and 30.2 points respectively, corresponding to about .69 and .95 standard deviations.

Although Table 5.1 gives only test scores, a range of other academic indicators yields similar profiles: Compared to youngsters in the high group, low SES children's report card averages in reading and math in the fall of first grade are both about .9 standard deviations lower, they are three times more likely to be held back at year's end (22% vs. 7%), and they are more than twice as likely to be referred for special education services in either first or second grade (17% vs. 9%).[4] Also low SES children are absent more often in first grade; receive lower work habit ratings on their report cards; and are described by their teachers as less cooperative, less invested in their schoolwork, and as more prone to "acting out." Thus, low SES youngsters not only lag behind initially in terms of cognitive skills, but they also apparently are less comfortable with the behavioral expectations that attach to the student role.

These first-grade comparisons indicate the extent to which public schools in places like Baltimore fall heir to the city's problems; these problems lead to the huge disparities in children's school readiness. Families do indeed "make the difference," as is plain from the Equality of Educational Opportunity (EEO) Report (Coleman et al., 1966) and other like studies (e.g., Hodgson, 1973). The comparison of test scores and of other academic indicators from the fall of first grade largely reflects family resources and related differences in learning oppor-

---

[3]See Entwisle and Alexander (1992) for a discussion of lack of ceiling effects.

[4]Special education figures apply to the first 2 years of children's schooling. Because we initially sampled regular classrooms only, special education placements are underrepresented in the first year data. The percentages reported combine assignment to separate special education classes and pull-out programs from regular classes.

tunities over the preschool years, differences that no doubt will continue to favor children from high SES households throughout their schooling (e.g., Hess & Holloway, 1984; Slaughter & Epps, 1987). The last point is worth repeating: Unless something happens to improve low SES children's prospects, the expectation probably would be for them to lose more ground over time, whereas to shrink the gap implies moving against the pull of out-of-school resources.

So what does happen as time passes? The remaining entries in Table 5.1 report year-end test scores over the ensuing 8 years for these same children. They show that low SES youngsters fall back further and further.[5] Beyond first grade and through the rest of elementary school, low SES youngsters' shortfall hovers in the vicinity of .8–1.0 standard deviations, a much larger relative difference than is seen in the fall of first grade, especially on the CAT-R. This pattern continues into Year 6, when about 61% of the cohort has made the transition into middle school,[6] while in Years 7 and 8—middle school years for almost everyone—low SES children fall yet further behind. In both reading and math, their test scores trail by well over a full standard deviation, the largest shortfall over the entire period.[7]

The cleavage across SES levels in the competencies tapped by the two CAT subtests thus widens substantially over time. It might be concluded from this trend that schools over this period have not served low SES youngsters especially well. But schools are not the only developmental context these students experienced over the 8 years in question. The trends by SES seen in Table 5.1 reflect all the influences in children's realm of experience, not just influences present in schools. In the United States, children attend school about 180 days a year, for perhaps 6 hours a day. Rutter and his colleagues (Rutter, Maughan, Mortimore, & Ouston, 1979) in their study of inner city London secondary schools emphasized the intensity of the experience in the title of their book: *Fifteen Thousand Hours*. But let's not forget the other 70,000 hours, as Heath and Clifford (1980) aptly reminded us of in their critical commentary on Rutter's research. The large

---

[5]These testing data come from BCPS records, so children only are covered so long as they remain in the City school system. Over the 8 years covered in Table 5.1, case coverage falls off substantially (by about 40%). However, the patterns displayed in Table 5.1, and also in Table 5.2, are virtually unchanged when averages are based only on youngsters who remain in City schools over the entire period.

[6]The school transition issue is complicated. Children in the lowest SES group are much more likely than those in the middle and high groups to be held back in elementary school, and so barely half (52%) are in sixth grade in Year 6, compared to 70% of those in the middle SES group and 82% of those in the high SES group. For a general overview of these children's complicated "pathways" through the elementary and middle school years, see Alexander, Entwisle, and Dauber (1994, chapter 2).

[7]There is considerable evidence that students' performance falls off in the middle grades (for overview, see Eccles & Midgley, 1990; Harvard Education Letter, 1992; Stipek, 1984). The trend in Table 5.1 suggests such problems are especially severe for low SES youngsters, whose academic foothold has been tenuous all along.

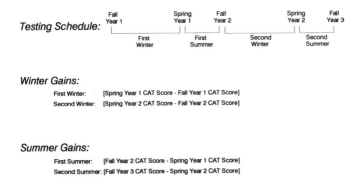

FIG. 5.1.   Illustrative time line for seasonal comparisons of cognitive growth.

majority of children's time during the year is spent outside school, so unless it is assumed no learning occurs when children are outside school, there obviously is a major confounding of school effects with the effects of the other institutional contexts that frame children's development—the family and the community. Table 5.1 shows that some children have a substantial edge at the start of their schooling, and they are the ones in high SES families. It is reasonable to assume that these favorable circumstances affect children's cognitive development on an on-going basis, even after their formal schooling commences.

The school's unique contribution to children's cognitive development can be clarified by comparing learning patterns season by season. When tests are administered fall and spring (the schedule used when BSS children were in elementary school),[8] the impact of schooling should be reflected in improvement during the fall–spring interval. However, in addition to being in school during this time, children also are "in" their families and "in" their communities, so cognitive gains during the school year respond to in-school and out-of-school influences in unknown proportions. The spring–fall testing interval, however, reflects gains over the summer break, when children are not in school. By comparing gains children make in winter with gains they make in summer, we can approximate a natural experiment: Because schools are not implicated in summer gains but are implicated in winter gains, differences between summer and winter in the amounts children learn can suggest how much schools specifically contribute to cognitive growth.[9] Figure 5.1 illustrates how this approach to parsing out annual gains season by season is implemented.

Table 5.2 reports seasonal comparisons for the first 5 years of the BSS youngsters' schooling, the elementary school years for most. Winter gains exceed summer gains by a wide margin each year, indicating that all children make more

---

[8]After elementary school (project Years 7 and 8) testing was done in spring only.

[9]The interval covered here is shorter than in Table 5.2 because the BCPS discontinued fall testing after project Year 6.

TABLE 5.2
School Year and Summer CAT Gains over the Elementary School Years by SES Level

	CAT-R SES Level			CAT-M SES Level		
	Low	Mid	High	Low	Mid	High
Winter Gains						
Year 1	56.7	68.6	60.8	50.0	52.9	45.0
	(327)	(165)	(161)	(340)	(166)	(158)
Year 2	48.0	45.4	40.1	42.9	43.5	42.2
	(323)	(151)	(151)	(322)	(154)	(150)
Year 3	31.2	35.6	33.7	36.0	35.9	35.6
	(294)	(120)	(118)	(296)	(120)	(118)
Year 4	33.1	41.0	31.7	33.2	33.6	35.7
	(291)	(128)	(109)	(291)	(128)	(108)
Year 5	24.3	29.1	24.6	24.7	30.7	27.8
	(315)	(142)	(102)	(307)	(141)	(102)
Total Winter Gains	193.3	219.7	190.9	186.8	196.6	186.3
Summer Gains						
Year 1	-3.7	-2.1	15.0	-4.8	-6.8	8.8
	(318)	(159)	(154)	(321)	(160)	(151)
Year 2	-3.5	1.8	8.5	-5.2	-.6	3.3
	(295)	(126)	(123)	(294)	(127)	(123)
Year 3	1.6	2.5	14.9	-1.9	5.1	1.3
	(299)	(123)	(114)	(299)	(123)	(114)
Year 4	4.5	1.6	10.4	4.9	4.8	5.6
	(285)	(126)	(91)	(283)	(125)	(90)
Year 5	2.0	-4.1	-2.2	-.9	1.6	5.9
	(274)	(113)	(88)	(277)	(110)	(87)
Total Summer Gains	.8	-.3	46.5	-7.9	4.0	24.9

progress when in school. More relevant, though, are seasonal differences in learning patterns that revolve around SES distinctions. These are easiest to see when gains are expressed per month rather than per season (roughly 8 months in the winter, 4 in the summer): The average monthly gain on the CAT-R for low SES children in the first winter is just over 7 points (i.e., 56.7/8 = 7.1), compared to an average *loss* over the first summer (4 months) of .9 points per month (−3.7/4). For high SES children, the corresponding figures are 7.6 (60.8/8) and 3.8 (15.0/4), *both positive*.

In Year 1, the winter rates for the high and low SES groups are almost the same: a difference of 4.1 points, corresponding to just .09 standard deviations (the *SD* for winter gains the first year is 46.07). The summer pattern is quite different, as the raw score difference of almost 19 points is just under .5 *SD*s, and the low group actually loses ground. The exact figures differ from year to year, but the same general pattern holds throughout Table 5.2. Even though the summer period is only half as long, the summer advantage that accrues to high SES children is striking.

The last entries in each panel show how this advantage cumulates over the 5 elementary years (see *Total Gain* entries in the last row for each panel). Across all five summers, the high SES group gains 46 points in reading comprehension and about 25 points in math, whereas the middle and low SES groups essentially stand still in reading and either gain a little or lose a little in math. Across the SES extremes, the summer disparity amounts to roughly 45 points on the CAT-R and 33 points on the CAT-M. In winters, by comparison, the total gains of the two SES groups over the elementary years are less than 5 points apart in both areas—only 1 point per year—and the middle group, not the high group, registers the largest gains.[10]

Thus the increasing gap across SES levels over the elementary years seen in Table 5.1 can be attributed almost entirely to gains that children from high SES households made when school was not in session. Children learn year round, yet most studies neglect seasonal variation in children's learning rates. This oversight may be most serious in the first few grades, which is when the largest seasonal disparities are registered. During this period of the beginning school transition, children are adjusting to the academic routine, learning fundamental skills, and developing at a much faster rate than they will later on.[11] Children also are

---

[10]Limiting the comparison just to children in the BCPS over the entire period yields quite similar *Total Gains*: in winter, 200.7, 222.5, and 191.8 points on the CAT-R for low, mid-level, and high SES youngsters respectively; in summer, the corresponding figures are −1.0, −3.8, and 33.2. The only noteworthy change is the reversal of the winter gain comparison, which favors the low SES group modestly in the revised figures, owing to small increases in their gains over the first two winters (4 points in the first winter; 3 in the second). Changes in the CAT-M comparisons are more minor still. These illustrate our earlier point that sample attrition due to movement out of the BCPS has little effect on testing trends overall or on trend comparisons across SES levels.

[11]Jencks (1985) suggested that learning in the early grades outpaces learning in the high school years by a factor of almost 10 to 1.

quickly channeled into trajectories that school organizational patterns reinforce (Alexander & Entwisle, 1994; Entwisle & Alexander, 1993). The transition from "home child" to "school child" is not part of large, national studies of schooling, like the NELS-88 project and High School and Beyond, which begin in eighth grade or later. Nevertheless, the trajectories implied by the BSS data in Table 5.1 are well established long before children reach middle school.

The impressive season-by-season differences in Table 5.2 are obscured when gains are computed spring to spring as is typical in large national studies. Scores based on annual gains invariably show positive correlations between family SES level and children's achievement gains, but this picture is misleading. Children reared in high SES settings advance year round, but children from disadvantaged circumstances are likely to spend the summer in environments where resources to support their learning are scarce. Disadvantaged children are dependent on schools for the experiences that help them move forward. They keep pace when they are in school, but not when they are out of school.

The BSS data, along with other studies that report broadly similar seasonal trends in cognitive growth (David, 1974; David & Pelavin, 1978; Hammond & Frechtling, 1979; Hayes & Grether, 1983; Hayes & King, 1974; Heyns, 1978, 1987; Murnane, 1975; Pelavin & David, 1977), thus point to an important conclusion: Schools do make a difference for poor children, because schooling offsets the dearth of learning resources in low SES youngsters' home environments, at least in the early years. What are the home learning resources that the school replaces in winter? While we cannot go very far in unpackaging the SES variable, other BSS analyses suggest that family structure and school racial composition are not major considerations (Entwisle & Alexander, 1992, 1994). One obvious area involves differences in specific learning materials, educational toys, books, and the like, and these no doubt play a role, but several other kinds of SES-linked resources that might not be so obvious could also play a role. The first is the emotional climate in homes where finances are short, the second has to do with the worldview of parents of different social levels, and the third hinges on how parents react to information about their children's progress in school.

Some authors report that children who live in poverty experience double jeopardy, first, because they are exposed more frequently to medical illnesses, family stress, and other negative life conditions and second, because they experience more serious consequences from these risks than do children of high SES, especially if their poverty is long term (Parker, Greer, & Zuckerman, 1988). It is difficult to reconcile the BSS data with this perspective, however, because our data also show that the number of negative life events in low SES families exceeds that in high SES families, but when school is in session, the two groups gain at about the same rate. This parity in school outcomes for children from different backgrounds suggests that in addition to seeing the school as a forum for learning, where teachers mobilize resources and so prompt pupils to achieve, we may also conceive of the school as a social environment that neutralizes or buffers home stresses.

A second possibility emphasizes the different roles that parents of various SES backgrounds set for themselves with respect to their children's education. Middle-class parents conceive of themselves as active partners in the education of their children, whereas often working-class parents prefer leaving the role of educator to the school (Lareau, 1987). If this holds generally, the strong seasonal patterns in test scores for BSS children could reflect parental involvement for better-off children, which when school is in session, tends to be redundant with school effects but which when school is not in session, adds importantly to student achievement. High SES parents take over the role of teacher in summer and because of close contact with school in winter, they know the level and kind of experiences their children are ready for. From this standpoint, the summer decrement in children's progress is not so much a consequence of a dearth of material resources in low SES homes as of a lack of a special kind of "human capital."

A third possibility relates to still another kind of parent capital. In every BSS analysis so far, parents' expectations are powerful predictors of children's performance, irrespective of SES level. Other researchers even report parents' expectations to be more potent than the child's IQ in predicting school performance (Parsons, Adler, & Kaczak, 1982). Low SES parents are just as likely to hold high expectations for their children as high SES parents are, but high SES parents' expectations for children are much more in tune with the child's performance level than are those of low SES parents (Alexander, Entwisle, & Bedinger, 1994). High SES parents, for example, recall their children's marks on prior report cards more accurately than do low SES parents. In other words, high SES parents are good at processing information furnished them by the school that will help them monitor their child's schooling. Perhaps because high SES parents are more informed about what to expect, their expectations are stronger predictors of the child's actual performance, or put another way, high SES parents' expectations are a more useful resource for the child.

We do not wish to suggest that any of the explanations proposed are necessarily correct or that the list is exhaustive. The data in this chapter can suggest only that the home resources found in high SES families have some role in promoting youngsters' achievement in the summer. These resources could encompass books, games, trips to museums and zoos, special lessons and organized summer activities, but emphasizing material resources may be deceptive. The human resources that usually accompany material resources may hold the key. Whatever the case, we need to define better the circumstances that make it possible for children to make a smooth transition into first grade and then to continue to move forward even when schools are closed.

WHAT WORKS: AVENUES FOR MORE EFFECTIVE INTERVENTION

The previous section demonstrates that schools do make a difference, but as presently constituted, they do not make enough of a difference to offset educational disparities that originate in out-of-school circumstances. There are large differences that separate high and low SES children's performance at the start of first grade and high SES children's advantage continues during the summer months. Directing attention, as we do, to the school's special contribution to disadvantaged children's learning in the early grades is not meant to paper over the problems that beset urban education. Still the pattern of winter test gains reveals that schooling helps promote educational equality, and indeed, just appreciating that schools are doing so well by less advantaged youngsters could itself go far toward improving teachers' and parents' morale and reviving the other intangibles that undergird a positive social climate in schools (see p. 80). The continuing challenge, though, is to find ways to make schooling even more effective than it is at present, and in this section we point to several areas that seem promising.

Attacking Problems Early

The Beginning School Study enrolled first grade students because we thought there was a particular need to understand better why some youngsters settle into the school routine successfully whereas others flounder. The period of early schooling sets the stage for virtually everything that follows: Achievement patterns and work habits are established, reputations are formed, a paper trail is put in place that will follow children for their rest of their schooling, and children's ideas about self and school begin to crystallize. Recovery from a shaky start is not impossible, but as a general rule it is better (and easier) to avoid problems in the first place than to have to fix them later: "Prevention and early intervention are much more promising than waiting for learning deficits to accumulate" (Slavin, Madden, & Karweit, 1989, p. 355).

As noted previously, low SES youngsters start school already badly disadvantaged and then proceed to fall further and further back over the years. But they would be worse off still were it not for the compensatory effects of schooling. One might reasonably suppose that if some school is good, then more school would be even better. Also, because children in countries that consistently outperform U.S. students in terms of test score comparisons also typically spend more time in school, often much more time, the idea of additional exposure is appealing (e.g., Stevenson & Stigler, 1992). Reflecting this logic, proposals to lengthen the school year, extend the school day, or begin school at earlier ages have all been advanced (e.g., Kagan & Zigler, 1987).

Thus far, summer programs that extend the school year have not proven especially helpful (e.g., Carter, 1984; Heyns, 1987); however, other interventions that add to disadvantaged children's academic time or otherwise supplement services routinely provided by schools do seem to make a difference. This holds for preschool programs like Head Start, Chapter 1 programs, and full-day versus half-day kindergarten programs (Entwisle, Alexander, Cadigan, & Pallas, 1987; also see various review chapters in Slavin, Karweit, & Madden, 1989; also, Haskins, 1989). Recently, center-based early childcare for children from impoverished families has proved effective (e.g., Caughy, DiPietro, & Strobino, 1994), as have formal programs for after-school care (Posner & Vandell, 1994).

Unfortunately, the benefits associated with such interventions, especially higher test scores, often do not last much more than a year or two beyond the period of participation (the so-called "spurt–fade-out" pattern). Even short-term gains can be important, however (e.g., Woodhead, 1988). For example, the most convincingly established *long-term* effects of preschool involve reduced retention rates and reduced need for special education services (Consortium of Longitudinal Studies, 1983; Lazar & Darlington, 1982). Head Start boosts children's IQ scores by about 8 points in first grade, but the gains are transient and all but disappear by third grade. Achievement test scores too are elevated, but again only temporarily. Nevertheless, these temporarily elevated scores may explain why pre-schooled children are less often retained and assigned to special education in the early grades.

In Baltimore, as elsewhere, the first grade retention rate is much higher than the rate in any later grade (Alexander, Entwisle, & Dauber, 1994; Shepard & Smith, 1989). BSS children of low SES are 41% more likely than high SES children to fail first grade, controlling for race and gender. Even controlling additionally for initial test scores, they are 15% more likely to fail first grade (Dauber, Alexander, & Entwisle, 1993). Once children are held back, they are effectively launched into trajectories that persist at least through the eighth grade, which is as far into their schooling as we have considered the question (Alexander, Entwisle, & Dauber, 1994). Grade retention predicts high school dropout (Cairns, Cairns, & Neckerman, 1989; Fine, 1991; Lloyd, 1978; Stroup & Robins, 1972), so many minority and low SES children's life chances seemingly are compromised by the time they finish first grade.

The evidence for lasting advantages from early interventions in terms of educational and later-life outcomes like grade retention, high school graduation, and later employment thus is encouraging (Consortium of Longitudinal Studies, 1983; Lazar & Darlington, 1982; Schweinhart, Berrueta-Clement, Barnett, Epstein, & Weikart, 1985), but more needs to be learned about how best to structure early interventions so as to enhance disadvantaged children's readiness skills *and* to help them to keep up in the early primary grades. Short-term Band-Aids clearly are not the answer. The problem is not just that low SES youngsters begin school already far behind. The out-of-school forces that set them back initially will continue to weigh on them all through their schooling, and to offset these disadvantages, extra supports very likely will also have to be long term.

What Are Good Schools Like?

From the early school effects literature (e.g., Coleman et al., 1966; Jencks et al., 1972; Mosteller & Moynihan, 1972), we learned that problems of low achievement and underachievement among disadvantaged student populations are not budget driven, at least not in any straightforward way (e.g., Hanushek, 1989; but see Hedges, Laine, & Greenwald, 1994, for another view). Instead, early studies in the "school climate" tradition (Brookover, Beady, Flood, Schwietzer, & Wisenbaker, 1979; McDill & Rigsby, 1973; Rutter et al., 1979) emphasized the importance of an ethic, ethos, or atmosphere that supports academic striving. The "effective schools" characterization of exemplary schools stresses agreement on the schools' goals, high and clear expectations for *all students'* performance, an orderly, disciplined environment, and the need to maintain a sense of community, so that the order and discipline are achieved consensually rather than imposed (e.g., Edmonds, 1986; Levine, 1990; Mackenzie, 1983; Rutter et al., 1979).[12] Science labs, library books, class size, teacher qualifications, and the like rarely make it onto such lists. No doubt it is preferable that schools be well equipped, but a dedicated, highly motivated administration and teaching staff can make a difference for the better even when such tangibles are in short supply. It is telling, we think, that these very same themes all surface in recent studies that compare the educational effectiveness of public and Catholic high schools in fostering cognitive skill development. This research gives a slight edge to Catholic schools even though their average per pupil expenditures are considerably less than in the public sector (Bryk, Lee, & Holland, 1993; Coleman & Hoffer, 1987; Coleman, Hoffer, & Kilgore, 1982).[13]

Schools in the public sector that work well evidence much the same "school quality" profile as Catholic schools (e.g., Bryk et al., 1993; Coleman et al., 1982), so for us the public–private distinction is secondary. More important, in our view, is that the kind of school organization that works best at engaging children's energies and moderating disadvantages associated with at risk background traits in public–Catholic comparisons aligns so well with other descriptions of effective schools. Such schools often are smaller, and they do not necessarily have the most modern, up-to-date facilities, but they manage to foster a sense of community, and they are characterized by high standards, high expectations, and infrastructure support for everyone's learning. There may be other distinguishing features that should be added, but these are the clearest. The challenge is to encourage this kind of school environment when it does not emerge "naturally."

---

[12]The descriptions of "effective schools" in this literature do not always emphasize the same qualities. Also, the methodology of this approach has its limitations. See Good and Weinstein (1986), Purkey and Smith (1983), and Rowan, Bossert, and Dwyer (1983).

[13]No such comparisons have been reported in the primary grades, so it is impossible to say whether this conclusion holds across the board (e.g., Jencks, 1985).

What to Do/Think About Tracking?

Tracking is one way schools manage diversity. It is a technical solution to a technical problem (Dreeben, 1984; see also Hallinan & Sørensen, 1983), and because the problem of diversity is near pervasive, tracking is near universal (see Epstein & MacIver, 1990, and McPartland, Coldiron, & Braddock, 1987, for surveys of practices through the middle grades).

Global assessments of the extensive literature on tracking in its various guises are almost uniformly negative (e.g., Oakes, 1992, 1994; Rosenbaum, 1980), although the underlying issues are complex and defy simple answers (for an excellent review, see Oakes, Gamoran, & Page, 1992). In the early primary grades, sizable racial/ethnic or socioeconomic biases rarely show up in ability group placements (e.g., Haller, 1985; Haller & Davis, 1980; Sørensen & Hallinan, 1984), but such disparities are more pronounced at the upper grade levels when curriculum placements are at issue. Even then, however, social biases typically are less important than "merit" criteria, like test scores, marks, and previous preparation (e.g., Alexander & Cook, 1982; Alexander, Cook, & McDill, 1978).

Tracking arrangements frequently structure learning opportunities unfairly for children placed low, the part of the picture emphasized in the "detracking/ restructuring" movement. However, tracking does not always hurt low-end children (Bryk et al., 1993; Gamoran, 1993), and it often seems to help high-end children (see, for example, Oakes, 1989). At the upper grade levels especially, tracking may be unavoidable in some form because prior preparation and relevant competencies are wildly disparate. This last point warrants elaboration. The vast majority of middle schools use tracks in at least some subjects (e.g., Epstein & MacIver, 1990) and only under unusual circumstances can tracking be avoided altogether. For example, Hoffer's (1992) comparison of tracked and untracked middle schools shows less variability in baseline achievement tests in schools that did not group than in those that did, and the number of middle schools that did not group in math dropped from 10 of 52 in seventh grade to 4 of 51 in eighth grade.

The more variability there is in children's competencies, the more the pressure to homogenize instructional groups. Consider the situation in Baltimore. *At the end of fifth grade,* just before the move to middle school, those BSS youngsters who in sixth grade took remedial English (42% of the total) averaged 443.1 on the CAT-R; their reading report card mark averaged 2.2 (just above *satisfactory*), and their reading level, at 4.1, was well below grade level. By comparison, children placed in advanced English (20%) averaged 571.3 on the CAT-R (a difference of 1.9 *SD*s), 3.2 in reading (1.3 *SD*s), and their average reading level already was 6.0 (1.5 *SD*s). These are the extremes, but the typical remedial student also lagged behind students in regular classes, especially in terms of test scores, which carry greater weight in initial middle school placements because they are relatively context free (e.g., Dauber, Alexander, & Entwisle, 1994)[14]: .87 *SD*s on the CAT-R (443.1 vs. 502.5), .25 *SD*s for reading marks (2.2 vs. 2.4), and .4 *SD*s for reading level (4.1 vs. 5.2). Our point here is not that placements in the BCPS are in any sense "optimal" (which cannot be determined by simply comparing qualifications), but that they reflect the technical logic of tracking.[15]

There also are large differences separating SES groups at the end of elementary school. As *fifth graders,* high SES children averaged .92 *SD*s above the low SES group on the CAT-R (539.8 vs. 477.1), .74 *SD*s above on the CAT-M (515.7 vs. 473.3), .89 *SD*s in terms of reading marks (3.2 vs. 2.3), .97 *SD*s in terms of reading instructional level (5.9 vs. 4.7), and .74 *SD*s in terms of math marks (3.1 vs. 2.3). These extreme differences between the "highs" and the "lows" at the end of elementary school have consequences, and some are immediate. In the fall of sixth grade, 59% of high SES youngsters took advanced English, half took advanced math, 56% began a foreign language, and just over a fourth were in remedial reading; 9% of low SES youngsters were in advanced English, 3% took advanced math, 14% began a foreign language, and almost 80% were in remedial reading.

Low level placements in middle school effectively hobble later prospects, as prerequisites and course sequencing constraints in high school make it hard, if not impossible, to switch then into the "fast track" (Oakes, 1988, 1989). Still, these middle school placement patterns are not arbitrary, because they reflect the history of these youngsters as they moved up through the grade structure.

The answers on tracking aren't all in (see Alexander, Entwisle, & Dauber, 1994, for comment on some of the outstanding issues), but several recommendations seem reasonably secure. First, and most important, children's skills need to be shored up in the early grades, so that gigantic disparities like those just reviewed don't force the issue later (see also Biemiller, 1993). Also, the most divisive kinds of tracking ought to be avoided (e.g., whole class, all day in the early grades); tracking should be done only when it serves a useful purpose (grade retention, for example, has mainly positive consequences for children in the BSS [see Alexander, Entwisle, & Dauber, 1994], whereas low placements for reading instruction have negative consequences [Pallas, Entwisle, Alexander, & Stluka, 1994]); placements should be flexible and reassignments made as

---

[14]Middle schools typically enroll students from several elementary schools, often crossing community boundaries. If marking standards differ greatly across elementary schools, as well they might, this would undermine the usefulness of marks as a guide for making initial middle school placements.

[15]Some studies suggest that remedial students would do well in regular or advanced classes and be better off there, but Hoffer (1992) and Gamoran and Mare (1989) reminded us that this outcome likely holds only for students "at the margin." No one knows what would happen with wholesale shifting about. In Hoffer's analysis hardly any lower track youngsters' estimated "placement propensity" would put them in upper track classes; upper track students who mirror the characteristics of those in lower tracks are similarly rare.

warranted, which gets harder in the upper grades when courses are sequenced; and, children placed low should not be shortchanged in terms of "opportunities to learn," which happens too often the way tracking at present is implemented[16] (see Hallinan, 1994, for additional comment).

Parent Involvement

Finally, there is the question of parent involvement. That so much of low SES youngsters' achievement shortfall relative to their high SES peers originates outside of school suggests the importance of interventions that work with and through families, but home–school partnerships that focus narrowly on getting "outsider" groups more involved in the schools address only part of the problem.

Low SES as well as high SES parents can help boost their children's schooling by being encouraging and supportive (for relevant evidence, see Alexander & Entwisle, 1988). Middle- and upper-class parents are more effective, though. They understand better how schools work and are in a better position to use that understanding to advance their children's prospects (e.g., Alexander, Entwisle, & Bedinger, 1994; Baker & Stevenson, 1986; Entwisle & Hayduk, 1982).

School initiatives probably cannot compensate fully for extreme differences across families in material well-being, lifestyle, attitudes, and values, but parent involvement programs and home–school partnerships show that motivated parents, even when poor economically, can learn to be more effective in support of their children's schooling. Teaching parents how to monitor homework, helping them understand the school's expectations for their children, opening lines of communication in both directions, and making parents feel welcome and respected may make a difference for low SES parents (see Lareau, 1987). Indeed, programs designed to break down home–school barriers have moderated somewhat the characteristic relationship between SES level and school performance (Epstein, 1991, 1992). Additional efforts along these lines are needed.

SUMMARY AND IMPLICATIONS

To understand the dynamics of academic development, it makes sense to begin early in life, and in our view the earlier the better. Beginning School Study data show that family disadvantage translates into educational disadvantage right at the start of children's formal schooling, and that the gap between low and high SES children's test scores widens over the years. Although from such a pattern it appears schools are doing little to help to compensate for family disadvantages, this conclusion is misleading. Comparisons of test gains season by season reveal that

---

[16]Catholic schools serve as one model (e.g., Bryk et al., 1993; see also Gamoran, 1993, for examples in the public sector).

low SES youngsters keep pace during the school year. They do not keep up during the summer months, however, as that is when high SES youth forge ahead. Nevertheless, the winter progress of low SES youngsters suggests schools already are succeeding to a greater extent than they are credited with.

In our view, lasting improvements are most likely to come from planned changes that are anchored in deep intuitions and firm evidence about the nature of human beings and their social institutions. And even then, progress will be slow and come in small steps. More effective time on task can help some; early interventions of high quality can help some; a better school climate can help some; improved tracking practices can help some, and so forth, but none of these is a solution. Effective preschool programs, for example, typically do not bring at risk children up to acceptable levels of performance (Hebbeler, 1985), nor does holding children back a year when they are far behind (Alexander, Entwisle, & Dauber, 1994), although both can be useful; differences in engaged time account for only a small portion of achievement variance (Karweit, 1989); the Catholic school advantage over public schools in boosting test performance, which has received much attention recently as reflecting school quality differences, is only about .1 *SD*s (Alexander & Pallas, 1984; Coleman et al., 1982), and we could go on. The seasonal comparisons presented herein show the "outside forces" that pull against the schools' success in helping disadvantaged youngsters keep pace are powerful and confer advantages that cumulate over time. Until strategies are devised that effectively offset these forces, school-based solutions can be expected to yield only partial victories.

REFERENCES

Alexander, K., & Cook, M. (1982). Curricula and coursework: A surprise ending to a familiar story. *American Sociological Review, 47,* 626–640.

Alexander, K., Cook, M., & McDill, E. (1978). Curriculum tracking and educational stratification. *American Sociological Review, 43,* 47–66.

Alexander, K., & Entwisle, D. (1988). Achievement in the first two years of school: Patterns and processes. *Monographs of the Society for Research in Child Development, 53*(2), Serial No. 218.

Alexander, K., & Entwisle, D. (1994, April). *Educational tracking during the early years: First grade placements and middle school constraints.* Paper presented at the Conference on Institutions and Careers, Duke University.

Alexander, K., Entwisle, D., & Bedinger, S. (1994). When expectations work: Race and socioeconomic differences in school performance. *Social Psychology Quarterly, 57,* 283–299.

Alexander, K., Entwisle, D., & Dauber, S. (1994). *On the Success of failure: A reassessment of the effects of retention in the primary grades.* Cambridge, MA: Cambridge University Press.

Alexander, K., & Pallas, A. (1984). School sector and cognitive performance: When is a little a little? *Sociology of Education, 58,* 115–128.

Baker, D., & Stevenson, D. (1986). Mothers' strategies for children's school achievement: Managing the transition to high school. *Sociology of Education, 59,* 156–166.

Biemiller, A. (1993). Lake Wobegon revisited: On diversity and education. *Educational Researcher, 22*(9), 7–11.

Bracey, G. (1991). Why can't they be like we were? *Phi Delta Kappan, 73,* 104–117.

Brookover, W., Beady, C., Flood, P., Schwietzer, J., & Wisenbaker, J. (1979). *School social systems and student achievement.* New York Praeger.

Bryk, A., Lee, V., & Holland, P. (1993). *Catholic schools and the common good.* Cambridge, MA: Harvard University Press.

Cairns, R., Cairns, B., & Neckerman, H. (1989). Early school dropout: Configurations and determinants. *Child Development, 60,* 1437–1452.

Carter, L. (1984). The sustaining effects study of compensatory and elementary education. *Educational Researcher, 13,* 4–13.

Caughy, M., DiPietro, J., & Strobino, D. (1994). Day-care participation as a protective factor in the cognitive development of low-income children. *Child Development, 65,* 457–471.

Coleman, J., Campbell, E., Hobson, C., McPartland, J., Mood, A., Weinfeld, F., & York, R. (1966). *Equality of educational opportunity.* Washington, DC: U.S. Government Printing Office.

Coleman, J., & Hoffer, T. (1987). *Public and private schools: The impact of communities.* New York: Basic.

Coleman, J., Hoffer, T., & Kilgore, S. (1982). *High school achievement: Public, Catholic and private schools compared.* New York: Basic.

Consortium of Longitudinal Studies. (1983). *As the twig is bent: Lasting effect of preschool programs.* Hillsdale, NJ: Lawrence Erlbaum Associates.

Dauber, S., Alexander, K., & Entwisle, D. (1993). Characteristics of retainees and early precursors of retention in grade: Who is held back? *Merrill-Palmer Quarterly, 39,* 326–343.

Dauber, S., Alexander, K., & Entwisle, D. (1994). *Tracking and transitions through the middle grades: Channeling educational trajectories.* Unpublished manuscript.

David, J. (1974). *Follow through summer study: A two-part investigation of the impact of exposure to schooling on achievement growth.* Harvard Graduate School of Education.

David, J., & Pelavin, S. (1978). Secondary analysis: In compensatory education programs. *New Directions for Program Evaluation, 4,* 31–44.

Dreeben, R. (1984). First-grade reading groups: Their formation and change. In P. Peterson, L. Wilkinson, & M. Hallinan (Eds.), *The social context of instruction: Group organization and group process* (pp. 69–84). San Diego: Academic Press.

Eccles, J., & Midgley, C. (1990). Changes in academic motivation and self-perception during early adolescence. In R. Montemayor, G. Adams, & T. Gulotta (Eds.), *From childhood to adolescence: A transitional period?* (pp. 134–155). Newbury Park, CA: Sage.

Edmonds, R. (1986). Characteristics of effective schools. In U. Neisser (Ed.), *The school achievement of minority children: New perspectives* (pp. 93–104). Hillsdale, NJ: Lawrence Erlbaum Associates.

Ensminger, M., & Slusarcick, A. (1992). Paths to high school graduation or dropout: A longitudinal study of a first-grade cohort. *Sociology of Education, 65,* 95–113.

Entwisle, D., & Alexander, K. (1989). Early schooling as a "critical period" phenomenon. In K. Namboodiri & R. Corwin (Eds.), *Sociology of education and socialization* (Vol. 8, pp. 27–55). Greenwich, CT: JAI.

Entwisle, D., & Alexander, K. (1992). Summer setback: Race, poverty, school composition, and mathematics achievement in the first two years of school. *American Sociological Review, 57,* 72–84.

Entwisle, D., & Alexander, K. (1993). Entry into schools: The beginning school transition and educational stratification in the United States. In J. Blake & J. Hagen (Eds.), *Annual review of sociology* (Vol. 19, pp. 401–423). Palo Alto, CA: Annual Reviews.

Entwisle, D., & Alexander, K. (1994). Winter setback: School racial composition and learning to read. *American Sociological Review, 59,* 446–460.

Entwisle, D., Alexander, K., Cadigan, D., & Pallas, A. (1987). Kindergarten experience: Cognitive effects or socialization? *American Educational Research Journal, 24,* 337–364.

Entwisle, D., & Hayduk, L. (1982). *Early schooling: Cognitive and affective outcomes.* Baltimore, MD: Johns Hopkins Press.

Epstein, J. (1991). Effects on student achievement of teachers' practices of parent involvement. In S. Silvern (Ed.), *Literacy through family, community, and school interaction: Vol. 6* (pp. 261–276). Greenwich, CT: JAI.

Epstein, J. (1992). School and family partnerships. In M. Alkin (Ed.), *Encyclopedia of educational research, sixth edition* (pp. 1139–1151). New York: MacMillan.

Epstein, J., & MacIver, D. (1990). *Education in the middle grades: National trends and practices.* Columbus, OH: National Middle School Association.

Featherman, D., & Stevens, G. (1982). A revised socioeconomic index of occupational status: Application in analysis of sex differences in attainment. In R. Hauser, D. Mechanic, A. Haller, & T. Hauser (Eds.), *Social structure and behavior: Essays in honor of William Hamilton Sewell* (pp. 141–182). New York: Academic Press.

Feldman, S., & Elliott, G. (1990). *At the threshold: The developing adolescent.* Cambridge, MA: Harvard University Press.

Fine, M. (1991). *Framing dropouts: Notes on the politics of an urban public high school.* Albany, NY: State University of New York Press.

Furstenberg, F., Brooks-Gunn, J., & Morgan, S. (1987). *Adolescent mothers in later life.* Cambridge: Cambridge University Press.

Gamoran, A. (1993). Alternative uses of ability grouping in secondary schools: Can we bring high-quality instruction to low-ability classes? *American Journal of Education, 102,* 1–22.

Gamoran, A., & Mare, R. (1989). Secondary school tracking and educational inequality: Compensation, reinforcement or neutrality? *American Journal of Sociology, 94,* 1146–1183.

Good, T., & Weinstein, R. (1986). Schools make a difference: Evidence, criticisms and new directions. *American Psychologist, 41,* 1090–1097.

Haller, E. (1985). Pupil race and elementary school ability grouping: Are teachers biased against black children? *American Educational Research Journal, 22,* 456–483.

Haller, E., & Davis, S. (1980). Does socioeconomic status bias the assignment of elementary school students to reading groups? *American Educational Research Journal, 17,* 409–418.

Hallinan, M. (1994). Tracking: From theory to practice. *Sociology of Education, 67,* 79–84.

Hallinan, M., & Sørensen, A. (1983). The formation and stability of instructional groups. *American Sociological Review, 48,* 838–851.

Hammack, F. (1986). Large school system's dropout reports: An analysis of definitions, procedures, and findings. *Teachers College Record, 87,* 324–341.

Hammond, P., & Frechtling, J. (1979, April). *Twelve, nine and three month achievement gains of low and average achieving elementary school students.* Paper presented at AERA Annual Meeting, San Francisco.

Hanushek, E. (1989). The impact of differential school expenditures on school performance. *Educational Researcher, 18,* 45–65.

Harvard Education Letter. (1992, January–February). The seventh-grade slump and how to avoid it. *Harvard Education Letter,* 1–4.

Haskins, R. (1989). Beyond metaphor: The efficacy of early childhood education. *American Psychologist, 44,* 274–282.

Hayes, D., & Grether, J. (1983). The school year and vacations: When do students learn? *Cornell Journal of Social Relations, 17,* 56–71.

Hayes, D., & King, J. (1974). *The development of reading achievement differentials during the school year and vacation.* Unpublished manuscript, Cornell University, Ithaca, NY.

Heath, A., & Clifford, P. (1980). The seventy thousand hours that Rutter left out. *Oxford Review of Education, 6,* 3–19.

Hebbeler, K. (1985). An old and a new question on the effects of early education for children from low income families. *Educational Evaluation and Policy Analysis, 7,* 207–216.

Hedges, L., Laine, R., & Greenwald, R. (1994). Does money matter? A meta-analysis of studies of the effects of differential school inputs on student outcomes. *Educational Researcher, 23,* 5–14.

Hess, R., & Holloway, S. (1984). Family and school as educational institutions. In R. Parke (Ed.), *Review of child development research: Vol. 7. The family* (pp. 179–222). Chicago: University of Chicago Press.

Heyns, B. (1978). *Summer learning and the effects of schooling.* New York: Academic Press.

Heyns, B. (1987). Schooling and cognitive development: Is there a season for learning? *Child Development, 58,* 1151–1160.

Higgins, E. T., & Parsons, J. E. (1982). Social cognition and the social life of the child: Stages as subcultures. In E. T. Higgins, D. N. Ruble, & W. W. Hartup (Eds.), *Social cognition and social development: A sociocultural perspective* (pp. 15–62). Cambridge: Cambridge University Press.

Hodgson, G. (1973). Do schools make a difference? *The Atlantic, 231,* 35–46.

Hoffer, T. (1992). Middle school ability grouping and student achievement in science and mathematics. *Educational Evaluation and Policy Analysis, 14,* 205–227.

Jencks, C. (1985). How much do high school students learn? *Sociology of Education, 58,* 128–153.

Jencks, C., Smith, M., Ackland, H., Bane, M., Cohen, D., Gintis, H., Heyns, B., & Michelson, S. (1972). *Inequality: A reassessment of the effect of family and schooling in America.* New York: Basic.

Kagan, S., & Zigler, E. (1987). *Early schooling: The national debate.* New Haven, CT: Yale University Press.

Karweit, N. (1989). Time and learning: A review. In R. Slavin (Ed.), *School and classroom organization* (pp. 69–95). Hillsdale, NJ: Lawrence Erlbaum Associates.

Lareau, A. (1987). Social class differences in family–school relationships: The importance of cultural capital. *Sociology of Education, 60,* 73–85.

Lazar, I., & Darlington, R. (1982). Lasting effects of early education: A report from the Consortium for Longitudinal Studies. *Mongoraphs of the Society for Research in Child Development, 47*(2–3).

Levine, D. (1990). Update on effective schools: Findings and implications for research and practice. *Journal of Negro Education, 59,* 577–584.

Lloyd, D. (1978). Prediction of school failure from third-grade data. *Educational and Psychological Measurement, 38,* 1191–1200.

Mackenzie, D. (1983). Research for school improvement: An appraisal of some recent trends. *Educational Researcher, 12,* 5–17.

McDill, E., & Rigsby, L. (1973). *Structure and process in secondary schools: The impact of educational climates.* Baltimore, MD: Johns Hopkins Press.

McPartland, J., Coldiron, J., & Braddock, J. (1987). School structures and classroom practices in elementary, middle and secondary schools (Tech. Rep. No. 14). Baltimore, The Johns Hopkins University, Center for Research on Elementary and Middle Schools.

Mosteller, F., & Moynihan, D. (1972). *On equality of educational opportunity.* New York: Vintage.

Murnane, R. (1975). *The impact of school resources on the learning of inner city children.* Cambridge, MA: Ballinger.

Natriello, G., McDill, E., & Pallas, A. (1990). *Schooling disadvantaged children: Racing against catastrophe.* New York: Teachers College Press.

Oakes, J. (1988). Tracking in mathematics and science education: A structural contribution to unequal schooling. In L. Weis (Ed.), *Class, race and gender in American education* (pp. 106–125). Albany: State University of New York Press.

Oakes, J. (1989). Tracking in secondary schools: A contextual perspective. In R. Slavin (Ed.), *School and classroom organization* (pp. 173–195). Hillsdale, NJ: Lawrence Erlbaum Associates.

Oakes, J. (1992). Can tracking research inform practice? Technical, normative and political considerations. *Educational Researcher, 21,* 12–21.

Oakes, J. (1994). More than misapplied technology: A normative and political response to Hallinan on tracking. *Sociology of Education, 67,* 84–89.

Oakes, J., Gamoran, A., & Page, R. (1992). Curriculum differentiation: Opportunities, outcomes and meanings. In P. Jackson (Ed.), *Handbook of research on curriculum* (pp. 570–608). New York: Macmillan.

Pallas, A., Entwisle, D., Alexander, K., & Stluka, M. (1994). Ability-group effects: Instructional, social or institutional? *Sociology of Education, 67,* 27–46.

Parker, S., Greer, S., & Zuckerman, B. (1988). Double jeopardy: The impact of poverty on early child development. *Pediatric Clinics of North America, 35,* 1227–1240.

Parsons, J. E., Adler, T. F., & Kaczak, C. M. (1982). Socialization of achievement attitudes and beliefs: Parental influences. *Child Development, 53,* 322–339.

Pelavin, S., & David, J. (1977). Evaluating long-term achievement: An analysis of longitudinal data from compensatory educational programs (Project 4537). Menlo Park, CA: SRI International.

Posner, J., & Vandell, D. (1994). Low-income children's after-school care: Are there beneficial effects of after-care programs? *Child Development, 65,* 440–456.

Purkey, S., & Smith, M. (1983). Effective schools: A review. *Elementary School Journal, 83,* 427–452.

Rosenbaum, J. (1980). Some implications of educational grouping. *Review of Research in Education, 8,* 361–401.

Rowan, B., Bossert, S., & Dwyer, D. (1983). Research on effective schools: A cautionary note. *Educational Researcher, 12,* 24–31.

Rutter, M., Maughan, B., Mortimore, P., & Ouston, J. (1979). *Fifteen thousand hours: Secondary schools and their effects on children.* Cambridge, MA: Harvard University Press.

Schweinhart, L., Berrueta-Clement, J., Barnett, S., Epstein, A., & Weikart, D. (1985). The promise of early education. *Phi Delta Kappan, 66,* 548–551.

Shepard, L., & Smith, M. (1989). Introduction and overview. In L. Shepard & M. Smith (Eds.), *Flunking grades: Research and policies on retention* (pp. 1–15). London: Falmer.

Slaughter, D., & Epps, E. (1987). The home environment and academic achievement of Black American children: An overview. *Journal of Negro Education, 56,* 3–20.

Slavin, R., Karweit, N., & Madden, N. (Eds.). (1989). *Effective programs for students at risk.* Boston: Allyn and Bacon.

Slavin, R., Madden, N., & Karweit, N. (1989). Effective programs for students at risk: Conclusions for policy and practice. In R. Slavin, N. Karweit, & N. Madden (Eds.), *Effective programs for students at risk* (pp. 355–372). Boston: Allyn and Bacon.

Sørensen, A., & Hallinan, M. (1984). Effects of race on assignment to ability groups. In P. Peterson, L. Wilkinson, & M. Hallinan (Eds.), *The social context of instruction: Group organization and group processes* (pp. 85–103). New York: Academic Press.

Stevenson, H., & Stigler, J. (1992). *The learning gap: Why our schools are failing and what we can learn from Japanese and Chinese education.* New York: Summit.

Stipek, D. (1984). The development of achievement motivation. In R. Ames & C. Ames (Eds.), *Research on motivation in education* (Vol. 1, pp. 145–174). New York: Academic Press.

Stroup, A., & Robins, L. (1972). Elementary school predictors of high school dropout among Black males. *Sociology of Education, 45,* 212–222.

Woodhead, M. (1988). When psychology informs public policy: The case of early childhood intervention. *American Psychologist, 43,* 443–454.

6

▼▼▼▼▼▼▼

Inequality in Educational Achievement: Families Are the Source, But Are Schools a Prophylactic?

Thomas D. Cook
Northwestern Univerity

Alexander and Entwisle (this volume, chap. 5) have written an important chapter on the origins of social class differences in the rate of change in reading and math. Their 8-year study of educational inequality follows 790 children who began as first graders in 20 Baltimore public schools that had been deliberately selected to vary in race and socioeconomic status (SES). Because the Baltimore elementary schools gave achievement tests in fall and spring of each year, this permitted Alexander and Entwisle to partition the total annual growth from spring to spring into its academic year and summer components (from spring to fall and fall to spring, respectively).

Analysis of the resulting data prompted Alexander and Entwisle to advance three knowledge claims:

1. During elementary and middle school, the gap in achievement between children of higher and lower social class widens.
2. This growth in inequality is due to class differences in summer learning.
3. It is not due to differential learning during the academic year, for then knowledge gains are independent of socioeconomic standing.

If we can trust them, these findings are important. Since the 1960s, billions of dollars have been spent on compensatory education designed to increase the learning of poor children. When such children are the only ones receiving the services in question, raising their achievement may also reduce the inequality in achievement associated with social class and its correlates, like race. One implication of the Alexander and Entwisle findings, then, is that schooling in the inner city reduces achievement inequality compared to what it would be if only home backgrounds were operating—as during summers. In Alexander and Entwisle's account, schools are not the villains causing or exacerbating cognitive inequality; they are the dams holding back the inequality that would otherwise erupt because of social class differences in educational advantages.

This perspective offers a challenge to the conventional wisdom in educational policy. This sees inner city public schools as so ineffective that only radical reforms like vouchers or privatization are worth considering. It also challenges much theory in the sociology of education. This assumes that schools do not explain much of the difference in children's cognitive performance—certainly not when compared to the influence of families. Given the importance of Alexander and Entwisle's knowledge claims, we think they deserve scrutiny by the highest standards. So, a major purpose of this chapter is to examine the warrant for their claims.

Another purpose is to examine some of the educational policy implications of the findings we consider more plausible—a task that Alexander and Entwisle also took upon themselves. However, the policy recommendation we find most compelling is a version of a recommendation they explicitly reject. It is based on increasing the amount of summer schooling for low-performing (but not necessarily lower class) children during the first elementary school years.

EXAMINING THE KNOWLEDGE CLAIMS

The Calendar Year Growth in Achievement Inequality. Alexander and Entwisle state that lower SES children fall back further and further as time passes, and they note that this increase in inequality occurs for both reading and math. To examine this proposition, we refer to their Table 5.1 (see p. 70). The data come from annual spring achievement testings, and so we refer to them as data on calendar year gains. The contrast is with academic year gains—from fall to spring—and summer gains—from spring to fall. Few school districts do twice-yearly achievement tests, but Baltimore is one.

As far as reading is concerned, both the mean differences and the differential between the high and low SES groups expressed as a percentage of the standard deviation reveal that: (a) an achievement differential is evident when the children begin elementary school; (b) this differential widens with age; but (c) the rate at which the gap increases slows with age; (d) it has essentially ceased to grow by the end of the third year, and certainly by the end of the fourth except for (e) a one-shot increase in inequality between the sixth and seventh years, when nearly all the children have completed the transition into middle school. Thus, there is indeed evidence of an increase in reading inequality. But the *rate* of increase is negatively accelerated and, by about the fourth year, the gap ceases to widen, except perhaps in one middle school year.

Consider, next, the math data. Examination of Table 5.1 reveals that the SES group difference increases steadily between the springs of Year 1 and Year 3, being constant thereafter except for an increase between the sixth and seventh years, when almost all the children are in middle school. This is the same data pattern obtained with reading. The raw differences in means between the high and low SES groups show one minor difference, however. The annual differences in gains are 25, 33, 47, 56, 53, 57, 81, and 82 units, suggesting a widening gap during the first four elementary school years—rather than the first three—plus the increase in the one middle school year also found with reading. Thus, the combined math and reading data suggest two empirical phenomena, each more specific than the over-generalized claim that low SES children fall back further as time passes:

1. Social class differences in reading and math consistently increase over the first 3 and perhaps the first 4 years of elementary school, but the resulting mean differences do not increase in any systematic fashion thereafter.
2. Between the sixth and seventh years of schooling, when nearly all of the original sample are in middle school, inequality increases in both math and reading. But this differential does not increase in the next year; it stays constant.

These more specific conclusions, like those of Alexander and Entwisle, depend on a variety of assumptions. One is that there are no scaling artifacts—that the math and reading subtests have equal intervals across their entire age range. The Baltimore school district presumably uses age-appropriate tests designed to avoid ceiling effects. But no variances or distributions are presented in Alexander and Entwisle to check on range restrictions, particularly in the high SES group. However, Alexander and Entwisle's Footnote 3 does assert that no ceiling effects were noted when an (undefined) check was made.

A more crucial assumption is that the content validity of the achievement tests is constant across age and social class. In the earliest elementary grades, there is considerable national consensus about the basic skills children should learn. But as they master these skills, children are then freed to explore other areas of learning in more advanced areas of reading or math or in social studies and science—areas that are not assessed in conventional reading and math tests for a given age level. We can have no confidence that the data patterns described previously would be replicated if other domains were added to the Baltimore test battery in order to assess achievement more broadly. At every age the high SES children do better than the low SES children and so may be freer to pursue knowledge in other domains not included on reading or math tests. If so, gaps would be even wider on broader assessment batteries.

The final assumption is that the annual differences in Table 5.1 are not influenced by selection confounds. We return to this issue in detail later. For now let us only note that Table 5.1 shows that the overall attrition rate from the high SES group is about three times higher than from the other groups. Moreover, this attrition differential is greatest in the early elementary years. The children leaving the study (and hence the Baltimore public schools) are predominantly White and presumably higher academic achievers. Indeed, they may even be the highest achievers among the Whites! If the data in Table 5.1 could magically be presented for each year for all the 790 children who began in the study, social class changes in cognitive inequality might look quite different from what we now see in Table 5.1.

Any conclusions about the growth in calendar year inequality that are drawn from the data in Table 5.1 have to assume: (a) that there are no selection confounds that vary with age or social class; (b) that there are no scaling artifacts that increase with age or class; and (c) that the relationship between children's performance in reading and math and their total knowledge is independent of age and social class.

Social Class Differences in Summer Learning Gains. Alexander and Entwisle claim that "the increasing gap across SES levels over the elementary years . . . can be attributed almost entirely to gains that children from high SES households made when school was not in session" (p. 75)—that is, during summers. Their claim is restricted to the elementary school years, for no spring to fall testing data are available for middle schools. Thus, we cannot probe whether summer learning differences account for the one-shot increase in achievement inequality found between Years 6 and 7. Moreover, because our analysis of the annual data reached a somewhat different conclusion from Alexander and Entwisle, our task is to see whether summers account for the initial increase and subsequent decrease in inequality in spring to spring testings rather than to test whether summers account for a continuously increasing social class differential.

Alexander and Entwisle do not pretend to be the first scholars to show differential summer learning gains, though they do show them at a younger age than others. Prior studies suggest that children from different social class backgrounds learn (and forget!) different amounts over the summer and that such inequalities accumulate across several summers. So, the reality of differential summer learning is not at issue. However, some more specific issues about such learning are worth examining.

One concerns *the temporal stability of class differences in summer achievement gains.* Using data from the high and low SES groups in the authors' Table 5.2 where spring to fall testing results are presented, our Fig. 6.1 plots the reported size of the summer learning gains with reading and math combined. It is apparent that the size of the social class difference in gains decreases with age. Indeed, by the fourth year the effect seems very modest, and by the fifth year it is nonexistent. That the size of the summer-caused differential decreases with age and has almost reached asymptote by the end of the third year corresponds with our interpretation of the annual data—that is, the gap grows initially wider, but with ever smaller increments so that by the end of the third or fourth elementary school year the increments cease and the differential remains constant. Thus, the summer data can account for the annual data as we interpret the latter. But neither the calendar year nor summer data show the increasing gap between low and high SES children that Alexander and Entwisle claim. And Fig. 6.1 makes clear that even if there were an ever-increasing annual gap in achievement, the summer data could not be a cause of it. This is because the size of the summer differential in gains decreases over the years and eventually reaches zero.

Another issue concerns *cumulative summer differences in achievement*. Indeed, Alexander and Entwisle make more of summer differences summed over the 5 study years than they do of the form of summer differences from year to year. In the low SES group, they report that the 5-year cumulative summer gain is .8 units; in the middle SES group, it is −.3 units; and in the high SES group, it is 46.5 units. Thus, all the cumulative summer differential seems attributable to the high SES group; there is not the theoretically expected difference in reading gains between the low and middle SES groups.

The data on which these estimates are based include all the children providing data at each time point. Hence, interpretation is clouded if there is differential attrition from the SES groups. Our Table 6.1, computed from details in Alexander and Entwisle's Table 5.2, shows that this is indeed the case—about 42% of the high SES children present at the first measurement wave were no longer providing data by the fifth wave, whereas the corresponding percentage was about 14% in the low SES group. Most of this attrition difference is because White students (overrepresented in the high SES group) are leaving the Baltimore school district, a selection process that would be even more problematic if the higher achieving White children were more likely to move than their lower scoring White counterparts.

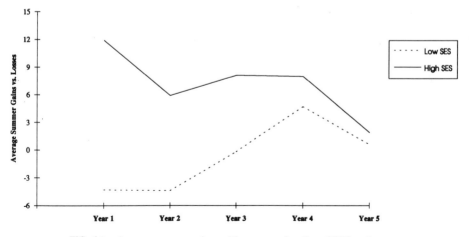

FIG. 6.1.   Average summer gains and losses as a function of SES and year.

TABLE 6.1
Sample Size as a Function of SES and Year

	SES		
	Low	Mid	High
Year 1	318	159	154
Year 2	295	126	123
Year 3	299	123	114
Year 4	285	126	91
Year 5	274	113	88

Longitudinal data restricted to the students present at each testing would get around this problem of differential attrition, though it would restrict conclusions to children remaining in Baltimore for their entire elementary school career. Footnote 10 of Alexander and Entwisle's report provides the summed gains from a purer longitudinal design. The summer gain in the low SES group is −1.0 units; the gain in the middle group is −3.8 units, and is 33.2 units in the high group. Such data are congruent with the hypothesis of differential summer gains by social class, but only if the high SES group is contrasted with the others and not when the low and middle SES groups are contrasted. But even in the maximal contrast between the high and low SES groups the differential is still 30% smaller in the longitudinal design than when the more cross-sectional (and attrition-plagued) design is used. In the latter case, the summer gains cumulated to 46.5 units rather than 33.2. Has Alexander and Entwisle's mode of presenting the data inadvertently capitalized on selection, providing a larger summed effect size estimate than is warranted?

Using the cross-sectional design, the summer effect size for math summed over 5 years is 30% smaller than the reading effect. That is, the low SES group loses −7.9 units, the middle group gains 4.0 units, and the high SES group gains 24.9 units. We see here the expected differences between the low and middle SES groups—is it statistically significant, though?—and between the high SES group and the two others. But the difference between the low and high groups is smaller for math (32.8) than reading (45.7), suggesting that the differential summer gains in the earliest elementary school years may affect reading more than math. Footnote 10 does not include the math gains from a longitudinal design but does assert that the nature of the design leads to changes that "are more minor still" than the changes in reading effect sizes. But if they were in the same direction as the reading changes, this would nonetheless entail reducing an estimate of differential summer gains that is already smaller for math than reading.

For a better sense of summer (and calendar year) effect sizes, we would like to see the annual and summer data displayed for both reading and math as year-by-year results from an analysis restricted to those children who were present at all data collection waves. This would be a less generalizable analysis than the one the authors used. But because it is less biased, it probably deserves at least as much prominence as the more biased cross-sectional test that Alexander and Entwisle actually used.

A third issue *concerns the generalizability of summer gains.* Although a longitudinal analysis might reveal smaller cumulative learning differentials, the greater attrition of more affluent White children from the Baltimore public schools may create a bias in the opposite direction. If these learn most over the summer (or during the school year), omitting them from the analyses will underestimate the cumulative summer and calendar year learning difference by some unknown amount. Longitudinal analysis will control for selection bias due to different students being in the analysis year by year. But it will still not be bias-free, because it loses those children we presume are most likely to show greater gains at all times. Indeed, Table 5.1 shows that rate of differential attrition by social class is greatest in the early elementary school years. If we could magically put the drop-outs from the research into the analysis, would the summer learning differential be greater than what Table 5.1 reveals for the first three elementary school years? Would we have found the ever-increasing gap in annual differences that Alexander and Entwisle postulated?

We cannot know the answers to such questions. But merely posing them illustrates how sensitive estimates of inequality growth are to the way the research question is framed. One framing treats as the population those children who stay in Baltimore public schools for all the years under study. Another framing treats as the population those children who provided data at the first wave of testing, which requires keeping in the study all those children who left the public schools, many to the suburbs. A third framing concerns school district differences in the types of students they attract and in the services they provide. Such differences might be a potent source of cognitive inequality, particularly when inner city and affluent suburban districts are compared. To probe the role of district-level factors in determining the form and magnitude of cognitive inequality requires sampling children from both the city and suburbs—a tall order, since few suburbs have fall and spring testings. Still, as a thought experiment, it is worth asking: If there were a sample of both city and suburban children, would one find an ever-widening gap? If so, would it be due to ever-larger growth increments—as Alexander and Entwisle claim—or to increments (a) that are positive each year, but that decline in magnitude as the children age; or (b) that are positive in the earliest school years but decline to zero thereafter? Each of these involves a widening gap, but at different rates and with different implications for whether the gap ever ceases to grow.

Framing the inequality issue only around children who are in an urban district at one time point—or even multiple time points—cannot provide a sensitive estimate of how inequality changes in those parts of our society where most concern about inequality in achievement is expressed. This is the difference between inner city and suburban school districts where population and expenditure differences are so large. With the data in Alexander and Entwisle's chapter, we cannot be sure how large the cumulative summer achievement differential is *either* within cities; *or* when children who stay in a city are contrasted with those who eventually move to the suburbs; *or* when city children are contrasted with children who have always lived in the suburbs.

Another issue with summer gains concerns specifying how social class should be understood. Alexander and Entwisle attribute the differences in summer learning gains to social class writ large. But we need to be more specific, given that their sampling design deliberately confounds race and class. Analyses are not presented for African Americans and Whites separately in order to probe if class differences in summer gains are comparable within race. It is impossible to know, therefore, whether we are dealing with *generalized* class differences in gains or with differences that depend on race and class being confounded. The two are, of course, related in the United States. Hence, in some demographic sense, the confounding may be justified. But still, a general statement about class biases assumes that the same bias is found wherever social class varies, including when it varies within various racial or ethnic groups. This last kind of inference is not yet warranted, perhaps because no statistically powerful test of class differences within race is possible with these data, especially after attrition is taken into account. A different sampling design would have been required for this purpose. But with the available sampling design we would have liked to see the data displayed several different ways, each making different assumptions about the population and potential bias.

We also think that there is a case for treating SES as a continuous rather than a categorical variable. This is because the reading and math summer gains seem to be nonlinearly related to the three SES categories, with the low and middle SES groups differing less from each other than either of them differs from the high SES group. Examination of how these three social class categories relate to individual SES indicators within Alexander and Entwisle's text shows the same nonlinear pattern. That is, the status difference between the high and middle SES groups is greater than the status difference between the middle and low groups. We suspect, therefore, that SES and learning gains are in fact linearly related and that a correlational analysis would be more efficient than creating three SES categories.

Combining a continuous SES measure with a longitudinal design suggests the advisability of exploring some kind of hierarchical linear modeling analysis. The simplest form of this would be a two-level design in which the first level is each child's series of achievement scores as an individual growth curve and the second is the child himself or herself. SES would then be used as one predictor at this second level in order to probe Alexander and Entwisle's hypothesis that learning curves differ by social class during the calendar year and summer but not during the academic year. A more complex analysis might also be feasible, using schools as a third level. But this requires assumptions about how to deal with moves between Baltimore schools during the period under study.

Notwithstanding, the design and analysis presented by Alexander and Entwisle make it difficult to estimate how large the summer learning differences are and to determine whether the form of learning differences is constant (as implied by their extensive use of the summed summer data) or decreases with age (as implied by Fig. 6.1). A longitudinal, multilevel analysis would shed some better light on these matters, though it cannot deal with the important restrictions to external validity associated with the differential loss of high SES children as they grow older.

If we are willing to assume that there is some type of a summer social class difference in achievement gains—a proposition that other study results also support—then another issue is to explain such differential gains. How much of them is the product, for instance, of differential formal instruction like summer classes or tutors? How much the product of informal instruction as adults read with children or do puzzles with them or even engage them with learning tools like computers? How much is due to adult language patterns as parents interact with children informally and enlarge their vocabulary, expand their active knowledge of more complex grammar, or encourage them to expand verbally on the answers they give? How much is due to reinforcement processes as parents and other adults reward children materially and psychologically? How much is due to the time adults spend with children in summer as opposed to asking siblings to baby-sit or expecting the child to spend time on the streets or alone? And how much is due to general summer enrichment opportunities that might have a secondary payoff in knowledge gains, such as summer camps? We could go on and on. The point, though, is to illustrate that summer is not a black box causal agent. It is a period of time in which knowledge-producing activities occur, and presumably, differentially by social class. It would be theoretically instructive, and perhaps practically useful, to describe what such activities are.

Gains During the Academic Year Are Not Related to SES. Alexander and Entwisle claim that during the school year children from high and low SES groups learn comparable amounts. They do this from quite different baselines, though, and this baseline difference is probably due to family factors that operate before formal schooling begins and during the summers of elementary school. Referring to the high and low SES groups and using "winters" as a literary contrast with "summers" rather than as a designation of period, Alexander and Entwisle write: "In winters . . . the total gains of the two SES groups over the elementary years are less than 5 points apart" (p. 75). They further note that it is the middle SES group, not the high group, that registers the largest gains. This last point reinforces the notion that academic year learning gains are not related to SES in the positive linear fashion implied by SES causing learning differences in some simple way. They draw these conclusions from a cross-sectional analysis. But they also provide the relevant reading results from the longitudinal design.

The same picture emerges of no-difference in learning gains during the school year. Whatever the design, SES does not seem to be related to learning gains during the academic year.

The greatest threat to the validity of this conclusion is the differential attrition noted earlier. There is a disproportionate loss of high SES students from the sampling design, which could suppress what would otherwise have been even larger academic year gains in later years. In their defense, Alexander and Entwisle might contend that they are only interested in urban inequality and hence in those children who remain in Baltimore, preferring not to frame the inequality issue in terms of whether selective outmigration to the suburbs reduces social class gaps in the city because the children most likely to benefit from academic year instruction have disproportionately left the city. If this selection account is empirically correct—and we do not know if it is—it would have another important implication. It entails an even larger academic year gap between the city and suburbs. And for many commentators on U.S. education, this is the inequality gap of greatest national significance, eclipsing the importance of social class gaps within cities.

Also plausible is the argument that restricting the analysis to reading and math underestimates the social class differences in academic year gains in other cognitive domains. For instance, the higher reading and math performance of high SES children might have improved their performance in social studies or science. Alexander and Entwisle might legitimately reply that to probe whether gaps open in other cognitive skills involves a research question they did not ask. However, as we have reframed the question above, it puts reading and math into a larger achievement framework which implies that the absence of academic year differences in reading and math may not generalize to other topics. Is it the case that, year after year, poorer children are working on the more basic skills that the reading and math tests assess whereas their economically more advantaged counterparts are moving on to different but not-assessed subject matters where academic year gaps are indeed opening up? We do not know. But from a falsificationist perspective, the onus lies on Alexander and Entwisle to rule out this possibility if they want to claim that their results are about the growth in inequality in general achievement and not just reading and math.

The absence of social class differences in learning during the elementary school academic year is the most surprising finding in the Alexander and Entwisle chapter. For this conclusion to hold even in Baltimore, we have to believe that some of the following propositions are true. The first is that the family and social class mechanisms leading to greater learning gains for the more advantaged students prior to school and during summers do not operate during the academic year. In other words, from September to June, parents stop doing what works for them in summers, perhaps because they think schools already do these things. It is difficult to assess the plausibility of this argument. We are not experts on the issue and do not know the literature. Note what is at stake here, though. It is not that the more affluent parents do less during the school year of what they do during summers and before the child entered school. It is that they eliminate such activities altogether, for unless some theory of countervailing forces is developed, the total absence of an SES differential in academic year gains implies that the SES differential in home activities promoting learning is also totally absent during the school year though it operates during summers.

It is also possible to argue that high SES families do indeed do more achievement-enhancing things at home during the academic year, but what they do is redundant with what schools do. Thus, the home activities have no marginal impact on test scores. But repeating the same material at school *and* at home should induce an overlearning that differs by SES, even if the initial acquisition of information is similar across classes. We suspect that few learning theorists would be willing to postulate that overlearning should not influence test score gains, for it is a major cause of long-term memory and of the active cognitive reorganizations that allow what has been learned to be used in novel contexts later.

The absence of social class differences in academic year learning gains also implies that none of the school practices that promote learning during the academic year operates differentially by class. Included here are the causes of learning that Alexander and Entwisle themselves discuss. How reasonable is it to assume that during the elementary school years SES is not correlated with tracking practices, homework practices, curriculum design, teachers' time on task, teachers' calling on students in class, teachers' expectancies for students, and peers' behavioral support for achievement? If SES is positively correlated with some of these practices—and not necessarily all of them—then social class differences in academic year gains should result, unless one is willing to postulate that SES is positively correlated with some practices but is negatively correlated with others in the same degree.

Sociologists of education and educators would have no problem, we suspect, postulating that social class is related to such practices at the high school and perhaps middle school levels; at issue with the Alexander and Entwisle chapter, however, is the elementary level. Here, literature on the availability and operation of inequality-causing processes is less developed, and we badly need systematic reviews that conceptualize SES differences in several ways—in terms of contrasts between districts varying in average SES levels, in terms of within-district contrasts between schools varying in average social class, and in terms of within-school contrasts between students of different advantagement levels. It will be a difficult task convincing most social scientists that SES plays no role whatsoever in the allocation of teaching processes that educational researchers claim are responsible for higher rates of achievement gain in the elementary school years. Yet that is one implication of the Alexander and Entwisle finding. Given the importance of the point, I would like to see from them a review in defense of their claim that there is no correlation between SES and achievement-enhancing practices in elementary schools.

If one accepts *either* that family practices facilitating achievement are correlated with social class and do not come to a halt during the academic year, *or* if one assumes that some teacher practices in elementary school favor the high SES children, then it has to follow that the city schools in Baltimore serving poorer children are outperforming the schools serving more affluent children. What might be responsible for this? Any causal mechanism has to be based either on poorer children having more of what makes a differences in achievement or on them benefitting more from whatever pedagogical factors are equally available to all students. In the education literature, it is rare to find claims that poorer children learn more than more affluent children when exposed to the same curriculum materials—assuming, of course, that there is no ceiling effect depressing the scores of the high SES children. Much more plausible is that poor children are exposed to more or better educational services. But from which sources? The likeliest contenders are compensatory education programs. By law these are supposed to be available only in educational settings with a given percentage of poor children, or in settings where certain language groups are represented that often tend to be of lower socioeconomic standing; alternatively, these compensatory services are restricted to children with specific learning disabilities, who again are more likely to come from the poorer sections of U.S. society.

We have no problem believing that compensatory education services like Chapter 1, bilingual education, and various special education services are generally more available in less financially advantaged school districts, and that the differential between many urban and suburban districts is substantial. However, it is less clear whether there is a large difference in program availability at the elementary level *within* a city like Baltimore. This is because public school SES differences are likely to be smaller within cities than between cities and suburbs, and also because many city administrators feel pressured to allocate resources to schools equally, or fairly equally, irrespective of formal program requirements. Administrators who want to minimize the focused inequality in treatment that compensatory education demands, but which causes them political headaches, can distribute the resources under their own control in ways that favor the schools with a higher percentage of affluent children. When they do this, they cancel out all or some of the differences in treatment that compensatory education is designed to create. Such speculations are not meant to deny all differences in the allocation of compensatory education across Baltimore elementary schools. We merely want to argue that large differences in the availability of compensatory services cannot be assumed willy-nilly. A strong justification needs to be offered, preferably based on direct measurement of program availability across the sample of schools under analysis.

For compensatory education to play a role in explaining why social class achievement gaps do not widen during the academic year, we would have to assume that it is more available in poorer city schools and that it is absolutely effective in enhancing achievement. This last proposition is not likely to go unchallenged. For the major compensatory education programs the available evidence about effectiveness is not based on sophisticated designs, and we are aware of no empirical claims that they produce cognitive effects that are large or even moderate; quite small relationships are typically invoked. However, the *cumulative* impact of all the programs targeted at poorer children is a more relevant concern. But little is known about how children fare when they are receiving multiple services simultaneously. The National Assessment of Educational Progress shows that racial gaps are slowly but systematically narrowing in the United States, and this *may* reflect the cumulative effects of many compensatory education programs. Even so, Alexander and Entwisle did not review the evidence about the effectiveness of compensatory education, though it is a central issue for understanding why academic year achievement gaps do not widen between SES groups.

Alexander and Entwisle's data on the absence of SES differences in academic year gains in reading and math are remarkable. If not due to selection or scaling artifacts, they present a picture of elementary schools that are eminently fair or that are even better for poorer children than others in the sense that the schools countervail against any home differences favoring the achievement of high SES children or any teacher tendencies to favor more economically advantaged children. This picture is much more positive than the description offered by many critics of urban education, and it suggests that compensatory education services are effective in preventing achievement gaps from growing wider.

POLICY IMPLICATIONS

The Assumptions of Alexander and Entwisle's Analysis. Alexander and Entwisle conducted an analysis of the policy implications of their dual claims that: (a) educational inequality is due to social class differences in family practices that enhance achievement during summers but not during the academic year, and (b) schools are effective in preventing class-based achievement gaps from growing even wider. The authors' analysis is essentially a review of factors that cause achievement gains with poorer children. They want to uncover "what works" in schools and preschools.

They particularly emphasize four factors. One is the importance of early childhood interventions like Head Start, although they note that program effects do not persist for very long in the majority of relevant studies. They also deal with the likely relevance of carefully designed and implemented tracking techniques during the elementary and middle school years, stressing those that do not require tracking children in all subjects for most of the school day. Their contention is that all students gain from careful tracking, including the lower performers. Next, Alexander and Entwisle discuss the literature on schools as "communities of learners," claiming that social and academic climates like those found in many private schools will increase children's knowledge, whatever their social background. The final school practice that "works" for Alexander and

Entwisle is parent involvement, and their literature review leads them to promote various forms of it in the expectation that it will positively impact on performance. We do not want to contest these reviews. They seem to us to be up-to-date, comprehensive, and balanced. But we do want to point to some assumptions behind the notion that a review of what works in increasing achievement for less economically privileged children constitutes an analysis of educational policy about inequality in achievement.

Such inequality can be reduced in two major ways. One is to make sure that the lowest performers are more likely to get access to educationally effective resources; the other is to ensure that, despite similar patterns of exposure, the nature of the materials or teachers leads to bigger learning gains by children from less advantaged home backgrounds.

It is possible for an effective educational resource to be universally available but to be used more often in ways that favor the more advantaged. As a result, children of all kinds learn in the aggregate, enhancing overall efficiency, but the more advantaged group also learns more, increasing inequality. Are the less advantaged helped by such a resource because they know more, or are they hurt more because they now fall even further behind other children? This is a difficult practical and ethical dilemma, and we face it with a universally available educational tool like *Sesame Street* that seems to be used more often in more affluent homes (Cook et al., 1975). But Alexander and Entwisle do not discuss how their four ways of enhancing academic achievement are distributed by social class or how they might be used in ways that enhance the achievement of poorer children more than others. As distasteful as such analyses are to some observers of U.S. education, unless they are carried out, treatises on "what works" to increase efficiency in learning do not uncover factors that will necessarily "work" to reduce inequality when that is a policy goal. And we presume it to be a goal of Alexander and Entwisle's analysis, which is, after all, an empirical study of the origins of inequality and of the role city schools play in reducing inequality.

In the short term, policy options are constrained by what is politically, financially, and culturally viable in a nation and school district and by what can actually be implemented in the hurly-burly of daily life in real homes and real schools. Alexander and Entwisle do not present such analyses for each of the options they favor, leaving that to readers. We do not have the space to conduct such analyses, though we will do so later for the policy option we prefer and that follows most closely from Alexander and Entwisle's findings. We want only to point out here how much more constraining these already constraining factors become once one views them in the context of reducing inequality by making effective educational resources more available to poorer districts or to poorer students within districts or by selecting techniques that promote higher achievement in poorer children though children of all backgrounds are equally exposed to them. Assumptions about the desirability of unequal opportunities or of engineering materials so that one group gains more from them than others are not widely shared in the U.S. culture. And the politics of promoting such goals through these mechanisms are explosive. Also, the technologies for helping lower class children benefit more from equal exposure are not well developed. We still do not know, for instance, whether multicultural education is effective, though it was developed to increase the academic motivation of racial minorities more than of other groups. Whether it actually does this and results in greater achievement gains by the minorities is an unknown. But we do know that multicultural education is highly controversial and could lead to a White backlash. Thus, even the barest outline of a policy analysis has to deal with values, culture, politics, money, and local implementability—matters that are especially complicated if reducing inequality is a policy goal rather than just enhancing overall efficiency.

A Policy Option Worth Considering. Although Alexander and Entwisle single out summer learning differentials as the major cause of educational inequality during the elementary and middle school years, they explicitly reject the idea of basing policy changes on increasing the amount of summer instruction. They do this because, in their view, studies of summer instruction have shown little or no beneficial impact. This is surprising, for even with only one summer of instruction, we would expect the increased time-on-task to result in learning in those areas actually covered by the teachers. Did the studies of summer programs use learning outcomes that were not content valid for what was actually taught? Were the summer curricula rigorous, or was the summer devoted to more recreational than pedagogic objectives? Were the studies they reviewed of the effects of a single summer or of multiple summers, of full-time or part-time programs, or of programs lasting a few weeks or most of the summer? We find it difficult to believe that summer programs will not be effective if time and serious curriculum design are devoted to them. Closer study of the specifics of past evaluations of summer school are called for, we believe. Only then would we be willing to consider seriously the hypothesis that summer school is not a source of leverage for enhancing the learning of poorer students in ways that will also reduce educational inequality. Indeed, two (and possibly three) of the strategies in Alexander and Entwisle's own list of effective pedagogic practices can be brought to bear just as easily over summer as during the school year.

The political, financial, and cultural viability of a policy based on expanding summer school opportunities is enhanced when we note two things. First, Alexander and Entwisle's own data suggest that such opportunities are most needed during the first three elementary school summers. Although this costs money, it is obviously less expensive than calling for many years of summer school. It is also worth noting that effective summer programs might reduce the need for special education services during the school year, and savings could result from this. Second, many Americans believe that interventions are more effective the younger the child, and public support for programs is powerfully influenced by public perceptions of their efficacy (Cook & Barrett, 1992). Intervening in the earliest years has a further advantage in terms of basic U.S. values. The younger children are, the easier it is to claim that differences in achievement are the product of different social backgrounds rather than personal character. Once again, the public is more willing to support those they think are at a disadvantage because of circumstances beyond their personal control. Finally, our guess is that younger children are, in general, more sympathetic to the public than are older students, certainly preadolescents and adolescents. Targeting the summer program to the first three summers of elementary school should help with the politics of support, fitting it into cultural belief systems about the need to help those in need for no fault of their own.

Although universal early summer school would be important for enhancing the overall efficiency of U.S. education, it is expensive and will become embroiled in debates about extending the school year. Moreover, it will only help reduce inequality if poorer children attend summer schools at a higher rate than other children or if they "somehow" learn more from similar exposure. If reducing inequality is the goal, then a scheme has to be devised for getting a higher percentage of poorer children into summer schooling. The current political Zeitgeist does not favor tax-supported services targetted exclusively at poor children or even racial minorities. The call should therefore be for well-designed summer educational services targeted at students performing in the bottom portion of each class, with the cutoff being set locally depending on resources. Low SES children fall disproportionately among the lower performers, of course, entailing that a new summer school program for academically weaker students would especially help them while not excluding the more affluent children who also need help. This design feature should make a summer program more financially, politically, and culturally viable, as well as contribute to preventing an increase in inequality because of SES differences in summer activities at home.

Given this particular program targetting, steps would have to be taken in each school district to prevent stigmatizing the program. What we propose would initially be a voluntary activity, and how it is presented to the local community is a key issue. It has to be a serious pedagogic activity that emphasizes teaching basic skills in interesting ways. No summer program for these children should be designed around a mostly recreational opportunity. There will be some students whose parents do not want them to attend, however skillful the district or school officials might be at making the program attractive. That is sad but not cause for rejecting the idea of quality, full-day 8-week summer schools for lower performing children, many of whom will need to attend for several years.

SUMMARY

Alexander and Entwisle have written an unusually important chapter to support their claim that inequality in educational performance is due to family factors that operate during both the preschool years and those summers while children are attending elementary schools. These home factors, they claim, do not influence inequality during the academic year, presumably because city schools are so effective for poorer children. Our analysis of their data suggests that there are indeed likely to be summer learning differentials. But these operate less strongly with each passing year and have essentially disappeared by the third or fourth year of elementary school. However, we would be more comfortable with this conclusion had Alexander and Entwisle presented their data longitudinally rather than cross-sectionally. There is one footnote about longitudinal analyses, and it suggests that for reading the 5-year cumulative summer differential was 30% less than it was in the cross-sectional results. Whether the annual summer gains would have become progressively smaller in the longitudinal analyses we cannot say.

The results just mentioned cannot be generalized beyond students who stay in the Baltimore city schools. White students, who tend to be more affluent than African-American students, are leaving these schools at a considerably faster rate, perhaps the most affluent Whites fastest of all. Had it been possible to follow up all the original sample, we might have noted quite different results than those presented. In particular, the possibility is strong that inequality would have been greater, especially in the later school years, and that summer differentials might not have decreased at the same rate.

Framing Alexander and Entwisle's research question around an original sample of both urban and suburban children might also have led to different patterns of inequality growth from those presented, for this particular location difference is correlated not only with race and SES but also with levels of school district expenditure. The within-district question framing of Alexander and Entwisle reduces expenditure differences.

Also, their framing of the research question around inequalities in reading and math entails that no general conclusions about cognitive achievement are warranted. The acquisition of better reading and math skills creates in students the wherewithal to explore topics like social studies and science that are not part of these tests. Such skills even make it possible for some of these children to go on to advanced topics in reading and math that standard tests do not assess. It is presumably the more affluent children who are most likely to know more than others in areas the tests do not cover, again leading to an underestimate of the true extent of inequality and of its growth. How Alexander and Entwisle framed their research question might, then, have led to their Tables 5.1 and 5.2 showing less growth in inequality than would have been obtained had they constructed their research question, not about reading and math among children who stay in the city, but about SES differences in achievement (a) within a population of children some of whom stay in the city but others of whom move to the suburbs; or (b) within a population of children attending both urban and suburban schools.

The policy discussion of Alexander and Entwisle is restricted to a thoughtful review of four factors that prior research has shown increase the academic performance of poorer children. However, a full policy analysis also requires consideration of values, culture, finance, and politics. Where educational inequality is concerned, it also requires an analysis of the mechanisms whereby greater gains are to be achieved by those most in need. Traditionally this has meant either restricting learning opportunities to the less fortunate or selecting learning opportunities from which they will benefit more than other children. Neither of these is likely to be popular.

The policy option we most discuss is an expansion of summer school for the earliest elementary grades. We suggest that this change meets many cultural and political needs and does not have to involve large new financial expenditures if it is voluntary and targeted at lower performing children of all social class backgrounds for only the first three summers of elementary school. Such a program should be pedagogic rather than recreational and based on the best available pedagogy for the particular population of children a school serves. Because these children have not been doing well during the academic year, "more of the same" might not be a good formula for summer curriculum design.

ACKNOWLEDGMENT

This chapter has benefitted from research supported by the John T. and Catherine D. MacArthur Foundation's Network on Successful Adolescent Development in High-Risk Settings.

REFERENCES

Cook, F. L., & Barrett, E. J. (1992). *Support for the American welfare state: The views of congress and the public.* New York: Columbia University Press.
Cook, T. D., Appleton, H., Conner, R., Shaffer, A., Tamkin, G., & Weber, S. J. (1975). *"Sesame Street" revisited.* New York: Russell Sage Foundation.

7

▼▼▼▼▼▼▼

Effects of Schooling
on Children and Families

Adam Gamoran
University of Wisconsin–Madison

How do school processes affect children and their families? Alexander and
Entwisle (chapter 5, this volume) adopt a useful framework for answering this
question. They pose three possibilities: Does schooling compensate for initial
inequalities that students bring with them to school? Alternatively, does schooling
reinforce initial differences, so that inequality is wider when students leave school
than when they enter it? Yet another possibility is that schooling is neutral with
respect to inequality, preserving but not magnifying initial differences. For Alexander and Entwisle, inequality refers to achievement differences between students from economically advantaged and disadvantaged families; the same framework can be applied to differences between boys and girls, minority students
and Whites, and among other social categories (Gamoran & Mare, 1989).

To address this question fully, one must consider two aspects of achievement
growth: the *level* of achievement, and its *distribution*. The first refers to educational productivity, and the second to inequality. Presumably, one would want
to reduce inequality while maintaining or enhancing productivity.

EFFECTS ON STUDENTS

Alexander and Entwisle respond to the question with evidence on achievement
growth in elementary school. They show that average achievement rises over
time, among students of all backgrounds. Inequality between students of high
and low socioeconomic status (SES) also grows as time goes by (Alexander &

Entwisle, Table 5.1). Thus, it appears at first that schooling reinforces inequality. As it turns out, however, differential growth is largely due to varied changes during the summer, when high SES students gain and low SES students fail to advance; by contrast, high and low SES students make progress at approximately the same rate during the school year (Table 5.2). This evidence (see also Heyns, 1978) suggests that elementary schooling does not reinforce initial differences. Whether schooling effects are compensatory or neutral, however, is a matter of interpretation.

Schooling Effects: Neutral or Compensatory?

One way of looking at the findings suggests that schooling is essentially neutral with respect to SES inequality. This interpretation points to the fact that differences that existed prior to first grade, and which expand each summer, are preserved during each school year. Schooling does not add to these gaps, but it does not reduce them, either. Hence, schooling neither adds to nor subtracts from inequality. (It does, however, add to productivity for students from both SES categories.)

Another interpretation, which is implied by Alexander and Entwisle, is that schooling compensates for inequality. This viewpoint does not claim that schooling makes up for initial inequality, but that it compensates for additional inequality that would occur in the absence of schooling. Figure 7.1 illustrates this point using Alexander and Entwisle's data on CAT reading scores for low and high SES students. The solid line and large dashes indicate actual achievement growth over the course of elementary school for low and high SES students, respectively. The dotted and smaller dashed lines indicate growth implied by schooling alone, and the dots-and-dashes sequences show growth implied by home life alone. (In Fig. 7.1, gains implied by schooling and home are calculated based on the separate trajectories observed during the school year and the summer.) Among high SES students, the three lines run closely together; gains implied by schooling are only modestly higher than gains implied by the home (until Year 6), and the actual gains are in between. By contrast, the lines for low SES students diverge dramatically: Gains implied by schooling are markedly higher than the actual gains, and the tiny gain implied by home effects lies far below. One can interpret the difference between the lines for schooling effects and the lines for home effects as the compensatory effects of schooling. Schooling does not eliminate the difference between advantaged and disadvantaged students, but it makes the gap a lot smaller than it would be if schooling did not occur.

Interestingly, the two interpretations about inequality also imply differing views for productivity. In the interpretation that says schooling is neutral for inequality because it neither adds to nor subtracts from inequalities students bring with them to school, schooling appears equally productive for advantaged and disadvantaged students. In contrast, when schooling is seen as compensatory because it makes inequality smaller than it would be if students did not attend,

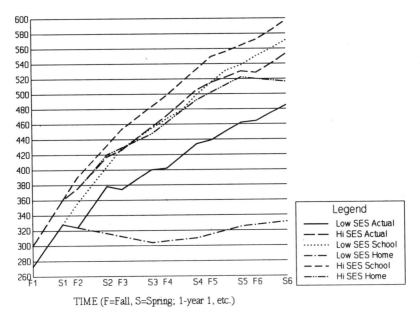

FIG. 7.1.   Compensatory effects of schooling.

it must appear that schooling is much more productive for low SES than for high SES students. The difference, of course, lies in the standard of comparison.

The interpretation in favor of compensatory effects may be overstated, because it seems unlikely that the gains of high SES students would persist to the observed extent over the summer if schooling actually ceased. Presumably, high SES students obtain tools during the school year that they use to enhance their skills during the summer (whereas low SES students, who gain the same tools during the school year, are unable to put them to good use during the summer). In the absence of winter schooling, summer gains could tail off quickly, and inequality between high and low SES students would not be as great as that implied by the lines for home effects in Fig. 7.1. Still, some difference in home effects would likely occur, so the interpretation is probably valid at least to some degree.

These findings (including those of Heyns as well as those of Alexander and Entwisle) are consistent with other research at the elementary school level. Effects of average school conditions on SES inequality are quite small (e.g., Coleman et al., 1966; Jencks et al., 1972). Conditions that vary within schools also have little impact on inequality between advantaged and disadvantaged students. Ability grouping, for example, does not contribute to net achievement inequality among students from varied socioeconomic backgrounds (e.g., Gamoran, 1989; Haller & Davis, 1980).

At the secondary level, results for SES inequality may be somewhat different. Although the research literature is not entirely consistent on this point, several recent studies suggest that between-school SES inequality widens during the high school years (Bryk, Lee, & Holland, 1993; Gamoran, 1992). Also, an enduring finding indicates that tracking inside schools leads to an increase in within-school achievement inequality by social background (e.g., Alexander & McDill, 1976; Gamoran & Mare, 1989; Heyns, 1974). That is, tracking tends to magnify initial differences in achievement among students from diverse family backgrounds. Interestingly, the story is not the same for race and ethnicity: Net of prior achievement and SES, tracking does not magnify achievement differences among Whites, Hispanics, and African Americans (Gamoran & Mare, 1989; Lucas & Gamoran, 1991). However, because minority groups have lower average socioeconomic status, tracking's total impact is to magnify race and ethnic differences in achievement (Lucas & Gamoran, 1991).

This evidence suggests that Alexander and Entwisle's picture of compensatory effects of schooling would look somewhat different if it were examined at the secondary level. Unfortunately, fall achievement was no longer measured after Year 6 of the Beginning School Study (BSS), so it is not possible to examine this further. As Alexander and Entwisle point out, national survey data do not permit such analyses, either.

Another way the findings would differ at the secondary level is that schooling would probably appear less productive. The deceleration of learning observed in Fig. 5.1 probably persists through the middle and high school years; this supposition is backed by research at the high school level that indicates that year-to-year gains are small (Alexander, Natriello, & Pallas, 1985; Gamoran, 1987). BSS data could be used to test this hypothesis, through Grade 9 when standardized testing ceased.

Reducing Inequality: Winter and Summer

Alexander and Entwisle discuss four types of initiatives that may help further reduce inequality among students: early intervention, improving school climate, changes in tracking systems, and parent involvement in schools. In considering these approaches, it is important to keep productivity as well as inequality in mind.

Available research indicates that all four approaches are promising for improving productivity, but their value for reducing inequality is open to question. Perhaps not coincidentally, these initiatives generally do not deal with the time period during which inequality most clearly expands, that is, the summer. Early intervention could reduce initial differences, but it is unlikely to change students' summertime trajectories, as witnessed by the fading of Head Start effects (Alexander & Entwisle, chapter 5, this volume). Improving school climate and modifying or eliminating tracking are targeted at inequality between and within schools, respectively, that occurs during the school year. Even parent involvement programs are usually aimed at improving students' school performance during the academic year.

Can these initiatives compensate not only for initial differences but also for differences that accumulate each summer? The answer is not clear. Effective parent involvement programs raise achievement for students whose parents participate, but some writers fear that the programs will do little to reduce inequality. For example, Gamoran (1992) and Useem (1992) have suggested that when parents are involved in decisions about high school track assignment, high SES students exhibit increased likelihood of assignment to the high track, but low SES students do not receive the same benefit.

Changes in secondary school tracking, as discussed by Alexander and Entwisle, may help lessen the reinforcing effects of tracking on SES inequality. Rethinking the way students are organized for instruction still does not go so far as to reduce achievement gaps between advantaged and disadvantaged students. In describing two cases of effective instruction in low-ability classes, Gamoran (1993a) reported on classes in which low-achieving students did not fall behind during the course of the school year. However, these cases consisted primarily of middle-class students, and although they did not fall further behind, they did not make up much ground, either. Similarly, White, Gamoran, and Smithson (1994) observed that new "transition math courses" aimed at bridging the gap between general and college-preparatory math provide substantial benefits over general-track classes—but they are still not as productive as the college-preparatory classes themselves.

EFFECTS ON FAMILIES?

Although Alexander and Entwisle discuss schooling effects on students and the role of families in schooling effects, they say little about how schools affect families (aside from effects on the child, who is of course a family member). This neglect is not theirs, however, but exists in the research literature: There is much more research on how families affect students' performance in schools than about how schools can or do affect families. Still, available research suggests a direction for future studies.

As Alexander and Entwisle note, research on school climate or "ethos" suggests that schools that foster feelings of belonging and membership produce greater learning than schools that are more fragmented or lacking in a cohesive mission (Bryk & Driscoll, 1988; Bryk et al., 1993; Coleman & Hoffer, 1987; Crain, Heebner, & Si, 1992; Gamoran, 1993b; Wehlage & Smith, 1992). Schools identified as having clear ideals and a sense of community have included career magnet schools, and, in particular, Catholic schools, Bryk et al., (1993) referred to such schools as "communally organized." Research to date has indicated that these schools produce higher achievement and, at least in the case of Catholic schools, lower inequality than comprehensive public high schools (e.g., Bryk et al., 1993).

Researchers have yet to examine the broader effects of communally organized schools on students' families or home lives. If communally organized schools have an impact on students' home environments, they may change the trajectory of summer learning as well as that of winter learning.

Theories about communally organized schools suggest this may be the case. Coleman and Hoffer (1987) argued that a school can serve as a functional community, that is, as a community in which social ties support the school's academic mission. Social relations in a functional community go beyond those strictly related to academics; they include relations among students and among students' parents, as well as between parents and teachers. Why are these non-academic relations important? A network of social ties can generate trust, commitment, and a sense of obligation among members (Coleman, 1990). In this environment, norms may emerge, including norms that support academic success. The greater the "closure" in the network (reciprocated ties among all participants) and the better the communication in the network, the more likely such norms can emerge.

If this theory is correct, social ties that support learning could extend across the summer as well as during the academic year. If school participants (staff, students, and parents) operate as a functional community, the norms generated by this community stand some chance of operating all year round. In this case, behavior that assists summer learning—reading, for example—might be supported by families, and students would engage in them.

Even if such norms exist, however, students from economically disadvantaged families may lack the resources to engage in behavior that would foster summer learning. They may have no money for books, for example, or no one to take them to the library. This dilemma suggests that communally organized schools should incorporate broader year-round services, such as summer programs, community centers, youth groups, and so on, to provide resources that allow norms generated during the academic year to be supported during the summer.

A proposal for extended services at school accords with research that bears on summer learning. First, it is consistent with findings cited by Alexander and Entwisle that summer school typically does little to forestall achievement losses among disadvantaged students (e.g., Heyns, 1978). The typical summer program may fail precisely because it is not embedded in a network of social relations that supports academic success. In contrast, extended services at communally organized schools may succeed by promoting the same norms during the summer as in winter. Second, the proposal is consistent with recent findings that year-round schools raise achievement for at-risk students but not for other students (Gandara & Fish, 1994). One explanation for such effects is that the year-round school provides a continuous normative environment for academic work, as well as the opportunities lacking in the summertime home environments of low-income students, thereby reducing the summer drop-off that is typically observed.

CONCLUSIONS

Alexander and Entwisle clearly demonstrate that elementary schools produce learning and compensate for achievement differences that would occur in the absence of schooling. However, schooling does not compensate for inequalities between poor and well-off students that exist when students enter school and that expand whenever school is not in session. At the secondary level, inequality grows during the school year as well as during the summer.

Current policies that address achievement inequality between advantaged and disadvantaged students generally focus on the academic year. Such programs hold promise, but effective summertime programs have the potential for even greater impact, because inequality typically expands so much during the summer. To date, summer programs have not done much to reduce inequality. Recent research suggests that year-round schools may be a more effective alternative. Research is needed to explore the proposal that extended services at communally organized schools, perhaps in the context of family–school partnerships (e.g., U.S. Department of Education, 1994), could foster summer learning as well as winter learning for disadvantaged students.

ACKNOWLEDGMENT

I am grateful to John Smithson for help with the figure.

REFERENCES

Alexander, K. L., & McDill, E. L. (1976). Selection and allocation within schools: Some causes and consequences of curricular placement. *American Sociological Review, 41*, 963–980.

Alexander, K. L., Natriello, G., & Pallas, A. M. (1985). For whom the school bell tolls: The impact of dropping out on cognitive performance. *American Sociological Review, 50*, 409–420.

Bryk, A. S., & Driscoll, M. E. (1988). *The high school as community: Contextual influences and consequences for students and teachers.* Madison, WI: National Center on Effective Secondary Schools.

Bryk, A. S., Lee, V. E., & Holland, P. (1993). *Catholic schools and the common good.* Cambridge, MA: Harvard University Press.

Coleman, J. S. (1990). *Foundations of social theory.* Cambridge, MA: Harvard University Press.

Coleman, J. S., Campbell, E., Hobson, C., McPartland, J., Mood, A., Weinfeld, F., & York, R. (1966). *Equality of educational opportunity.* Washington, DC: U.S. Government Printing Office.

Coleman, J. S., & Hoffer, T. (1987). *Public and private high schools: The impact of communities.* New York: Basic Books.

Crain, R. L., Heebner, A. L., & Si, Y.-P. (1992). *The effectiveness of New York City's career magnet schools: An evaluation of ninth-grade performance using an experimental design.* Berkeley, CA: National Center for Research in Vocational Education.

Gamoran, A. (1987). The stratification of high school learning opportunities. *Sociology of Education, 60,* 135–55.

Gamoran, A. (1989). Rank, performance, and mobility in elementary school grouping. *Sociological Quarterly, 30,* 109–123.

Gamoran, A. (1992). Access to excellence: Assignment to honors English classes in the transition from middle to high school. *Educational Evaluation and Policy Analysis, 14,* 185–204.

Gamoran, A. (1993a). Alternative uses of ability grouping in secondary schools: Can we bring high-quality instruction to low-ability classes? *American Journal of Education, 101,* 1–22.

Gamoran, A. (1993b, August). *Achievement in city high schools.* Paper presented at the annual meeting of the American Sociological Association, Miami.

Gamoran, A., & Mare, R. D. (1989). Secondary school tracking and educational inequality: Reinforcement, compensation, or neutrality? *American Journal of Sociology, 94,* 1146–1183.

Gandara, P., & Fish, J. (1994). Year-round schooling as an avenue to major structural reform. *Educational Evaluation and Policy Analysis, 16,* 67–85.

Haller, E. A., & Davis, S. (1980). Does socioeconomic status bias the assignment of elementary school students to reading groups? *American Educational Research Journal, 17,* 409–418.

Heyns, B. (1974). Social selection and stratification within schools. *American Journal of Sociology, 79,* 1434–1451.

Heyns, B. (1978). *Summer learning and the effects of schooling.* New York: Academic Press.

Jencks, C. L., Smith, M., Ackland, H., Bane, M. J., Cohen, D. K., Gintis, H., Heyns, B., & Michelson, S. (1972). *Inequality: A reassessment of the effects of family and schooling in America.* New York: Basic Books.

Lucas, S. R., & Gamoran, A. (1991, August). *Race and track assignment: A reconsideration with course-based indicators of track locations.* Paper presented at the annual meeting of the American Sociological Association, Cincinnati.

U.S. Department of Education. (1994). *Strong families, strong schools: Building community partnerships in education.* Washington, DC: Author.

Useem, E. (1992). Middle schools and math groups: Parents' involvement in children's placement. *Sociology of Education, 65,* 263–279.

Wehlage, G. G., & Smith, G. A. (1992). Building new programs for students at risk. In F. M. Newmann (Ed.), *Student engagement and achievement in American secondary schools* (pp. 92–118). New York: Teachers College Press.

White, P., Gamoran, A., & Smithson, J. (1994). *Upgrading the high school math curriculum: Math course-taking patterns in New York and California.* Madison, WI: Consortium for Policy Research in Education.

8

▼▼▼▼▼▼▼

Schools, Children At Risk, and Successful Interventions

Claude Goldenberg
California State University, Long Beach

In their usual thorough and rigorous way, Professors Alexander and Entwisle make two critical points in their chapter (chap. 5, this volume). These provide the starting point for my own comments. Ultimately I would like to address questions of intervention for children at risk—what are we intervening for and how successful can we be?

INEQUALITY, IN AND OUT OF SCHOOL

First, Alexander and Entwisle demonstrate that it is during nonschool time—before they start and during the summer months—that low SES children fall academically behind their higher SES peers and get progressively further behind. During the school months (at least through elementary school), the rate of progress is virtually identical for high and low SES children. If anything, it seems slightly greater for low SES children.[1] Regression effects might exaggerate low SES students' school-year gains while minimizing those of high SES students. But this wouldn't explain the strikingly different patterns during the winter and summer months. At least with respect to measured achievement, schools seem to contribute to, not work against, educational equity. Schools hold the line during the year; there would be more inequity in cognitive outcomes in the absence of

---

[1] I must note the puzzling finding that Alexander and Entwisle mention only in passing—the mid-level SES group registered the greatest academic growth during the winter months, almost .5 *SD* when added over the 5 years. I'm curious as to their interpretation of this.

schooling. Alexander and Entwisle put it this way: "Despite surface indications that seem to suggest the opposite, the public schools in places like Baltimore are a more powerful, positive force in children's lives than is generally realized" (p. 69). This is certain to be a controversial point, yet it is the clearest demonstration of it I have seen.

Second, given that the inequalities in cognitive outcomes are a result of out-of-school contexts—family and community—Alexander and Entwisle warn against unrealistic expectations about the extent to which schools can offset the "outside forces" that create, sustain, and aggravate achievement differences between high and low SES students. Although they clearly take the position that we must continue to work to make schools even more effective than they presently are, they are just as clearly sober in their appraisal of how far and how fast we can expect to go: "In our view, lasting improvements are most likely to come from planned changes that are anchored in deep intuitions and firm evidence about the nature of human beings and their social institutions. And even then, progress will be slow and come in small steps" (p. 84).

It seems to me these conclusions, given Alexander and Entwisle's data and the data of many others, are unassailable: *Schools do contribute to academic development, but by themselves they cannot make up for the lack of resources (material and otherwise) many students experience outside of school.* It is simply a fact that there is enormous variability in the access children have outside of school to opportunities and experiences that influence their academic development and performance *in* school.

These conclusions have a number of implications, of course. One is that all the bad things critics accuse the schools of doing to poor children—putting them in low groups, having low expectations, being insensitive to their cultures and learning styles, or the one I usually nominate, just plain failing to teach—might be grossly overstated, if not outright fantasies. To the contrary, these data seem to show that when in school, and at least with respect to what standardized tests measure, these children progress as do their more advantaged peers. So if our concern is with equity of educational outcomes, schools seem to be doing their share. Achievement gains during the school year are indeed independent of SES. This conclusion too is likely to be very controversial because, as Cook (chap. 6, this volume) reminds us, it flies in the face of mountains of evidence that low SES children are at a disadvantage while they are in school, due to a wide range of SES-related processes. These include, but are certainly not limited to, academic grouping (low SES children tend to be in lower ones), teacher expectations (lower for low SES children), and parent involvement (also lower for low SES children). In addition, as Cook also pointed out, replications and other more rigorous analyses of the data would be well-advised. Nonetheless, assuming Alexander and Entwisle's conclusions hold up, this is a major finding of enormous significance.

WHAT ARE WE INTERVENING FOR?

But what, exactly, is its significance? And what do these conclusions mean for intervention efforts aimed at helping at risk children to be more successful? It depends, it seems to me, largely on what we mean by success and what we are trying to accomplish in our interventions. If our definition of success is having low SES children's performance become comparable to that of high SES children—what Gamoran (chap. 7, this volume) calls the issue of "distribution"—then Alexander and Entwisle's conclusions present a very grim scenario. At a minimum, this definition of success says that without a comprehensive, highly intensive effort to marshal and deploy resources at home, school, and in the community, schools are wasting their time. And even with such colossal efforts, we might be disappointed. Let us not delude ourselves about the enormity of the task. This is what Lisbeth Schorr and others who have argued for integration of programs, policies, and services—the school being but one of many agencies implicated—have maintained: "Everyone agrees that it takes a village to raise a child. But in the inner city, the village has disintegrated. That is why we need bold and comprehensive strategies. Incrementalism will not do it. There are chasms you cannot cross one small step at a time" (Schorr, 1994, p. 237).

Never mind that we might think we know how to accomplish the goal of closing high–low SES gaps. Maybe we do, and I suspect most everyone would be in favor of doing so. I know I would. But in reality, closing the gap and following through with what Schorr talked about will require local, regional, and national political acts of will towards which we must continually work, but that at the moment remain dreamy visions.

But what if we have another definition of success? What if we define success in terms of helping *all*, or almost all, children achieve at least at some reasonable level, for example "on grade level" according to tests or textbooks, or at the "proficient" level according to National Assessment of Educational Progress (NAEP) standards or according to any one of many possible criteria? This would then turn the problem into, as Gamoran and others (e.g., Walberg, 1984) have called it, a "productivity" issue. What if we define success as fundamentally improving educational productivity for low SES (and other) children, instead of defining success in terms of narrowing the SES achievement gap? If this is how we operationalize success, then Alexander and Entwisle's conclusions carry less weight. They are no less important or useful to know. They just don't matter as much for the business at hand. Because now what we are interested in is a very different sort of problem—helping all children achieve at least at satisfactory levels in school, that is, helping them learn to read, write, think, compute, speak, and be knowledgeable about the world so that they might function productively in school and (we hope) beyond. Of less interest is whether, as a group, they do any of this better or worse than children from more advantaged backgrounds.

Now you might say this a distinction without a difference, because one would necessarily lead to the other, or stated somewhat differently, that this is an evasion because the one can't be done without the other. Worse yet, I might be accused of being disingenuous or at best naive, trying to induce a Lake Woebegone effect, where all children will be above average. But I do not think any of these is a valid criticism. Under the assumption that a rising tide lifts everything that floats (and virtually all children float), no cap needs to be placed on what more advantaged students can accomplish. The entire student population could certainly benefit from substantial bump up academically, witness the consistent NAEP findings that large majorities—from two thirds to three fourths of students—have at most only basic reading proficiency skills (Mullis, Campbell, & Farstrup, 1993). Our goals simply become to help all students achieve at some reasonable academic level (and I recognize that defining such a level is not without its complexities), regardless of how far those at the top go and regardless of what we define as "average."

In any case, whether focusing on satisfactory achievement levels *for all* necessarily implies a narrowing of the achievement gap, I think the strategic difference is important. The issue is no longer the SES "cleavage," as Alexander and Entwisle call it. The issue becomes helping children attain levels of achievement that promote functional, productive, and satisfying lives, which is what all the parents who have either participated in my studies or had children in my classroom seem to me to want more than anything else.

INTERVENING FOR SCHOOL SUCCESS

I think if we define success in this second way—as a matter of improving educational productivity—the problem is less overwhelming. It's still a challenge, let us be very clear about that. But there is every indication that it's a manageable challenge. We need not—indeed, must not—give up on the other definition of success, that of eliminating or at least minimizing the SES cleavage. But I think that is a fundamentally different challenge, one that is going to require very hard and protracted work in the political arena. Ultimately this challenge refers to a more equitable distribution of resources in our society, and there are clearly limits to what schools can do. I think Jencks was right more than 20 years ago when he said (I am paraphrasing) that if you want to redistribute resources, do it through monetary and fiscal policy, not through educational policy (Jencks et al., 1972).

We really are talking about two different (although obviously not unrelated) views of what the problem is and therefore what would constitute success—closing the gap or having all students succeed in school. In case there is still doubt about this difference in perspectives, let me engage in a bit of textual exegesis, drawing on Alexander and Entwisle's chapter and a piece by their colleagues at Johns Hopkins University, Slavin, Madden, Karweit, Dolan, and Wasik (1994).

Alexander and Entwisle's chapter makes frequent references to "differences across SES lines" and "gaps," "cleavages," "distinctions," and "stratification." Consider this excerpt: "Unless something happens to improve low SES children's prospects, the expectation probably would be for them to lose more ground over time, whereas to shrink the gap implies moving against the pull of out-of-school resources" (p. 72). In fact, the bulk of their analysis revolves around SES differences and the countervailing forces of the school and the society. Tensions, fissures, and cracks run throughout their paper. Maybe I am particularly sensitive to these images coming from California, and in particular Los Angeles, where both the social and geological faults run hard and deep. But the images are clearly there; I do not think I am making it up. And when Alexander and Entwisle talk about intervention, they mean intervention to reduce the gap: "As presently constituted [schools] do not make enough of a difference to offset educational disparities that originate in out-of-school circumstances" . . . "In this section we point to several areas that seem promising" (p. 78)—promising, that is, for reducing the gap between high and low SES students.

In contrast, consider an earlier publication by Slavin, Madden, Karweit, Livermon, and Dolan (1990) describing their widely cited program to improve disadvantaged children's achievement, "Success for All" (SFA). Slavin et al. began their report like this: "Every child can learn." Call me a misty-eyed romantic, but I love that line. I wish every American Educational Research Association (AERA) publication could scale those rhetorical heights. Throughout the article, the focus is on indicators of satisfactory and less-than-satisfactory achievement, not in relation to how more advantaged children achieve (although normative standards are implicit), but in relation to levels of achievement that indicate mastery of basic academic skills and successful adaptation to school—being on grade level and avoiding retention, special education placement, truancy, and so on. SFA, the authors noted, is "designed to bring every child in an inner-city elementary school to the third grade with adequate reading, mathematics, and language skills. . . . [It] attempt[s] to guarantee every child a level of basic skills sufficient to serve as a basis for success in the later grades" (Slavin et al., 1990, p. 257). In subsequent reports, the focus on success as being "grade level performance" is even more explicit. Most recently, in a review of SFA implementations and evaluations involving nearly two dozen cohorts, seven of which had completed third grade, Slavin et al. (1994) asked the bottom-line question: "Will Success for All ultimately bring all children to grade level in reading?" (p. 190). Note the absence of any comparison with the achievement of more advantaged children. In this view of success, narrowing the gap or minimizing the cleavage is not the issue, at least not in any explicit way. Improving the school performance of at risk children so that they might be successful and productive in their school careers is.

The latter view of the issue is, I believe, the more productive one for people working in schools. We should certainly attend to the other, far more difficult issue—narrowing the gap between the advantaged and the disadvantaged—but we should do so in our roles as citizens and political activists committed to a just and free society.

INTERVENTIONS TO HELP DISADVANTAGED CHILDREN: HOW SUCCESSFUL CAN WE BE?

Having spent so much time pondering what we are intervening for and what constitutes success in interventions, what do we know and what can we say about intervening to help promote success among disadvantaged children? In the simplest terms we can say we know this: It can be done. We know of many ways to increase average achievement levels and increase the probability that disadvantaged children will be more successful, that is, achieve at what we might call grade level norms or standards (e.g., Bliss, Firestone, & Richards, 1991; Comer, 1980; Goldenberg & Gallimore, 1991; Slavin et al., 1994; Tharp & Gallimore, 1988). Certainly the home–school link offers one set of important ways (Epstein, chapter 14, this volume; Goldenberg, 1993).

But there are two catches at the moment. The first is no surprise to anyone: It usually—but not always—takes additional resources. Some of the work by Slavin and colleagues suggests that rearranging how currently available moneys[2] are used can make a substantial difference; but still, additional resources produce stronger effects, particularly for the very lowest achieving students (Slavin et al., 1994). Evidence reviewed by Alexander and Entwisle and others suggests that some nonmaterial resources—for example, sense of community, shared purpose and commitment—are also extremely important. But as a general rule, we can probably conclude that material resources help, assuming of course they are used well.

The other catch is that we are still short of finding ways to help *all*, or virtually all, students succeed. Even Success for All, a comprehensive, rigorously research-based effort that its developers described as a "relentless approach to prevention and early intervention," falls short of this goal. Across various sites in Baltimore, only 46% of third grade children in SFA schools were on or above grade level in reading according to the latest data I have seen. This was in contrast to 26% of children in control schools (Slavin et al., 1994). Although clearly a significant and meaningful effect, it is still far short of success for *all*, if we define success as attainment on grade level.

Let me turn last to a somewhat different sort of effort in which I have been involved over the past 4 years to improve the academic achievement of children in a largely Latino immigrant school district in Southern California (Goldenberg

---

[2]Chapter 1 and other forms of assistance can be considered currently available moneys, but they can also be seen as extra resources already provided.

& Sullivan, 1994). I've been working in this district for about 10 years, first as a doctoral student, then as a teacher, and most recently as a researcher-collaborator with teachers and administrators. The children who attend school in the district are typically seen as at risk for underachievement. Parents were born either in Mexico or Central America; about three fourths of the children were born in the United States, mostly Southern California. Most children and parents speak Spanish as their first language. Parents average about 7 years of formal schooling. About 90% of the children qualify for free meals; most of the rest qualify for reduced-price meals.

Language and immigration add several dimensions to these children's at-risk status. But in many ways the issues surrounding these children's poor school performance are very similar to those surrounding the poor school performance of other low-income, minority children. This in itself could be the topic for an extended treatment. In any case, in 1990, the principal and I embarked on a project to improve academic achievement across the board at the school. There is far too little time to go into any detail here about what we did, but let me try to summarize very briefly.

First, we developed a model of school change, based on our experience and our reading of the literature, that we thought would help guide our efforts. This model posits four "change elements" that can be manipulated to bring about productive change in schools. At least three of these elements sound familiar: *goals* that are set and shared; *indicators* that measure success; *assistance* by capable others; and *leadership* that supports and pressures (Goldenberg & Sullivan, 1994). Our model is designed to help us do what Alexander and Entwisle quite rightly said is the challenge faced by schools who want to embrace student achievement: foster a sense of community, and maintain high standards, high expectations, and an infrastructure that supports everyone's learning (including, I would add, teachers' learning).

Then, informed and guided by this model, we embarked on a several years' project that has produced some gratifying results. Without going into any of the operational details, let me just give a flavor of some of the processes involved. We developed a set of academic expectations or goals, grade level by grade level. This was a 2-year operation. When interviewed in mid 1993–1994 about the role of these expectations at the school, teachers reported that they had made a difference for them. The expectations were specific guidelines teachers could use to focus their teaching, and despite the additional work involved in developing them, they were seen as critical:

Q: Do you hold higher expectations now?
A: I think so. . . . I've always held high expectations, but I think even higher [now]. No, they're maybe not . . . they're more specific.

......

Q: Over the last couple of years has your workload increased?
A: Yeah, but that's what happens if you want to be involved with something, then that's what happens . . . we have a lot of autonomy at this school. . . . here we had that opportunity to develop [goals and expectations] ourselves.

......

A: I've always felt the problem of getting it all in. . . . Now, because of the goals and expectations, it is more cut and clear what goes in the back burner. . . . because of the goals and expectations I'd say I'm more focused. (Goldenberg & Sullivan, 1994, pp. 12–13)

Teachers work together in workgroups, developing instruction and materials in areas they choose. They have opportunities to share and compare what they and others are doing. We've developed a school-wide set of authentic assessments, administered by project staff and aides at the school. We also have in-services from time to time on selected topics. For example, we've had some on parent involvement and the use of homework to enhance learning. There is quite a solid research basis showing the beneficial effects of homework on student achievement (e.g., Cooper, 1989; Paschal, Weinstein, & Walberg, 1984). Homework positively influences achievement because it affects the proximal learning environment at home, one of the most important influences on student achievement (Wang, Haertel, & Walberg, 1993).

Here is what some of the teachers said about homework and the homework in-service:

Where I notice the difference is in how their reading improves when they read at home. I can tell the difference with the new students I received. One teacher didn't have her students read at home and the other did. The students who read at home do much better in my class than those from the teacher who never had them read at home.

...

The upper grade teachers now give more [homework], and they give it more consistently. Less of it is busywork. . . . I think the students respond positively. They're more serious and responsible about schoolwork when they have homework regularly. The homework in-service reminded teachers how homework fits into classroom lessons, how valuable homework is for the kids. (Goldenberg & Sullivan, 1994, p. 15)

We've had a fair amount of success with our model-based school change project. When the project began in 1989–1990, average achievement at the school was below state, national, and district norms. Within 3 years, achievement at the school had surpassed the rest of the district (which is demographically comparable), and in some respects matched or surpassed state and national norms. Spanish literacy scores in the primary grades have improved considerably. In the

1990 first grade Spanish cohort, only 30% of students were on grade level according to national norms. By the time this cohort reached third grade, students at the school outperformed other Spanish-speaking third graders in the district who had attended their respective schools since first grade; 60% were reading at or above grade level, in contrast to less than 50% on grade level around the district. The following year the succeeding cohort did even better: 69% of the school's Spanish-speaking third graders were on grade level in reading, according to national norms. Fourth graders tested in English reading (California Learning Assessment System, CLAS) in 1993 were more likely to score at the highest levels (4 and up) than were fourth graders throughout the district—28% versus 17% (comparable state figure, 30%; Goldenberg & Sullivan, 1994).

So again we see some evidence of progress. Nearly 70% of our third graders are on grade level in reading in Spanish; 28%—just 2% fewer than the state average—of our fourth graders are at the proficient and above level in English. Still, not **all** our students are where they need to be. The data show this, and we and the teachers know it. "We're working very slowly," one fifth grade teacher said last year. "But there's more to do. There's much more to do."

These are surely sentiments Alexander and Entwisle would endorse. But are we making progress, or are we running into a ceiling that Alexander and Entwisle seemed to foreshadow? Maybe both. Most important, is this the best we can do? I don't think so, or rather I hope not. But we must acknowledge, whether we're talking about success as narrowing the cleavage or success as getting all children "on grade level," there are no simple or easy answers. To this extent, Alexander and Entwisle's cautious conclusions should serve as reminders of the work and the challenges that lie ahead.

ACKNOWLEDGMENTS

Funding for the research reported here has been provided by the Spencer Foundation, the U.S. Dept. of Education Office of Educational Research and Improvement, and the California State Dept. of Education. No endorsement from any source is implied nor should be inferred.

REFERENCES

Bliss, J., Firestone, W., & Richards, C. (Eds.). (1991). *Rethinking effective schools: Research and practice.* Englewood Cliffs, NJ: Prentice-Hall.

Comer, J. (1980). *School power: Implications of an intervention project.* New York: The Free Press.

Cooper, H. (1989). *Homework.* New York: Longman.

Goldenberg, C. (1993). The home-school connection in bilingual education. In B. Arias & U. Casanova (Eds.), *Bilingual education: Politics, research, and practice* (pp. 225–250). Yearbook of the National Society for the Study of Education.

Goldenberg, C., & Gallimore, R. (1991). Local knowledge, research knowledge, and educational change: A case study of first-grade Spanish reading improvement. *Educational Researcher, 20*(8), 2–14.

Goldenberg, C., & Sullivan, J. (1994). *Making change happen in a language-minority school: A search for coherence.* Washington, DC: Center for Applied Linguistics.

Jencks, C., Smith, M., Ackland, H., Bane, M., Cohen, D., Gintis, H., Heyns, B., & Michelson, S. (1972). *Inequality: A reassessment of the effect of failure and schooling in America.* New York: Basic.

Mullis, I., Campbell, J., & Farstrup, A. (1993). *NAEP 1992 reading report card for the nation and the states* (Rep. No. 23-ST06). Washington, DC: U.S. Department of Education.

Paschal, R. A., Weinstein, T., & Walberg, H. J. (1984). The effects of homework on learning: A quantitative synthesis. *Journal of Educational Research, 78*(2), 97–104.

Schorr, L. (1994). Looking ahead: Integrating urban policies to meet educational demands. In K. Wong & M. Want (Eds.), *Rethinking policy for at-risk students* (pp. 221–238). Berkeley, CA: McCutchan.

Slavin, R., Madden, N., Karweit, N., Dolan, L., & Wasik, B. (1994). Success for All: A comprehensive approach to prevention and early intervention. In R. Slavin, N. Karweit, & B. Wasik (Eds.), *Preventing early school failure: Research, policy, and practice* (pp. 175–205). Needham Heights, MA: Allyn and Bacon.

Slavin, R., Madden, N., Karweit, N., Livermon, B., & Dolan, L. (1990). Success for All: First-year outcomes of a comprehensive plan for reforming urban education. *American Educational Research Journal, 27*, 255–278.

Tharp, R., & Gallimore, R. (1988). *Rousing minds to life: Teaching, learning and schooling in social context.* Cambridge: Cambridge University Press.

Walberg, H. (1984). Improving the productivity of America's schools. *Educational Leadership, 41*(8), 19–27.

Wang, M., Haertel, G., & Walberg, H. (1993). Toward a knowledge base for school learning. *Review of Educational Research, 63*, 249–294.

9

Further Comments
on Seasonal Learning

Doris R. Entwisle
Karl L. Alexander
Johns Hopkins University

We appreciate the time and attention all three reviewers have devoted to our paper, and our ongoing research will profit from their suggestions. We limit our remarks here to Cook's (chap. 6, this volume) comments, because they raise a number of points about issues that need further clarification and that can usefully be addressed here.

The major issues we address in Cook's comments are: the framing of the Beginning School Study (BSS), using achievement tests as criteria for cognitive growth, sample attrition, and policy questions about summer school. The overall design of the BSS, the strengths or weaknesses of achievement tests when used to measure schooling outcomes, and sample attrition are all fairly straightforward technical issues, and our previously published work offers some discussion of each (see Entwisle & Alexander, 1990, 1992, 1994a).

As a preamble, we review some details of the BSS. It began in 1982 by identifying a two-stage random sample of about 800 Baltimore youngsters. Only 3% of the selected families declined to participate. To our knowledge, it is the only longitudinal study of both White and African-American urban children, spanning a range of SES levels, who have been followed closely for over a dozen years since they began first grade. Also it may be the only nonnational study with a sample selected randomly at the start. Semiannual direct interviews of the children themselves, starting in the fall of Grade 1, have been supplemented with data collected almost every year directly from teachers and school records. Achievement test data were collected every fall and spring over the 5 elementary school years. To our knowledge, Heyns' (1978) research with Atlanta sixth and seventh graders is the only other study with fall and spring test scores that covers more than 1 school year.

Study Design

We find it curious for a reviewer to critique a 12-year long study by suggesting that we should have conducted an entirely different study—for example, a study spanning several school districts (pp. 95–96), or one involving the determination of how much parents' language patterns enlarge offsprings' vocabulary (p. 97), or one that measures growth in social studies or science (p. 99). Aside from the severe cost restrictions that any item on this wish-list ignores, limiting the sample to Baltimore City reduced several kinds of extraneous variation: (a) teachers' salary scales across schools are the same; (b) the same texts and curricular materials are used in all schools; (c) standards for marking and test taking are the same across schools; (d) record keeping is the same, for example, how absences and lateness are counted; (e) the school calendar is the same, and so on.

For reasons of cost, we did not have the option to sample children in more than one district, but even if we had, there are strengths and weaknesses that need to be carefully weighed. One strength is that by carefully selecting a random sample and then taking great pains to implement it almost exactly (with a 3% refusal rate), we avoided many of the pitfalls of selectivity that plague studies of this genre. So, pitting randomness and the uniformity of children's school experience against almost any alternative design within our budget, we placed our bets as we did. A random sample was selected, not so much because we wished to generalize back to the Baltimore City "universe," but because any kind of self-selection of families into a study of schooling tends to recruit those who are most interested, "advantaged," or savvy about school. Because the initial sample was two-stage random, any framing of the study subsequent to its inception, especially for achievement test gains, has to be around the population who provided data on first testing. Sample attrition has to be calculated from this starting point. Given this feature of the design, Cook's suggestions about alternative framing (p. 95) seem inappropriate.

Another study design issue concerns socioeconomic status and the way it is conceptualized. Cook recommends that it be conceptualized as a continuous rather than as a categoric variable. Actually how best to measure relatively poor children's family background at present is not entirely clear, and it was even less clear when we began the BSS. Some current recommendations (Entwisle & Astone, 1994) are that for relatively low SES children, it is probably best to use three separate measures of household structure, plus household income and mother's education. However, investigators are necessarily constrained by the data available. In our chapter (this volume, chap. 5) we used a five-component measure that combined *each* parent's education and occupation, and whether the child was eligible for meal subsidy. The five variables were transformed to standard scores and averaged. Though arbitrary, the high, middle, and low SES divisions capture sizeable differences on each of the underlying measures. Documentation of this is provided in our chapter. There was never any attempt to make a linear scale for SES or to define SES in any way other than operationally as described previously. For a relatively disadvantaged population like children in Baltimore City Public Schools, variability in SES is severely reduced compared to other populations. Even in the high group, for example, about one third of the children are on meal subsidy (i.e., their family income and size placed them at or below 1.85 times the federal poverty level).

Because our chapter states how SES was conceptualized and measured, it is perplexing that Cook would look for "theoretically expected difference in reading gains between the low and middle SES groups" (p. 94), or speak about "social class writ large" (p. 96), or expect SES to be linear or linearly related to learning gains (p. 96). Cook chooses to interpret low, middle, and high SES in his own terms rather than as defined for our analysis, and this choice detracts from the usefulness of the discussion.

Attrition

There are many ways to examine attrition, as Cook implies. Here, however, attrition *must* involve reference to the full random sample of youngsters chosen in the fall of 1982. In what follows, we take two approaches to attrition over the first 5 years of the study because these are the years for which we have seasonal test data.

The first approach is to tally children's meal subsidy status at successive test points. Meal subsidy identifies families who are close to or below the poverty line. (Both full and partial meal subsidy are scored 0; no subsidy is scored 1.) The proportion above subsidy across low, middle, and high SES groups, as defined for our chapter, is listed in Table 9.1. For example, in the fall of 1982, when the study began, only 33% of children in the full sample received no subsidy; when grouped by SES level, about 87% of high SES youngsters did not qualify for subsidy, 44% of middle SES youngsters did not qualify for subsidy, but only 5% of low SES youngsters did not qualify for subsidy. Through the first 5 years, drift in this measure is small. For example, by the fall of 1986, there was an increase of about

TABLE 9.1
Proportions of Children Above Subsidy Level

	Total	Low SES	Mid SES	High SES	N
Fall 1982	0.33	0.05	0.44	0.87	701
Fall 1983	0.33	0.08	0.41	0.87	646
Fall 1984	0.32	0.08	0.46	0.88	614
Fall 1985	0.31	0.05	0.45	0.89	557
Fall 1986	0.29	0.05	0.44	0.87	574

1% in the proportion of children in the low group not requiring subsidy. The meal subsidy indicator gives little indication of selective attrition, within or between SES groups. It is also clear from the distribution of meal subsidy recipients that low, middle, and high are labels that apply only to the BSS.

An even more relevant way to assess attrition for our chapter is to examine children's standardized test scores in reading comprehension and math concepts for the fall of 1982 when the study began and then to tally these same beginning California Achievement Tests (CAT) scores (Level 11) for the samples of children each fall—in second grade, third grade, and so on. As noted, the BSS sample is two-stage random, and only 3% of the parents whose children were randomly designated refused to participate. The question at issue, then, is whether the successively smaller samples retain the features of the original random sample, or, put another way, do the means and variances of the 1982 test data for the sample of children for whom there are test scores in succeeding years approximate those same parameters as measured in 1982?

Through 5 elementary years of the BSS, Table 9.2 gives the fall 1982 reading comprehension and math concepts test scores for the samples of students for whom test scores are available in later years. For example, the overall mean for 1982 reading comprehension scores is 279 for the fall 1986 sample of students, compared to a mean of 281 when the study began (about .05 SD difference). The average 1982 test scores for the low, middle, and high SES groups in 1986 are all within 1 point of their 1982 levels (272 vs. 273; 279 vs. 280; and 301 vs. 300). These figures seem extremely close.

The means and standard deviation by SES groups for the math test are also quite close. For example, the mean for the low SES group in fall 1986 (end of elementary school) exactly matches the mean for fall 1982, and the means in the rest of the table are all less than one tenth of a standard deviation different from the fall 1982 means.

Although, as Cook says, the overall attrition from the high SES group is greater than for the low groups (pp. 95, 98) the *nature* of the attrition is such that the *original parameters of the test distributions in 1982 within each social class group are preserved*. The nature of attrition is of keen interest for reasons of bias; the amount of attrition is relevant mainly in terms of power of statistical tests. We and he are concerned mainly with bias.

Clearly, to retain the entire sample is always the aim, and we have worked hard to follow all students. (In Year 11, we are still in touch with 85% of students in the original sample.) In any given analysis, however, missing data as well as case loss contribute to attrition. The distribution of test scores over the first 5 years looks random in terms of fall 1982 test scores, however, and this strengthens the seasonal comparisons across SES groups.

Another issue is also related to attrition. Cook expects a review of the relevant literature . . . "[showing] no correlation between SES and achievement-enhancing practices in elementary schools" (p. 99). First, to our knowledge, ours are the

TABLE 9.2
Average Fall 1982 Cat Scores for Children Whose Later Scores Are Available

Reading Comprehension

	Sample Size	Total		Low SES		Middle SES		High SES	
		Mean	SD	Mean	SD	Mean	SD	Mean	SD
Fall 1982	675	281	41.0	273	36.0	280	38.1	300	47.0
Fall 1983	605	282	41.0	274	36.3	280	38.7	302	45.9
Fall 1984	544	281	40.3	273	35.8	280	38.1	304	44.9
Fall 1985	502	282	40.9	272	36.0	282	38.6	308	44.4
Fall 1986	518	279	39.4	272	35.8	279	39.6	301	41.9

Math Concepts

	Sample Size	Total		Low SES		Middle SES		High SES	
		Mean	SD	Mean	SD	Mean	SD	Mean	SD
Fall 1982	693	293	31.9	282	27.2	296	27.4	312	35.8
Fall 1983	620	295	31.5	284	27.0	298	27.2	315	34.5
Fall 1984	560	293	31.7	283	27.4	299	26.1	315	34.6
Fall 1985	566	292	32.0	281	27.1	299	26.7	316	35.5
Fall 1986	585	291	282.0	282	296.0	297	27.3	312	34.4

only data that explicitly point to the invariance of winter gains, so a review is not possible from a seasonal perspective. Some published data by Heyns (1978, pp. 45–46), do suggest invariance of winter gains in fifth and sixth grade tests of word knowledge, but she does not comment on this. Second, research projects that turn up "null" findings seldom cross editors' desks, so a thorough stock taking may not even be possible. To show that some teaching practice or class activity does *not* work or that some relationship is nil has, unfortunately, little appeal for U.S. researchers.

The winter pattern implies that schools function, on balance, so that low SES children's learning is on a par with that of their more advantaged classmates. Such an equalizing effect of school is at odds with the view that school practices are stacked against such youngsters. Research that evaluates specific practices— like grouping or retention—is useful but cannot inform us directly about the basic nature of schooling. There is more to the "black box" of schooling than is generally appreciated.

Achievement Tests

Again, we focus on only the first 5 years because it is in those years that seasonal differences in test scores are at issue.

We chose the CAT subtests in verbal comprehension and math concepts for several reasons:

1. Unlike other CAT subtests, they are available at every grade level over the 12-year span that public schools cover.
2. They contain enough items in the early grades to be of satisfactory reliability.
3. We found them free of ceiling and floor effects for our sample by plotting the full distributions of test scores and studying both extremes.
4. They represent the core of the elementary school curriculum in that they tap higher level skills in the two subject domains universally agreed to be most essential.

We had no choice about *which* set of standardized tests to use, because the school system made that determination. The CAT was validated on a national sample in 1976, about 5 years before the BSS started. Cook wishes we had expanded our search beyond reading and math (p. 99), but the longitudinal test information to do this did not exist. Other tests in the CAT battery (vocabulary, computation, language, and so on) taken by BSS children were either included in the battery for only 2 or 3 years and/or could not be used because of ceiling effects.

A summary of scale scores by grade level (Table 9.3) taken from the 1976 standardization of the CAT (California Achievement Test, 1979) suggests that many of Cook's points questioning the relationships among scores across grade

TABLE 9.3
Information on the CAT Standardized Sample (1976) Taken From Technical Bulletin 1 (California Achievement Test, 1979)

Grade Level	Math Concepts				Reading Comprehension			
	Mean Score (SD)	Successive Differences	Annual Differences (12 month)	First Differences	Mean Score	Successive Differences	Annual Differences (12 month)	First Differences
Fall 0.8	284 (32.5)				271 (47.5)			
Spring 1.2	299 (32.0)	15			284 (43.5)	13		
Fall 1.8	334 (36.4)	35	50		336 (47.2)	52	65	
Spring 2.2	352 (37.3)	18		8	362 (50.7)	26		13
Fall 2.8	376 (41.6)	24	42		388 (52.7)	26	52	
Spring 3.2	389 (45.3)	13		5	401 (55.5)	13		16
Fall 3.8	413 (46.6)	24	37		424 (57.2)	23	36	
Spring 4.2	425 (46.0)	12		4	441 (60.2)	17		0
Fall 4.8	444 (50.7)	19	31		460 (69.5)	19	36	
Spring 5.2	454 (49.1)	10		2	472 (66.1)	12		8
Fall 5.8	473 (56.8)	19	29		488 (68.4)	16	28	
Spring 6.2	482 (55.9)	9			498 (68.5)	10		

levels or across subject areas are moot. Table 9.3 gives mean scores for the Form
C reading comprehension and math concepts subtests by grade level over the
range of ages appropriate for comparison with the BSS sample (see California
Achievement Test, 1979, pp. 93–95). These standardization scores begin with
Year 0.8 (before first grade) and continue to Year 6.2 (the beginning of sixth
grade) in Table 9.3. The decimal portions of the grade designation do not conform
to months in a year (12). The technical bulletin manual says only: "Item difficulties are based on standardization testing in the fall of 1976 and the spring of
1977" (p. 31). Thus, fall scores are listed by "years" with a 2 after the decimal
point—0.2, 1.2, and so on; spring scores are listed by "years" with 8 after the
decimal point—0.8, 1.8, and so on. However, we cannot identify the specific fall
or spring month in which tests were given. It does not seem accidental, however,
that in all years for the math test and in the first 2 years for the reading test,
gains in the summer interval (0.4 year units) are around half the size of gains in
the prior winter interval (0.6 year units, see Table 9.3). Because the standardization sample is not divided into SES groups, the differences by season
cannot be analyzed further.

The beginning baseline for the reading test (Year 0.8) is considerably less
than the lowest baseline for math (271 vs. 284), and the upper boundary in fall
1986 (Year 6.2) is higher for the reading score than for the math score (498 vs.
482). Accordingly, over the first five grades there is a test range of 228 for
reading and of 198 for math (30 points difference). Also the disorderly first
differences in annual gains for reading (13, 16, 0, 8) and the more orderly
differences for math (8, 5, 4, 2) suggest that the growth curves are decelerating in both cases but would be hard to fit with any simple function or the same
function. Obviously, the verbal and math tests are not calibrated to the same
scale score parameters, so to compare means from one subject domain to
means from the other, or to add math and verbal scores as Cook did, is inappropriate.

The inappropriateness of "pooling domains" is even more convincingly borne
out by comparing the relationships between test score gains and predictor variables for each domain (see Entwisle & Alexander, 1990, 1992, 1994a). For
example, African-American children in integrated schools do as well as their
White counterparts in math but not in reading, and we suspect (but cannot prove)
that this difference in performance in reading and math is because of dialect and
other linguistically based interference in reading in mixed-race classrooms.

We therefore believe that Cook's suggestions for "[plotting] the . . . summer
learning gains with reading and math combined" (p. 93), and worrying that "the
summer effect size for math . . . is 30% smaller than the reading effect" (p. 94),
are not sensible, and that to conclude that "differential summer gains in the
earliest elementary school years may affect reading more than math" (p. 94) on
the basis of evidence here is inappropriate.

As an aside, the "decelerating growth" pattern manifest in the CAT scale scores, which concerns Cook, is not at all peculiar to this particular set of CAT data. This pattern is apparent in much historical as well as modern test data. Two figures in Stephens (1956, pp. 162–163), plot gains in Stanford achievement scores over Grades 2 to 6 and speed of silent reading over Grades 2 to 8. Stephens said: "Although students push steadily ahead, they do so at a decreasing rate. Although they gain something every year, they gain more in the early years than in the later years . . . [and] the trend . . . shown . . . is by no means unique" (p. 162). Schneider (1980) remarked on the same phenomenon.

In sum, the general patterns in longitudinal test data seen for the BSS, which resemble those seen in other data sets, render Cook's question about the constancy of learning differences (p. 97) irrelevant. The pattern of decelerating gains is very general. Stephens (1956) suggested that the deceleration in performance curves can be attributed to approaching an asymptote. This explanation makes most sense for skills involving speed or physical dexterity. It is not as appealing as an explanation for decelerating growth in verbal comprehension or math reasoning, especially by the end of Grade 5. Although its significance is not clear, both the published norming data specific to the CAT and many other standardized tests show the same general patterns of growth that we observed in the BSS.

We have some guesses about the sources of this trend. It is important to recognize that a scale at a given age level is good to a linear transformation, but the operations used to join the vertical scale scores for the CAT are nonlinear. Thurstone's method of absolute scaling, which was used to develop the vertical scale scores for the CAT, seems preferable to other methods but is obtained by forcing raw scores within a given percentile range at the "top" of one age level to conform to an equal probability chunk of the normal distribution for the same percentile range at the "bottom" of the next age level. Ascertaining that the monotonically increasing size of scores is not seriously violated from one age to the next (the litmus test reported by the test makers) is reassuring but does not guarantee equal intervals at different ages. For one thing, because the variance of test scores increases with age (the raw score data in the technical bulletin [California Achievement Test, 1979] show increasing variance with age), the higher of the two overlapping tails in two contiguous age distributions of scores likely will be "squeezed" smaller to accomplish the calibration of scores for one year with scores in the next year at each joint in the scale. If so, the scale units of the higher level test will be compressed a little at each age "joint" in the vertical scale—perhaps explaining not only why the CAT scores show decelerated growth, but why other tests show this as well. The tails of the distributions are the critical portions of the original scores that overlap from grade to grade. Tests at contiguous levels, especially if the amount of squeezing is small relative to the scales' range, may not be much affected, but when tests are used over many ages, as in the BSS, these squeezes may be nontrivial. Clearly, before projected national studies of preschool and elementary school children are fielded later in this decade, vertical scaling issues need careful scrutiny.[1] We have been careful to check for ceiling and floor effects, to verify increasing score variance with age, and to check test–retest reliability both short and long-term, but the equal interval feature of tests remains a challenging issue.

Using tests purported to measure comparable kinds of achievement over a long time to measure growth in the same children raises many thorny issues related to psychometrics and modeling strategies. Present day achievement tests may be "equal interval," as advertised, in the restricted range of one or two grades, but there is no guarantee that an interval in Grade 1 is equal to an interval in Grade 5, and strictly speaking, no certain way to ascertain whether scale units over a range of ages or even with one specific grade are the same. Regretfully, therefore, in terms of Cook's assumptions (pp. 91, 92):

1. we cannot assume there are no scaling artifacts,
2. hopefully, validity of tests is constant across age and social class (and no way to check this), but
3. selection confounds in our sample are minimal.

There are other vexing problems connected with seasonal scores that Cook does not notice. For test scores obtained only a few months apart, error components are not independent. This dependence negates the use of regression models, including the hierarchial models that Cook suggests, because such models assume that disturbances of dependent variables are unrelated to independent variables in the same equation. LISREL models in theory can overcome this drawback by use of instrumental variables to identify models with correlated error components, but so far, despite considerable effort, we have not been able to locate suitable instrumental variables. To circumvent difficulties associated with correlated disturbances, as we explained in detail in Entwisle and Alexander (1992, 1994a) where seasonal gains are analyzed, we resorted to repeated measures MANOVA models. In these models only the within-student variance is relevant, so only the dependent variable can be continuous. Interactions with SES are the focus of interest in those analyses, so SES of necessity must be treated as categoric.

---

[1] Other problems may plague the tests as well. The sampling procedure to obtain the norming populations suggests that even if children's reading comprehension or math concepts abilities are normally distributed by grade in the total U.S. school population, the norming groups used to develop the 1976 CAT could well depart from that ideal. Without describing the sampling frame in detail (see California Achievement Test, 1979), we note that once a high school was selected, *all* grades in its set of feeder schools were tested. This lack of independence in sampling units may reduce the range of the score distribution, especially in the lower grades where sample sizes are less than a thousand per geographic area.

Summer School

Like Heyns (1978), we find it paradoxical that summer school programs, at least as so far evaluated, have not helped disadvantaged children. Cook misreads our comments about previous research as implying we see no promise in summer programs. This is incorrect. In fact, in prior articles (Entwisle & Alexander, 1992, 1994a, and elsewhere), we speculated that summer school may actually prevent losses by the most disadvantaged students—that is, summer school may enable them to retain what they knew at the beginning of the summer. "Zero gains" between spring and fall scores could be interpreted pessimistically as "no gain," as typically is done, but if those students had no summer school, they might show losses instead. If no gain more optimistically signifies "no losses," this puts quite a different face on the matter.

Unfortunately our data are not sufficient to open the "black box" of summer activities related to differential progress made in summer by children of varying SES backgrounds (Cook, this volume, p. 97). Contextual effects, however, are a possibility still to investigate as an impetus to summer gains. We showed that boys in more affluent neighborhoods gain more on math tests than do boys in less affluent neighborhoods over the first 2 years of school (Entwisle & Alexander, 1994b). Is summertime more helpful for learning of high SES than low SES children because of neighborhood resources? Because family SES and neighborhood SES are correlated, perhaps the actual SES resources that prompt the summer gains we found are linked to neighborhood rather than to family or only to family.

We also found another contextual effect: Youngsters in the first two grades gain more in reading comprehension if they attend segregated rather than integrated schools, even though children in integrated schools come from families with more economic resources (Entwisle & Alexander, 1994a). We speculate that integrated classrooms may create "noise" in terms of dialect and other linguistic differences between subcultural groups that interferes with leaning to read. This noise is absent when segregated neighborhoods surround children in summer.

Our purpose in outlining these two contextual possibilities is not so much to suggest that they "explain" summer learning as to suggest that the hypotheses currently in vogue relating family SES to school learning are exceedingly narrow. Our chapter offers speculation on other family resource possibilities that we feel also deserve consideration.

REFERENCES

California Achievement Test. (1979). *Technical Bulletin 1, Forms C and D, Levels 10–19*. Monterey, CA: McGraw-Hill.
Entwisle, D. R., & Alexander, K. L. (1990). Beginning school math competence. *Child Development, 61*, 454–471.

Entwisle, D. R., & Alexander, K. L. (1992). Summer setback: Race, poverty, school composition, and mathematics achievement in the first two years of school. *American Sociological Review, 57,* 72–84.

Entwisle, D. R., & Alexander, K. (1994a). Winter setback: School racial composition and learning to read. *American Sociological Review, 59,* 446–460.

Entwisle, D. R., & Alexander, K. (1994b). The gender gap in math: Its possible origins in neighborhood effects. *American Sociological Review, 59,* 822–838.

Entwisle, D. R., & Astone, N. M. (1994). Some practical guidelines for measuring youth's race/ethnicity and socioeconomic status. *Child Development, 65,* 1521–1540.

Heyns, B. (1978). *Summer learning and the effects of schooling.* New York: Academic.

Schneider, B. L. (1980). *Production analysis of gains in achievement.* Paper presented at the annual meeting of the American Educational Research Association, Boston, MA.

Stephens, J. M. (1956). *Educational psychology.* New York: Henry Holt.

III

HOW IS CHANGING FAMILY STRUCTURE AFFECTING SCHOOL OUTCOMES?

10
▼▼▼▼▼▼

Family Change and Student Achievement: What We Have Learned, What It Means for Schools

Nicholas Zill
Westat, Inc.
Rockville, MD

The family situations in which U.S. children are cared for and raised have changed dramatically over the last 30 years, that is, between 1964 and 1994. Divorce and childbearing outside of marriage have both become much more common. These are by no means the only changes that have occurred in U.S. family life, but they are the trends that have received the most attention and generated the greatest anxiety.

The number of children who live with only one parent, with a birth parent and a stepparent, or with neither of their parents has increased substantially. In 1981, 33% of all children under 18 in the United States did not live in a traditional two-parent family, that is, with both of their biological parents. By 1992, that figure had risen to 43% of all children. Estimates are that half of all children today will spend some time in a single-parent family before they reach age 16.

Currently, more than 40% of all first marriages end in divorce (Norton & Miller, 1992). The U.S. divorce rate doubled between the late 1960s and the late 1970s (Fig. 10.1). The rate has stabilized and even declined slightly since then but remains at very high levels (National Center for Health Statistics, 1994). Each year, more than 1.5 million children—nearly 2.5% of all U.S. children—undergo the painful experience of having their parents separate or become divorced (Bianchi & McArthur, 1991; Zill & Nord, 1994).

In addition to divorce, the number of children born to unmarried mothers has grown greatly in recent years. In 1992, the nationwide count of such births amounted to 1.2 million, or 30% of all births. This was nearly triple the percentage of births that occurred outside marriage in 1970. Among births to White women,

Divorce Rate

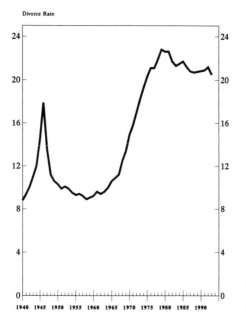

FIG. 10.1. Divorces per 1,000 married women ages 15 and over, 1940–1993. Data are from National Center for Health Statistics (1994).

the percentage that occurred outside marriage quadrupled between 1970 and 1992, going from 5.5% to 23%. Among births to African-American women, the unmarried percentage rose from 38% in 1970 to 68% in 1992 (see Fig. 10.2). There are signs that unmarried birth rates are starting to level off, however; the 1992 figures were little changed from those in 1991 (Ventura, Martin, Taffel, Mathews, & Clarke, 1994).

What have these changes meant for the academic achievement, school behavior, and educational attainment of young people who grow up in single-parent families, stepfamilies, or other nontraditional family types? What, if anything, should schools be doing to adapt to the new realities of family life in the United States? For years, discussions of these issues have been dominated by those holding extreme views. On one side were those who contended that coming from a disrupted family was a serious impediment to a young person's academic success and later life chances and that the increased prevalence of divorce and unmarried childbearing constituted *the* major negative developments affecting the well-being of children in the United States.

On the other side were those who argued that the fact that a child came from a single-parent family or stepfamily had no particular bearing on how well he or she did in school or in life. Single-parent families and stepfamilies were simply different from, not necessarily more stressful or less supportive than, two-parent families in which both biological parents were present in the household. Indeed, many of the nontraditional families were believed to have "hidden strengths," such as warm, nurturing grandmothers who taught the children about their heritage and bolstered their self-esteem.

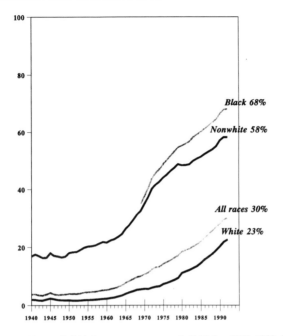

FIG. 10.2. Nonmarital births as a percentage of all births, 1940–1992. Data are from Ventura et al. (1994).

Much of the debate between proponents of these conflicting positions took place on the anecdotal level or relied on evidence from limited studies based on small samples that were not necessarily representative of the general population. Fortunately, however, over the last decade and a half, social scientists have generated a considerable body of solid research on family disruption and student achievement and behavior. In the last year alone, two major new studies on the topic have been published. One is the book *Parents, Their Children, and Schools* (1993), edited by Barbara Schneider of the National Opinion Research Center and James S. Coleman of the University of Chicago, which includes a chapter by Seh-Ahn Lee (1993) on "Family Structure Effects on Student Outcomes." The other is the book, *Growing up with a Single Parent: What Hurts, What Helps* (1994), by Sara McLanahan of Princeton and Gary Sandefur of the University of Wisconsin, which analyzes data from four different national surveys.

These new works add to an already rich literature that has previously been reviewed and synthesized by Hetherington (1979; Chase-Lansdale & Hetherington, 1990), Longfellow (1979), Emery (1982, 1988), Furstenberg and Cherlin (1991), Wallerstein (1991), and Amato (1993, 1994; Amato & Keith, 1991a, 1991b), among others. One of the ways that the more recent research on children in nontraditional families has differed from earlier research is that many of the newer studies have made use of data from surveys and longitudinal studies based on large probability samples of students or families with children. Amazingly enough, different studies by different researchers from a variety of disciplines have produced fairly consistent results.

What the findings of these studies show is that neither of the extreme positions described previously is correct. It seems quite unlikely, based on the research results now at hand, that divorce and unmarried childbearing are *the* major causes of school failure in the United States today or that academic achievement has declined over time because of the increased prevalence of marital disruption and parenthood outside of marriage. As we shall see, the data simply do not support such interpretations.

On the other hand, it is also incorrect to assert that divorce and single parenthood have *no* significant effects on students' achievement, behavior, or educational attainment. Coming from a single-parent family or stepfamily is clearly a risk factor for lower achievement and attainment and, especially, for school-related conduct problems. The fact that family structure is only one of several factors that help determine a student's chances of school success does not imply that we should dismiss its importance. Likewise, the fact that other personal or familial assets may enable a student to overcome the negative influence of family turmoil should not cause us to minimize the potential impact of such turmoil on students who lack those other assets.

What this chapter attempts to do is briefly review what the research on family change and student achievement has found and make inferences about what the findings imply for school policies and practices. As part of the research review, I consider several mediating factors or processes that may help to explain why students from different types of families differ in their achievement and behavior. Among these factors are: income and other family resources, parent–child relationships and interactions, parent involvement in school-related activities, and family moves.

MAJOR FINDINGS OF RESEARCH ON FAMILY STRUCTURE AND STUDENT ACHIEVEMENT

Nearly a dozen large-scale, high-quality studies have collected data on the kind of family a child lives in and related the family living arrangements to the student's performance and conduct in school.[1] Illustrative data from several of these studies are presented later. With remarkable consistency, the studies have arrived at the following conclusions:

---

[1] See Allison and Furstenberg (1989); Amato and Keith (1991b); Astone and McLanahan (1991, 1994); Dawson (1991); Dornbusch et al. (1985); Guidubaldi, Perry, and Cleminshaw (1984); Haveman, Wolfe, and Spaulding (1991); Hetherington, Camara, and Featherman (1983); Krein and Beller (1988); Lee (1993); McLanahan and Sandefur (1994); Peterson and Zill (1986); Sandefur, McLanahan, and Wojtkiewicz (1992); Wojtkiewicz (1993); Zill (1988); and Zill and Schoenborn (1990).

1. Students' academic performance and school behavior relate significantly to family structure, with students from single-parent families, stepfamilies, and, indeed, all family types other than intact two-parent families showing lower achievement and a higher incidence of school conduct problems than students from mother–father families.

2. The relationship between family structure and academic performance is diminished but not eliminated when other related factors, such as parent education and race, are controlled. The extent to which the diminution occurs varies with both the type of dependent measure and the type of family involved.

3. The "adjusted" relationships between family structure and student achievement and misconduct are modest in magnitude (average effect sizes of about .15 of a standard deviation for achievement measures and about .25 of a standard deviation for behavior or disciplinary measures). However, these modest associations produce substantial increases in the risk that students will experience negative events, such as having to repeat a grade or being suspended from school.

4. The strength of the "adjusted" relationship between family structure and student performance varies across different outcome measures. The weakest relationships are found with standardized test scores and other measures that are heavily reflective of innate talent. Intermediate strength relationships are found with grades, grade repetition, and other measures that reflect motivation, application, and conduct, as well as talent. The strongest relationships are found with direct measures of student misbehavior and with measures of school disciplinary actions that result from misconduct, such as the student being suspended or the parent being required to come in for a conference with the teacher or principal.

5. The strength of the relationship between family structure and academic performance varies across different family types. However, after adjustment for background factors, students from the three major forms of alternative family do not differ greatly or consistently in the extent to which they show lower academic performance or more frequent problem behavior than students from intact mother–father families. The three most common forms of nontraditional family are mother-only families in which the mother has separated or divorced, mother-only families in which the mother has never married, and mother–stepfather families.

6. The effects of family structure on educational outcomes are visible in long-term effects, such as higher rates of high school dropout and lower rates of college enrollment and completion, as well as in short-term disturbances in pupil achievement and behavior.

DATA THAT ILLUSTRATE THE FINDINGS

Data from nationwide studies done for three different federal agencies help to illustrate the principles summarized previously. The studies are the National Health Interview Survey on Child Health, the National Education Longitudinal Study of 1988, and the National Longitudinal Survey of Youth.

Achievement and Conduct Problems
in Elementary and Secondary Students
(National Health Interview Survey)

The first set of data, presented in Fig. 10.1 and Fig. 10.2, comes from the National Health Interview Survey on Child Health. This was an in-person household survey conducted in 1988 by the National Center for Health Statistics of the U.S. Department of Health and Human Services (Zill & Schoenborn, 1990; Dawson, 1991). The children in the subsample analyzed here were 10,027 students aged 7–17 from communities across the United States.

Figure 10.3 shows how the percentage of children experiencing problems in school varies across students from four different types of families: mother–father families, mother-only families in which the mother was formerly married, mother-only families in which the mother has never married, and mother–stepfather families in which the child's mother was divorced and subsequently remarried. The specific problems examined are: being in the bottom half of the class in the current school year; ever having to repeat a grade in school; the child's parents being asked to come in for a meeting with teachers or administrators during the current school year because of the child's problematic behavior in school; and the child ever having been suspended or expelled from school. The determination as to whether or not a given child had each of these problems is based on the reports of a parent respondent, usually the child's mother. For simplicity, estimates for children from less common family types, such as father-only or father–stepmother families are not shown separately, but data from these children are included in the *all children* totals.

Looking first at the frequencies of learning and school behavior problems in the general population of students aged 7–17, we see that 44% were described as being in the middle to the bottom of their class, 18% had to repeat at least one grade, 18% had had a conduct problem at school during the current school year that led to the teacher or principal requesting a meeting with the child's parents, and 8% had been suspended or expelled at some point.

Comparing the frequency of these problems across the four family types (see the bars labeled *Observed* in Fig. 10.3), we see that children in the single-parent and stepparent families were significantly more likely to exhibit each type of problem than were children from mother–father families. Students living with single mothers who had never married had the highest observed problem frequencies, with 60% of them in the bottom half of the class (compared to 38% of students from mother–father families), 33% having repeated a grade (compared with 13% of the students from mother–father families), 30% having required a parent conference this year (compared with 13% of the students from mother–father families), and 17% having been suspended or expelled (compared to 5% of the students from mother–father families).

Students living with single mothers who had separated or divorced also showed significantly higher rates of school-related problems than students from intact

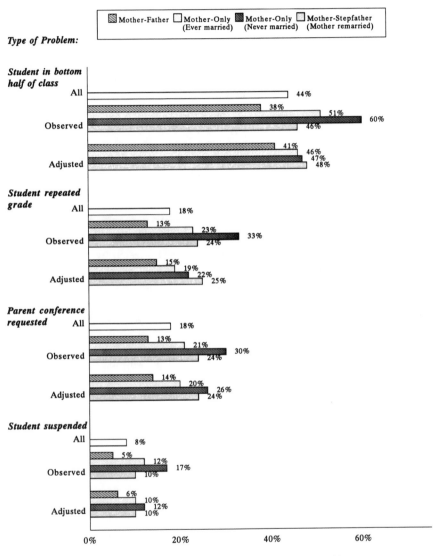

Type of Problem:

| Mother-Father | Mother-Only (Ever married) | Mother-Only (Never married) | Mother-Stepfather (Mother remarried) |

Student in bottom half of class

All 44%
Observed 38% / 51% / 60% / 46%
Adjusted 41% / 46% / 47% / 48%

Student repeated grade

All 18%
Observed 13% / 23% / 33% / 24%
Adjusted 15% / 19% / 22% / 25%

Parent conference requested

All 18%
Observed 13% / 21% / 30% / 24%
Adjusted 14% / 20% / 26% / 24%

Student suspended

All 8%
Observed 5% / 12% / 17% / 10%
Adjusted 6% / 10% / 12% / 10%

0%   20%   40%   60%

Percentage of students with specified problem

FIG. 10.3. Percentage of students with school related problems from mother–father, mother-only, and mother–stepfather familes, U.S. children ages 7–17, 1988. Data are from Zill and Coiro (1991).

145

families, although only about half as elevated as the problem rates for students with never-married mothers. Fifty-one percent of these students ranked in the bottom half of their class, 23% had repeated a grade, 21% had misbehaved to an extent that prompted a parent–teacher conference, and 12% had been suspended. Students living with divorced mothers who had remarried also showed elevated rates of learning or behavior problems, of about the same magnitude as those for students from the ever-married mother-only group.

The different marital groups show substantial variation in other characteristics that are relevant to the frequency of school-related problems, such as average parent education levels, racial composition, frequency of poverty and welfare dependence, and average age of the children in the group. When multiple regression methods were used to adjust the comparisons for these background disparities, the differences among the marital groups in the frequency of school-related problems were considerably diminished. (See the bars labeled *Adjusted* in Fig. 10.3).[2] Nevertheless, even with the adjustments, school-related problems continued to be significantly more frequent among children in the single-parent and stepparent groups than in the nuclear family group.

The never-married mother-only group was most affected by the adjustments, inasmuch as never-married motherhood is considerably more common among African Americans than Whites, Asians, or Hispanics, and unmarried mothers tend to have lower education levels than either stably married or formerly married mothers, as well as higher rates of poverty and welfare dependence (Dawson, 1991, Table 2; Zill, 1988; Zill & Nord, 1994). For example, after adjustment, the percentage of children in this group who were in the bottom half of the class declined from 60% to 47%, whereas the percentage who had repeated a grade fell from 33% to 22%.

The mother–stepfather group was least affected by the adjustments, because this group has a similar ethnic composition as the mother–father group, and parents in the group have only slightly lower education levels and slightly higher poverty levels than parents in nuclear families. Thus, children in the mother–stepfather group showed about the same frequencies of school-related problems before and after the statistical adjustments were made.

Children living with separated or divorced mothers who had not remarried fell between the mother–stepfather and never-married mother groups in terms of ethnic composition, parent education, and poverty frequency: They were more disadvantaged than the mother–stepfather group but less disadvantaged than children living with never-married mothers. Hence, the effects of the statistical adjustments on this group were more pronounced than those for the mother–

---

[2]Multiple classification analysis was used to correct the family structure comparisons for the main effects of parent education, race and Hispanic origin, sex of child, age of child, region, metropolitan residence, number of children in family, and welfare/poverty status. The analyses were carried out by the author in collaboration with Mary Jo Coiro of Child Trends.

stepfather group but less marked than those for the never-married mother group. For example, after adjustment, the percentage of children in this group who were in the bottom half of the class declined from 51% to 46%, whereas the percentage who had repeated a grade fell from 23% to 19%.

Variations Across Outcome Measures. Note that the effects of the statistical adjustment were greater on the indicators of class standing and grade repetition than on the parent conference and student suspension indicators. This may be seen more clearly in Fig. 10.4, which presents the same data in the form of percentage increases in risk of school-related problems that were found for students from mother-only and mother–stepfather families over the risks faced by students from intact mother–father families. For the never-married mother group, the adjusted percentage increase in risk for class standing was only about one quarter of the unadjusted percentage increase in risk, and the adjusted increase for grade repetition was only about one third of the unadjusted increase. By contrast, the adjusted increase for suspension was about half the unadjusted increase, and the adjusted increase for the parent conference measure was about two thirds of the unadjusted increase. A similar pattern may be seen in the raw and adjusted differences in risk for the ever-married mother-only group. One reason for the differential effects of adjustment across measures is that the class standing and grade repetition indicators were more strongly related to parent education level than were the student suspension and parent conference indicators.

Figure 10.4 also illustrates the principle that the adjusted relationship between family structure and school outcomes is stronger for measures that deal with student behavior than for measures dealing with academic aptitude or achievement. Observe that the size of the adjusted percentage increase for the mother-only groups over the mother–father group goes up from class standing to grade repetition to parent–teacher conference to student suspension. The mother–stepfather group exhibits a slightly different pattern, with grade repetition as well as the conference and suspension measures showing larger percentage increases than the class standing measure.

Variations Across Family Types. Another principle mentioned previously was that the size of the relationship between family structure and school outcome measures varies across different kinds of nonnuclear families, but that students from the three major forms of nontraditional family, namely, mother-only ever-married, mother-only never-married, and mother–stepfather, do not differ greatly or consistently in the extent to which they show lower academic performance or more frequent misbehavior than students from intact mother–father families. This point is also well illustrated by the adjusted data shown in Fig. 10.3 and Fig. 10.4. Other data, examined later, show more sizable differences involving other nontraditional family forms.

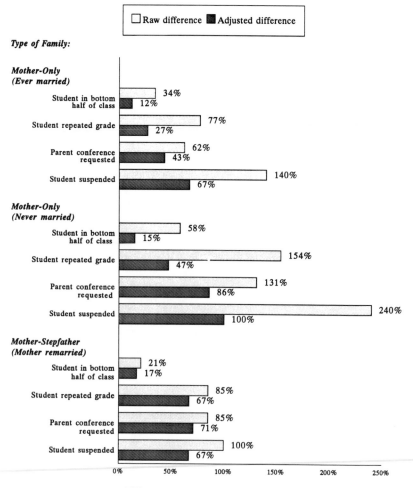

FIG. 10.4. Percentage increase in risk of school-related problems for students from mother-only and mother–stepfather families over students form mother–father families, U.S. children ages 7–17, 1988. Data are from Zill and Coiro (1991).

Adjusting for Poverty. In making the adjustments shown in Fig. 10.3 and Fig. 10.4, the variable of poverty and welfare status was included as one of the control variables.[3] This is a debatable procedure, because poverty and welfare

---

[3]The poverty/welfare status variable was a tripartite variable with the following three categories: (a) families that received Aid to Families with Dependent Children during the previous 12 months; (b) families whose income was below the official poverty line, but which did not receive welfare; and (c) nonpoor, nonwelfare families.

dependence are often consequences of family disruption and unmarried parent-hood, rather than (or as well as) correlates or causes of single parenthood (Bianchi & McArthur, 1991). Thus, in adjusting for poverty, we may be, in effect, removing some of the actual effect of family structure on pupil achievement and behavior. It is noteworthy, though, that significant differences between students from two-parent and single-parent families remain after making this adjustment. This implies that the effects of family structure are not due solely to economic factors, as some have argued. I return to this issue later in the chapter.

The Question of Effect Size. What should one make of the adjusted differ-ences in achievement and behavior between traditional and single-parent families? Even though the differences may be statistically reliable, they seem not to amount to much in practical terms. I consider this question further after examining the other data sets. But two observations are worth making at this point. One is that a risk of serious student misconduct and suspension that is twice as great or nearly twice as great as that shown by students from stable mother–father families hardly seems inconsequential. Yet this is what students from mother-only and mother–stepfather families exhibited, even after adjustment for related family risk factors like low education, race, and poverty.

On the other hand, although coming from a single-parent family or stepfamily significantly increased the relative risk that a child would experience problems in school, the majority of students from the nontraditional families did *not* show these problems.[4] This bolsters the conclusion that family structure is not, in itself, a major determinant of school failure.

Test Scores, Grades, and Misconduct in Eighth Graders (National Education Longitudinal Study of 1988)

We now turn to data from the National Education Longitudinal Study of 1988 (NELS:88), a nationwide panel study conducted by the National Center for Edu-cation Statistics (NCES) of the U.S. Department of Education. The study admin-istered standardized achievement tests and questionnaires to a national probability sample of 24,599 eighth graders in 1988 and also collected data from the students' parents, teachers, and schools (Schneider & Coleman, 1993). NCES reinterviewed and retested the young people in the sample as high school sophomores and seniors (or dropouts), and will continue to study them as college students or young workers.

Figure 10.5 shows how the standardized achievement test scores, grades, and misbehavior of eighth grade students from five different nontraditional family types

---

[4]The one case in which a majority of children *did* have negative outcomes was on the class standing measure, where one would expect about half of all students to be in "the bottom half of the class."

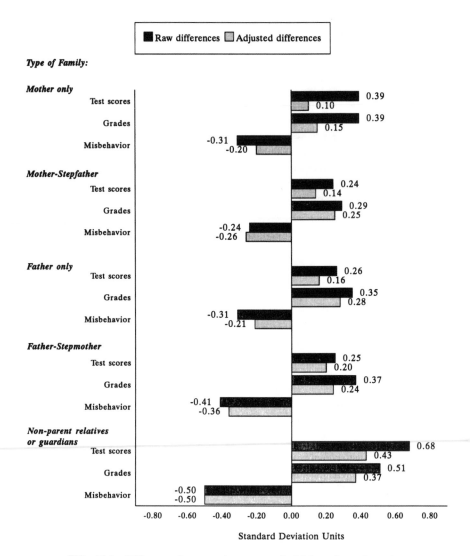

FIG. 10.5. Differences between the scores of eighth-grade students from mother–father families and other family types. Data are from Lee (1993). Effect sizes were calculated by N. Zill from data presented in Tables 3.2 and 3.4 of Lee (1993).

compared with those of students from intact mother–father families.[5] The five family types are mother-only families (with no distinction made between ever-married and never-married mothers), mother–stepfather families, father-only families, father–stepmother families, and families in which the student lives with neither parent but with nonparental relatives or unrelated foster parents or guardians.

The data shown are the differences between the average scores of the students from mother–father families and the average scores of students from each of the other family types. Both raw differences and adjusted differences are presented, with all the differences being expressed in standard deviation units, that is, as effect sizes. Positive differences for the test scores and grades variables mean that students in the mother–father group showed higher achievement and better grades, on average, than students in the specified type of nontraditional family. Negative differences for the misbehavior scale mean that students in the mother–father group reported less misbehavior, on average, than students in the specified type of nontraditional family. Adjusted differences were standardized for the effects of parent education, race, and gender of child. Effect sizes were calculated by the present author from a published analysis of the NELS data carried out by Seh-Ahn Lee (1993) of the University of Chicago.

These data extend our illustration of the principles summarized previously to other school outcome measures and other types of nontraditional families. Again we see that family structure relates to academic performance, with the comparisons all favoring students in mother–father families and the raw differences between single-parent families or stepfamilies and nuclear families ranging in magnitude from one quarter to four tenths of a standard deviation. As before, however, the differences were considerably reduced when adjusted for the effects of other background variables. Indeed, the adjusted difference in achievement test scores between students from mother–father families and mother-only families amounted to only one tenth of a standard deviation.

Also as before, the adjusted differences between nuclear and nonnuclear family types varied across the different types of outcome measures. Standardized test scores showed the smallest differences (with effect sizes ranging from .10 to .20 of a standard deviation), grade averages showed somewhat larger differences (.15 to .28 of a standard deviation), and the misbehavior measure showed the largest differences (.20 to .36 of a standard deviation). (The ranges given include only the single-parent family and stepfamily groups, not the nonparental relatives or guardians group.)

---

[5]The test scores were a composite of student scores on reading and math achievement tests that were administered to the students as part of the NELS base year assessment. The grades score was an average calculated from students' reports of the grades they received in major academic subjects. The misbehavior score was a scale score based on students' reports of whether they had been sent to the office for misbehaving, whether their parents had received warnings about the students' attendance or behavior, and whether they had gotten into a fight with another student.

Family Types That Show Larger Effect Sizes. After adjustment, the various single-parent and stepparent family types showed roughly the same magnitudes of effects, with two notable exceptions. First, students in father–stepmother families showed more elevated misbehavior scores than the other single-parent families or stepfamilies. Second, students living with neither parent, but with grandparents or other nonparent relatives only or with unrelated foster parents or guardians, showed significantly larger differences (ranging in magnitude from about four tenths to half a standard deviation) than did students from all the other family types. With respect to test scores and grades as well as misbehavior, students in the neither-parent group showed the greatest elevation in unfavorable outcomes over students from mother–father families.

Young people who live apart from both of their birth parents are often ones who have had a good deal of turmoil in their lives and, not infrequently, histories of parental neglect or abuse. As far as students who live in father–stepmother families are concerned, there may be a selection process at work such that adolescents from divorced families who are creating disciplinary problems that the biological mother feels she cannot handle are sent to live with the father and his new wife. Thus, being in a father–stepmother family may be a sign, rather than a cause, of especially severe behavioral difficulties (Zill, 1988).

High School Dropout Rates Among Young People From One-Parent and Two-Parent Families (National Longitudinal Survey of Youth)

For the last illustration of family structure effects on school outcomes, we turn to the National Longitudinal Survey of Youth (NLSY) for evidence of longer-term impacts of family disruption on young people's educational attainment. The NLSY is a panel study of a nationally representative sample of almost 14,000 young men and women born between 1958 and 1965. The study was sponsored by the Bureau of Labor Statistics of the U.S. Department of Labor to provide information on the education, labor force participation, and military service of young Americans born in these years. Participants in the study were first interviewed in 1979 when they were between 14 and 21 years of age and have been reinterviewed every year since then.

Figure 10.6 presents data based on a subset of 5,246 youth from the NLSY sample, those who were between the ages of 14 and 17 in 1979 and who were, for the most part, still living at home with their families. Shown are the percentages of young people from this subsample who went on to drop out of high school at some point, broken down by family structure, race and Hispanic origin, and parent education. The figure is based on a table prepared by McLanahan and Sandefur for their recent book, *Growing Up With a Single Parent: What Hurts, What Helps* (1994, p. 58).

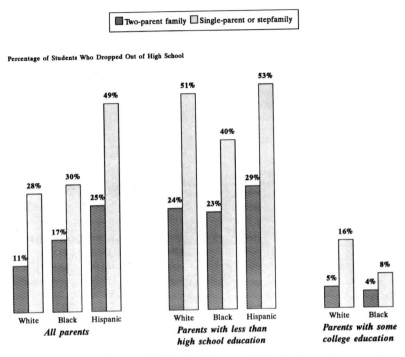

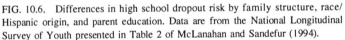

FIG. 10.6. Differences in high school dropout risk by family structure, race/Hispanic origin, and parent education. Data are from the National Longitudinal Survey of Youth presented in Table 2 of McLanahan and Sandefur (1994).

Overall, the risk of dropping out of high school was about twice as great for students from single-parent families or stepfamilies as for students from intact two-parent families: 29% of the former group dropped out, as opposed to 13% of the latter. (These figures were adjusted for the effects of mother's and father's education, race and sex of the child, number of siblings, and place of residence). A similar two-fold dropout risk for young people who had experienced parental divorce by age 16 was found by Zill, Morrison, and Coiro (1993), analyzing longitudinal data from the National Survey of Children. Comparable results were also obtained by McLanahan and Sandefur (1994, pp. 40–43) from their analyses of three other national data sets, namely, the Panel Study of Income Dynamics, High School and Beyond, and the National Survey of Families and Households.

As shown in Fig. 10.6, the increased risk of dropout in one-parent families was observed in African-American and Hispanic families as well as White families, and in families in which the parents both had at least some college education as well as in families in which neither parent was a high school graduate. The proportionate increase in risk associated with single parenthood was greater for White students than for African-American or Hispanic students. Nonetheless, the increase for minority students was still considerable. Family disruption increased the chances of dropout by two-and-a-half times for White students (from 11% to 28%), by two times for Hispanic students (from 25% to 49%), and by 1.8 times for African-American students (from 17% to 30%).

The chances of students dropping out of high school were considerably lower if the parents had some college education than if they were less educated. Nevertheless, if they were in one-parent families, the chances of dropout increased by a factor of three for White students with college-educated parents (from 5% to 16%), and by a factor of two for Black students with college-educated parents (from 4% to 8%). (There were not enough Hispanic youth with college-educated parents in the NLSY subsample to make stable estimates for their differential risk of dropout by family type).

Clearly, family structure is not the only factor that affects a student's chances of completing high school on time. Parent education plays an important role, as does race and ethnic background. Hispanic students in two-parent families were more than twice as likely to be dropouts as White students in two-parent families (25% vs. 11%), and African-American students in two-parent families were one-and-a-half times as likely to be dropouts (17% vs. 11%). White students in two-parent families were five times as likely to be dropouts if their parents had less than a high school education than if their parents were college educated (24% vs. 5%).

As McLanahan and Sandefur (1994, pp. 42–43) pointed out, though, the doubling of the risk of dropout associated with family disruption is far from trivial. It is equivalent to the increase in risk associated with having a mother who was a high school dropout, as opposed to a mother who was a high school graduate. Moreover, the NLSY data imply that if all students came from two-parent families, the overall dropout rate would decline by one third. It is also noteworthy that the combination of living in a single-parent family or stepfamily *and* having a mother with a relatively low education level increased the risk of dropout to the point that a majority of young people in these circumstances interrupted or failed to complete their schooling.

Post High School Differences in Educational Attainment. Based on their analyses of data from three different data sets, the National Longitudinal Survey of Youth, High School and Beyond, and the National Survey of Families and Households, McLanahan and Sandefur (1994, pp. 46–48) concluded that family disruption continues to reduce a child's educational attainment after high school. They found that adjusted rates of college enrollment were 12% to 15% lower in single-parent families and stepfamilies than in two-parent families. In the High School and Beyond data, for example, 50% of high school graduates from one-parent families enrolled in college, compared to 57% of graduates from two-parent families.

Differences in college completion were more pronounced, with students from one-parent families showing adjusted graduation rates that were 25% to 35%

lower than those of students from two-parent families. In the National Survey of Families and Households data, for example, 15% of high school graduates from single-parent families and stepfamilies graduated college, whereas 23% of those from two-parent families did so. However, not all of the available evidence supports the conclusion that family disruption reduces the chances of post high school attainment. For example, data from the Panel Study of Income Dynamics did not show statistically significant differences in college attendance or graduation associated with family structure.

MEDIATING FACTORS

What are the mediating factors and processes that might explain why students who live with a single-parent family or in a stepfamily get lower grades, misbehave more in school, and are more likely to repeat a grade, be suspended, and drop out of high school than students who live with both of their parents? Nearly everyone acknowledges that conflict between parents and the process of divorce are stressful for both the children and parents involved. That stress can distract students from concentrating on their studies and lead to "acting out" in school of the anger and helplessness that many young people feel as their parents attack each other and their families disintegrate.

But these are relatively short-term responses to the crisis of marital strife and family transition. Given the power of the human organism to recuperate from stress and the diverse experiences that different families have after divorce, why would one expect long-term impairments in young people's academic performance and behavior? Also, why should we see school-related problems in children who live with never-married mothers? These children have not necessarily experienced parental conflict or family disruption.[6]

As we have seen, part of the answer to the previous questions is that the lower academic performance of children from single-parent families or stepfamilies is not due to family structure as such. Rather, it is due to the fact that adults who are younger, have lower education levels, lower earnings, and minority ethnic backgrounds are somewhat more likely to separate or get divorced and much more likely to have children outside of marriage. Their children do less well in school partly because of these other negative background factors. When these correlated factors are controlled, the strength of the relationship between family structure and school outcomes is considerably reduced, especially the association with lower achievement test scores.

---

[6]Children born and raised outside of marriage may have witnessed fighting between the unmarried mother and father or the mother and other boyfriends or the breakup of informal cohabitation arrangements. But the occurrence of these events is less certain than when legal marriages break up, and the crises surrounding them tend to be less prolonged. Also, they are less wrenching for the child, who has usually not had the chance to build up a close relationship with the mother's partner.

Some even argue that adults with less scholastic aptitude or antisocial personality patterns are more likely to enter into unstable marriages and have children outside marriage. Then their lower aptitude levels or antisocial behavioral tendencies are genetically transmitted to at least some of their children, and this is a reason why we see higher frequencies of school failure and misconduct in students from one-parent families.

Whether or not the last position has any merit, the fact is that there are significant associations between family structure and school outcomes that remain after related background factors are controlled. What intervening processes account for these associations? A number of different theories have been put forth about the mechanisms that may be involved. Amato (1993) considered five distinct explanatory factors in a recent review and appraisal of theories on children's adjustment to divorce. They were: the absence of the noncustodial parent, the adjustment of the custodial parent, interparental conflict, economic hardship, and stressful life changes. He concluded that existing research provides the most consistent and convincing support for the interparental conflict perspective (Emery, 1982). But he also argued that a model combining insights from all five perspectives may be needed to fully account for current research findings.

Is Money All That Matters?

Given the apparent accuracy of Amato's appraisal that no single model does full justice to current findings, it is dismaying that McLanahan and Sandefur (1994) and a number of other sociologists and economists came out with statements contending that much of the effect of family structure is attributable to differences in family income. McLanahan and Sandefur also made fairly strong policy recommendations that grow out of this interpretation of the data.

There is no doubt that family disruption and single parenthood are associated with lower income levels and that family income is one of the determinants of a child's life chances and future success (Bianchi & McArthur, 1991). In 1993, the median family income level for a U.S. child in a two-parent family was about $43,600, whereas the median family income for a child in a mother-only family was about $12,100 (Zill & Nord, 1994, p. 15). Indeed, the association between family structure and low-income or poverty status is stronger than the correlation between family structure and a child's achievement or misbehavior. But there are several reasons for arguing that lower income is not *the* major intervening factor that explains why single parenthood is associated with lower achievement and increased misconduct.

The Case Against the Income Explanation. First, there are the data on children from stepfamilies. Primarily because of the presence of a male wage earner, mother–stepfather families have dramatically higher income levels than mother-only families. Yet, as we have seen, students from mother–stepfather families have achievement and misconduct problems that are about as frequent as those of students from mother-only families. Why does higher income not have its supposed beneficial effect in these families? Advocates of the income explanation argue that it is because the insertion of a new adult into the family constellation is itself a source of stress, strain, and rivalry for the offspring of a disrupted marriage. Or they contend that there is something else about students from stepfamilies, such as having higher rates of residential mobility, or going to lower quality schools, or receiving less supportive parenting, that accounts for the elevated rate of school-related problems in these students (McLanahan & Sandefur, 1994, chapter 7).

It seems implausible, however, that income, which supposedly exerts such a powerful positive influence on children in mother-only families, suddenly becomes so weak in stepfamilies that its influence can be undone by the stress of a family transition or a residential move. Also, what about the noneconomic factors that the economic hardship theorists invoke to explain the puzzling findings for stepfamilies? Why are these same noneconomic factors (i.e., nonsupportive parenting, residential moves) not relevant for mother-only families? Again, it seems unlikely that factors and dynamics that are important for one type of family could really be so unimportant in another type of family.

A second argument against the "it's all income" position is that controlling for postdisruption income does not always work the way the hardship theorists contend that it should work, that is, to substantially reduce the relationship between family structure (or at least single parenthood) and child outcome measures. Adding controls for family income does seem to reduce the relationship between being in a mother-only family and academic performance measures such as class standing, grade repetition, test scores, or high school dropout. (See Table 10.1 and Table 10.2 for examples of the effect on class standing and grade repetition. See McLanahan & Sandefur, 1994, chapter 5, for the effect on high school dropout; and Schneider & Coleman, 1993, chapters 3 and 4, for the effect on achievement test scores.) But it does not do the same for the relationship between being in a mother-only family and misconduct measures such as school suspension or having the parent asked to come in for a conference about the student's behavior. (See Table 10.3 and Table 10.4 for examples of this lack of effect with respect to parent conference and school suspension variables. See Schneider & Coleman, 1993, pp. 58–61, for an example with respect to self-reported misbehavior in school.) Hetherington and Jodl (1994) also reported that income is a fairly weak predictor of child behavioral disturbances in their longitudinal studies of both divorced and remarried families.

A third question to be raised about the economic hardship argument is: What is really being controlled when we adjust for family income in mother-only families? In these families, income is primarily a function of the mother's employability and earning power (because child support payments are so infrequent and small, and welfare payment levels do not vary over much of the income

TABLE 10.1

Predicting Child's Academic Standing in Upper Half of Class From Family Structure, Income, Parent Involvement, and Family Background Characteristics (Multiple Logistic Regression)

Predictor Variables	Basic Model		Control for Income		Control for Parent Involvement		Control for Both Income and Parent Involvement	
	Standardized Coefficient	Odds Ratio	Standardized Coefficient	Odds Ratio	Standardized Coefficient	Odds Ratio	Standardized Coefficient	Odds Ratio
Family Structure								
Mother only	-.05***	.81	-.01	.97	-.04**	.85	-.00	1.00
Mother–stepfather	-.07***	.69	-.06***	.72	-.06***	.73	-.05***	.75
Other parents	-.02	.87	-.01	.92	-.01	.93	-.01	.97
Parent Involvement								
Moderate or high vs. low involvement	—	—	—	—	.15***	1.74	.14***	1.68
Family SES								
Family income	—	—	.13***	1.08	—	—	.11***	1.07
Parent education	.24***	1.45	.20***	1.35	.20***	1.37	.17***	1.29
Mother's Employment								
Full time	-.00	1.00	-.02	.92	-.01	.96	-.03*	.90
Part time	.02	1.11	.02	1.08	.02	1.07	.01	1.05
Looking for work	-.01	.94	-.00	.99	-.01	.92	-.00	.97
Ethnic Background								
Black	-.11***	.59	-.09***	.64	-.11***	.60	-.09***	.65
Hispanic	-.04***	.79	-.03**	.86	-.03**	.82	-.02	.88
Asian	.02	1.34	.03*	1.39	.03*	1.48	.03**	1.52
Child's Age and Sex								
Age in years	-.09***	.93	-.09***	.93	-.07***	.94	-.07***	.94
Sex (f = 1, m = 0)	.20***	2.03	.20***	2.03	.19***	2.01	.19***	2.01
Multiple R (Somer's D)	.37***		.38***		.39***		.40***	

Note. From Running in Place: How American Families Are Faring in a Changing Economy and an Individualistic Society by N. Zill and C. Nord, 1994 (Table III-7). Washington, DC: Child Trends. Additional analyses of data from the 1993 National Household Education Survey.
*p = <.05; **p = <.01; ***p = <.001.

TABLE 10.2

Predicting Child's Grade Repetition From Family Structure, Income, Parent Involvement, and Family Background Characteristics (Multiple Logistic Regression)

Predictor Variables	Basic Model		Control for Income		Control for Parent Involvement		Control for Both Income and Parent Involvement	
	Standardized Coefficient	Odds Ratio	Standardized Coefficient	Odds Ratio	Standardized Coefficient	Odds Ratio	Standardized Coefficient	Odds Ratio
Family Structure								
Mother only	.07***	1.33	.02	1.08	.06***	1.30	.02	1.07
Mother–stepfather	.13***	2.06	.12***	1.97	.12***	2.00	.11***	1.93
Other parents	.06***	1.41	.05**	1.32	.05***	1.38	.04**	1.29
Parent Involvement								
Moderate or high vs. low involvement	—	—	—	—	-.07***	.78	-.06***	.81
Family SES								
Family income	—	—	-.15***	.92	—	—	-.15***	.92
Parent education	-.27***	.66	-.22***	.72	-.26***	.68	-.20***	.73
Mother's Employment								
Full time	.00	1.00	.03	1.11	.01	1.02	.03	1.12
Part time	-.03	.89	-.02	.91	-.02	.90	-.02	.92
Looking for work	.04**	1.47	.04**	1.40	.04**	1.48	.04**	1.42
Ethnic Background								
Black	.10***	1.64	.08***	1.46	.10***	1.62	.08***	1.45
Hispanic	.01	1.06	-.01	.96	.01	1.04	-.01	.96
Asian	-.04	.64	-.04*	.61	-.04	.62	-.04*	.59
Child's Age and Sex								
Age in years	.25***	1.24	.25***	1.25	.24***	1.23	.25***	1.24
Sex (f = 1, m = 0)	-.20***	.48	-.20***	.49	-.20***	.49	-.20***	.49
Multiple R (Somer's D)	.45***		.46***		.46***		.47***	

Note. From *Running in Place: How American Families Are Faring in a Changing Economy and an Individualistic Society* by N. Zill and C. Nord, 1994 (Table III-5). Washington, DC: Child Trends. Additional analyses of data from the 1993 National Household Education Survey.

*p = <.05; **p = <.01; ***p = <.001.

TABLE 10.3

Predicting Teacher's Contact About Child's Behavior From Family Structure, Income, Parent Involvement, and Family Background Characteristics (Multiple Logistic Regression)

Predictor Variables	Basic Model		Control for Income		Control for Parent Involvement		Control for Both Income and Parent Involvement	
	Standardized Coefficient	Odds Ratio	Standardized Coefficient	Odds Ratio	Standardized Coefficient	Odds Ratio	Standardized Coefficient	Odds Ratio
Family Structure								
Mother only	.09***	1.46	.07***	1.35	.09***	1.44	.07***	1.35
Mother–stepfather	.08***	1.58	.08***	1.55	.08***	1.56	.07***	1.53
Other parents	.10***	1.77	.09***	1.72	.09***	1.74	.09***	1.71
Parent Involvement								
Moderate or high vs. low involvement	—	—	—	—	-.03*	.88	-.03	.90
Family SES								
Family income	—	—	-.05**	.97	—	—	-.05*	.97
Parent education	-.10***	.86	-.08***	.89	-.09***	.88	-.07***	.90
Mother's Employment								
Full time	.00	1.01	.01	1.04	.01	1.02	.01	1.05
Part time	.01	1.03	.01	1.04	.01	1.04	.01	1.05
Looking for work	-.00	.96	-.01	.94	-.00	.97	-.01	.95
Ethnic Background								
Black	.13***	1.91	.12***	1.84	.13***	1.89	.12***	1.83
Hispanic	.08***	1.60	.07***	1.54	.08***	1.59	.07***	1.54
Asian	.01	1.20	.01	1.18	.01	1.17	.01	1.16
Child's Age and Sex								
Age in years	-.20***	.84	-.19***	.84	-.20***	.84	-.20***	.84
Sex (f = 1, m = 0)	-.27***	.38	-.27***	.38	-.27***	.38	-.27***	.38
Multiple R (Somer's D)	.38***		.39***		.39***		.39***	

Note. From *Running in Place: How American Families Are Faring in a Changing Economy and an Individualistic Society* by N. Zill and C. Nord, 1994 (Table III-7). Washington, DC: Child Trends. Additional analyses of data from the 1993 National Household Education Survey.
*p = <.05; **p = <.01; ***p = <.001.

160

TABLE 10.4

Predicting Whether Child Ever Suspended or Expelled From Family Structure, Income, Parent Involvement, and Family Background Characteristics (Multiple Logistic Regression)

Predictor Variables	Basic Model		Control for Income		Control for Parent Involvement		Control for Both Income and Parent Involvement	
	Standardized Coefficient	Odds Ratio	Standardized Coefficient	Odds Ratio	Standardized Coefficient	Odds Ratio	Standardized Coefficient	Odds Ratio
Family Structure								
Mother only	.14***	1.84	.13***	1.73	.13***	1.76	.12***	1.70
Mother–stepfather	.13***	2.07	.12***	2.04	.12***	1.96	.12***	1.95
Other parents	.08***	1.63	.08***	1.60	.07***	1.54	.07***	1.52
Parent Involvement								
Moderate or high vs. low involvement	—	—	—	—	-.15***	.58	-.15***	.58
Family SES								
Family income	—	—	-.05*	.97	—	—	-.03	.99
Parent education	-.16***	.79	-.14***	.81	-.12***	.84	-.11***	.85
Mother's Employment								
Full time	-.03	.91	-.02	.93	-.02	.95	-.01	.96
Part time	-.04	.84	-.04	.85	-.03	.87	-.03	.87
Looking for work	.00	1.00	-.00	.99	.00	1.02	.00	1.02
Ethnic Background								
Black	.23***	3.18	.23***	3.07	.23***	3.14	.23***	3.07
Hispanic	.04*	1.26	.03*	1.22	.04*	1.23	.03	1.21
Asian	-.01	.85	-.01	.84	-.02	.79	-.02	.79
Child's Age and Sex								
Age in years	.16***	1.15	.16***	1.15	.14***	1.13	.14***	1.13
Sex (f = 1, m = 0)	-.31***	.32	-.31***	.32	-.31***	.32	-.31***	.32
Multiple R (Somer's D)	.49***		.49***		.51***		.51***	

Note. From *Running in Place: How American Families Are Faring in a Changing Economy and an Individualistic Society* by N. Zill and C. Nord, 1994 (Table III-6). Washington, DC: Child Trends. Additional analyses of data from the 1993 National Household Education Survey.
*p = <.05; **p = <.01; ***p = <.001.

range). Thus, one could argue that by controlling for income we are really controlling for the mother's competence. This is less true in mother–stepfather families, because the stepfather's earnings are a major determinant of total income.

More competent single mothers tend to earn more *and* have better achieving children, but the higher earnings are not necessarily the cause of the better achievement. The children achieve better because at least some of them have inherited her innate capabilities, and because the mother provides a more stimulating and supportive home environment. If this argument is true, then if we had some independent measure of the mother's competence, such as an aptitude or achievement test score, controlling for it should reduce the relationship between income and child achievement. This is exactly what was found by Moore and Snyder (1991) in a study of the children of women in the National Longitudinal Survey of Youth (NLSY) who became unmarried teenage mothers. In predicting to vocabulary test scores of these children, Moore and Snyder found that the best predictors were the mother's score on the Armed Forces Qualifying Test, which was given as part of the NLSY, and the HOME Scale, a measure of the stimulation and support that the mother provided to the child at home. Income added little to the regression when these variables were included.

The point I am making is not that income is irrelevant to the development and behavior of children in single-parent families, but that it is not, as the economic hardship theorists contend, the only thing that matters. I certainly believe it would be a good thing if more children in impoverished or near-poor single-parent families could live in more comfortable circumstances. But I doubt that this would solve all their school-related problems.

Quality of Childrearing and the Relationship Between Parent and Child

Rather than focusing primarily or exclusively on income as a mediator of family structure effects, research tells us that we need to pay attention to what actually happens inside nontraditional families that may put the children in those families at educational risk. As Amato (1993, pp. 28–30) pointed out in his review of theories on children and divorce, there is a good deal of evidence that supports the hypothesis that the well-being of children in single-parent families and stepfamilies is positively associated with the way the custodial family functions as a childrearing organization and the general quality of the relationship between the child and the custodial parent or parents. There is also evidence that the well-being of the children is positively associated with the psychological adjustment of the parent who lives with the child.

Various studies have found ineffective childrearing behavior to be more common in single-parent families and stepfamilies than in intact mother–father families (Forgatch, Patterson, & Skinner, 1988). In a well-known longitudinal study, for example, Hetherington and her colleagues (Hetherington, Cox, & Cox, 1977, 1982) found recently divorced mothers to be less communicative and affectionate with their children, less consistent in their use of discipline, and more punitive than a control group of married mothers from the same socioeconomic and cultural backgrounds. They also found the custodial single mothers to be more anxious, depressed, angry, and self-doubting. Some of these differences were a short-term result of the stress of parental conflict and marital disruption. But even short-term impairments in family functioning can have long-term effects if they come at critical junctures in the child's life, such as when the young person gets involved in his or her first sexual relationship or starts disengaging from school to the extent that she or he is in danger of dropping out.

According to an influential and well-supported theoretical perspective, Hirschi's control theory (1969), the existence of a strong, positive bond with at least one and preferably both parental figures is an indication of successful socialization and a powerful deterrent to delinquency and other forms of deviant behavior. Yet in a longitudinal study of the long-term effects of divorce in young adulthood, Zill et al. (1993) found that two thirds of young adults from divorced families had poor relationships with their fathers, and 30% had poor relationships with their mothers. These were both double the proportions found to have poor relationships in nondivorced families. In their meta-analysis of studies on the effects of divorce on children, Amato and Keith (1991b) found that children in divorced single-parent families had less positive relationships with custodial parents than did children in intact families.

The proportion of eighth grade students in the National Education Longitudinal Study of 1988 who were left unsupervised for long periods of time after school was found to be significantly greater in single-mother and stepfather families than in intact two-parent families, especially if the mother worked full-time (Muller & Kerbow, 1993, pp. 24–26). In the same data set, the amount of after-school supervision that a student received was found to be positively related to both test scores and grades, even when other family, school, and parental behavior factors were controlled (Muller, 1993, pp. 82, 89).

Even though McLanahan and Sandefur (1994) argued for the primacy of income in their policy recommendations, they actually present analyses that show that parenting behavior can account for as much of the difference in high school dropout risk between children from single-parent families and two-parent families as income can (pp. 109–112). In these analyses, they used data from the longitudinal High School and Beyond study and controlled for differences in parental activities with the child, supervision, and educational aspirations. Because of limitations of the data sets, they were unable to control for both income and parenting behavior in the same analyses. They also note that other researchers found weaker parenting effects (Astone & McLanahan, 1991; Thomson, Hanson, & McLanahan, in press).

The Role of Parent Involvement

Two recent studies have examined whether lower levels of parent involvement in school-related activities might help to explain the higher incidence of achievement and behavior problems in students from single-parent families and stepfamilies. One study (Lee, 1993) used data from the National Education Longitudinal Study of 1988, whereas the other (Zill & Nord, 1994) employed data from the National Household Education Survey of 1993 (see Table 10.5 and Fig. 10.7). Although they used somewhat different measures of parent involvement and student achievement and behavior, both studies arrived at similar conclusions.[7]

The studies found that controlling for parent involvement reduced but did not totally compensate for the negative effects of coming from a mother-only family or stepfamily (Tables 10.1 through Table 10.4). Controlling for both parent involvement and family income did compensate for the negative effects of coming from a mother-only family as far as test scores, class standing, and grade repetition were concerned (see Table 10.1 and Table 10.2). It did not do so with respect to the criterion measures of teacher contact about the child's behavior and student suspension (see Table 10.3 and Table 10.4), nor with respect to self-reported misbehavior (Lee, 1993).

In addition, both studies found that higher levels of parental involvement were associated with better student outcomes on nearly all of the achievement and behavior measures. This was true within mother-only families and mother–stepfather families, as well as in intact two-parent families. (See Fig. 10.8 and Fig. 10.9). These findings lead to the conclusion that school-based efforts to encourage and increase parent involvement can have beneficial effects in nontraditional families and may help to lower some if not all of the increased risk that students from these families face in their academic careers.

WHAT FAMILY CHANGE MEANS FOR SCHOOLS

I turn now to the question of what the research findings reviewed previously imply for the policies and practices of elementary and secondary schools across the United States. What, if anything, should schools be doing to deal with the negative consequences for children of parental conflict, family disruption, and

---

[7]In the National Household Education Survey of 1993, parents of students in Grades 3 through 12 were asked about three activities: "Since the beginning of the school year, have you or [child's other parent] . . . attended a general school meeting, for example, back to school night or a meeting of a parent–teacher organization? . . . attended a school or class event such as a play, sports event, or science fair? . . . acted as a volunteer at the school or served on a school committee?" Parents who had done none or only one of these things were categorized as displaying a *low* level of involvement in school-related activities. Those who answered "yes" to two of the questions were classified as having a *moderate* level of involvement, whereas those who had done all three were said to have a *high* level of involvement.

TABLE 10.5
Predicting Moderate and High Levels of Parent Involvement From
Family Structure and Other Child and Family Characteristics
(Multiple Logistic Regression)

| | Moderate and High Levels | | High Levels | |
Predictor Variables	Standardized Coefficient	Odds Ratio	Standardized Coefficient	Odds Ratio
Family Structure				
Mother only	−.05***	.81	−.10***	.66
Mother–stepfather	−.07***	.66	−.12***	.51
Other parents	−.07***	.64	−.13***	.45
Family SES				
Parent education	.28***	1.53	.24***	1.44
Family income	.16***	1.10	.15***	1.09
Mother's Employment				
Full time	.07***	1.27	−.03	.88
Part time	.06***	1.31	.04*	1.18
Looking for work	.02	1.17	−.05*	.67
Racial/Ethnic Background				
Black	−.05**	.80	−.05*	.77
Hispanic	−.06***	.72	−.04**	.77
Asian	−.07***	.39	−.08***	.38
Child's Age and Sex				
Age in years	−.08***	.93	−.00	1.00
Sex (female = 1, male = 0)	.06***	1.23	.02	1.09

Note: From *Running in Place: How American Families Are Faring in a Changing Economy and an Individualistic Society* by N. Zill and C. Nord, 1994 (Tables III-2 and III-3). Washington, DC: Child Trends. Data from the 1993 National Household Education Survey.
*p = <.05; **p = <.01; ***p = <.001.

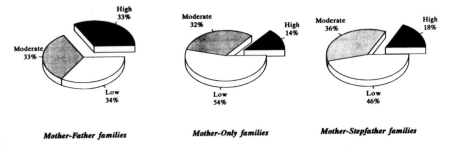

Mother-Father families   **Mother-Only families**   **Mother-Stepfather families**

FIG. 10.7. Level of parent involvement in school activities by family type, U.S. students in Grades 6–12. Data are from Zill (1994).

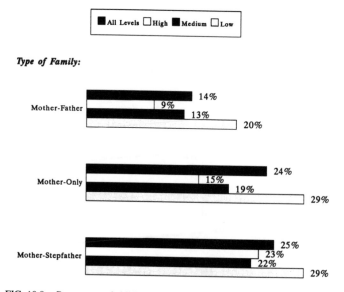

■All Levels ☐High ■Medium ☐Low

Type of Family:

Mother-Father
14%
9%
13%
20%

Mother-Only
24%
15%
19%
29%

Mother-Stepfather
25%
23%
22%
29%

FIG. 10.8. Percentage of children who repeated a grade, by family type and level of parental involvement. Data are from Zill (1994).

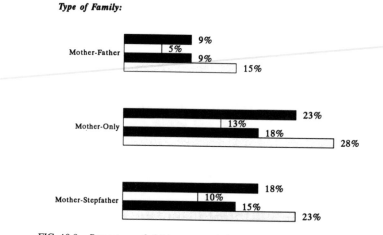

■All Levels ☐High ■Medium ☐Low

Type of Family:

Mother-Father
9%
5%
9%
15%

Mother-Only
23%
13%
18%
28%

Mother-Stepfather
18%
10%
15%
23%

FIG. 10.9. Percentage of children suspended or expelled from school, by family type and level of parental involvement. Data are from Zill (1994).

166

childrearing outside of marriage? What, if anything, can schools do to help reduce the incidence of family disruption and high-risk family formation in the future?

I make seven recommendations regarding things schools should and should not do to ameliorate the negative effects of family change on children. I follow these with three recommendations regarding longer-range efforts that schools might undertake to prevent family disruption and unwise family formation when the pupils of today become the marriage partners and parents of tomorrow. These recommendations grow out of the research findings summarized previously, but they go beyond the findings to draw on other research and my own observations and opinions on how schools can function most effectively.

Ameliorating the Negative Effects of Family Change on Individual Students

Schools Cannot Duck the Issue of Family Change. The first thing that schools clearly cannot do is to avoid the issue of family change entirely. Much as teachers and school administrators might like to consider parental conflict and family disruption to be private matters that are of no proper concern to the school, they cannot do so. As the research review demonstrated, the effects of conflict and disruption show up in the classroom in the form of student inattentiveness, noncompletion of assignments, poor performance on tests, disruption of the class, aggressive behavior toward classmates, and other manifestations. These are things that teachers, counselors, and principals must deal with if the school is to continue to function as a learning environment and if the individual student who displays the signs and symptoms of family stress is to be assisted.

It might be argued that the academic problems and misconduct of students from disrupted families could be handled without reference to the family turmoil that caused or contributed to them. This might be so, but it does not seem as productive an approach as one which also addresses the underlying family problems. Indeed, ignoring the family context might lead to actions that could aggravate parental conflict and worsen the effects of family turmoil on the student's academic career.

Students From Disrupted Families Should Not Be Treated in Stereotypical Fashion. It should be obvious from the research findings that students from single-parent families and stepfamilies are not all alike in their academic performance and classroom behavior. Although many display temporary impairments in response to family stress, most recover and go on to do as well in school as they were doing before the disruption. Likewise, the performance and behavior of students with parents who have never married is more dependent on their overall family backgrounds than on the single fact of parental nonmarriage. Thus, it is a serious mistake for teachers and school administrators to have a fixed image of students from nontraditional families and, especially, to see them all as doomed to be troublemakers and dropouts. An expectation that most will do all right and many will do just fine in school is much closer to the facts.

Schools Should Be Understanding But Maintain Standards. Teachers and school administrators should be understanding and supportive of students with disruption-related problems, but they should also maintain standards of achievement and conduct. School officials have an obligation to not let the misconduct or nonperformance of some students interfere with the learning opportunities of others. In addition, a firm but not rigid set of standards is something that many students from disrupted families seem to need. Perhaps because they feel guilty about the family situation, divorced and unmarried parents are sometimes overly indulgent in their treatment of their children, unwilling to make demands for completion of chores and homework, and too prepared to overlook transgressions of decorum and family rules. Or the parents are inconsistent in their disciplinary practices, veering unpredictably from permissiveness to punitiveness and back again (Hetherington, 1979; Forgatch et al., 1988). A school that insists on adherence to a reasonable set of rules and performance requirements can help the family to develop (or regain) a balanced regimen that is supportive of the student's emotional needs but also cultivates responsible behavior.

Ground Rules for School–Home Coordination and Communication Should Not Exacerbate Conflict Between Parents. In order to satisfy legal requirements and not get enmeshed in conflicts between divorcing or unmarried parents, schools and families need to have mutually agreed-upon ground rules covering such matters as who receives report cards and other school-to-home communications, which parent is entitled to sign permission slips authorizing the student to go on class trips, and so on. This becomes more of an issue as joint legal custody arrangements become more common. Although these ground rules are necessary, the rules should not be structured in ways that exacerbate conflict between parents. For example, sending out a duplicate set of grade advisories to both parents when they have joint legal (but not physical) custody and request it, seems like a small burden for the school to bear in order to avoid potential battles between the parents over who should receive such information.

Schools Should Not Try to Resolve Conflicts Between Parents. Although schools have a role to play in supporting parents in their childrearing tasks, there are some things that schools should clearly not try to do. One of those "don'ts" is trying to resolve conflicts between parents. If the conflict is serious enough that it is interfering with the child's academic performance, then it is certainly appropriate for school officials to urge parents to get professional help. But teachers and school administrators should not try to act as divorce mediators or family court judges themselves. School officials are not trained for such roles, nor do they have professional standing in performing these functions. Also, there are potential hazards and liabilities that schools expose themselves to in attempting to mediate between warring parents. The greatest service that a school can perform for a family in crisis is to be a good school in the traditional sense of providing good teaching and a positive learning environment for students.

Schools Should Encourage Participation by Parents From Nontraditional As Well As Traditional Families. The research reviewed previously suggests that parental involvement in school-related activities can be just as beneficial for students in single-parent families and stepfamilies as it is for students from intact mother–father families. Thus, schools should actively encourage participation by parents from all kinds of families. One of the things that schools can do in response to the changing family landscape is to take pains to insure that events and activities involving parents are not set up in ways that might discourage or embarrass unmarried or remarried parents. The school or the PTA could also plan activities that are responsive to the special concerns and interests of parents from single-parent families and stepfamilies, if sufficient interest exists among parents to support such activities.

Schools Should Be Prepared to Refer Families to Counselling Programs. School-based counselling programs for children experiencing problems as a result of their parents' separation or divorce have been developed by innovative clinicians such as Pedro-Carroll, Kalter, and others (Pedro-Carroll & Cowen, 1985; Pedro-Carroll, Cowen, Hightower, & Guare, 1986). Research has shown that such programs can be effective in reducing and preventing negative effects of family stress on school-aged children (Kalter & Schreier, 1993). Thus, schools should be prepared to refer families to such counselling programs, when such services are needed and desired by the families in question. If sufficient resources exist, school systems should offer such programs themselves.

More problematic is how to assist single-parent families and stepfamilies with older elementary or adolescent children in which parents are having difficulty maintaining control of their offspring (Patterson & Stouthamer-Loeber, 1984). The dilemma is particularly critical in inner-city schools in which out-of-control youngsters may become involved in gangs, drug trafficking, and violent crime (Caspi, Elder, & Bem, 1987; Robins, West, & Herjanic, 1975). Clinicians such as Patterson (Patterson, Reid, Jones, & Conger, 1975) and Forehand (Forehand, Wells, & Griest, 1980) developed behavioral intervention programs for assisting parents to modify deleterious interaction patterns with their adolescents that may promote or reinforce defiant and aggressive behavior (Kazdin, 1987). But when delinquent behavior patterns are too far developed, new kinds of interventions that involve parents, therapists, and school and juvenile justice officials may be needed (Patterson, DeBaryshe, & Ramsey, 1989). Applied research to develop and test the effectiveness of such interventions should be given high priority by federal, state, and private funding agencies.

Preventing Family Disruption and High-Risk Family Formation in the Future

Schools are increasingly asked to perform functions that we used to expect families or other social institutions to perform. Schools are also being called on to solve a broad array of social problems, when many public school systems are having difficulty in carrying out their basic function of educating young people. At the risk of adding to these unreasonable expectations, I conclude this chapter by suggesting three things that schools could be doing to help prevent family disruption in the future. Such efforts should not be aimed primarily at lowering the incidence of divorce or unmarried childbearing per se but at preventing the formation of multirisk families. These are families that involve not only single parenthood but low parent education levels, low incomes, parental immaturity, and negative parental behaviors such as drug or alcohol abuse. The research findings indicate that young people who grow up in these kinds of families are the ones who are most vulnerable to academic failure, classroom misconduct, and later poverty, dependency, and deviant behavior (Loeber & Dishion, 1983; McCord, McCord, & Howard, 1963; Zill & Nord, 1994).

Schools Should Strengthen Programs for the "Forgotten Half" of Students Who Are Not College Bound. The first thing that schools could do to help improve family stability in the future is to improve job training, apprenticeship, and early employment opportunities for those teenagers and young adults who are not college bound, the so-called "forgotten half" of students. The reason for emphasizing these programs is that research has clearly shown that limited employment opportunities, unstable employment, and low wages are important causes of family disruption. The lack of career opportunities is also an important reason why young people become parents when they are financially not ready to support their children. Finding ways to provide young people who are not doing well in conventional academic studies with positive career alternatives should be given a high priority by school systems.

Schools Should Not Teach That All Family Forms Are Equally Viable. A second step that schools can take that may affect family life in the future is to not teach that all family forms are equally viable. The facts that researchers have learned about how children do in different kinds of families should form the basis for what young people are taught about family life, parenting, and child development. Without exaggerating the risks, or "putting down" individuals who come from these families, teachers and counselors should be honest about the known drawbacks of single-parent families and stepfamilies. As efforts to end smoking have shown, knowledge of risks can make a difference in people's behavior. But the knowledge has to be communicated in order to have any effect.

Schools Should Teach That Unprepared Parenthood Is Unwise. A third, related step that schools should undertake is to insure that teachers and counselors communicate clearly and consistently to older students that it is unwise to have children when they are emotionally and financially unprepared to care for them. Unmarried teenage parenthood before high school graduation is not a cost-free experiment with alternative lifestyles; it is a major cause of child poverty, welfare dependency, and school failure. Schools should be making that clear to students and emphasizing that young people are doing themselves and their offspring no favors by engaging in unprepared parenthood. Simply providing young people with condoms or other contraceptive technologies without a strong, consistent message about the reasons for making use of them is much less likely to be effective.

Getting schools to implement these recommendations will not be easy, and the steps themselves will not work miracles. They will not, for instance, create jobs where none exist. But combined with efforts by other public and private institutions, such efforts may make a tangible difference in the lives of many young people, and hence have a beneficial effect on family life in the future.

REFERENCES

Allison, P. D., & Furstenberg, F. F. (1989). How marital dissolution affects children: Variations by age and sex. *Developmental Psychology, 25,* 540–549.

Amato, P. R. (1993). Children's adjustment to divorce: Theories, hypotheses, and empirical support. *Journal of Marriage and the Family, 55,* 23–38.

Amato, P. R. (1994). Life-span adjustment of children to their parents' divorce. In R. E. Behrman (Ed.), *The future of children* (Vol. 4, pp. 143–164). Los Altos, CA: Center for the Future of Children, The David and Lucile Packard Foundation.

Amato, P. R., & Keith, B. (1991a). Parental divorce and adult well-being. *Journal of Marriage and the Family, 53,* 43–58.

Amato, P. R., & Keith, B. (1991b). Parental divorce and the well-being of children: A meta analysis. *Psychological Bulletin, 110,* 26–46.

Astone, N. M., & McLanahan, S. S. (1991). Family structure, parental practices, and high school completion. *American Sociological Review, 56,* 309–320.

Astone, N. M., & McLanahan, S. S. (1994). *Family structure, residential mobility, and education: A research note.* Unpublished manuscript.

Bianchi, S., & McArthur, E. (1991). Family disruption and economic hardship: The short-run picture for children. *Current Population Reports* (Series P-70, No. 23). Washington, DC: U.S. Government Printing Office.

Caspi, A., Elder, G. H., & Bem, D. J. (1987). Moving against the world: Life course patterns of explosive children. *Developmental Psychology, 23,* 308–313.

Chase-Lansdale, P. L., & Hetherington, E. M. (1990). The impact of divorce on life-span development: Short- and long-term effects. In D. L. Featherman & R. M. Lerner (Eds.), *Life-span development and behavior* (pp. 105–150). Hillsdale, NJ: Lawrence Erlbaum Associates.

Dawson, D. A. (1991). Family structure and children's health and wellbeing: Data from the 1988 National Health Interview Survey on Child Health. *Journal of Marriage and the Family, 53,* 573–584.

Dornbusch, S. M., Carlsmith, J. M., Bushwall, S. J., Ritter, P. L., Leiderman, H., Hastoff, A. H., & Gross, R. T. (1985). Single parents, extended households, and the control of adolescents. *Child Development, 56,* 326–341.

Emery, R. E. (1982). Interparental conflict and the children of discord and divorce. *Psychological Bulletin, 92,* 310–330.

Emery, R. E. (1988). *Marriage, divorce, and children's adjustment.* Beverly Hills, CA: Sage.

Forehand, R., Wells, K., & Griest, D. (1980). An examination of the social validity of a parent training program. *Behavior Therapy, 11,* 488–502.

Forgatch, M. S., Patterson, G. R., & Skinner, J. (1988). A mediational model for the effect of divorce on antisocial behavior in boys. In E. M. Hetherington (Ed.), *The impact of divorce and step-parenting on children* (pp. 135–154). Hillsdale, NJ: Lawrence Erlbaum Associates.

Furstenberg, F. F., & Cherlin, A. J. (1991). *Divided families: What happens to children when parents part.* Cambridge, MA: Harvard University Press.

Guidubaldi, J., Perry, J. D., & Cleminshaw, H. K. (1984). The legacy of parental divorce: A nationwide study of family status and selected mediating variables on children's academic and social competencies. In B. Lahey & A. E. Kazdin (Eds.), *Advances in child psychology* (Vol. 7, pp. 109–155). New York: Plenum.

Haveman, R., Wolfe, B. L., & Spaulding, J. (1991). Educational achievement and childhood events and circumstances. *Demography, 28,* 133–158.

Hetherington, E. M. (1979). Divorce: A child's perspective. *American Psychologist, 34,* 851–858.

Hetherington, E. M., Camara, K. A., & Featherman, D. L. (1983). Achievement and intellectual functioning of children in one parent households. In J. T. Spence (Ed.), *Achievement and achievement motives* (pp. 205–284). San Francisco: Freeman.

Hetherington, E. M., Cox, M., & Cox, R. (1977). The aftermath of divorce. In J. H. Stevens, Jr., & M. Matthews (Eds.), *Mother–child, father–child relations.* Washington, DC: National Association for the Education of Young Children.

Hetherington, E. M., Cox, M., & Cox, R. (1982). Effects of divorce on parents and children. In M. Lamb (Ed.), *Nontraditional families* (pp. 233–288). Hillsdale, NJ: Lawrence Erlbaum Associates.

Hetherington, E. M., & Jodl, K. M. (1994). Stepfamilies as settings for child development. In A. Booth & J. Dunn (Eds.), *Stepfamilies: Who benefits? Who does not?* (pp. 55–79). Hillsdale, NJ: Lawrence Erlbaum Associates.

Hirschi, T. (1969). *Causes of delinquency.* Berkeley: University of California Press.

Kalter, N., & Schreier, S. (1993). School-based support groups for children of divorce. In J. E. Zins & M. J. Elias (Eds.), *Promoting student success through group interventions* (pp. 39–66). Ann Arbor, MI: Haworth.

Kazdin, A. E. (1987). Treatment of antisocial behavior in children: Current status and future directions. *Psychological Bulletin, 102,* 187–203.

Krein, S. F., & Beller, A. H. (1988). Educational attainment of children from single-parent families: Differences by exposure, gender, and race. *Demography, 25,* 221–234.

Lee, S. (1993). Family structure effects on student outcomes. In B. Schneider & J. S. Coleman (Eds.), *Parents, their children, and schools* (pp. 43–75). Boulder, CO: Westview.

Loeber, R., & Dishion, T. J. (1983). Early predictors of male delinquency: A review. *Psychological Bulletin, 94,* 68–99.

Longfellow, C. (1979). Divorce in context: Its impact on children. In G. Levinger & O. C. Moles (Eds.), *Divorce and separation: Context, causes, and consequences* (pp. 287–306). New York: Basic Books.

McCord, W., McCord, J., & Howard, A. (1963). Familial correlates of aggression in nondelinquent male children. *Journal of Abnormal and Social Psychology, 62,* 72–93.

McLanahan, S., & Sandefur, G. (1994). *Growing up with a single parent: What hurts, what helps.* Cambridge, MA: Harvard University Press.

Moore, K. A., & Snyder, N. O. (1991). Cognitive attainment among firstborn children of adolescent mothers. *American Sociological Review, 56,* 612–624.

Muller, C. (1993). Parent involvement and academic achievement: An analysis of family resources available to the child. In B. Schneider & J. S. Coleman (Eds.), *Parents, their children, and schools* (pp. 77–113). Boulder, CO: Westview.

Muller, C., & Kerbow, D. (1993). Parent involvement in the home, school, and community. In B. Schneider & J. S. Coleman (Eds.), *Parents, their children, and schools* (pp. 13–42). Boulder, CO: Westview.

National Center for Health Statistics. (1994). Annual summary of births, marriages, divorces, and deaths: United States, 1993. *Monthly Vital Statistics Report, 42*(13). Hyattsville, MD: Public Health Service.

Norton, A. J., & Miller, L. F. (1992). Marriage, divorce, and remarriage in the 1990s. *Current Population Reports* (Special Studies Series P-23–180). Washington, DC: U.S. Bureau of the Census.

Patterson, G. R., DeBaryshe, B., & Ramsey, R. (1989). A developmental perspective on antisocial behavior. *American Psychologist, 44*, 329–335.

Patterson, G. R., Reid, J. B., Jones, R. R., & Conger, R. E. (1975). *A social learning approach to family intervention: Vol. 1. Families with aggressive children.* Eugene, OR: Castalia.

Patterson, G. R., & Stouthamer-Loeber, M. (1984). The correlation of family management practices and delinquency. *Child Development, 55*, 1299–1307.

Pedro-Carroll, J., & Cowen, E. L. (1985). The Children of Divorce Intervention Project: An investigation of the efficacy of a school-based prevention program. *Journal of Consulting and Clinical Psychology, 53*, 603–611.

Pedro-Carroll, J., Cowen, E. L., Hightower, A., & Guare, J. (1986). Preventive intervention with children of divorce: A replication study. *American Journal of Community Psychology, 14*, 277–290.

Peterson, J. L., & Zill, N. (1986). Marital disruption, parent–child relationships, and behavioral problems in children. *Journal of Marriage and the Family, 48*, 295–307.

Robins, L. N., West, P. A., & Herjanic, B. L. (1975). Arrests and delinquency in two generations: A study of Black urban families and their children. *Journal of Child Psychology and Psychiatry, 16*, 125–140.

Sandefur, G. D., McLanahan, S. S., & Wojtkiewicz, R. A. (1992). The effects of parental marital status during adolescence on high school graduation. *Social Forces, 71*, 999–1017.

Schneider, B., & Coleman, J. S. (Eds.). (1993). *Parents, their children, and schools.* Boulder, CO: Westview.

Thomson, E,, Hanson, T. L., & McLanahan, S. (in press). Family structure and child well-being: Economic resources vs. parental behaviors. *Social Forces.*

Ventura, S. J., Martin, J. A., Taffel, S. M., Mathews, T. J., & Clarke, S. C. (1994). Advance report of final natality statistics, 1992. *Monthly Vital Statistics Report, 43*(5), suppl. Hyattsville, MD: National Center for Health Statistics.

Wallerstein, J. S. (1991). The long-term effects of divorce on children: A review. *Journal of the Academy of Child Adolescent Psychiatry, 30*(3), 349–360.

Wojtkiewicz, R. A. (1993). Simplicity and complexity in the effects of parental structure and high school graduates. *Demography, 30*(4), 701–717.

Zill, N. (1988). Behavior, achievement, and health problems among children in stepfamilies: Findings from a national survey of child health. In E. M. Hetherington & J. Arasteh (Eds.), *The impact of divorce, single parenting and stepparenting on children* (pp. 325–368). Hillsdale, NJ: Lawrence Erlbaum Associates.

Zill, N. (1994). Understanding why children in stepfamilies have more learning and behavior problems than children in nuclear families. In A. Booth & J. Dunn (Eds.), *Stepfamilies: Who benefits? Who does not?* (pp. 97–106). Hillsdale, NJ: Lawrence Erlbaum Assocites.

Zill, N., & Coiro, M. J. (1991). [Unpublished analysis of data from the 1988 National Health Interview Survey on Child Heath.] Washington, DC: Child Trends.

Zill, N., Morrison, D. R., & Coiro, M. J. (1993). Long-term effects of parental divorce on parent–child relationships, adjustment, and achievement in young adulthood. *Journal of Family Psychology,* 7(1), 91–103.

Zill, N., & Nord, C. W. (1994). *Running in place: How American families are faring in a changing economy and an individualistic society.* Washington, DC: Child Trends.

Zill, N., & Schoenborn, C. A. (1990). Health of our nation's children: Developmental, learning, and emotional problems. United States, 1988. *Advance Data from Vital and Health Statistics, 190,* 1–18.

11

Changes in Families and Trends in Schooling

Robert D. Mare
University of Wisconsin–Madison

Nicholas Zill's chapter (this volume, chapter 10) highlights the relationships between important dimensions of family and household structure and education-related behaviors. The chapter considers a number of outcomes, including behavioral problems exhibited by children while in school, such as suspensions, grade repeats, scores on scholastic aptitude/achievement tests, and high school dropout. Zill's approach to family structure is to compare children raised in mother–father households to those raised in several household forms that result from divorce or childbearing outside of marriage, including children raised by never-married mothers, by formerly married mothers, and by mothers who have remarried. Using a variety of high-quality sets of nationwide data that were collected in the 1980s, he demonstrates large differences in education-related outcomes among children and teenagers raised in alternative family types. He also shows that although these differences are considerably reduced when other sociodemographic characteristics are controlled, substantial differences remain. Zill considers a number of possible interpretations of the links between family structure and educational outcomes and provides a pointed critique of recent commentaries on family structure effects that interpret the effects of family structure as being largely the result of the economic hardships experienced by children who are raised in single-parent families. The strengths of Zill's chapter lie in its demonstration of family and household effects on schooling across a variety of high quality sets of data and in providing a balanced assessment of the existence and magnitude of these effects. Zill puts the estimated negative effects of being raised outside of a mother–father household in a sensible perspective. The estimated effects are large, statistically robust, and well worth worrying about. They are not so large, however, as to overshadow the effects of other major social determinants of educational success and failure, especially the socioeconomic characteristics of the families in which children are raised.

Zill has summed up what is known about the effects of family structure on student achievement. He has drawn on not only the analyses that he reports in the present chapter and his other work in this area, but also on the big body of research on this topic that has poured forth from many other researchers during the past decade. In this discussion I point out some of the things that we *do not* know and where further research might be directed. In the balance of these comments I emphasize some neglected areas of research on the links between family and school. In keeping with my expertise as a demographer and student of social stratification, I focus on aggregate and macrolevel aspects of family and household-related demographic trends and on their implications for educational performance and educational inequality.[1]

AGGREGATE IMPLICATIONS OF FAMILY AND HOUSEHOLD CHANGES

The poignant testimonials of teachers and school officials, as well as many journalistic accounts, emphasize that today's teachers are required to do many more things than teach. Teachers have become counselors, nutritionists, and law enforcement officers, as well as sponsors of extracurricular activities. The time spent in these roles cuts into academic instruction but is unavoidable given the needs of today's students. Many of these accounts make two points, either explicitly or implicitly, that are relevant to the issues discussed by Zill: (a) The extra demands placed on teachers are attributable in no small part to the inability of students' families to meet their needs for social support, and (b) this is a much more serious problem than it was in the past. Zill provides some support for point a inasmuch as he shows that children who are not raised in mother–father households are more likely to have poor academic performance and conduct problems and that their parents have a lower level of involvement in their schooling.

Point b presumes an answer to the question, "How is changing family structure affecting school outcomes?" Despite the title of Zill's chapter, neither it nor

---

[1]An important set of issues that I do not address concerns the methodology of obtaining unbiased estimates of the effects of family structure on educational outcomes. These issues include nonrandom selection of children into alternative family types, the possibly confounding effects of variables that are omitted from the models, the potential simultaneous relationship between family structure and some child outcomes, and the proper specification of the family structure effect. For a good discussion and an imaginative approach to the problem of selection bias in the assessment of family structure effects, see Manski, Sandefur, McLanahan, and Powers (1992).

much of the literature to which it refers reports a direct examination of the ways in which changes in the distribution of family types in the population have induced changes in educational outcomes. Rather, the analysis of change is left implicit. For changing family and household structure to bring about changes in educational outcomes, four conditions must be met:

1. The educational outcomes for each cohort of children must vary systematically across children who have been raised in alternative family structures.
2. The effects of family and household structure must be roughly similar across cohorts of children.
3. The distribution of family and household structures must change across cohorts of children to a substantial degree.
4. Changes in other characteristics of children or the environments that they experience must not offset the effects of changes in family structure.

The literature on the effects of family and household structure on educational outcomes, including the results discussed by Zill, provides considerable support for condition 1. Relatively little research focuses on condition 2, but the relationships reported by Zill have been reported for a number of distinct sets of data that have been collected from the 1960s into the 1990s. Although a well-designed study that focuses explicitly on whether the effects of family and household structure have been stable over recent cohorts of children is still needed, it seems likely that changes in these effects are small relative to their absolute magnitudes. We do know that the distribution of household structures has changed over time (condition 3) and certainly in a direction that implies more behavioral problems in schools and lower academic achievement (e.g., Bumpass & Sweet, 1992; Garfinkel & McLanahan, 1986). Yet whether these changes are large enough, given the effects of family structure within each cohort, to induce major changes in school-related behavior problems or academic achievement is not known.

Most problematic is condition 4, namely whether changes in family and household structure are big enough relative to changes in other aspects of the lives of children that also affect their educational success. Among other aspects of family and household environments that affect education-related outcomes include parents' educational attainments, family income, number of siblings, and whether or not mothers are employed. During the past several decades, cohorts of children have changed considerably in the types of family and household circumstances that they have experienced. The growth of female-headed households is but one of these changes. Another important change is a dramatic increase in the average educational attainment of parents. Between 1980 and 1990, for example, the percentage of children whose mothers had at least some college education increased from about 30% to about 40% (Mare, 1995). The proportion of children who have large numbers of siblings has declined during this period, whereas the proportion of young children whose mothers are employed has sharply increased. During the 1980s, average family incomes were stable, but the proportion of children whose parents had very high or very low incomes increased sharply, whereas those raised in middle-income families declined. This latter trend reflects a population-wide drift toward increased income inequality over the period.

The effects of these trends on educational attainment and other school-related outcomes are only partially understood and are certainly complex. Parents' educational attainment positively affects most desirable educational outcomes, and the large increases in average parental attainment have been a strong force toward improving the educational performance of children (e.g., Mare, 1995). Educational attainment varies inversely with the number of siblings (e.g., Blake, 1989), and the trend toward smaller families tends, at the margin, to improve most education-related outcomes, although recent changes in family size may have been too small to induce much change in the average performance of children. The effects of family income on average attainment are ambiguous, inasmuch as there is a growing representation of the least and most advantaged students. It does seem clear, however, that change in the income distribution may have widened the variance in educational outcomes, a point to which I return later.

Taken together, these changes may have more than offset the aggregate deleterious effects of changing family and household structure. We do know that on most educational outcomes, conditions on balance improved during the 1980s. Rates of high school dropout declined, average levels of completed attainment increased, and, for most age groups, performance on standardized tests of academic achievement improved, especially for members of traditionally disadvantaged racial and ethnic minorities. These trends are partly attributable to the favorable sociodemographic trends that I have mentioned, although they may also be linked to changes in educational policies, including those related to early childhood education, teacher compensation, and coursework requirements (Mare, 1995). By the same token, hard-pressed educational practitioners, who are convinced that the growth of female-headed households is a major source of (the perceived) worsening classroom conditions, may well ask how badly off they would be in the absence of these offsetting demographic and policy trends. When we get to the bottom of it, however, we do not know how these various trends have combined to produce observed trends in educational outcomes. As Zill points out, we now have almost a dozen national-level surveys with which one can analyze the effects of family structure and other factors on educational achievement. Although these surveys were concentrated in the 1980s, good data for at least some important outcomes are available for at least the last 30 years. Although these data have often not been collected with an eye to exactly replicated measurement over time, they are nonetheless suitable for answering the sorts of aggregate questions about social change that I discuss in this section. Instead of only analyzing these surveys as independent studies of cross-section relationships, we should be combining them in creative ways to assess the actual effects of changes in family and household structure.

WHAT ABOUT EDUCATIONAL INEQUALITY?

In considering educational outcomes, it is natural first to do as I have just done, and ask whether changes in family and household structure and other factors affect average *levels* of student achievement, problem behaviors, and ultimate attainment. Of equal significance, however, is whether these trends affect the *distribution* (that is, inequality) of educational outcomes (e.g., Gamoran & Mare, 1989). Educational inequality bears upon the organization of schools, lifetime patterns of inequality within cohorts of children, and the distribution of family advantages and disadvantages in subsequent generations. Yet little, if any, of the literature on the effects of family structure pays attention to issues of educational distribution. Despite the lack of research on the effects of trends in family and household structure on the distribution of educational outcomes, there is considerable reason to expect such effects to be present.

Inequality in an index of student achievement (whether for problem behaviors, scholastic achievement, or ultimate educational attainment) depends on the variability of the various family factors that affect the level of achievement plus the *covariance* (i.e., the degree of association) among these family factors. Obviously, when parents' educational attainment is highly variable, student outcomes are more variable than when parental schooling is more equally distributed. Perhaps less obviously, when parental educational attainment is positively (negatively) associated with another family factor that favorably (unfavorably) affects student achievement, such as the existence of a mother–father family, student achievement will be more unequal than when parents' schooling and other family factors are independent. Households headed by unmarried or divorced mothers tend to have lower incomes and lower levels of parental schooling than mother–father families, indicating that, within a cohort, the covariances among family factors magnify educational inequality. In assessing the consequences of family change, however, the issue is whether these covariances have grown and thereby engendered increases in inequality of educational outcomes. Some recent commentators have suggested that the growth of female-headed families has occurred disproportionately for women who are more poorly educated and less able, increasing inequality among children from varying socioeconomic backgrounds (Herrnstein & Murray, 1994). My own view is that this is an interesting and researchable hypothesis on which creative and careful studies still need to be done. The many large-scale national surveys of children and families that have been conducted in recent decades should be used to assess trends in educational inequality and in the joint distributions of family and household structure and other factors that affect children's educational success.

A BROADER AND DEEPER VIEW OF FAMILY
AND HOUSEHOLD STRUCTURE

In considering family structure, Zill focuses on whether a child is raised in a mother–father household or a household in which the child's mother is never-married, formerly married, or remarried. As he acknowledges, this is not the only important change in American families, but it is the one that has stimulated the greatest amount of public discussion. In thinking about the effects of family and household on student achievement, however, one should keep in mind some of the other changes in family patterns that may have also altered the level and distribution of student achievement. These other changes are of two types: (a) changes in the demographic processes that underpin changes in the frequency of one- and two-parent households and (b) changes in other aspects of family structure not reflected in the marital status of the mother. Although none of these trends by themselves is as dramatic and unambiguous in its import for student achievement as the growth of single-parent households, it is important to keep them in mind.

The classification of family types considered by Zill and others, which is based on the marital status of the mother, is a simplification of a complex set of demographic processes and structures. For example, children may vary greatly in the amount of time that they spend in a single-parent household and in the ages at which they have this experience. They may also vary in how many marital transitions their mothers experience and in the timing of those transitions during their childhood (Haveman & Wolfe, 1994; Wu & Martinson, 1992). The sorts of family and household structure effects documented in this chapter are robust and basic conclusions remain unchanged when more complex specifications of the effects of single-parent status are used (McLanahan & Sandefur, 1994; Wojtkiewicz, 1993). Not all of the complexities have been fully studied, however, and one should keep them in mind when interpreting family and household structure effects. In particular, there is reason to believe that the demographic meaning of mother-only households has shifted in recent years.

One aspect of household structure that is captured by Zill's classification is the distinction between children born to unmarried mothers and the children of formerly married women. With delays in marriage and the rise in fertility to unmarried women, children raised by never-married mothers have become a significantly larger fraction of all children who are not living in mother–father families (e.g., Bumpass & Raley, 1993). One potential implication of this trend, not observable in the sort of cross-section analyses that Zill presents, is that mother–father households have become a more select population than they were in the past. On average, they consist of older parents and may include fewer conflict-ridden marriages. This suggests that the observed advantage of mother–father families may be growing, albeit for reasons of selectivity rather than a growing structural advantage to that family structure (Furstenberg & Cherlin, 1991).

What is not fully captured by Zill's classification are the family and household relationships experienced by children who are raised by unmarried or formerly married mothers. As age at marriage has increased and rates of marriage have declined, rates of cohabitation between unmarried persons have increased and an increasing number of children are born to cohabiting couples (Bumpass & Raley, 1993). Moreover, many formerly married mothers are also cohabiting and thus exposing their children to such relationships. We know relatively little about how these kinds of family environments compare to those provided by single mothers who are not cohabiting in their effects on children's achievement. Nor do we know much about how the effects of the environments provided by cohabiting biological fathers compare with those provided by other male cohabitors.

A further complication to the structure of mother-only households is that a large proportion of fatherless children are born or reside in their grandparents' homes. During the 1970s and 1980s, more than one third of single mothers spent some time living in their parental household after giving birth; about two thirds of women who gave birth before their first marriage spent some time living with their parents (Bumpass & Raley, 1993). We know relatively little about the extent to which these experiences modify the disadvantages suffered by children in mother-only households. These patterns suggest that speculations about the home environment of such children need to take account of the more complex web of kin that some mother-only households provide.

In addition to the subtle demographic processes that underpin the family types considered by Zill and other researchers on the effects of family structure on educational outcomes, the family has undergone other changes that may have affected children's academic achievement in complex ways:

1. One important change is in the size of families, brought about by secular reductions in fertility (Blake, 1989; Hauser, 1989). Given the large negative effect of size of sibship on student achievement, the greater preponderance of only and two-child families in recent cohorts may, *ceteris paribus*, be more conducive to student achievement. At the same time, however, a reduction in the number of siblings may, under some conditions, be unfavorable to intellectual development. Some theorists point to the capacity of children to learn from their older siblings and to learn by serving as teachers to their younger siblings (e.g., Zajonc, 1976). Although the empirical support for these types of mechanisms is limited (Retherford & Sewell, 1991), they are nonetheless potentially important aspects of family change.

2. Family structure includes not only the marital statuses of adult members of the family but also their patterns of work and time allocation more generally. A dramatic change in the lives of children during the past five decades has been the increasing proportion of mothers who are employed. Changes in the amount of time that mothers devote to paid work as well as the quality of employment that they experience have changed the character of early child care that is pro-

vided, the amount of direct parental supervision that children receive, and the quality of interaction between mothers and children. The cross-section and longitudinal effects of these factors on child development and student achievement are complex and do not point unambiguously to either a favorable or an unfavorable trend in educational outcomes (Parcel & Menaghan, 1994). They are nonetheless a key aspect of family change in recent decades.

3. Among households that include married couples, family structure also encompasses patterns of assortative mating between men and women with varying socioeconomic characteristics. Parental resemblance on socioeconomic characteristics has a major effect of the level and range of cultural and socioeconomic environments that a child experiences. At the individual level, children whose parents are both highly educated and hold well-paying jobs are clearly more advantaged than children who have only one parent with these characteristics (and, of course, compared to children who have only one parent at all). At the aggregate level, moreover, tighter resemblance between spouses increases the inequality in family environments across children from more and less socioeconomically advantaged families. As I noted previously, inequality depends on not only the variance of parental characteristics but also the degree to which several parental characteristics are associated. During the past five decades, there has been a significant increase in the association between mothers' and fathers' educational attainments, owing to trends in age at leaving school, age at marriage, and women's employment (Mare, 1991). For mother–father families, this trend has altered the socioeconomic structure of families and, *ceteris paribus*, augurs increasing educational inequality in the next generation.[2]

THE NEED FOR MODELS AND THE EFFECT
OF PARENTAL INCOME

All of the family and household structure effects reported in Zill's chapter are based on elementary regression equations that provide net coefficients for the classification of family types and other predictors of student behavior and achievement. These models are serviceable for describing basic patterns in the data, but they have weaknesses when it comes to drawing inferences about the causal processes that underpin these patterns. In the absence of a more explicit model about the ways that the several determinants of student achievement work together, it is hazardous to make inferences about the relative importance of these

---

[2]A potentially offsetting factor to the increasing covariance of mothers' and fathers' schooling is the decreasing educational inequality of each parent considered separately. As average levels of parental schooling have increased, they have approached a ceiling that results in some compression of the distribution of mothers' schooling and fathers' schooling (Mare, 1991, 1995).

influences or policy inferences that might be drawn from the results. This point can be seen most clearly in Zill's commentary on the effects of income on student achievement. Zill makes several useful observations about the limitations of interpretations of the effects of family and household structure that focus solely on the economic hardships suffered by children raised in female-headed households. In suggesting that other factors—for example, parental involvement—may be at least as important, however, his argument is weakened by a lack of specification of the way that income may affect child outcomes. His Table 10.1 (see p. 158) shows that family income has a strong effect on parental involvement. If parental involvement is one of the factors that transmits the effect of income on student achievement, then it is hard to make the claim that parental income is a more or less important determinant of achievement than involvement. Rather, an increase in income will raise parental involvement and independently improve child outcomes. The total effect of income is the combination of these direct and indirect effects. Although it is possible to make this interpretation of Zill's calculations, the discussion in the chapter seems more concerned with emphasizing the effect of one variable at the expense of another. A more explicit specification of the model would clear up this ambiguity.

Zill is sharply critical of researchers, such as McLanahan and Sandefur (1994), who have drawn policy inferences from the strong income effect. It is unfair to characterize their position as "it's all income" inasmuch as they say that only about 50% of the outcomes that they study can be attributed to income differences among household types. McLanahan and Sandefur did emphasize income redistribution as a tool for remedying the hardships borne by children raised in single-parent households. Although they were not explicit on this point, I suspect that their emphasis on such policies is not motivated only by the size of the income effect. Rather, they regarded income redistribution as a feasible policy instrument. The historic successes of Social Security show that this is indeed an effective measure. Although such redistributive efforts may be unpopular in today's political environment, we know more about how to make families better off economically than we do about how to directly change parental childrearing practices. Indeed, as McLanahan and Sandefur pointed out, reducing economic hardship may be an effective way of changing parents' behavior toward their children.

ACKNOWLEDGMENTS

While preparing this chapter, the author was supported by grants from the University of Wisconsin-Madison, the National Science Foundation, and the Office of the Assistant Secretary for Planning and Evaluation, U.S. Department of Health and Human Services, to the Institute for Research on Poverty. The author is grateful to Judith A. Seltzer for helpful comments on an earlier draft.

REFERENCES

Blake, J. (1989). *Family size and achievement.* Berkeley: University of California Press.

Bumpass, L. L., & Raley, R. K. (1993, April). *Redefining single-parent families: Cohabitation and changing family reality.* Paper presented at the annual meeting of the Population Association of America, Cincinnati, OH.

Bumpass, L. L., & Sweet, J. A. (1992). *Family experiences across the life course: Differences by cohort, education, and race/ethnicity.* NSFH Working Paper No. 42. National Survey of Families and Households, University of Wisconsin-Madison.

Furstenberg, F. F., & Cherlin, A. J. (1991). *Divided families: What happens to children when parents part.* Cambridge, MA: Harvard University Press.

Gamoran, A., & Mare, R. D. (1989). Secondary school tracking and stratification: Compensation, reinforcement, or neutrality? *American Journal of Sociology, 94,* 1146–1183.

Garfinkel, I., & McLanahan, S. (1986). *Single mothers and their children: A new American dilemma.* Washington, DC: The Urban Institute.

Hauser, R. M. (1989). Review of Judith Blake, "Family size and achievement." *Population and Development Review, 15,* 561–567.

Haveman, R., & Wolfe, B. (1994). *Succeeding generations: On the effects of investments in children.* New York: Russell Sage Foundation.

Herrnstein, R. J., & Murray, C. (1994). *The bell curve: Intelligence and class structure in American life.* New York: The Free Press.

Manski, C. F., Sandefur, G., McLanahan, S., & Powers, D. (1992). Alternative estimates of the effect of family structure during adolescence on high school graduation. *Journal of the American Statistical Association, 87,* 25–37.

Mare, R. D. (1991). Five decades of educational assortative mating. *American Sociological Review, 56,* 15–32.

Mare, R. D. (1995). Changes in educational attainment, school enrollment, and skill levels. In R. Farley (Ed.), *State of the Union: America in the 1990s. Vol. 1: Economic trends* (pp. 155–213). New York: Russell Sage Foundation.

McLanahan, S., & Sandefur, G. (1994). *Growing up with a single parent: What hurts, what helps.* Cambridge, MA: Harvard University Press.

Parcel, T. L., & Menaghan, E. G. (1994). *Parents' jobs and children's lives.* New York: Aldine de Gruyter.

Retherford, R. D., & Sewell, W. H. (1991). Birth order and intelligence: Further tests of the confluence model. *American Sociological Review, 56,* 145–158.

Wojtkiewicz, R. A. (1993). Simplicity and complexity in the effects of parental structure on high school graduation. *Demography, 30,* 701–717.

Wu, L., & Martinson, B. (1992). Family structure and the risk of a premarital birth. *American Sociological Review, 58,* 210–231.

Zajonc, R. B. (1976). Family configuration and intelligence. *Science, 192,* 227–236.

12

▼▼▼▼▼▼▼

Family Composition, Family Interaction, and Children's Academic and Behavior Problems: Interpreting the Data

Elizabeth G. Menaghan
Ohio State University

Zill (this volume, chap. 10) uses data from several major United States data sets to summarize very clearly the evidence that variations in current family composition are linked to variations in current child outcomes. He considers both academic performance and behavior problems and presents evidence that children living with their two biological parents currently fare better on average than children in other common family arrangements—including mother–stepfather families and mothers rearing children alone. He draws attention to the need to control background factors that may be correlated with family income and investigates several mediating pathways by which these family composition differences in child outcomes are produced. In explaining mediating factors, Zill mentions parental conflict and parents' emotional adjustment but devotes most of his discussion to family income and parent–child interaction; he argues that although the poorer economic circumstances of mother-only families help to explain some of the observed differences in child outcomes, these income differences do not go far in explaining the worse outcomes of mother–stepfather families. Zill emphasizes the need to consider the extent to which differences in family interaction patterns, parental investments, and parental involvement may account for differences in family outcomes; he summarizes national evidence suggesting both that families with varying composition differ, on average, on parent–child relationships and parental involvement in school-related activities and that these factors are important in affecting children's outcomes.

Zill argues that "we need to pay attention to what actually happens inside nontraditional families that may put the children in those families at educational risk" (p. 162). In addition, we need to pay attention to such processes in *all* families, traditional as well as nontraditional. The data he summarizes show that higher levels of parental involvement at school, for example, are associated with better student outcomes for children from all types of families. More generally, we need to better distinguish the antecedents and correlates of current family circumstances from the consequences of those circumstances and specify the conditions under which these consequences are most benign and most damaging. I organize my own comments around three major issues: first, issues of selection effects—that is, the extent to which current differences in both processes and outcomes may be reflecting other, antecedent differences between adult family members; second, the need to consider both work and family conditions in our models; and third, the complexities embedded in the measurement and meaning of family composition. I then briefly comment on some of Zill's recommendations for schools, focusing on his suggestions regarding what schools should teach children about the risks and benefits of specific family arrangements.

ANTECEDENTS OF FAMILY COMPOSITION

A major difficulty in efforts to attribute causal status to current living arrangements is the competing hypothesis that such linkages may be largely spurious. Human capital arguments draw attention to the differences in intelligence, initiative, educational attainment, physical health, and social competencies that shape individuals' prospects in the labor force and in family life. Individuals are not randomly assigned to occupations or to marital statuses, and observed differences between individuals who are also in differing occupational and family circumstances may reflect such pre-existing differences as much or more than they reflect causal effects of those conditions themselves. Further, selection effects are not merely due to differences among individuals. Social stratification arguments also point to average *group* differences in opportunities and obstacles.

The unobserved variables that lead to exit from high school without a diploma or exit from college without a bachelor's degree, to an early marriage or pregnancy, or to an unfortunate partner choice may explain later outcomes as much or more than the subsequent occupational conditions or marital status that we observe. Although it is unlikely that selection into more or less stressful contests completely "explains" outcomes independent of the social stressors themselves, we *are* likely to overestimate the effects of social circumstances if we do not take antecedent factors into account. In addition, variations in individual and family vulnerability are likely to *interact* with social stressors, with the adverse effects of difficult current conditions more powerful for adults with fewer resources. Conversely, the psychosocial and interpersonal strengths that adults can bring to stressful situations make a difference in the way their children are affected. It is critical to control for individual characteristics and resources as well as membership in disadvantaged ethnic groups, and to evaluate potential interactions between current circumstances and individual resources, when trying to assess the causal impacts of family and economic factors on families and individual lives.

A major contribution of Zill's chapter is his summary of data analyses that *do* control for some of the major confounds—mother's educational attainment and race/ethnicity. It is noteworthy that elevated risks for children not living with their two biological parents persist even after such controls. And although they do not formally test interactions between education and ethnicity and family composition, their data suggest that family composition differences hold within all education levels and ethnic groups.

Even these studies, however, do not control for differences in age at child-bearing; mother's own cognitive skills; maternal attitudes/resources such as self-esteem, sense of mastery, or planfulness (Clausen, 1991); or maternal propensities toward antisocial and risk-taking behavior. Zill does refer to such variables and suggests that maternal aptitudes, attitudes, and behavior are likely to have their effect on the next generation's school problems and misconduct via *genetic* transmission. This hardly seems like the only possible or even the most plausible pathway by which such characteristics affect children. He himself refers to the possibility that such variables may contribute to marital instability and nonmarital childbearing as well as to later maternal earnings (reflecting selection processes), and others have noted that these characteristics are linked to more positive mother–child interaction as well (Menaghan, 1994; Menaghan & Parcel, 1991; Patterson, DeBaryshe, & Ramsey, 1989; see also Moore & Snyder, 1991). It is important to consider how such variables may qualify our claims regarding the causal impacts of family arrangements.

CHANGING OCCUPATIONAL AND FAMILY CIRCUMSTANCES

In evaluating the changes in family arrangements that have occurred over the last 50 years, I argue that we need to consider the extensive changes in employment and occupational opportunities that have also occurred over the same time period (see also Menaghan & Parcel, 1990; Parcel & Menaghan, 1994). Examining the composition of family households with children, it is apparent that there are fewer biological fathers present and more new husbands and partners who are biologically unrelated to at least some of the children living there. On a daily basis, there are also fewer mothers there, because of the large increase in labor force involvement of mothers with young children. Despite increasing proportions of mothers in the labor force, there has been only limited change in the type of work they do or in the economic rewards of typical women's jobs; thus, although more mothers are working, they are not likely to be able to provide an adequate family income. As many manufacturing jobs have moved to other countries, young men's earnings prospects have also deteriorated, and the real earnings of young men with limited educations have diminished over the last decade. These two sets of trends are not unrelated: As Zill points out at the very end of his chapter, "Research has clearly shown that limited employment opportunities, unstable employment, and low wages are important causes of family disruption" (p. 170). These economic problems also discourage marital formation (Schor & Menaghan, in press) and encourage marital disruption (South, 1985).

These changes in men's and women's labor force participation and in their family composition also reflect in part the profound cultural shifts in normative male and female rights and obligations. Thompson and Walker (1989) commented on the uneven pace of these gender shifts, with men registering only small increases in household labor despite women's increasing hours in paid work. Hochschild (1989; see also Lennon & Rosenfield, 1994) documented the tensions between spouses that this "stalled revolution" fosters, and certainly the ambiguities and resentments surrounding contemporary divisions of labor within households contribute both to family conflict and to disruption of relationships. Continuing gender-linked inequality in wages and in household labor fuels conflict at the level of individual households. These trends help call attention to the fact that family composition, observed at a single point in time, is not simply an exogenous variable having effects on other outcomes but is itself dependent on other factors.

Just as it is the quality of parenting, not simply family status, that matters for children, it is not simply employment status but also the quality of employment that matters. Work socialization arguments such as those proposed by Kohn and Schooler (1983) suggest that work conditions that permit greater autonomy and increase adults' sense of mastery and competence will have positive effects on how parents treat their children. Conversely, work that is routinized, heavily supervised, and low in autonomy and substantive complexity produces a sense of powerlessness and alienation that both colors beliefs about the possibility of control in other aspects of life and arouses psychological distress (see also Mirowsky & Ross, 1989). If we compare two mothers who have the same education, income, family composition, and family size, we find that the mother who is working in an occupation that gives her greater opportunity to solve problems and to work at a variety of tasks provides more support to her children at home. She provides a greater range of stimulating materials and is warmer in her interaction. Conversely, the mother worn down by repetitive routine work seems less available to her children and less able to assist their development (Menaghan & Parcel, 1991). Thus, family interaction, investments, and involvement with children are not dependent only (or even mostly) on family compositional differences but reflect the effects of the full array of familial resources and vulnerabilities. This fuller array includes the intellectual and psychosocial resources discussed previously that affect family patterns, parents' employment status, and the quality of their employment. These employment factors affect the quality of the relations among the adults in family households, as well as the income streams on which families can depend (Menaghan, 1991). All of these contribute to what parents do—and not necessarily in a straightforward way—and need to be considered jointly.

Over the last few years, and with a range of collaborators including Kowaleski-Jones, Mott, Parcel, and Rogers, I have tried to bring these differing strands of research together in investigating the effects of work and family circumstances on children's home environments and on their academic and social outcomes. All of these studies have taken advantage of the rich information on both mothers and children available in the Child–Mother datasets of the National Longitudinal Surveys of Youth, which include annual interviews with these mothers since 1979 and biennial assessments of their children since 1986 (Baker & Mott, 1989).

One example of the complexities in such relationships is a study I recently completed with Parcel (Menaghan & Parcel, 1995). This study examined changes in the quality of children's family environments as a function of changes in family and occupational conditions over a 2-year period for parents with young children (5 to 8 years old at the second time point). We used an overall global measure of the quality of children's home environments that embraces parents' provision of intellectual stimulation and support, warmth and responsiveness in mother–child interaction, and a safe and organized physical environment. All analyses controlled for parents' background and education, maternal ethnicity, child gender, and child health. We found that, on average, persistent nonmarriage, disruption of marriage, and the birth of additional children were all associated with a decline in the quality of home environments. These negative effects of nonmarriage are consistent with the data that Zill summarizes. But we also examined interactive effects and found that the negative effect of remaining unmarried varied depending on mothers' employment status and the quality of her employment: Effects were more positive for mothers employed at higher wages and more negative for unmarried mothers who remained without employment at both time points. In fact, for mothers whose wage levels were high, remaining unmarried had no significant negative impact on the changing quality of their children's home environments. (Defined as one standard deviation above the sample mean, "high wages" were $ 9.50 per hour, implying annual 1988 earnings of $19,760 if mothers worked full time, year round.) The combination of persistent single status and persistent nonemployment had more negative consequences than either of these statuses considered alone: Mothers both persistently unmarried and persistently nonemployed experienced a decline in home environments that was more than three times that experienced on average by other persistently unmarried mothers. Thus, this study suggests that the effects of single motherhood on children's everyday family environments are contingent of the fact and quality of employment.

In the second study (Menaghan, Kowaleski-Jones, & Mott, 1994) we focused on somewhat older children (10 through 14 years old in 1990), an age period in which behavior problems and school difficulties have increasingly serious consequences for adult well-being (McLanahan & Bumpass, 1988). We considered how difficult family conditions, including larger numbers of children, fewer adults, and greater conflict between parents, as well as overall family economic pressures and parents' occupational circumstances, including employment status, occupational complexity, and work hours, affected family interaction (cognitive stimulation, emotional warmth, and active parental negotiation of family rules and involvement with school performance) and in turn children's academic problems (tapped by low class standing, being behind in grade, and taking remedial classes) and social difficulties (tapped by maternal reports of behavior problems).

All the children studied lived with their biological mothers; we distinguished mothers living alone or with female relatives, those living with the child's biological father, and those living with a husband or partner who was not the study child's biological father. For both of the latter groups, we also measured the quality of the partner relationship, as indicated by the frequency of disagreements and positive interactions. All models controlled for mothers' early resources (her self-concept and her cognitive skills), measured a decade earlier, because these relatively enduring attributes of the mother were hypothesized to have influenced her current economic and family circumstances and to continue to influence her interaction with her children. All models also controlled for mother's age and ethnicity as well as child's age, gender, and birth weight. Thus, in contrast to many studies of family composition, we included both spouses and male partners who were living with the children and controlled for marital quality, employment status, and occupational quality, as well as maternal cognitive and psychosocial resources. We also expanded on prior literature by explicitly modeling plausible interactions among maternal background resources, social stressors, and family interaction patterns. And, unlike the studies of parent involvement by McLanahan and Sandefur (1994) noted by Zill, which could not account simultaneously for both parent activities and family income, we could control for family income adequacy when considering the effects of family interaction patterns in our models.

Focusing here on effects of current family composition, we found that variations from mother–father families did have some consequences, but these consequences were not uniform. For example, mothers rearing children alone, whom we anticipated would be most disadvantaged, did provide lower levels of cognitive support overall, but they expressed less warmth toward their children only when income adequacy was low, and they were less active in structure and involvement only when the number of children was high.

For both mother–father and mother–stepfather families, troubled partner relationships significantly reduced parental cognitive and emotional supports and increased the likelihood of children's academic difficulties. This is consistent with prior research that levels of conflict in two-parent families significantly undermine the quality of children's lives. Compared to mother–father families, we did observe some mother–stepfather differences: Although they provided similar levels of intellectual stimulation and active structuring, they were lower on average in warmth, and the children in these families tended to have higher levels of academic and behavior problems. However, warmth differences were sharply reduced when mothers had higher cognitive skills and were employed, and problem levels were less when family size was small and the parents were more actively engaged in setting and negotiating rules and intervening when school problems arose. These qualifications suggest that negative effects are not inevitable to this family arrangement, which is likely to be part of an increasing number of children's lives, but can be significantly diminished by other factors, including the interaction patterns that parents establish.

FAMILY COMPOSITION: SOME COMPLICATIONS

In our own studies and those of other researchers, we observed a wide range of definitions of family structure. Some researchers considered current composition for children of various ages, whereas others focused on family structure caught at some specific age, typically age 14 or 16. These different measurement rules may yield different findings. In addition, it is not always clear whose point of view is taken in classifying families. If we characterize families from the point of the view of the individual children in a family, the same family may be classified differently depending on which child is the focal child. That mothers are currently in their first marriage does not mean that the spouse is the father of all of the children studied, particularly for women who married for the first time some time after the birth of children. Men may be fathers to some of the children and stepfathers to others. Thus, parent–child relationships even at a single point in time can be quite complicated. In one of the few studies focused on father–child interaction, Fondell and Cooksey (1994) used data from the first wave of the National Survey of Family Households (NSFH) to study variations by family composition in what men who live with children do. They distinguished men who live only with their own biological children, those who live only with stepchildren, and those who live with both their own biological children and stepchildren; they also took into account what other adults were present in the household and what their relationship was to the focal child. This example suggests the heterogeneity typically glossed over in broader categorizations.

Even these complex categorizations are limited to cross-sectional *snapshots* of the current situation. As Zill points out, however, some family living arrangements represent a recent change that may have been *prompted* by child difficulties, whereas others probably proxy for a prior history of child neglect or abuse. The total number of changes in family composition, rather than or in addition to the current situation, may be critical in shaping children's behavior and emotional well-being (but see Wojtkiecwicz, 1993). More generally, it is important to treat family history, as well as current family composition, as itself a dependent variable in need of investigation, not only an explanatory variable aiding our understanding of child outcomes.

In addition, the increasing numbers of informal unions creates analytic and measurement problems. Thirty percent of the families we classified as mother–stepfather families were not married couples; another researcher might have classified these same families as single-mother families. Similarly, our measures of family income will vary depending on whether we decide to include or exclude unmarried stepfathers' earnings (see Manning & Lichter, 1994). As family forms become more complex, the dangers of serious misclassifications increase as well, and comparison across studies may be hampered by differences in decision rules about measures of family arrangements.

IMPLICATIONS FOR GENERALIZATIONS ABOUT FAMILY STRUCTURE

In these comments, I have emphasized the need to understand why and under what conditions specific family arrangements have better and worse effects. Studies that include strong controls for parental background and that test for interactive effects suggest that the *causal* links between specific family arrangements and either family interaction or children's outcomes are not as strong or as invariant as we sometimes portray them.

To fully understand the effects of parents on children, our research must be focused on understanding the total set of conditions that make parent–child interactions more difficult, including family arrangements but also encompassing parental resources, culturally shaped gender roles, and occupational and economic conditions. Our research needs to focus as much attention on social factors that *influence* family composition and interaction as it does on how family composition and interaction affect children. It must consider interactions between the resources that parents, particularly mothers, bring to difficult situations, and it must also take seriously the likelihood that work and family conditions, and changes in those conditions, interact in their effects. These interactions tend to take two forms. First, combinations that increase the total set of family demands are more negative than other combinations. Second, work and family conditions may interact in an offsetting or compensatory way, with more positive occupational circumstances, for example, buffering the effects of some difficult family conditions. We have only begun to specify such conditions.

Although such interactions may provide some basis for optimism—specific family arrangements are not necessarily or invariably negative in their consequences for children—they may also be interpreted more pessimistically. Those families facing more difficult family circumstances are also likely to be lower in the personal psychosocial and intellectual resources that might buffer adverse effects, and they are also likely to have poorer occupational and economic prospects. Unmarried mothers with jobs that provide high wages, for example, the group of unmarried mothers who were similar to married mothers in the quality of family environments they provided, are clearly an advantaged subset of all unmarried mothers in the U.S. today. Similarly, although mother–stepfather families characterized by high parental rule negotiation and involvement have children who are doing well, we know from other research that many mother–stepfather families do not match this description (Astone & McLanahan, 1991).

It is such considerations that make it so difficult to answer questions, like that posed at this conference, about whether, if all else were equal, family forms other than two biological parents would necessarily have negative impacts on children. The easy answer is no: If all else were truly equal—if these families were equal in the resources that parents had; in their economic and occupational prospects; in the numbers and ages of children; in the time that parents had to devote to children; and in the stimulation, support, and structuring they provided—we would have no reason to expect differences in outcomes, precisely because there would be no variation in the means by which currently observed differences are produced. But this simple no is misleading in the image it suggests and the promise it makes—that families differing in family composition *could* be equal in all these aspects in any real world (in contrast to our statistically adjusted models). To take one example, consider how income could be equal. Zill documents the large average income differences between families with and without a male wage-earner (p. 156). Other data show that the median weekly earnings for women working full time were $381 in 1992, compared with $505 for men working full time. This gender gap in earnings implies an annual income advantage of nearly $6,500 for two-parent families supported by a working man compared to a one-parent family supported by a working woman. These families would have equal earnings only if this gender gap in earnings were erased—an unlikely prospect in the near future at least. (It also applies only to the advantaged subset of single-mother families in which the mother had full-time employment at median female wages; Zill reports that the actual annual median income for all single-mother families was only about $12,000 in 1993.) Even if male and female workers had equal earnings, the presence of a wife who is not in the labor force would make the families very different in the total amount of available parental time.

In any case, this calculation underestimates the typical income gap between families supported by employed women and two-parent families because, as Lichter points out (chap. 17, this volume), the latter are increasingly likely to have both a higher paid man's salary and also earnings from his wife. Combining the median earnings of a full-time male worker and a full-time female worker yields a median weekly income of $886, implying an annual income of approximately $46,000 and an annual income gap of more than $25,000 between dual-earner families and female-earner families. Although this gap might be narrowed somewhat by nonresidential fathers' contributions for child support, this is currently not a dependable or substantial source of income for many single mothers. Typically, the "everything else equal" argument can only hold for the highly unusual subset of single women who earn as much by themselves as the combination of earnings of a typical man *and* a typical woman. Such women are not likely to be equal to other women in education, occupation, or work hours; again, the notion of families "alike in all other ways" is an elusive idea. Indeed, it makes one hope, for the sake of children in various family arrangements, that Zill is right that differences in income per se are not as causally implicated in producing child academic and social problems as other investigators have concluded and that parents' own investments in their children and involvement in their lives—which are linked only imperfectly to family composition and income—are at least as critical as income per se.

In his closing comments, Zill identifies the real problem as being the prevention of "multirisk" families—characterized by low parental education, low income, parental immaturity, and parental deviance, including drug and alcohol use—not simply family composition other than biological mother and father. Family composition variables may proxy (rather poorly) for the subset of families with this constellation of problems. To understand the independent contributions of these factors, we need to tease apart these intercorrelated risks and consider their relative importance. If schools are to stress that all family forms are not equally viable, as Zill suggests, this must be done with greater explicit attention to the *conditions under which* these drawbacks are most and least. For example, Zill comments that "unmarried teenage parenthood before high school graduation" (p. 171) has negative consequences. This pattern includes variations in age at childbirth and in educational attainment as well as differences in marital status at the time of the birth. The negative consequences associated with this pattern partly reflect the poor prospects that such parents have for employment and earnings. It is difficult to measure how much such negative consequences reflect marital status per se, or how much better would be "*married* teenage parenthood before high school graduation." Yet our emphasizing marital status in the constellation seems to suggest that the key to good outcomes for a young mother without a high school diploma is marriage—most likely to a young man who has also dropped out of high school without a diploma and who also has poor prospects for employment and earnings. This suggestion is unwarranted.

In seeking to educate children and adolescents about family life, it seems more useful to emphasize to them that both their own fulfillment, achievement, and well-being and also their children's outcomes are positively linked to their investing in their own education, to their attempting to form and preserve equitable and harmonious relations with potential parenting partners, to their achieving adequate income levels, and to their providing their children with sufficient time, attention, supervision, warmth, and economic security. It is, on average, probably easier to accomplish this in some family forms than in others.

Attaining these conditions is also more difficult today for U.S. families of all types, given changes in wage levels and in the distribution of occupations, the persistence of large gender disparities in earnings potential, and the increasing employment insecurities and overload created by downsizing and other cost-cutting measures taken by employers. These goals will continue to be inordinately difficult for a significant proportion of individual families without greater societal attention to the cultural and economic barriers hampering such individual efforts.

REFERENCES

Astone, N., & McLanahan, S. (1991). Family structure, parental practices, and high school completion. *American Sociological Review, 56*, 309–320.

Baker, P. C., & Mott, F. L. 1989. *NLSY child handbook 1989: A guide and resource document for the National Longitudinal Study of Youth 1986 child data.* Columbus, OH: Center for Human Resource Research, The Ohio State University.

Clausen, J. (1991). Adolescent competence and the shaping of the life course. *American Journal of Sociology, 96*, 805–842.

Fondell, M., & Cooksey, M. (1994, August). *Time well-spent: The role of fathers in a child's life.* Paper presented at the annual meeting of the American Sociological Association, Los Angeles, CA.

Hochschild, A. (1989). *The second shift.* New York: Viking.

Kohn, M. L., & Schooler, C. (1983). *Work and personality: An inquiry into the impact of social stratification.* Norwood, NJ: Ablex.

Lennon, M. C. & Rosenfield, S. (1994). Relative fairness and the division of housework: The importance of options. *American Journal of Sociology, 100*, 506–531.

Manning, W., & Lichter, D. (1994, August). *Measuring children's economic well-being in single-parent, cohabiting, and married couple families: Evidence from the 1990 census.* Paper presented at the annual meeting of the American Sociological Association, Los Angeles, CA.

McLanahan, S., & Bumpass, L. (1988). Intergenerational consequences of family disruption. *American Journal of Sociology, 94*, 130–152.

McLanahan, S., & Sandefur, G. (1994). *Growing up with a single parent: What hurts, what helps.* Cambridge, MA: Harvard University Press.

Menaghan, E. G. (1991). Work experiences and family interaction processes: The long reach of the job? *Annual Review of Sociology, 17*, 419–444.

Menaghan, E. G. (1994). The daily grind: Work stressors, family patterns, and intergenerational outcomes. In W. Avison & I. Gotlib (Eds.), *Stress and mental health: Contemporary issues and future prospects* (pp. 115–147). New York: Plenum.

Menaghan, E. G., Kowaleski-Jones, L., & Mott. F. L. (1994, May). *The intergenerational costs of parental social stressors: Academic and social difficulties in early adolescence.* Paper presented at the meeting of the Population Association of America, San Francisco, CA.

Menaghan, E. G., & Parcel, T. L. (1990). Parental employment and family life: Research in the 1980s. *Journal of Marriage and the Family, 52*, 1079–1098.

Menaghan, E. G., & Parcel, T. L. (1991). Determining children's home environments: The impact of maternal characteristics and current occupational and family conditions. *Journal of Marriage and the Family, 53*, 417–431.

Menaghan, E. G., & Parcel, T. L. (1995). Social sources of change in children's home environments: Effects of parental occupational experiences and family conditions over time. *Journal of Marriage and the Family, 57*, 69–84.

Mirowsky, J., & Ross C. (1989). *Social causes of psychological distress.* New York: Aldine de Gruyter.

Moore, K., & Snyder, N. O. (1991). Cognitive attainment among firstborn children of adolescent mothers. *American Sociological Review, 56,* 612–624.

Parcel, T. L., & Menaghan, E. G. (1994). *Parents' jobs and children's lives.* New York: Aldine de Gruyter.

Patterson, G. R., DeBaryshe, B. D., & Ramsey, E. (1989). A developmental perspective on antisocial behavior. *American Psychologist, 44,* 329–335.

Schor, E., & Menaghan, E. G. (in press). Family pathways to child health: Social determinants of family functions and functioning. In S. Levine, D. Walsh, & B. Amick (Eds.), *Society and health.* NY: Oxford University Press.

South, S. (1985). Economic conditions and the divorce rate: A time-series analysis of the postwar United States. *Journal of Marriage and the Family, 47,* 31–42.

Thompson, L., & Walker, A. (1989). Gender in families: Women and men in marriage, work, and parenthood. *Journal of Marriage and the Family, 51,* 845–871.

Wojtkiecwicz, R. A. (1993). Simplicity and complexity in the effects of parental structure on high school graduation. *Demography, 30,* 701–717.

13

Toward a Balanced View
of Family Change

Diane Scott-Jones
Temple University

Dismay about the negative effects of changes in family structure can be heard throughout our society, from many parts of the political spectrum. President Clinton and former Vice President Quayle each sounded the alarm about family structure in recent speeches (Ingwerson, 1994; Office of the Press Secretary, 1994). Many of us would agree that raising a child and educating that child are difficult tasks, even when two biological parents devote themselves to their parental responsibilities. Those two parents, it would seem, need an adequate income, a safe home, and a safe neighborhood. The two biological parents also would need the support of a network of extended kin and friends and the support of social institutions, such as schools, all acting in the best interests of the child.

Many children, however, are not reared in what we consider ideal family situations. In Zill's chapter (this volume, chap. 10), the two-biological-parent family is taken as the standard and is compared to three other family structures: single-parent families in which a divorced or separated mother has custody of her children, single-parent families in which the mother never married, and mother–stepfather families. Zill asks how family structure is related to three important outcomes: academic achievement, misbehavior in school, and educational attainment. To answer the questions he raised, Zill turns to data from three national surveys: The National Health Interview Survey on Child Health, the National Education Longitudinal Study of 1988 (NELS88), and the National Longitudinal Survey of Youth (NLSY). Zill also relies heavily on McLanahan and Sandefur's analyses of national survey data, which are reported in their recent book, *Growing Up With a Single Parent* (1994).

I read Zill's chapter with great interest. At the end of my reading, however, many questions remained. What can we say with certainty about the importance of the two-biological-parent family for children's performance in school? More importantly, what can we do to enhance children's school achievement or to enhance the well-being of families, based on our knowledge of the role of two biological parents? My concerns are centered around three main issues. First, the differences between two-biological-parent families and other families often were small in magnitude and may shift focus away from other important issues that affect a broad range of families. Second, in the large-scale surveys reported, the multidimensional nature of families was acknowledged only through the use of statistical controls, and there was no fine-grained analysis of family ecologies. Finally, the large-scale surveys employed imprecise measures of important constructs.

SMALL DIFFERENCES

Zill acknowledges that some differences between single- and two-parent families are small in magnitude and, although statistically significant in large data sets, may be of questionable practical significance. An example is Zill's report of High School and Beyond data, analyzed by McLanahan and Sandefur (1994). These data show college enrollment rates of high school graduates from single-parent families and from two-parent families of 50% and 57%, respectively. Should these data cause us to focus on the damage done by single-parent families or on the fact that approximately half of all U.S. adolescents do not go on to college? These adolescents, termed the *forgotten half* (William T. Grant Commission, 1988), may not be well served by our educational system. Rather than focus on single-parent families, perhaps we should focus on the academic preparation of noncollege-attending adolescents, as in Hamilton's (1990) important work.

Similarly, the National Survey of Families and Households data, again as analyzed by McLanahan and Sandefur (1994), show that college graduation rates for high school graduates from single-parent families and from two-parent families are 15% and 23%, respectively. Again, instead of focusing on the damage done by single-parent families, we need to be concerned that only a small percentage from either family type will complete college. Our economy may not be able to absorb the high percentage of young people who are not college graduates. Perhaps we should provide for noncollege graduates to seek additional education and job training at later points in the life course.

Small but statistically significant differences in high school performance between two-biological-parent families and other-parent families are reported by McLanahan and Sandefur (1994) in their analyses of the High School and Beyond data set. In these analyses, the *one-parent* designation included stepparent families. In addition, statistical controls were employed for parents' education, gender, ethnicity, family size, and region of residence—but not for income, a point to which I return later. Students from two-biological-parent families did better than their peers on four of five indicators of high school performance: standardized test scores, college expectations, grade point average, and school attendance. What was most striking about these data, however, was not the difference between two-biological-parent families and other families. Instead, an important story was that no difference was found in school attitude. In both family types, the majority of students—80%—reported liking school and would be disappointed if they didn't complete college. Yet, less than 40% in either family arrangement actually expected to attend college.

An important question is what parents do with their children in single-parent and two-biological-parent families. McLanahan and Sandefur (1994), analyzing data from the National Survey of Families and Households, found few significant differences across family structures in mothers' behavior with their children; the significant differences were relatively small in magnitude. It should be noted that fathers' behavior with children was not included in these analyses. Fathers in two-biological-parent families typically are not actively involved in childrearing, although father involvement is increasing (see Bronstein & Cowan, 1988; Snarey, 1993). These analyses are important, however, because the effect of the biological father on children may be indirect, not only through his interactions with the children or through his income, but also through his impact on the mother's well-being and her behavior with her children.

Generally, mothers' having meals with the child, reading to the child, hugging and praising the child, and scolding or spanking the child were not significantly different across family structures, and any differences were very small. For example, mothers and children in two-biological-parent families have meals together more often than mothers and children in other families but the difference is only about one half a meal per week. Similarly, McLanahan and Sandefur found few significant differences across family structure for variables representing mothers' supervision of their children. These data are reassuring in that almost all mothers report knowing the child's whereabouts but somewhat disturbing is that less than 10% report a regular bedtime, and only about one fifth to about one third report having rules for television or never leaving the child alone.

Given the relatively small differences, one must wonder about the persistence with which researchers pursue simple comparisons of two-parent and single-parent families. The consensus from research 10 years ago (see Scott-Jones, 1984, for review) is remarkably similar to conclusions we can draw now. Ten years before that 1984 review, Herzog and Sudia's (1973) conclusions also were similar. Ten years from now, we may still debate the significance of the differences between two-parent and single-parent families. Our framing of questions and our interpretation of results are indications of the value we place on two biological parents as the ideal agents for childrearing. Yet, differences within a given family structure make simple comparisions misleading (Scott-Jones, 1984). "Living with two biological parents" is not a uniform family scenario. This family designation includes both harmonious and conflictful families, affluent and poor families, dual-career and single-career families, and families of various ethnic groups. Family life is likely to be very different for the adults and children in these ostensibly similar two-biological-parent families.

STATISTICAL CONTROL OR ECOLOGICAL NICHE

In surveys of the kind reported by Zill, the multidimensional nature of families is addressed through the use of statistical control. These surveys are important and essential national resources, but the statistical adjustments are not good substitutes for research focusing on a variety of families. Controlling for the effects of income, parental education, ethnicity, and child's age is not equivalent to building a strong base of studies that examine particular ecological niches. We need to understand ethnicity, income, and other variables not merely as statistical controls but as important contexts for children—as ecological niches that define children's lives. The data Zill provides are a starting point, but these data need to be filled in with a richer and more detailed understanding of children's and families' lives.

Some controls are controversial, such as the control for income. McLanahan and Sandefur (1994) argued that income is a mechanism through which families affect child outcomes and thus should not be controlled. The issue is complicated, because it is also true that single-parenthood occurs more frequently among low-income families; without a control for income, some of the negative effects of low income will be attributed to single-parent status. Zill rejects an economic explanation of the problems children experience in single-parent families, and he contrasts his view with that of McLanahan and Sandefur (1994). As Zill correctly notes, family income is not the sole mechanism through which family structure is related to educational outcomes. My own reading of McLanahan and Sandefur, however, is that these authors propose a more complex model in which economic, parental, and community resources are lacking in single-parent families.

I would like to add to this discussion the role of ethnicity. In our society, ethnic group membership is an important feature of a child's ecological niche. Ethnic differences exist in both family structure and school outcomes. Overall, White children are more likely than African-American and Hispanic children to live in two-biological-parent families and are more likely to graduate from high school. As Zill illustrates in his Table 10.4, based on McLanahan and Sandefur's (1994) analyses of the National Longitudinal Survey of Youth, the proportionate increase in dropout rates for children from single-parent families is greatest for White students, followed by Hispanic students, and least for African-American students. For Whites, at all educational levels, the dropout rates double from two-biological-parent families to other families. In each of the three ethnic groups, for parents with less than high school education, high school dropout rates are substantial even in two-biological-parent families—close to one fourth or more of these students do not complete high school. Among parents with some college education, two-biological-parent families' dropout rates do not differ for African Americans and Whites; among other-parent families, the dropout rate for Whites is 16% and is double that of African Americans. These data suggest that it is important to examine variables other than two-biological-parent status; ethnicity and parents' educational level are important as well. In addition, historical changes in educational attainment do not correspond to changes in family structure. Family structure changed dramatically between 1940 and 1980; however, educational attainment did not decline. The percentage of high school graduates among African-American young adults, 18–24 years of age, increased during this time (Furstenberg & Condran, 1988).

Among two-biological-parent families, African Americans have lower incomes than do Whites and experience lower increases in income over time. McLanahan and Sandefur (1994) reported data from the Panel Study of Income Dynamics showing that over a 5-year period, when the child in the family went from 12 to 17 years, the median family income of African-American two-biological-parent families increased by less than $2,000. For White two-biological-parent families during this same time period, the average family income increased almost $5,000. In addition, African-American parents earn less than White parents at the same educational level.

McLanahan and Sandefur (1994) reported that White children in single-parent families live in much better community settings than do African-American families in two-biological-parent families. For quality of neighborhood, ethnicity is a much more important factor than family structure. A large part of what the two-biological-parent family contributes to the child is a safe home, a safe neighborhood, and community resources. Therefore, the containment of low-income African-American single-parent families in urban housing projects and the extreme segregation or "hypersegregation" of African-American families of all types must be an element in children's school performance.

Massey and Denton (1993), in their book *American Apartheid*, presented a persuasive argument for their thesis that segregation confines African Americans to a "circumscribed and disadvantaged niche" (p. 149) in the neighborhoods in which they are able to live. Other ethnic groups are able to move to better neighborhoods, with better schools and other resources, whenever their incomes allow. Both institutional actions and private decisions prevent African-American parents from providing good neighborhoods for their children. Massey and Denton used Philadelphia to illustrate the differences in neighborhoods of African Americans and Whites as they move from poverty to affluence. In Philadelphia, both poor Whites and poor African Americans live in neighborhoods where the median value of homes is low, the percentage of births to single mothers is high, and well over one third of students score below the 15th percentile on high school standardized achievement tests. Differences between poor African Americans and Whites on these neighborhood indices are in favor of African Americans. At higher levels of individual income, however, the neighborhood indices are markedly better for Whites than for African Americans. Denton and Massey concluded: "Because of segregation, the same income buys Black and White families educational environments that are of vastly different quality" (Denton & Massey, 1993, p. 153).

Another important aspect of African-American family life is the relatively high proportion of births to adolescent mothers. In his comments, Zill mentions briefly the need to prevent adolescent childbearing, which is a widely agreed upon goal. At least part of current concern about adolescent childbearing stems from the fact that births to adolescents tend to occur outside marriage. This situation is in contrast to the 1950s, when rates of births to adolescents were higher but public concern about adolescent childbearing was not strong. Then, the young couple was far more likely to marry and remain in a stable, economically viable family. In our analyses of birth records, we found that fewer than 10% of 18- and 19-year-old African-American childbearers were married. In contrast, more than half of Hispanic childbearers at this age were married. Educational attainment, however, was much higher for African Americans than for Hispanics, and the educational level of Hispanic childbearers who remained unmarried was higher than that of Hispanics who married (Scott-Jones, 1991). In our analyses of data from the National Survey of Family Growth, educational attainment was a stronger predictor of adult income than was the experience of adolescent childbearing (Scott-Jones & Turner, 1990). Thus, forming a two-parent family may not be the best choice for adolescent childbearers in current social and economic conditions.

IMPRECISE MEASURES

The force of the large data sets based on national probability samples is undermined by the simplicity of the questions asked. Student misbehavior, one of the important school outcomes in Zill's chapter, is not measured in a very complex manner. In the National Health Interview Survey, suspension from school and requests that parents come to a school conference may be biased measures of student misbehavior. Suspensions and being called in for conferences are not "pure" measures of misconduct; suspensions are more likely to occur in children from poor and ethnic minority families. Thus, what we construe as the impact of family structure on children's school outcomes may be magnified by school policies and practices that affect suspensions. Further, these variables were assessed via maternal report; school records may be a more accurate source of such data. At the very least, these data need to be qualified as maternal perceptions of student behavior and achievement.

In the NELS data, girls' misbehavior may be underestimated by the use of fighting in the misbehavior score; in the analyses, gender is a statistical adjustment rather than an aspect of the child's life to be studied and understood. In addition, problems may exist in children who do not get suspended from school. Suspensions and being called in to conferences may be inconvenient for the adults involved, but internalizing disorders—anxiety, depression—may be as damaging to children as the more noticeable externalizing disorders that lead to suspension or other disciplinary measures. Forehand, Long, Brody, and Fauber (1986), for example, included internalizing behaviors, as well as externalizing behaviors and grade point average, as dependent measures in a study of predictors of school outcomes in two-parent families.

RECOMMENDATIONS

We can ask what, if anything, schools should do to accommodate variation in family structure in our society. We also can ask what message trickles down from social science research to parents and to the U.S. public in general about the causes of school failure and school success.

Included in Zill's speculation about causes of school failure and misconduct in children from single-parent families is a genetic explanation, which is raised briefly and left dangling. Zill suggests, without presentation of evidence, that school failure and misconduct may result from genetically transmitted "lower aptitude levels" and "antisocial behavioral tendencies" (p. 156) in single-parent families. This suggestion without accompanying evidence is particularly disturbing, given the current controversy surrounding Herrnstein and Murray's *The Bell Curve* (1994).

Further, Zill writes that "If all students came from two-parent families, the overall dropout rate would decline by one third" (p. 154). No clear policy recommendations follow from this type of statement. All students are not from two-parent families, and no policy now acceptable to the U.S. public can force this family structure. We cannot force marriage, prohibit divorce, or simply wish for more two-biological-parent families. Zill urges schools not to stigmatize students from single-parent families and offers some positive practical suggestions. Zill's suggestions, however, do not flow from the data he presented and do not form a consistent set of recommendations.

McLanahan and Sandefur (1994) ended their book with three recommendations. First, they recommended that we work to increase the economic well-being of single-parent families. Zill is skeptical of this recommendation. Granted, an adequate family income will not guarantee educational success. The evidence appears strong, however, that an adequate family income, and the resources that typically follow, will greatly increase children's likelihood of success in school.

A second recommendation from McLanahan and Sandefur (1994) is that we share responsibility for raising children more equally between men and women and between parents and nonparents. Noncustodial fathers, in particular, will need to share the substantial costs of raising and educating children. In addition, families with no school-aged children of their own will need to feel a commitment to other people's children in order to support public education and other appropriate programs and policies. This latter point is important, given the decline in the percentage of families with school-aged children, which could result in an erosion of public support for education (Scott-Jones, 1986).

Finally, McLanahan and Sandefur (1994) recommended that programs for children and families be universal. This recommendation is especially important, given that the problems children experience are not dramatically different between two-biological-parent families and other family arrangements. The problems are more pronounced and more urgent in single-parent families, but no family arrangement results in children untouched by problems that can affect their school performance.

Zill begins his chapter by setting up the extreme positions regarding family structure. Extremes, as Zill points out, usually do not fit data very well. We do not have empirical support for stigmatizing all family forms other than the two-biological-parent family, and we do not have support for ignoring changes in family arrangements. Between these extremes is a level of objectivity and tolerance we aim for as researchers and practitioners.

REFERENCES

Bronstein, P., & Cowan, C. P. (Eds.) (1988). *Fatherhood today: Men's changing role in the family.* New York: Wiley.

Forehand, R., Long, N., Brody, G. H., & Fauber, R. (1986). Home predictors of young adolescents' school behavior and academic performance. *Child Development, 57,* 1528–1533.

Furstenberg, F. F., Jr., & Condran, G. A. (1988). Family change and adolescent well-being: A reexamination of U.S. trends. In A. J. Cherlin (Ed.), *The changing American family and public policy. The changing domestic priorities series* (pp. 117–155). Washington, DC: Urban Institute Press.

Hamilton, S. F. (1990). *Apprenticeship for adulthood: Preparing youth for the future.* New York: The Free Press.

Herrnstein, R. J., & Murray, C. (1994). *The bell curve: Intelligence and class structure in American life.* New York: Free Press.

Herzog, E., & Sudia, C. (1973). Children in fatherless families. In B. M. Caldwell & H. N. Ricciuti (Eds.), *Review of child development research* (Vol. 3, pp. 141–232). Chicago: University of Chicago Press.

Ingwerson, M. (1994, September 13). Both conservatives and liberals decry rapid increase in single-parent families. *Christian Science Monitor,* pp. 1, 4.

Massey, D. S., & Denton, N. A. (1993). *American apartheid.* Cambridge, MA: Harvard University Press.

McLanahan, S., & Sandefur, G. (1994). *Growing up with a single parent.* Cambridge, MA: Havard University Press.

Office of the Press Secretary, The White House. (1994, September 9). [Remarks by the President in speech to National Baptist Convention, New Orleans.]

Scott-Jones, D. (1984). Family influences on cognitive development and school achievement. *Review of Research in Education, 11,* 259–304.

Scott-Jones, D. (1986). The family. In J. Hannaway & M. E. Lockheed (Eds.), *The contributions of the social sciences to educational policy and practice* (pp. 11–31). Berkeley: McCutcheon.

Scott-Jones, D. (1991). Educational levels of adolescent childbearers at first and second births. *American Journal of Education, 99,* 461–480.

Scott-Jones, D., & Turner, S. L. (1990). The impact of adolescent childbearing on educational attainment and income of Black females. *Youth and Society, 22*(1), 35–53.

Snarey, J. (1993). *How fathers care for the next generation: A four-decade study.* Cambridge, MA: Harvard University Press.

William T. Grant Commission on Work, Family, and Citizenship. (1988). *The forgotten half: Pathways to success for America's youth and young families.* Washington, DC: Author.

IV

BUILDING RESEARCH
AND POLICY AGENDAS:
NEW DIRECTIONS

14

▼▼▼▼▼▼

Perspectives and Previews on Research and Policy for School, Family, and Community Partnerships

Joyce L. Epstein
Johns Hopkins University

Over the past decade, the field of school–family–community partnerships has been energized before our very eyes by activities in research, policy, and practice. In research, scholars from different disciplines are applying various methodologies to study connections of schools and communities with families of various backgrounds and cultures and with students at different age and grade levels. The number of master's and doctoral dissertations are increasing as graduate students and their professors become familiar with the field and seek to make new contributions.

In policy, in 1994 Congress added a new national educational goal for school and family partnerships to the major federal legislation called Goals 2000: Educate America Act. Also, Title I regulations were revised and include mandates for specific family–school connections in order for states, districts, and schools to obtain and keep federal funds. Other federal, state, and local policies have been and are being developed that mandate or encourage partnership activities.

In practice, school administrators, teachers, parents, students, and others in communities are increasingly working together to meet various mandates and guidelines, and, more importantly, to design their own programs and practices. Along with curriculum, instruction, evaluation, and staff development, a program of school–family–community connections is now viewed as one of the components of school organization that may help to promote student learning and success in school.

AN EMERGING FIELD OF STUDY

A selective summary may help to illustrate some of the changes that have occurred in this growing field of study. Traditionally, studies of families, or schools, or communities were conducted as if these were separate or competing contexts. For example, in the late 1960s and 1970s, researchers argued heatedly about whether schools *or* families were more important. When heads cleared, the dual contributions of schools and families were acknowledged: Students are advantaged or disadvantaged by the economic and educational resources and guidance offered by their families, *and* students are advantaged or disadvantaged by the quality of their experiences in schools. The debate changed as it became increasingly clear that neither schools nor families alone can do the job of educating and socializing children and preparing them for life. Rather, schools, families, and communities share responsibilities for children and influence them simultaneously.

In the 1960s, the topic of "parent involvement" gained prominence with the implementation of federal Head Start and Follow-Through programs in preschool and early elementary grades. These programs legislated the involvement of low-income parents in the education of their young children to prepare them for successful entry to school. At the same time, other factors increased the involvement of middle- and high-income parents in their children's education. For example, more women were graduating from college and entering and staying in the work force; more mothers were equal with teachers in education; and more parents were active in decisions about early care for their children. Thus, there were pressures and opportunities for families with more and with less formal education to increase their awareness of the importance of their participation in children's education and in their continuous interactions with their children's schools (Connors & Epstein, 1995).

Other early policies changed basic connections of schools and families, based on demographic data, family demands, and goals for greater nutritional equity for all children. For example, schools began to serve lunch at school to all children, responding in part to the increasing numbers of working mothers who were not at home midday. Schools began to provide free breakfasts as well as free and reduced-price lunches to help poor families and their children. Research on these policies progressed from studies of whether to which food should be served in breakfasts and lunches to help students and their families.

The new policy agenda about partnerships is being driven by more complex family and community conditions, but emerging policies are still responses to poverty and other demographics, family demands, and goals for equity and excellence in students' education. The problems are well known: There are more two-parent homes in which both parents are employed; more young, single parents and more of them working outside the home; more children in poverty; more migrant and homeless children and families; more family mobility during the school year; and other factors that make it imperative to redesign and improve policies and practices for linking schools, families, and communities. But programs of partnership are not only responses to problems of families facing difficult conditions. The new policy agenda about partnerships reflects the advances in understanding how all families need better information about their children, the schools, and the part they play across the grades to influence children's well-being, learning, and development.

Some mandates and emphases in earlier federal programs (such as the parent councils required in Title I) were limited, often perfunctory activities that informed and involved only a few parents (Keesling & Melaragno, 1983). Other demonstration programs were quite comprehensive with home visits, assistance to parents in understanding their very young children, good communications with teachers, opportunities to volunteer, and other active interactions (Gordon, 1979). The early efforts to understand parent involvement were largely unsystematic, with few measures of the effects of specific practices of involvement. The first frameworks focused mainly on the roles that parents needed to play and not the work that schools needed to conduct in order to organize strong programs to involve all families in their children's education.

In the 1970s, the effective schools movement—a first wave of recent school reform—captured the attention of educators of students who were at risk of failing (Edmonds, 1979). Although it was not one of the initial elements of effective schools, parent involvement was quickly added to an expanding list of components that research and practice suggested would improve schools and increase student success. By the mid-1980s, the report *A Nation at Risk* (National Commission on Excellence in Education, 1983) directed attention to the need to improve all schools, not just those for students from economically distressed homes and communities. The *effective* schools litany evolved into lists of requirements for *restructured* schools. The school reform movements may continue to change its vocabulary: There already are discussions of *renewed, reinvented, redefined, responsive,* and *reconstituted* schools. Whatever the vocabulary, all school reform efforts recognize the need to improve the quality of education for all students. Each new initiative has sharpened the focus on curriculum, instruction, and connections with families.

In the 1980s, studies began to clarify the amorphous term *parent involvement,* and recast the emphasis from parent involvement (left up to the parent) to *school and family partnerships,* or, more fully, *school, family, and community partnerships,* in order to recognize the shared responsibilities for children within and across contexts. The concept of "shared responsibility" removed part of the burden from parents to figure out on their own how to become or stay involved in their children's education from year to year and put part of that burden on schools to create programs to inform and involve all families. Researchers collected data to identify separable components of involvement and began to focus more rigorously on measuring results of involvement for students, parents, and for educators (Epstein, 1987a, 1987b, 1992).

Growth in this field of study also was assisted by the federal government's creation in 1990 of the national Center on Families, Communities, Schools and Children's Learning to conduct an active research and development program on school and family partnerships from birth through high school. The Center includes over 20 researchers who are conducting research, development, evaluations, and policy studies in two research programs on the early years (focusing on students and their families from birth through age 10) and on the years of early and late adolescence (focusing on students and their families from age 11–19). The Center's researchers are from several disciplines, use varied methods and measurement models, and often work closely with educators and parents to design and study new approaches for productive partnerships.

In addition to its research agenda, the Center created an International Network of over 300 researchers in the United States and more than 40 nations to encourage and to share work on many topics related school, family, and community partnerships.Some researchers in other nations have followed the Center's format to establish interdisciplinary networks in their own countries (e.g., Australia, Portugal, and Denmark) and to work with and assist educators to improve school programs of partnerships with families and communities. The discussions and debates among international colleagues and collaborative cross-national projects (Davies, 1993) have added energy to this field.

For several years, the Center on Families, Communities, Schools and Children's Learning and the Institute for Responsive Education have joined forces to conduct a day-long roundtable for U.S. and international colleagues to share their research and development activities prior to the annual meeting of the American Educational Research Association (AERA). The Center also organized international symposia for several years for the formal AERA meetings. The number of countries, researchers, topics, questions, methods and measures, and quality of work at these meetings have grown each year.

There is other evidence of the growth of interest and action in this field of study. A dozen years ago, the AERA had few papers at its annual meeting on topics concerning families. Now, multiple labels are needed to index presentations on family involvement, school partnerships, parent participation, fathers, mothers, and other related terms. The Families as Educators Special Interest Group (SIG) at AERA has grown in membership for more than a decade. The annual meetings of nearly every major social science and policy-related professional association include presentations of research and often interdisciplinary panels on topics of schools, families, communities and their connections.

As should be expected in a maturing field, new theories, studies, policies, and practices generate heat as well as light. Researchers debate assumptions, definitions, and interpretations of results (Coleman, 1987; Lareau, 1989, and this volume, chap. 4). Policy leaders and educators take different paths toward varied goals. In short, the field of school, family, and community partnerships is growing and improving with better questions, methods, and approaches. The emerging field is strengthened by three characteristics of the participants and their work:

Academic Disciplinary Boundaries Have Blended. Progress in research on family, school, and community connections has been made across disciplines, within and across academic specialties. Researchers in sociology, psychology, social work, anthropology, education, history, economics, and other fields are conducting studies, building on each others' work, and contributing new perspectives that are, in turn, assisting policy and practice. These investments will continue to improve the understanding of families, schools, communities, and their connections.

Professional Boundaries Have Blurred. Researchers, policy leaders, and educators are working with and learning from each other. More than for most topics in social and educational research, there has been a short time line between research and its application in practice. More than for most topics, researchers, educators, and parents have been working together to identify the goals, problems, and potential solutions to create more successful partnerships to assist more students. These cross-context connections of university researchers, educators and policy makers have transformed how some research is designed, conducted, and interpreted (also see Moles, this volume, chap. 15).

The Main Questions Have Changed. We have moved from the question, Are families important for student success in school? to *If* families are important for children's development and school success, *how* can schools help all families conduct the activities that will benefit their children? Researchers and educators have common questions, such as: What do we need to know and do to help all children succeed in school and to enable their families to help them do so? How can schools communicate with families and community groups to enable more families (indeed all of them) to guide their children on positive paths from birth through high school? How can these communications be family friendly, feasible for schools, and acceptable to students? What are the effects of alternative designs and implementation processes of practices of partnership?

From my view, the main goal of partnerships is *to develop and conduct better communications with families across the grades in order to assist students to succeed in school.* Research should question, elaborate, or clarify all of the definable parts of that goal: to develop and conduct better communications (How? Which connections, interactions, and exchanges are promoted by different types of involvement? Which supporting policies are needed?); with more families (How? With which strategies to reach most or all families? With which guidance for all teachers and administrators?); to assist more students (How? With which roles for students? With which interactions of students and adults to motivate students to work hard and learn to their full potential?); to succeed in school (How? With which definitions and measures of success—that is, which results or outcomes of schooling?).

Research, policies, and practices are accumulating that inform all parts of this goal, but more studies and efforts in the schools are needed to fully understand whether and how the processes work. The next sections of this chapter take a *look back* to review some of the results of my and colleagues' earlier work to describe a knowledge base on which to build; then, a *look around* to discuss issues that are emerging in current research and in practice; and a *look ahead* to preview some of the questions that I believe need continued or new attention.[1, 2]

A LOOK BACK: A BASE ON WHICH TO BUILD

For many years, my colleagues and I have been conducting studies to identify and understand what schools need to know and do to develop and implement full or comprehensive programs of partnership. This work produced a theory, framework, and vocabulary that enables researchers and educators to communicate with, learn from, and assist each other. This is still a skeletal structure, however, that needs to grow to a full body of knowledge.

In the 1980s, I developed a theoretical perspective called "overlapping spheres of influence," based on data collected with colleagues from teachers, parents, and students in the elementary grades. The results of the data analyses could not be explained by older sociological theories that stressed that social organizations would be most effective if they set separate goals and worked efficiently and effectively on unique missions. Rather, a social organizational perspective was needed that posited that the most effective families and schools had overlapping, shared goals and missions concerning children, and conducted some work collaboratively.

The model of overlapping spheres of influence includes external and internal structures. The external structure can, by conditions or design, be pushed together or pulled apart by three main forces (background and practices of families, background and practices of schools and classrooms, and time). These forces create conditions, space, and opportunities for more or fewer shared activities of schools, families, and communities. The internal structure of the model specifies institutional and interpersonal communication lines and locates where and how social interactions occur within and across the boundaries of school, home, and

[1]This research was supported by the U.S. Department of Education, Office of Educational Research and Improvement (OERI) (R117Q00031). The opinions expressed are the authors' and do not represent OERI positions or policies.

[2]An earlier version of this chapter was presented at the national symposium: Family–School Links: How Do They Affect Educational Outcomes? Pennsylvania State University, October 31–November 1, 1994.

community. Institutional level interactions involve all members or groups within schools, families, and communities; individual interactions involve one student, parent, teacher, or community member; and combinations of these interactions also may occur within the areas of overlap. This theory integrates and extends a long line of ecological, educational, psychological, and sociological perspectives on social organizations and relationships (e.g., Bronfenbrenner, 1979; Leichter, 1974; Litwak & Meyer, 1974; Seeley, 1981; and a long line of research on school, family, and community environments and their effects. For details, references, and summaries see Epstein, 1987a, 1992.)

To study the usefulness of the theory, other researchers and practitioners and I conducted surveys of and field studies with teachers, parents, and students at the elementary, middle, and high school levels. Among other questions, we wanted to know: Which practices of partnership fall in the area of overlap or shared responsibility? What can be learned about the range and the results of the activities and interactions between families and schools and among schools, families, and communities? What can be learned about the policies and practical approaches that help schools develop and implement strong programs of partnership that engage all families?

Several studies helped to identify and improve a framework of six major types of involvement that fall within the areas of overlap in the spheres of influence model. Each type of involvement may be operationalized by hundreds of practices that schools may choose to develop their programs. There will be more or less overlap and shared responsibility depending on whether many of few practices on the six types of involvement are working; and each practice that is implemented opens opportunities for varied interactions of teachers, parents, students, and others across contexts. In short form, the six types explain how schools can work with families and communities to assist them to become or stay informed and involved in children's education at home and at school (Epstein, 1992). Briefly, the six types are:

Type 1—Parenting: Assist families with parenting and childrearing skills, family support, understanding child and adolescent development, and setting home conditions to support learning at each age and grade level.

Type 2—Communicating: Communicate with families about school programs and student progress with school-to-home and home-to-school communications.

Type 3—Volunteering: Improve recruitment, training, work, and schedules to involve families as volunteers and audiences at the school or in other locations to support students and school programs the school and students.

Type 4—Learning at Home: Involve families with their children in learning activities at home, including homework and other curricular-linked activities and decisions.

Type 5—Decision Making: Include families as participants in school decisions, governance, and advocacy activities through PTA, committees, councils, and other parent organizations.

Type 6—Collaborating With Community: Coordinate the work and resources of community businesses, agencies, colleges or universities, and other groups to strengthen school programs, family practices, and student learning and development.

Each of the six types poses specific challenges for its successful design and implementation; each type leads to some different results or outcomes for students, parents, and teachers; and each benefits from investments and commitments by the various members of the school–family–community partnership (Epstein, 1987b; Epstein & Connors, 1995).

The framework also helps researchers locate measures of involvement and the results of their studies in the same scheme that is useful to educators. That is, research on family or community volunteers at school or in other locations (Type 3) could contribute results that extend knowledge about the organization and effects of volunteers, and the results and knowledge gained could be particularly useful to schools interested in improving their volunteer programs (e.g., Epstein & Dauber, 1995.)

The results of the early studies raise many new questions. For example, one of the most consistent results in our and other surveys is that teachers have very different views of parents than parents have of themselves (Dauber & Epstein, 1993; Epstein & Dauber, 1991). Most teachers do not know most parents' goals for their children, nor do they understand the information parents would like to have to be more effective at home. Most parents do not know what most teachers are trying to do each year in school nor about school improvement activities. Similarly, neither parents nor teachers fully understand what students think about family–school partnerships. Indeed, most adults think students want to avoid or minimize family involvement in their education. Data from students, however, suggest the opposite. Students want their families to be knowledgeable partners with their schools in their education and available as helpful sources of information, assistance, or guidance. The studies show why it is important to measure teachers', parents', and students' views to identify gaps in knowledge that each has about the other and to identify their common interests in good communications and in children's success in school.

Although the early studies confirm that there are positive connections between family involvement and student achievement, we still know relatively little about which practices, how, when, for whom, and why particular practices produce positive student outcomes. There also is evidence of some negative connections of family involvement with student behaviors, when students are in trouble or need help, but little evidence about whether the interventions help solve the problems over time. The early studies show that school and family partnerships produce a variety of results for families, for teachers, and for students. Three results illustrate how broadly future questions must be cast:

School Practices Influence Family Involvement. Teachers' practices to involve families are as or more important than family background variables such as race or ethnicity, social class, marital status, or mother's work status for determining whether and how parents become involved in their children's education. And, family practices of involvement are as or more important than family background variables for determining whether and how students progress and succeed in school. At the elementary, middle, and high school levels, surveys of parents, teachers, principals, and students reveal that *if* schools invest in practices to involve families, then parents respond by conducting those practices, including many parents who might not have otherwise become involved on their own (e.g., Dauber & Epstein, 1993; Epstein, 1986a).

Teachers Who Involve Parents Rate Them More Positively and Stereotype Families Less. Teachers who frequently involve families in their children's education rate single and married parents and more and less formally educated parents equally in helpfulness and follow-through with their children at home. By contrast, teachers who do not frequently involve families give more stereotypic ratings to single parents and to those with less formal education, marking them lower in helpfulness and follow-through than other parents (Becker & Epstein, 1982; Epstein, 1990).

There Are Subject-Specific Links Between the Involvement of Families and Increases in Achievement by Students. Practices to involve parents at home with their children in interactions about a specific subject are likely to benefit student achievement in that subject. For example, with data that connected teacher practices, parent responses, and student achievement:

- Teachers' practices to involve parents in learning activities at home were mainly limited to reading, English, or related activities; also, principals encouraged teachers to involve parents in reading;
- Parents reported more involvement on reading activities; and
- Students improved their reading scores over one school year if parents were involved, but their math scores were not affected by frequent parent involvement in reading (Epstein, 1991).

These results suggest that specific practices of partnership may help boost student achievement in particular subjects. Research is needed to clarify whether family involvement with a child in one subject transfers to benefit the child in other subjects over time.

Other results from the early studies provide a base for new questions. For example: *On the importance and extent of involvement, on average:*

- Teachers, parents, and students agree that parent involvement is important.
- Teachers and parents report low contact with each other—even on traditional communications.

On the variations in patterns of partnership:

- Some teachers in urban, suburban, and rural schools are leaders in involving parents in many ways; other teachers avoid partnerships.
- Teachers and parents in the elementary grades (or self-contained classes) presently report more home–school connections than in the middle and high school grades (or in departmentalized programs).
- Teachers presently contact more parents if their children have problems in school; parents presently become involved more on their own if their children are doing well in school.
- The student is an important "transmitter" of information from school to home and from home to school.

On the types of involvement:

- Few parents are involved frequently at the school building.
- Most parents want to know how to help their own child at home each year.

Many other basic findings are summarized and discussed in Epstein, (in press-a).

Most of these results have been confirmed and extended by several researchers in studies of diverse populations of teachers, parents, and students (e.g., Ames, 1993; Brian, 1994; Davies, 1991; Davies, Burch, & Johnson, 1992; Dornbusch & Ritter, 1988; Eccles, & Harold, this volume, chap. 1; Epstein & Jacobsen, 1994; Epstein & Lee, 1993, in press; Lee, 1994; Montandon & Perrenoud, 1987; and many others). But there is much more to learn. Research about school, family, and community connections needs to improve in many ways. Early research was often based on limited samples, too global or too narrow measures of involvement, and limited data on student outcomes. As research proceeds with clearer questions and better data, measurement models should be more fully specified, analyses more elegant, and results more useful for policy and practice.

A LOOK AHEAD: PERSPECTIVES AND PREVIEWS

Studies conducted by researchers in the Center on Families, Communities, Schools and Children's Learning and by many other researchers are adding new knowledge on school, family, and community connections at various age and grade levels from birth through high school; in urban, suburban, and rural locations; with families of various backgrounds and cultures; new ways to understand and conduct studies of community connections with families and with schools; and new understandings of policy contexts. Studies in progress include surveys, case studies, experimental and quasi-experimental longitudinal data collections, field tests, evaluations, and program and policy development. The results of these studies will extend the field considerably, but they also raise new questions. Five topics have emerged from the ongoing research that are particularly compelling and need continued and additional study:

1. *points of transition* from one grade level to the next, from one school to the next, and across the years of high school;
2. *results or consequences*—positive or negative—of particular types of involvement at all levels for students, families, and for teaching practice;
3. the *components of community* in school and family partnerships;
4. the *roles of students* in school–family–community partnerships; and
5. *collaborations of researchers with policy leaders and educators.*

Each of these topics represents an extensive research agenda, and each has implications for policy and practice.

1. Perspectives and Previews:
Which Practices of Partnership Are Effective
at Important Points of Transition,
From One Grade Level to the Next,
Across School Levels, or at Other Times
That Students Change Teachers or Schools?

Students and their families age and grow and change grades, classes, and teachers every year. School and classroom programs and curricula become more complex each year and across levels. Schools also change as improvement plans and new programs are implemented. Teachers change as they become more experienced and as they add new approaches to their teaching repertory. Communities change as leaders, resources, services, and citizens come and go. All parts and participants of school, family, and community connections change constantly. Studies of partnerships, even at one point in time, must be aware of the inevitable developmental patterns of schooling.

The theory of overlapping spheres of influence encourages the measurement of concepts of change. It posits the pushing and pulling of these contexts as they are drawn together or forced apart each year by the philosophies, backgrounds, and practices of teachers, families, students, and others. Longitudinal data, case study histories, and other methods are important for learning more about the changing nature of partnerships across the grades.

Studies of change and transitions are demanding. Several studies by researchers in the Center on Families, Communities, Schools and Children's Learning are exploring continuity and change of family and community involvement with data collected over time on various topics. The studies use various methods, including surveys, interviews, observations, journals, and other reports from educators, from parents, and students. Some of these studies use mixed methods (e.g., small-sample, local case studies contrasted with large-sample surveys on the same topics) to examine how families are involved in their children's education, how involvement changes, and how the changes affect students, families, and teachers.

Regular Transitions Across the Grades. Research is accumulating on patterns of partnership across the grades. For example, longitudinal studies are in progress on how family involvement changes from kindergarten to Grade 2 in families with different cultural backgrounds (Bright, 1994; Hidalgo, 1994; Siu; 1994; Swap, 1994) and on how school programs to involve families change from Grades 2 to 5 (Ames, 1993). Many studies still are needed, however, to learn how partnerships change or remain the same across the grades from birth through high school; the challenges that families meet at each stage of their children's development; and the results for students, parents, and the schools of partnerships across the grades.

New issues about grade level changes are emerging. Students and their families change teachers every year, but little is known about these regular events that alter school and family connections. For example, the Center's research on families in different cultural groups reveals that children's new teacher may have different definitions of success than their prior teachers. Research is needed on how families learn about new teachers' ideas of how children succeed in their classrooms. A related question of equal importance is: How do teachers collect information from families about their children each year and periodically during a school year? Programmatic studies are needed on the organization and effects of various approaches to renew partnerships each year.

Alexander and Entwisle's research (this volume, chap. 5) raises another question about the annual transitions that students and their families make from the summer to the fall of the school year. Regardless of the school organization or length of the school year, home is a year-round resource. More information is needed on the question: What do schools need to do to help families maximize their influence year round? Presently, except in year-round schools, the summer is treated as a time that is separate from school. Research on summer learning and forgetting shows that summer is an influential time that affects students' skills and readiness for the next school year.

One study of the effects of summer learning packets suggests that marginal students, at risk of failing, are assisted in the fall by activities they conduct to keep their skills active in the summer (Epstein, Herrick, & Coates, in press). Another study indicates that a summer community component in a family literacy program has positive effects for the family and for students (Connors, 1993). Questions abound, however, about the best designs for active, interesting summer learning opportunities for students with their families and peers at home and in the community. Research and development are needed on effective approaches to integrate the summer time in the school year. For example, should (and how should) summer activities be organized for students and their families as part of the *concluding* school year or as part of the *oncoming* school year?

Key Points of Transition to New Levels of Schooling. Another important focus for future work is on changes in practices of partnership when children change schools. Particularly, dramatic declines in involvement are reported after each transition point from preschool to regular school, from elementary to middle school, and from middle to high school (Baker & Stevenson, 1986; Epstein & Dauber, 1991). Studies indicate, however, that these declines are not fixed. For example, a national survey of principals reports that middle grades schools that conduct strong transitional activities (such as inviting parents to visit the middle school while the children are still in the elementary grades) tend to continue more practices of partnership with families through the middle grades (Epstein & MacIver, 1990). Only about 40% of the middle grades schools in the United States, however, conduct strong transitional activities for families. Another survey shows that only 22% of the parents in a regional sample of six urban, rural, and suburban schools report that they visited the high school when their children were in the middle grades, and only 40% of the students did so (Connors & Epstein, 1994).

Research is needed on the design and effects of strategies and activities to help students and their families make successful transitions from the elementary to middle schools, middle to high schools, and high schools to postsecondary settings, and on how to maintain appropriate family involvement across school levels. Educators are providing some insights in their practices. For example, an inner city middle school conducted a formidable "orientation day" program for families and students on the first day of school and received high ratings for the effort from teachers, parents, and students (Epstein & Herrick, 1991). Such demonstration projects are informative, but studies of well-planned interventions will be needed to learn which kinds of orientation practices help most students, families, and schools. Newburg (1991) worked with educators to better understand the contacts and interactions that teachers need to make as students move from one school to the next. Research is needed on how families can be included in these transitional processes to help students prevent failure and maximize success in their new schools. What are the responsibilities of schools to conduct activities that inform families ahead of time about the changes that their children will experience when they move to new schools and what families can do to understand and assist the transitions? Should feeder or receive schools, or both, conduct these activities? What are the results of alternative approaches to communications about transitions? A parallel set of questions concerns the nature of family involvement in students' decisions about their postsecondary paths.

Unscheduled Transitions Due to Family Moves. Other questions about changing partnerships are raised by patterns of mobility, such as when families move in and out of schools and communities mid-year. Special problems must be solved when migrant, homeless, or other families move often (e.g., see PRIME, 1992). Unscheduled or unplanned transitions affect children, families, and their connections with schools. These transitions also affect what schools and teachers know or need to know about the entering children and families. Research is needed on the organization and effects of various approaches to partnerships with families in highly mobile schools and communities.

Other unscheduled transitions raise good research questions about the design and effects of school, family, and community partnerships. For example, when students are suspended from school, meetings with parents are required before the students are readmitted; or, when students are expelled from school, they—and their families—may enter new schools in new communities; or, when students drop out of school, they—and their families—may elect alternative schools or other programs in communities. Neither research nor practice has paid much attention to the design and results of connections with families that could assist students at times of dramatic, unscheduled changes in schools, and how to prevent these upheavals.

Transition to and Through High School. Of all the topics of continuity and change, the field has the least information about connections with families when students are in high school. Building on a handful of studies that raise numerous questions (Bauch, 1988; Clark, 1983; Dornbusch & Ritter, 1988), researchers in the Center are conducting surveys and field studies that ask: Which practices of partnerships are important for students, families, and schools at the high school level? How should practices to inform and involve families change from the freshman to senior years in high school? And, what are the results of partnerships for high school students, parents, and teachers?

The Center's research includes six high schools—two city, two suburban, and two rural schools—who agreed to work with researchers to design and administer surveys of teachers, parents, and students on their attitudes and ideas about partnerships in high schools (Epstein, Connors, & Salinas, 1993). The surveys are linked to the theory of overlapping spheres of influence and the framework of six types of involvement with questions that help a high school chart present practices and plan a multiyear, full program of partnership. The high schools are continuing to implement and improve practices such as involving families with students in goal setting, improving information systems, increasing attendance, bolstering student morale, creating stronger connections with community services for students and families, and other activities (Epstein & Connors, 1994; Connors & Epstein, 1994).

Many questions about partnerships in high schools remain to be addressed. The NELS:88 Base-Year and Follow-Up surveys offer important data from middle and high schools, from 8th, 10th, and 12th grade students and teachers, and from 8th and 12th grade parents, and from students in postsecondary settings. One Center study of partnership in high schools using the NELS data from students shows that when parents continue their involvement over time (i.e., from middle school Grade 8 to high school Grade 10), students report better attitudes, behaviors, report card grades, and attendance in high school (Lee, 1994). Standardized achievement test scores are harder to change in the upper grades and are not directly affected by continued involvement from Grades 8 to 10.

The NELS survey data from a large sample of schools, students, and families in Grades 8, 10, 12, and postsecondary years will be useful to many researchers because they offer broad coverage of many types of family involvement over time. But the NELS data also are limited, as practices of partnership are measured mainly by single items indicators. Deeper data from purposeful local or regional samples also will be needed to study in detail the design and effects of partnerships at the high school level.

At each higher level of schooling, questions about partnerships with families and communities become more difficult because the students, contexts, and all participants become more diverse and complex. All of the topics discussed in this chapter need further study at the high school level, including transitions, outcomes, community connections, the roles of students, and how researchers and educators work together.

2. Perspectives and Previews: What Are the Results or Outcomes of Particular Types of Involvement for Families, Students, and for Teaching Practice at All Levels of Schooling?

One of the most persistent misperceptions of many researchers, policy leaders, and educators is that any family involvement leads to all good things for students, parents, teachers, and schools. It is important to restate that the major types of involvement in the framework for research and practice are expected to affect different important outcomes for students, parents, and educators (Becker & Epstein, 1982; Epstein, 1982, 1986a, 1992). That is, not all activities to involve families lead quickly or directly to student learning, better report card grades, or higher standardized test scores. Rather, practices of the different types of involvement are expected to have theoretically linked results in the short term. For example, communications and interactions about parenting should first affect parents' informal interactions with their children; communications and interactions about reading should first affect a family focus on reading. If families continue to influence or reinforce student attitudes, behavior, or motivation, then student learning may improve over time. The pathways from particular family-school interactions to results for students, parents, or schools must be studied more rigorously than in the past, particularly with longitudinal data. Such studies are needed by educators in order to understand and predict the likely results of selecting and implementing particular practices to involve families in the schools and in their children's education.

For example, some Type 1 activities—such as workshops with parents or information about child development—may lead first to increasing (or, if poorly designed, to decreasing) parents' confidence about their understanding, supervision, and interaction with their children. Other practices, categorized in Type 3—such as new ways to organize, recruit, and train productive volunteers—may lead first to more effective (or, if poorly designed, to less effective) supervision by adults of student activities, more willingness of teachers to communicate in other ways with all families, or to a more varied curricular or extracurricular programs for students. By contrast, Type 5 practices—such as opening school decisions for input from parents or others in the community—may lead first to adults feeling more (or, if poorly organized, less) attachment to or support for the school. The positive or negative results of different involvement activities depend on the effectiveness of the design, implementation, measures, and improvements that are made over time.

Studies are needed on whether and how results of particular types of involvement generalize over time. For example, a chain of events may, hypothetically, take this pathway: Involvement of families in reading at home leads students, first, to greater attention to and motivation in reading. This may help students maintain or improve their reading skills. Over time, parental involvement in reading may lead to family discussions and interactions with children about other subjects. Also, teachers who communicate clearly with families about reading may, over time, improve their information to families about other subjects. This may help children see that their teachers want their families involved in their education, and that their families are interested in what they are learning and in talking with them at home about school and school plans. This support from families may motivate students to do their work in their school subjects and activities and plan for their future education and careers.

This line of events and effects may progress at different rates and with different degrees of success, depending on how much and how well the school informs and involves families and how the families and students participate. Activities, progress, and success may vary by teacher, by grade level, by students' starting skill levels, and by other student, family, and school characteristics. For example, some types of family involvement may affect skills or test scores more in the lower grades when achievement test scores are more changeable. Change in standardized test scores may be made more easily by students with low scores and "room to grow," particularly if the involvement of families is clearly focused on specific achievement topics (Epstein, 1991). Or, changes in new classroom skills and knowledge may be made by better students, who respond more quickly to new information (Epstein & Dauber, 1995). All of these variations raise researchable questions that need to be asked to more fully understand the results of particular school and family partnerships.

Improving Definitions of Achievement for Studies of Effects of Partnerships on Students. The achievement question must start with clearer definitions and measures of achievements. There are many measures of achievement besides standardized test scores that indicate students' success in school. And, some of these may be more responsive to school, home, and community conditions and, therefore, easier to change in the short term.

For example, specific-subject knowledge and skills may change from the pretest to posttest in units of work in science, math, social studies, or English, depending on the teachers' presentation of content, students' classwork, extra activities conducted with volunteers at school, and homework. In one evaluation, a program of parent volunteers working with teachers to introduce art appreciation to social studies classes significantly increased students' familiarity with art work. The subject-specific knowledge gained by students was linked directly to the content of the presentations by the volunteers (Epstein & Dauber, 1995). Several studies suggest that subject-specific family involvement affects learning in the related subject in the short term (Epstein, 1991; Epstein et al., in press).

Homework completion is another measurable achievement that influences student success in school and that may be affected by particular activities that involve families (Epstein, 1987c; Epstein, Jackson, & Salinas, 1994; Scott-Jones, 1995). If students complete their homework, they may attain higher report card grades, particularly if homework completion is counted by teachers as one component of students' marks. Or, homework completion may help students be better prepared for a class test, gain higher test scores, and, thereby, boost report card grades. New studies can help identify the effects of explicit processes and connections that are important for researchers, educators, families, and students to understand and apply.

There are other indicators of achievement. Good school attitudes, behavior, attendance, and the development of talents, interests, and other personal qualities are important for success in school. All of these may be affected (positively or negatively) by home and school practices of partnerships. Wise course choices and plans for the future also are important achievements in the upper grades that may be influenced by school, family, and student connections. These alterable outcomes that represent and contribute to success in school stand in contrast to narrow concerns with students' relative placements on standardized achievement test scores.

Because all students gain skills over time, it is difficult for many students to change their relative placement on tests or grades. There are, of course, exceptions, for example, students who dramatically find their way and become much better students than they were before or students who lose their way and fall farther and farther behind. Studies are needed on the part that family involvement plays to increase or maintain student motivation to learn and positive attitudes and behaviors under these different conditions, or to spur greater effort by students who could do better in school.

Positive and Negative Results of Involvement. Extant studies have generated compelling questions about the results or outcomes of partnerships. Although positive results of family involvement on various student outcomes are consistent and have been given the most attention (Henderson & Berla, 1994), some studies report negative correlations of some types of involvement with student achievements and behaviors and parental attitudes. For example, one study showed that students who are lower achievers spend more time on homework and receive more help with homework (Epstein, 1987c). The link of help with homework and low achievement is provocative because it either indicates that families who help are lowering their children's skills *or* that students who need more help are given more help by their families.

Another negative correlation reported in several studies, even under highly controlled statistical procedures, links parent and teacher contacts (e.g., frequent phone calls, conferences, and other communications) with students' academic problems and bad behavior (Lee, 1994). Also, frequent parent–teacher communications about student behavior are linked to parents' low ratings of the school and to parents' reports that their students like school less, are poorer students, are absent more, and have other negative attitudes and behaviors (Epstein & Jacobsen, 1994). These patterns stand in contrast to positive results in the same studies that are reported for other types of school–family links. The patterns are provocative because they could be interpreted to mean that home–school communications produce academic and behavioral problems, *or* that, presently, schools and families make contact more often when students run into difficulties in order to try to solve the problems.

There are clues that the negative correlations described previously occur because educators reach out to many sources, including parents, to obtain extra help, attention, and resources for students who are having academic or behavioral problems. These good intentions may not pay off, however, if the only communications between school and home are about trouble. Educators who are working to develop programs of partnership recognize that they need to conduct positive communications to establish a base of good relationships to draw on if they need families to help students solve academic or behavioral problems. In some high schools, for example, educators designed activities to start the school year with a positive meeting or phone call from a "key contact person" who is available as a resource to parents all year, or use "positive post cards" that send home good news about a student's work or contributions through the school year (Epstein & Connors, 1994).

To address this issue in practice, Seattle took a comprehensive approach in two middle schools with full-time, school-based "parent outreach coordinators" who contacted and worked with students and families if, on their report cards, students failed two or more courses. The goal was to prevent students from failing again in the next report card period. Contacts, guidance, and follow-ups with students, families, teachers, school counselors, and others were designed to alert and involve all who had a stake in students' success. A parent room at each school, facilitated by the parent outreach coordinators, made all parents welcome. The parent outreach coordinators received very positive evaluations for involving families, creating a welcoming school climate and establishing positive relationships to help solve difficult academic and other problems (Earle, 1989).

Any practice can be done well or poorly. There are risks, of course, that poorly designed or badly implemented practices to involve families will be ineffective or cause problems for students, for families, and for the schools (Scott-Jones, 1987). But studies by many researches using many methods show that well-designed and well-implemented practices yield positive results on various outcomes for students, parents, and the schools (Ames, 1993; Clark, 1983; Dornbusch & Ritter, 1988; Epstein & Dauber, 1991; Scott-Jones, 1987; and many others).

Studies are needed that determine if students who are having academic or behavioral difficulties in school improve over time if their families contact or are contacted by the schools, and if the students, families, and schools work together to solve the problems. It is not enough to measure family–school contact alone—the reaching out—to determine whether family involvement helps students improve their behavior or skills. The results of those efforts must also be measured. Longitudinal studies will be needed to determine if after receiving attention from home and school, students improve their attendance, behavior, pass their courses, and stay in school. We need to know: Which contacts and follow-up activities are most successful in helping students get back on successful paths? Which students and families respond best to various interactions? For how long should schools try to get students to solve their own problems before families are involved? How do these patterns of problem solving change across the grades?

To answer such questions about the effects of family involvement on achievements and other outcomes over time, research must statistically control for students' prior achievement, other prior outcomes, and families' prior involvement. Using a full effects model with the NELS:88 Base-Year and First Follow-Up surveys of students, Lee (1994) showed that family involvement in monitoring and interacting with students about homework and, particularly, family discussions about schoolwork, courses, grades, and the future have positive effects on high school students' report card grades and attitudes about school and teachers, even after statistically accounting for family involvement and student outcomes in the middle grades.

There are indications that effects of particular types of involvement may vary by level of schooling and by reporter or participant. For example, in the middle grades, according to principals, many types of school practices of partnership appear to boost one outcome—student attendance (Epstein & Lee, 1993). At the high school level, according to students, one type of involvement—family discussions about school, courses, and the future—appears to have positive effects on many outcomes, including attitudes, behaviors, and grades (Lee, 1994). These results reflect the strengths and weaknesses of the available data and raise many questions about effects of family involvement on students, parents, and teaching practice that must be addressed with better data and varied methods of analysis.

A detailed agenda for research on the outcomes of school, family, and community involvement can be drawn with questions about how each type of involvement is implemented in a comprehensive program. The following are examples of targeted questions on specific practices and their results that could extend research and contribute immediately useful information to teachers and administrators:

For Type 1—Parenting: How are workshop topics selected, conducted, and disseminated so that all families (not just those who can come to school) can obtain and apply information on topics that are important to parents? What are the short- and long-term effects for parents, students, and schools of parental participation in or information from workshops on parenting and childrearing across the grades? How does information from families about their children assist educators or other parents?

For Type 2—Communicating: How are report cards explained so that all families can understand them? How can families be helped to work with their children and teachers if they (and the students) believe that better grades are attainable? What are the results of these efforts on student report card grades? How can conferences be designed, scheduled, and conducted to increase the attendance of parents who work outside the home? How are students included in and affected by parent–teacher or parent–student–teacher conferences about student attendance, behavior, attitudes, achievement, goal setting, or other topics? How is information provided on school programs or course choices so that all families can understand and discuss the options and consequences of choices with their children? How do such discussions affect the patterns of choices that are made?

For Type 3—Volunteering and Supporting School Programs: How are volunteers recruited, welcomed, trained, and evaluated? How are the skills and talents of volunteers identified and matched with needs of teachers, students, and administrators? How do various volunteer programs and activities affect student learning, attitudes, and behavior; teacher attitudes toward parents; parent attitudes and skills; and other families?

For Type 4—Learning Activities at Home: In which forms can information about students' classwork and homework be offered to help families assist their children with their school responsibilities? How can activities be designed to enable families to use their unique "funds of knowledge" (Moll, Amanti, Neff,

& Gonzalez, 1992) to motivate their youngsters to learn new things at home? to enable students to interact with their families about things they are learning? How do activities at home that promote student and family interactions affect students' attitudes, skills, and homework?

For Type 5—Decision Making: How can all families give information to and receive information from parent leaders who represent them on councils and committees? How do family or community representatives on school site councils, school improvement teams, or committees alter (a) school improvement plans and activities or (b) the knowledge and attitudes of all parents about the school?

For Type 6—Connections With Community: How can schools help families obtain useful information about and access to community programs, services, and resources that may benefit them and their children? Which forms or approaches are most effective for sharing this information with all families? What effects will these approaches have on students' work in school? How can schools, families, and students contribute to their communities, and with what effects?

Focused evaluations on these and many other questions for each type of involvement should contribute to a menu of practices and their results. Information on the likely results—positive or negative and the possibilities, difficulties, and solutions to problems of involvement—would assist educators make more purposeful choices among practices of partnership to help them reach specific school or family goals.

3. Perspectives and Previews: How Can We Better Understand Components of Community in School, Family, and Community Partnerships?

Community is an old and vast term in sociology that demands new and focused attention in studies of school, family, and community partnerships. A broad definition of community refers to all individuals and institutions—in and out of school—who have a stake in the success of children in school and in the well-being of children and families. This includes schools, families, neighborhood groups, clubs and associations, businesses, libraries, local government, religious organizations, parks and recreation departments, police and juvenile justice offices, social service and health agencies, and others who serve children and families as a matter of course or in times of trouble. Presently, there is great interest in the potential and the problems of connecting schools, families, and communities in ways that will benefit student learning and development. There is widespread interest in integrating services across community agencies and in creating structures and processes that encourage interagency cooperation and collaborations to promote family support, family and student health, and student success in school. (See, for example, a report series from the National Center for Service Integration, e.g., Kinney, Strand, Hagerup, & Bruner, 1994; and Wynn, Costello, Halpern, & Richman, 1994.)

The community is one of the overlapping spheres of influence on student learning and development in the theoretical model of partnerships (Epstein, 1988, 1992). The relationships and resources of people and groups in a community are expressed in family–community, school–community, and family–school–community interactions.

Researchers often define and represent community using aggregated data about families or citizens in an area. For example, a community is sometimes defined by the average education level of all of the parents of students in a school or geographic location; by the percentage of families with particular qualities (e.g., single parents, race or ethnic minority group, poverty level, or other economic indicators in a neighborhood); by the average educational aspirations that parents have for their children or that students have for themselves; or by an average or percentage of other descriptive variables. In the same way, U.S. Census (or similar) data have been used to characterize populations in geographic areas surrounding particular schools (such as the percentage of citizens below the poverty line in a census tract around a school).

These variables represent some but not all factors that may influence children's learning. They are limited because they rate communities in terms of more or less of selected economic, intellectual, and social qualities or resources—such as high/low income, predominately Black/White, employed/unemployed, or married/single parents. One variable is too simple a descriptor of communities. That is, a high-income community may also be predominately minority; a low-income community may be highly supportive of their schools and eager for their children to attend college. Even if several descriptive variables are considered simultaneously, the resulting combined scores set communities on a continuum that labels them as high or low. Also, such labels are limiting because of the distance they place between a rating and the actual connections and activities of families and schools with children that influence student learning, attitudes, and behavior.

There are more proximate ways to characterize and study the resources and exchanges in communities that may assist students and families. Researchers in the Center on Families, Communities, Schools and Children's Learning are taking some different approaches to define and study community by focusing on strengths that are available in people, programs, and organizations in all communities. The idea is to get closer to what communities do, in contrast to what communities are. The same change was important for understanding families and family–school connections—that is, focusing on what schools and families can arrange to accomplish together, rather than only on their immutable (if more easily measured) characteristics. The redirection leads to new ways to measure and to influence family, school, and community connections from infancy to adolescence.

Some Center researchers are studying the impact of community programs on very young children and their families, including studies of programs to help parents read with toddlers (Morisset, 1993) and studies of the organization and effects of family literacy programs for parents of preschool, elementary, and middle school students (Connors, 1993, 1994; Dolan, 1992). Another study involves the design, development, implementation, and effects of a process to train low-income women in a community for employment in child care and to improve their own parenting and involvement activities and their children's school readiness (Kagan, Neville, & Rustici, 1993).

Other researchers are studying the impact of community programs for older students and families including studies of coaching processes and programs in which adults share their skills and talents with youth (Nettles, 1992, 1993). Other studies focus on the organization of child care programs to assist teenage mothers to continue to attend high school (Scott-Jones, in press); and on alternative approaches and results of interagency collaborations for high school students that include health, recreation, job training, child care, and other services (Burch, Palanki, & Davies, 1995; Dolan, in press-a).

The programs for younger and older children and their families may be based in community locations to provide services or in school locations to more easily contact and serve families and children. Community agencies, school districts, or community or parent volunteers may be responsible for staffing these and other programs that connect students and families with the strengths and services in their communities. Other connections may be made to enable students, families, or educators to contribute to their communities.

Even limited connections—such as when one school works with one community agency—pose many challenges. For example, one community-run family literacy program conducted in a school building required collaborative activities such as cross-agency planning, sharing of time, space, staff, responsibilities, and budgets (Connors, 1993). These new relationships needed to be developed by the community and school staffs. Programs operating over the long term are working to solve these problems (Dolan, in press-a, in press-b; Palanki et al., 1995), but the challenges and solutions and the effects of interagency or integrated services programs are mainly uncharted.

Questions about interagency connections open a formidable research agenda: What are the pros and cons, possibilities and problems, benefits and disadvantages of relatively simple connections of schools or families with one or two groups or programs in the community, or of more complex interagency collaborations? How should programs with connections to community be organized, implemented, and monitored to benefit children and families, schools, and the community?

Researchers also are exploring the strengths of parents and communities with various race, ethnic, and cultural characteristics (Delgado, 1992; Hidalgo, 1992, 1994; Hidalgo, Bright, Siu, Swap, & Epstein, 1995; Perry, 1993; Siu, 1992, 1994; Swap, 1994; Swap & Krasnow, 1992). These studies identify resources and strengths in families and communities that would be labeled "poor" or "deficient" if only aggregated economic statistics or census-type data were used to define them. For example, these studies suggest that resources within families and communities include rituals, traditional values, family dreams and aspirations, cultural norms for student behavior, racial identity development, practices that involve families in their children's education and schools, and formal and informal community organizations that support families.

These studies are adding new information that may help schools understand the complex nature of families and communities. For example, Hidalgo (1992) noted that immigrant families who aim to retain cultural identities and ties in their local communities require schools to change more than do immigrant families who aim to assimilate in the mainstream community. The former group wishes to be recognized and respected by their schools for their differences. Their cultures and backgrounds are potential resources for the schools. The unique needs of these families and children may require some special attention from the schools. The latter group, emphasizing assimilation, wishes to avoid attention by the schools to their newness or differences, even if they maintain their cultural traditions and identities in the home and community. They may work to change their own behaviors and attitudes to meet the expectations and demands of the schools.

In another study, Delgado (1992) identified the potential strengths of "natural support systems" in Puerto Rican communities. These include networks of extended families, religious groups, merchants, social clubs, and other individuals or groups that people contact for assistance instead of (or in addition to) seeking help from formal institutions such hospitals, health centers, and schools. Community strengths are not often recognized or counted in studies that employ traditional economic, educational, or social statistics. Yet, the informal networks may help families and children with many basic personal, economic, spiritual, and social needs. Delgado contended that community resources could be used in better ways by formal organizations, such as schools, to communicate with students and families.

Nettles (1992) identified coaching as one way to tap communities' strengths. By coaching, adults share their skills and talents with children, including public speaking, chess, sports, music, dance, art, science, and many other interests. She proposed a framework for how to think about, organize, and implement coaching programs. To use the framework in practice, she discussed strategies of how successful coaches teach, assess, structure environments, and offer social support to students (Nettles, 1993).

Parent rooms or parent centers aim to establish a school community by welcoming parents to the school building. In these centers, parents may help each other, help the school, and receive assistance or information from the school and from the community. As described by Johnson (1993, 1994) and Coates (1992), a parent room, parent center, or parent club is a place that draws parents, teachers, students, and community participants together and increases the frequency, duration, and types of connections that could help more children succeed in school. The first studies and descriptions of parent centers in schools and family resource centers in communities raise many questions for research on whether and how these organizational structures make it easier for schools to help families meet their responsibilities to their children and to help families help students solve academic or behavioral problems, should they arise.

The Center's studies of community work from the inside out—starting with the traditions and talents of families or other groups. The research asks questions about how to harness the strengths that are in all communities to assist students, engage families, and improve schools. Many questions remain, however, about the organization of community resources and patterns and effects of school, family, and community interactions. For example: How can all communities' strengths be tapped in ways that support families, children's growth and development, success in school, in infancy, childhood, and adolescence? Who will organize this work? How might schools draw on the strengths of families' language and cultural differences and other family and community skills and talents to improve the education of all children and to improve the schools' relationships with families? How should partnerships change or remain the same for families with various cultural, racial, or economic backgrounds, across the grades in order to create both a sense of community among all families in a school and still meet the needs of particular families? How does the community foster learning, reinforce schooling, and recognize accomplishments? Results of such studies should contribute new ideas about how to define, measure, and mobilize communities' strengths and how to promote school, family, and community partnerships that, ultimately, benefit students who are the future citizens, leaders, and families in communities.

4. Perspectives and Previews: How Can We Better Understand the Role of the Student in School, Family, and Community Partnerships?

An important, emerging theme in the Center's work is the role of the student in school, family, and community partnerships. The theory of overlapping spheres of influence places students at the center of the model (Epstein, 1987a). The theory assumes that families, schools, and communities share an interest in and responsibility for children all across the school years and that the main reason that educators, parents, and students interact is to assist students to succeed in school and in life. It is important to focus on how schools develop good programs of partnerships and on what parents want their schools to do to inform and involve them each year. It is more important, indeed crucial, to recognize that the student is the active learner, ultimately responsible for his or her education, and the main communicator between school and home.

Research is needed to define, design, and study students' roles in school, family, and community partnerships at different grade levels. This topic ties student development to the design and effects of family involvement in education. It promotes, even demands, interdisciplinary attention to stages of youngsters' development, interactions and relationships of many individuals, and the multiple contexts or environments in which students learn and in which family–school–community links occur.

Most studies of family–school links have not paid attention to the students' roles in partnerships. This is true despite the fact that students have long been reporters about their schools and their families. A few examples show, however, that the student role has been hovering in research on partnerships—waiting for and deserving more attention. Bronfenbrenner (1979) advised that socialization and education should be organized so that, over time, the balance of power is given to the developing person. Also, in an earlier study, Epstein (1983) found that age-appropriate decision-making opportunities at school and at home increase students' independence and other positive outcomes. Most often, however, literature on schools or families assumes that students are "acted on" rather than the actors or "done to" rather than the doers. The different assumptions about the students' roles in education raise questions for research about optimal designs for schooling and for school and family partnerships.

This theme is finding voice in other areas of school reform such as in reciprocal teaching, cooperative learning, constructivist approaches, and other active learning strategies. The role of the student in partnerships is being addressed in a few studies that have asked students directly about how they view the connections of their families and schools and how they participate as partners (Ames, 1993; Dornbusch & Ritter, 1988; Epstein, 1982; Montandon & Perrenoud, 1987). Students' opinions are informative and often surprising. For example, students express an overwhelming desire to be active participants in parent–teacher conferences and to be represented on school committees (Connors & Epstein, 1994).

In practice, educators are keenly aware that students play *the* key role in their own education. For example, many important activities in high school (e.g., choosing courses, finding career interests, planning for the future, understanding school policies) are presently often left up to the student *alone*. New approaches to partnerships with families focus on how middle and high schools design and conduct activities to enable families to provide extra support, as appropriate, on important decisions that affect the lives of students and their families (Epstein & Connors, 1994, 1995).

Importantly, students at all grade levels report that they want their families to be more involved and that they are willing to be the communicators and to conduct important exchanges with their families about school work and school decisions (Connors & Epstein, 1994; Epstein & Herrick, 1991). Earlier studies show that when they know their families are involved, students report that their schools and families are more similar, that their teachers and parents know each other, that they do more homework on weekends, and that they like school better (Epstein, 1982). In high school, students who report that their families are involved in many different ways at school and who discuss school and their futures at home have more positive attitudes, better attendance, and better grades than other students, even after accounting for their scores on these outcomes in the middle grades (Lee, 1994).

If youngsters do not define themselves as "student," then they must be something else, with no need to be in school. Those who feel the support of their family, teachers, peers, and community for their work as students are more likely to maintain that view of themselves and stay in school. Thus, ironically, students' participation in school, family, and community partnerships may contribute to their increasingly independent decisions about their education.

Research is greatly needed on such questions as: How shall activities be organized to enable students to take appropriate leadership for their learning at all grade levels? How much guidance and support, rules and regulations, independence and self-direction are needed by students across the grades? in diverse communities? There are many other questions about students' motivations, goals, and achievements. Questions about the roles that students play in partnership are importantly linked to all of the preceding topics. That is, studies are needed on students' roles in partnerships at points of transition from one grade or school to the next; the results or outcomes of all six types of involvement that include or exclude students; and the results of activities that involve students and their families with the community.

Students' roles and student development have not yet been well integrated into studies of school, family, and community partnerships nor in policies and practices of involvement. These topics may be crucial for understanding, implementing, and succeeding with partnerships across the grades. Undoubtedly, students are key to the success of all aspects of school reform, including family and community involvement.

5. Perspectives and Previews: How Can Researchers, Policy Leaders, and Educators Collaborate to Develop, Study, and Improve School, Family, and Community Partnerships?

Collaborative work and thoughtful give-and-take by researchers, policy leaders, and educators are largely responsible for the progress that has been made over the past decade in understanding and developing school, family, and community partnerships. Similar collaborations will be important for future progress in this and other topics of school reform. There are two requirements for successful collaboration—multilingualism and mutual respect. That is, researchers and educators must talk each others' languages and understand and respect each others' expertise in order to combine talents to improve schools. For researchers, this means learning the vocabularies and communication skills that are needed to converse with and to write for diverse audiences, including educational policy leaders, principals, teachers, and parents. For educators, this requires a readiness and capacity to use research to address topics of school improvement. Also, researchers need to gain familiarity with the challenges of teaching highly diverse students and the daily life of schools. Educators need to gain understanding of the challenges of collecting useful data to analyze processes and effects of school and classroom programs. Collaborations increase conversations and mutual respect as researchers, educators, parents, and students learn about their common goals and complementary strengths (Epstein, in press-b). The same requirements hold as families and students are included as planners, implementers, evaluators, and in other roles. Researchers and educators need to build communication skills and mutual respect with families and students and an understanding that parents are, indeed, partners in their children's continuing education and that students are the main actors in education.

Sharing the Role of Expert. The requirements for educators and researchers to speak with and develop respect for each other are addressed in a collaborative approach called "sharing the role of expert" (Epstein, 1986b; Epstein et al., in press). This approach recognizes that educators (policy leaders, teachers, and administrators) have particular talents and opportunities that are vital to the successful design and implementation of research-based practices. For example, administrators and teachers are responsible for implementing new strategies to involve families in their schools or classrooms as volunteers or to engage students with their families on math homework. Researchers, too, have particular talents and opportunities to design, evaluate, report, and disseminate the effects of school improvement efforts. Parents also have unique perspectives, concerns, and skills that relate to their children's success in school and that expand researchers' and educators' views. Together, educators, researchers, and parents plan new practices, collect, analyze and interpret data, and revise and improve plans, drawing on each other's expertise. The assumption is that these collaborations should lead to better practices, better processes, and better evaluations and interpretations of results than would be accomplished if the participants worked alone.

Sharing the role of expert alters how research is conducted. For example, when working directly with schools, a two-step process of evaluation is useful. The first step is to assess whether a practice actually is implemented and how its design could be improved; the second step is to study whether a practice (as implemented and improved) has measurable effects on students, families, or teaching practice. This sequence of collaborative activities helps educators and researchers get used to working with each other and assures that measures of results will not be made before a program is actually in place.

There are several emerging forms of collaborative work by researchers and educators, all of which require sharing the role of expert: school–university cooperation ("Alliance for Learning," 1994; Goodlad, 1988; Harkevy & Puckett, 1990; Miller & O'Shea, 1995); teacher research, teacher-led inquiry, reflective teaching (Cochran-Smith & Lytle, 1993; Cohn & Kottkamp, 1993; Lieberman, 1993; Maher & Alson, 1990; Newburg, 1991); parent–teacher action research (Burch & Palanki, 1994; Davies, Palanki, & Burch, 1993); and action teams for school, family, and community partnerships (Epstein & Connors, 1994; Epstein et al., in press). The various forms have different implications for the nature and products of the work of teachers and researchers. All, however, aim to encourage education policy leaders, educators, and researchers to work together, extend and share knowledge, conduct research on actions taken to improve schools, and take actions based on the results of research to continue improvements. Several include parents, and some include students or others from the community as participants in planning programs and practices, as well as in conducting and evaluating them.

Collaborations of Researchers and Education Policy Leaders.   Two examples of productive collaborations of researchers and policy leaders for increasing family–school partnerships include the development of a state policy on parent involvement in California (Solomon, 1991) and the design and work of Utah's Center on Families in Education (Lloyd, this volume, chapter 16). In these cases, educators read, adapted, and extended research for their locations and purposes, and researchers supported and assisted the policy leaders and educators in those locations with their work. Many other researchers and educators have worked to together to produce better school, family, and community partnerships (e.g., see articles by Chrispeels, Warner, Davies, D'Angelo, and others in the special section of *Phi Delta Kappan,* 1991; also, several examples of programs based on researchers' and educators' collaborations in Fagnano & Werber, 1994; Fruchter, Galletta, & White, 1992; Rioux & Berla, 1993).

Collaborations of Researchers and School Teams.   Two examples of productive collaborations of researchers, educators, and parents to increase family–school–community partnerships include Parent–Teacher Action Research Teams and Action Teams for School, Family, and Community Partnerships.

Parent–Teacher Action Research Teams, designed by Davies and his colleagues, include teachers and parents in site-based units for school improvement and problem solving (Burch, 1993; Davies et al., 1993; Palanki, Burch, & Davies, 1995). Educators and parents work together as change agents and as researchers to improve practices of partnerships in their schools. The teams define problems or needs, identify approaches to solve the problems, design and implement interventions, examine results, and follow up their work in meetings with further plans. They may choose one problem to solve or work on several aspects of partnership. This approach aims to develop "teacher researchers" and "parent researchers" who will continue to work together on projects to improve partnerships and other aspects of school reform. In the Center projects using this approach, paid facilitators assist the work of the Parent–Teacher Action Teams, and researchers are focusing on cross-site policy studies.

Action Teams for School, Family, and Community Partnerships, designed by Epstein and her colleagues, establish teams of teachers, administrators, parents, and where possible, students and members of the community who work for 3 years or more as the "action" arm of the school council or school improvement team on the topic of partnerships. The Action Team works with others to assess their school's present practices of partnership, parents, teachers, and students needs, and desired practices. The team members become chairs or co-chairs to oversee and to lead the implementation of multiyear plans of projects on each of the six types of involvement in our framework for partnership. They assess and share progress, problems, and new plans each year, link and report to the school improvement council, and communicate with the total school community about the school's activities to involve families. This approach is useful for developing ongoing programs of partnerships in elementary, middle and high schools (Epstein & Connors, 1994; Epstein & Dauber, 1991; Epstein et al., in press). It has been implemented in useful forms in Utah's and Wisconsin's state grants programs (Lloyd, this volume, chap. 16; Wisconsin Department of Public Instruction, 1994) and in many districts and schools. Other Action Teams could be arranged for other topics on the school improvement agenda.

In Center projects, researchers worked with educators and parents to develop and improve this approach and to study particular practices of partnership and their effects. For example, the Teachers Involve Parents in Schoolwork (TIPS) interactive homework process (Epstein et al., 1994) and the volunteers in social studies and art process (Epstein & Salinas, 1991) were developed collaboratively by researchers and educators, based on sharing the role of expert and the two-step evaluation process. Now, other educators may use the Action Team approach and the research-based TIPS interactive homework and volunteers processes. Using these strategies, other researchers may become partners with school teams in their local districts, states, or regions to assist them assessing the effectiveness of their practices.

The Center's studies demonstrate different but related routes to increasing schools' capacities to plan, implement, and continue to build programs of partnership. The emerging collaborative approaches have different emphases, however. In Parent–Teacher Action Research, the goal is for teachers and parents to design and conduct research on specific practices that they add to their programs. In Action Teams for School, Family, and Community Partnerships, the goal is for teachers, administrators, parents, and others to plan a multiyear program including the six types of involvement, informally monitor or evaluate progress, update plans, and improve practices. The collaboration of educators, parents, and researchers on these Action Teams relieves some of the burden on educators who, with limited time, may not be able to transform into statistical experts; and the collaboration relieves some of the burden on researchers who cannot become instant classroom experts with knowledge of what will work in daily practice. Also, this approach preserves a role for researchers in action research and increases chances of improving the research base and of assisting many schools with their work.

Research is needed on the impact of these and other forms of collaborative work by researchers with policy leaders, educators, and parents. But more pointedly, collaborative strategies could be particularly helpful for addressing the four topics discussed earlier in this chapter. Topic 1, on understanding changes across the grades and other important transitions, is of interest to researchers who seek better information on student development and change. Educators, in turn, need better solutions to problems of student adjustment in transitions from grade to grade, school to school, or developmental stage to stage. Researchers and educators, working collaboratively, could address common questions about how one teacher should link with the next, how information might flow from school to school at points of transition, how families should be engaged in their children's transitions, and other issues discussed with Topic 1 previously.

Topic 2, on understanding the results or outcomes of programs and practices that involve families, is a major interest to researchers of school effects. Educators, in turn, pay attention to the bottom line—results of their educational programs. Researchers and educators, working collaboratively, could address common questions about the effects of programs and practices to improve the school climate; increase teachers' effectiveness; assist mothers, fathers, or other family members in their interactions with their children and the school; increase student learning and development—all expected outcomes of productive partnerships—and other issues discussed with Topic 2 previously.

Topic 3, on understanding connections of schools and families with community services, resources, and organizations, challenges researchers to study the organization and effects of integrated services and to better define communities' roles in supporting children as students. Educators, in turn, need feasible ways to mobilize support from and connect to the school community, the students' home communities, and various communities that surround the school with potential strengths and resources. Some innovative activities to identify and tap into school communities have been designed by educators working with researchers (e.g., Floyd, 1994; Goode, 1990), but relatively little is known about the optimal organization of school, family, and community connections. Researchers and educators, working collaboratively, could address common questions about how connections with individuals, groups, and organizations in proximate and distant communities could improve the school, strengthen students' skills, assist families, benefit the community; and other issues discussed with Topic 3 previously.

Topic 4, on understanding roles that students play in school–family–community partnerships, interests researchers in many disciplines who study child and adolescent development. Educators, in turn, want better information about ways to develop students' responsibility, including the optimal mix of guidance from school and home and the design opportunities to develop independence. Researchers and educators, working collaboratively, could address common questions about student motivation; how students should be participants in school, family, and community partnerships; and other issues discussed with Topic 4 previously. Linked to this topic, researchers and educators working collaboratively also might explore questions on the most productive roles in school, family, and community partnerships for principals, district and state leaders, on-site coordinators, and families in relation to the roles of students in their own education.

In the next few years there will be many opportunities for new collaborations of researchers with policy leaders and educators to study the design and effects of guidelines, mandates, and other policies about school, family, and community connections. Two 1994 federal laws (Goals 2000: Educate America Act and Title I of the Elementary and Secondary Education Act) offer directives and funding to all states to enable districts and schools to design and test ideas for productive partnerships with families. The diverse responses to these federal laws across states, districts, and schools open countless opportunities for researchers to work with policy leaders and educators to address the five topics discussed in this chapter and other questions that emerge in local planning sessions. Comparative studies also will be informative on the effects on partnership programs of states' contrasting decisions about budgets, staff responsibilities, and elements of the new programs.

By sharing the role of expert with those who design and implement programs in the schools, researchers could assist educators and increase the knowledge available on alternative approaches for organizing, funding, and implementing school, family, and community partnerships. Studies will be important on such topics as: How will states identify effective practices among demonstration programs and extend options for implementing successful programs to other districts and schools? How can schools be assisted to move from very limited investments in one type of involvement (e.g., volunteers or school councils only) to more comprehensive programs? Overall, what would a supportive policy structure look like at the federal, state, district, and local school level that would support school activities to plan, implement, and evaluate practices of partnership? On many topics, then, researchers and educators can combine talents to study the effects of the growing number of investments in partnerships, with the goal of identifying effective practices and their results that may be considered by many schools, districts, and states as they plan and improve their programs.

CONCLUSION

Over the next half dozen years or so there will be intense national attention on whether and how students succeed in school, how schools improve their instructional programs, and how families are informed and involved in schools and in their children's education. Attention also will increase on whether and how communities assist schools, families, and students. These practical concerns open important opportunities for researchers to work with educators to design and study many topics for school improvement, including school, family, and community partnerships.

Studies have accumulated that indicate that (a) students do better in school if their parents are involved in various ways; (b) more parents become involved when schools establish and conduct good programs of partnership; (c) schools can be assisted by federal, state, district, and school leadership and policies to develop strong and responsive programs; (d) research and evaluation activities can identify differences between strong and weak policies, good and bad practices; (e) results of many studies have produced a research-based framework that should enable any school to plan and implement practices for the six major types of involvement, including practices to help meet specific goals for school improvement.

Despite real progress in understanding the potential and challenges of partnerships, there are many more questions to ask. This chapter previewed five topics that will benefit from the attention of researchers, policy leaders, educators, and families: partnerships at points of transition in schools and at the high school level; the effects of particular practices and full programs of partnership in the short and long term; the connections of communities with schools and families for student learning and development; the roles of students in partnerships; and forms of collaborative research and development by researchers, policy leaders, educators, and parents.

Other questions may be raised. For example, we need to know more about the nature and effects of fathers' participation in school and family partnerships across the grades; the effects on partnerships of particular federal, state, and local policies separately and in combination; the impact of contrasting forms of staff development and teacher and administrator preservice and advanced education on practices of partnership; the connections of parent education programs with broader programs of school and family partnerships; the connections of partnerships with other topics of school reform. These important issues can be targeted within the five topics discussed in this chapter.

The complex questions for research and for practice ensure that family–school links will remain a dynamic field of study.

REFERENCES

Alliance for Learning. (1994, April 13). *Education Week, XIII* (25, Suppl.), 1–24.

Ames, C., Khoju, M., & Watkins, T. (1993). *Parents and schools: The impact of school-to-home communications on parents' beliefs and perceptions* (Center Rep. No. 15). Baltimore: Center on Families, Communities, Schools and Children's Learning, Johns Hopkins University.

Baker, D. P., & Stevenson, D. L. (1986). Mothers' strategies for children's school achievement: Managing the transition to high school. *Sociology of Education, 59,* 156–166.

Bauch, P. A. (1988). Is parent involvement different in private schools? *Educational Horizons, 66,* 78–82.

Becker, H. J., & Epstein, J. L. (1982). Parent involvement: A study of teacher practices. *The Elementary School Journal, 83,* 85–102.

Brian, D. (1994, April). *Parental involvement in high schools.* Paper presented at the annual meeting of the American Educational Research Association, New Orleans.

Bright, J. A. (1994, Winter). Beliefs in action: Family contributions to African-American student success. *Equity and Choice, 10*(2), 5–13.

Bronfenbrenner, U. (1979). *The ecology of human development: Experiment by nature and design.* Cambridge, MA: Harvard University Press.

Burch, P. (1993). Circles of change: Action research on family–school–community partnerships. *Equity and Choice, 10*(1), 11–16.

Burch, P., & Palanki, A. (1994). Action research on family–school–community partnerships. *Journal of Emotional and Behavioral Problems, 1*(4), 16–19.

Burch, P., Palanki, A., & Davies, D. (1995). *From clients to partners: Four case studies of collaboration and family involvement in the development of school-linked services* (Center Rep. No. 29). Baltimore: Center on Families, Communities, Schools and Children's Learning, Johns Hopkins University.

Clark, R. M. (1983). *Family life and school achievement: Why poor Black children succeed or fail.* Chicago: The University of Chicago Press.

Coates, L. (1992). The parent club. In C. Hyman (Ed.), *The school–community cookbook* (pp. 122–125). Baltimore: Fund for Educational Excellence.

Cochran-Smith, M., & Lytle, S. (1993). *Inside/outside: Teacher research and knowledge.* New York: Teachers College Press.

Cohn, M. M., & Kottkamp, R. B. (1993). *Teachers: The missing voice in education.* Albany, NY: SUNY Press.

Coleman, J. S. (1987). Families and schools. *Educational Researcher, 16,* 32–38.

Connors, L. J. (1993). *Project Self Help: A family focus on literacy* (Center Rep. No. 13). Baltimore: Center on Families, Communities, Schools and Children's Learning, Johns Hopkins University.

Connors, L. J. (1994). *Small wins: The promises and challenges of family literacy* (Center Rep. No. 22). Baltimore: Center on Families, Communities, Schools and Children's Learning, Johns Hopkins University.

Connors, L. J., & Epstein, J. L. (1994). *Taking stock: The views of teachers, parents, and students on school, family, and community partnerships in high schools* (Center Rep. No. 25). Baltimore: Center on Families, Communities, Schools and Children's Learning, Johns Hopkins University.

Connors, L. J., & Epstein, J. L. (1995). Parents and schools. In M. Bornstein (Ed.), *Handbook of parenting* (pp. 437–458). Hillsdale, NJ: Lawrence Erlbaum Associates.

Dauber, S. L., & Epstein, J. L. (1993). Parents' attitudes and practices of involvement in inner-city elementary and middle schools. In N. Chavkin (Ed.), *Families and schools in a pluralistic society* (pp. 53–71). Albany, NY: SUNY Press.

Davies, D. (1991). Schools reaching out: Family, school and community partnerships for students success. *The Phi Delta Kappan, 72,* 376–382.

Davies, D. (1993). A more distant mirror: Progress report on a cross-national project to study family–school–community partnerships. *Equity and Choice, 19*(1), 41–46.

Davies, D., Burch, P., & Johnson, V. (1992). *A portrait of schools reaching out: Report of a survey on practices and policies of family–community–school collaboration* (Center Rep. No. 1). Baltimore: Center on Families, Communities, Schools and Children's Learning, Johns Hopkins University.

Davies, D., Palanki, A., & Burch, P. (1993). *Getting started: Action research in family–school–community partnerships* (Center Rep. No. 17). Baltimore: Center on Families, Communities, Schools and Children's Learning, Johns Hopkins University.

Delgado, M. (1992). *The Puerto Rican community and natural support systems: Implications for the education of children* (Center Rep. No. 10). Baltimore: Center on Families, Communities, Schools and Children's Learning, Johns Hopkins University.

Dolan, L. J. (1992). *Project Self Help: A first-year evaluation of a family literacy program* (Center Rep. No. 8). Baltimore: Center on Families, Communities, Schools and Children's Learning, Johns Hopkins University.

Dolan, L. J. (in press-a). *Implications of New Jersey's School-Based Youth Services for community interagency and school collaborations.* Baltimore: Center on Families, Communities, Schools and Children's Learning, Johns Hopkins University.

Dolan, L. J. (in press-b). An evaluation of social service integration in six elementary schools in Baltimore. In L. Rigsby & M. Wang (Eds.), *School/community connections.* San Francisco: Jossey-Bass.

Dornbusch, S. M., & Ritter, P. L. (1988). Parents of high school students: A neglected resource. *Educational Horizons*, *66*, 75–77.

Earle, J. (1989). *Restructuring Seattle's middle schools*. Alexandria, VA: National Association of State Boards of Education.

Edmonds, R. R. (1979). Effective schools for the urban poor. *Educational Leadership, 37*(2), 15–24.

Epstein, J. L. (1982). *Student reactions to teacher practices of parent involvement*. (Rep. No. P-21). Baltimore: The Johns Hopkins University Center for Research on Elementary and Middle Schools.

Epstein, J. L. (1983). Longitudinal effects of family–school–person interactions on student outcomes. In A. Kerckhoff (Ed.), *Research in sociology of education and socialization* (Vol. 4, pp. 101–128). Greenwich, CT: JAI.

Epstein, J. L. (1986a). Parents' reactions to teacher practices of parent involvement. *The Elementary School Journal, 86*, 277–294.

Epstein, J. L. (1986b, April). Sharing the role of expert: Cooperative researcher/teacher efforts in developing a process for teachers to involve parents in schoolwork. Paper presented at the annual meeting of the American Educational Research Association, San Francisco.

Epstein, J. L. (1987a). Toward a theory of family–school connections: Teacher practices and parent involvement. In K. Hurrelmann, F. Kaufmann, & F. Losel (Eds.), *Social intervention: Potential and constraints* (pp. 121–136). New York: DeGruyter.

Epstein, J. L. (1987b). What principals should know about parent involvement. *Principal, 66*, 6–9.

Epstein, J. L. (1987c). *Homework practices, achievements, and behaviors of elementary school students* (CREMS Rep. No. 26). Baltimore: Center for Research on Elementary and Middle Schools, Johns Hopkins University.

Epstein, J. L. (1990). Single parents and the schools: Effects of marital status on parent and teacher interactions. In M. Hallinan (Ed.), *Change in societal institutions* (pp. 91–121). New York: Plenum.

Epstein, J. L. (1991). Effects on student achievement of teacher practices of parent involvement. In S. Silvern (Ed.), *Literacy through family, community, and school interaction* (pp. 261–276). Greenwich CT: JAI.

Epstein, J. L. (1992). School and family partnerships. In M. Alkin (Ed.), *Encyclopedia of educational research, 6th edition* (pp. 1139–1151). New York: MacMillan.

Epstein, J. L. (in press-a). *School and family partnerships: Preparing educators and improving schools*. Boulder, CO: Westview.

Epstein, J. L. (in press-b). New connections for sociology and education: Contributing to school reform. *Sociology of Education, 68*.

Epstein, J. L., & Connors, L. J. (1994). *Trust fund: School, family, and community partnerships in high schools* (Center Rep. No. 24). Baltimore: Center on Families, Communities, Schools and Children's Learning, Johns Hopkins University.

Epstein, J. L., & Connors, L. J. (1995). School and family partnerships in the middle grades. In B. Rutherford (Ed.), *Creating family/school partnerships*. Columbus, OH: National Middle School Association.

Epstein, J. L., Connors, L. J., & Salinas, K. C. (1993). *High school and family partnerships: Surveys and summaries—Questionnaires for teachers, parents, and students, and How to summarize your high school's survey data*. Baltimore: Center on Families, Communities, Schools and Children's Learning, Johns Hopkins University.

Epstein, J. L., & Dauber, S. L. (1991). School programs and teacher practices of parent involvement in inner-city elementary and middle schools. *Elementary School Journal, 91*, 289–303.

Epstein, J. L., & Dauber, S. L. (1995). Effects on students of an interdisciplinary program linking social studies, art, and family volunteers in the middle grades. *Journal of Early Adolescence, 15*, 237–266.

Epstein, J. L., & Herrick, S. C. (1991). *Improving school and family partnerships in urban middle grades schools: Orientation days and school newsletters* (CDS Rep. No. 20). Baltimore: The Johns Hopkins University Center for Research on Effective Schooling for Disadvantaged Students.

Epstein, J. L., Herrick, S. C., & Coates, L. (in press). Effects of summer home learning packets on student achievement in language arts in the middle grades. *School Effectiveness and School Improvement.*

Epstein, J. L., Jackson, V., & Salinas, K. C. (1994). *Manual for teachers: Teachers Involve Parents in Schoolwork (TIPS) language arts, science/health, and math interactive homework in the middle grades* (Rev. ed.). Baltimore: Center on Families, Communities, Schools and Children's Learning, Johns Hopkins University.

Epstein, J. L., & Jacobsen, J. (1994, August). *Effects of school practices to involve families in the middle grades: Parents' perspectives.* Paper presented at the annual meeting of the American Sociological Association, Los Angeles.

Epstein, J. L., & Lee, S. (1993, August). *Effects of school practices to involve families on parents and students in the middle grades: A view from the schools.* Paper presented at the annual meeting of the American Sociological Association, Miami, FL.

Epstein, J. L., & Lee, S. (in press). National patterns of school and family connections in the middle grades. In B. A. Ryan & G. R. Adams (Eds.), *The family–school connection:Theory, research and practice.* Newbury Park, CA: Sage.

Epstein, J. L., & MacIver, D. J. (1990). *Education in the middle grades: National practices and trends.* Columbus, OH: National Middle School Association.

Epstein, J. L., & Salinas, K. C. (1991). *TIPS volunteers in social studies and art manual.* Baltimore: Center on Families, Communities, Schools and Children's Learning. Johns Hopkins University.

Fagnano, C. L., & Werber, B. Z. (1994). *School, family, and community interaction: A view from the firing lines.* Boulder, CO: Westview.

Floyd, S. (1994). *In their own voices: A case of collaboration and innovation in the English Language Arts.* Saginaw, MI: Saginaw High School (mimeo).

Fruchter, N., Galletta, A., & White, J. L. (1992). *New directions in parent involvement.* Washington, DC: Academy for Educational Development.

Goode, D. A. (1990). The community portrait process: School community collaboration. *Equity and Choice, 6*(3), 32–37.

Goodlad, J. (1988). *School–university partnerships in action.* New York: Teachers College Press.

Gordon, I. J. (1979). The effects of parent involvement in schooling. In R. S. Brandt (Ed.), *Partners: Parents and schools* (pp. 4–25). Alexandria, VA: Association for Supervision and Curriculum Development.

Harkevy, I., & Puckett, J. L. (1990). *Toward effective university–public school partnerships: An analysis of three contemporary models.* Philadelphia: University of Pennsylvania Graduate School of Education (mimeo).

Henderson, A. T., & Berla, N. (1994). *A new generation of evidence: The family is critical to student achievement.* Washington, DC: National Committee for Citizens in Education.

Hidalgo, N. (1992). *"i saw puerto rico once": A review of the literature on Puerto Rican families and school achievement in the United States* (Center Rep. No. 12). Baltimore: Center on Families, Communities, Schools and Children's Learning, Johns Hopkins University.

Hidalgo, N. M. (1994). Profile of a Puerto Rican family's support for school achievement. *Equity and Choice, 10*(2), 14–22.

Hidalgo, N., Bright, J., Siu, S., Swap, S., & Epstein, J. (1995). Research on families, schools, and communities: A multicultural perspective. In J. Banks (Ed.), *Handbook of research on multicultural education* (pp. 498–524). New York: MacMillan.

Johnson, V. R. (1993). *Parent/family centers: Dimensions of functioning in 28 schools in 14 states* (Center Rep. No. 20). Baltimore: Center on Families, Communities, Schools and Children's Learning, Johns Hopkins University.

Johnson, V. R. (1994). *Parent centers in urban schools: Four case studies* (Center Rep. No. 23). Baltimore: Center on Families, Communities, Schools and Children's Learning, Johns Hopkins University.

Kagan, S. L., Neville, P., & Rustici, J. (1993). *Family education and training: From research to practice—implementation plan.* (Center Rep. No. 14). Baltimore: Center on Families, Communities, Schools and Children's Learning, Johns Hopkins University.

Keesling, J. W., & Melaragno, R. J. (1983). Parent participation in federal education programs: Findings from the federal programs survey phase of the study of parental involvement. In R. Haskins & D. Adams (Eds.), *Parent education and public policy* (pp. 230–254). Norwood, NJ: Ablex.

Kinney, J., Strand, K., Hagerup, M., & Bruner, C. (1994). *Beyond the buzzwords: Key principles in effective frontline practice* (Working paper series). Falls Church, VA: National Center for Service Integration.

Lareau, A. (1989). *Home advantage: Social class and parental intervention in elementary education.* Philadelphia: Falmer.

Lee, S. (1994). *Family–school connections and students' education: Continuity and change of family involvement from the middle grades to high school.* Unpublished doctoral dissertation, Johns Hopkins University, Baltimore.

Leichter, H. J. (1974). *The family as educator.* New York: Teachers College Press.

Lieberman, A. (1993). The meaning of scholarly activity and the building of community. *Equity and Choice, 10*(1), 4–10.

Litwak, E., & Meyer, H. J. (1974). *School, family, and neighborhood: The theory and practice of school–community relations.* New York: Columbia University Press.

Maher, C., & Alson, A. (1990). Teacher development in mathematics in a constructivist framework. In R. B. Davis, C. Maher, & N. Noddings (Eds.), *Constructivist views on the teaching and learning of mathematics: Journal for research in mathematics education.* Monograph No. 4. (pp. 147–165). Reston, VA: National Council of Teachers of Mathematics.

Miller, L., & O'Shea C. (1995, Winter). Partnership: Getting broader, getting deeper. *Resources for Restructuring* (pp. 1–6). National Center for Restructuring Education, Schools and Teaching, NCREST, Teachers College.

Moll, L. C., Amanti, C., Neff, D., & Gonzalez, N. (1992). Funds of knowledge for teaching: Using qualitative approach to connect homes and classrooms. *Theory into Practice, 31*(2), 132–141.

Montandon, C., & Perrenoud, P. (1987). *Entre parents et enseignants Ün dialogue impossible?* [Between parents and teachers: An impossible dialogue?] Berne: Lang.

Morisset, C. E. (1993). *Language and emotional milestones: On the road to readiness* (Center Rep. No. 18). Baltimore: Center on Families, Communities, Schools and Children's Learning, Johns Hopkins University.

National Commission on Excellence in Education. (1983). *A nation at risk: The imperative of educational reform.* Washington, DC: U.S. Government Printing Office.

Nettles, S. M. (1992). *Coaching in community settings* (Center Rep. No. 9). Baltimore: Center on Families, Communities, Schools and Children's Learning, Johns Hopkins University.

Nettles, S. M. (1993). *Coaching in communities: A practitioner's manual.* Baltimore: Center on Families, Communities, Schools and Children's Learning, Johns Hopkins University.

Newburg, N. (1991). A systems approach to school reform. In D. A. Schon, (Ed.), *The reflective turn* (pp. 53–76). New York: Teachers College Press.

Palanki, A., & Burch, P. with Davies, D. (1995) *In our hands: A multi-site parent–teacher action research project on family-school-community partnerships.* (Center Rep. No. 30). Baltimore: Center on Families, Communities, Schools and Children's Learning, Johns Hopkins University.

Perry, T. (1993). *Toward a theory of African American school achievement* (Center Rep. No. 16). Baltimore: Center on Families, Communities, Schools and Children's Learning, Johns Hopkins University.

Phi Delta Kappan. (1991). Paths to partnership (Special section on parent involvement). *72,* 344–388.

PRIME. (1992). Parental Resources for Involvement in Migrant Education (Newsletter series). Geneseo, NY: BOCES Geneseo Migrant Center.

Rioux, W., & Berla, N. (Eds.). (1993). *Innovations in parent and family involvement.* Princeton Junction, NJ: Eye on Education.

Scott-Jones, D. (1987). Mother-as-teacher in the families of high-and low-achieving low-income Black first-graders. *Journal of Negro Education, 56,* 21–34.

Scott-Jones, D. (1995). Activities in the home that support school learning in the middle grades. In B. Rutherford (Ed.), *Creating family/school partnerships* (pp. 161–181). Columbus, OH: National Middle School Association.

Scott-Jones, D. (in press). Outcomes for adolescent mothers and their children in child care. Baltimore: Center on Families, Communities, Schools and Children's Learning, Johns Hopkins University.

Seeley, D. S. (1981). *Education through partnership: Mediating structures and education.* Cambridge, MA: Ballinger.

Siu, S. (1992). *Toward an understanding of Chinese-American educational achievement* (Center Rep. No. 2). Baltimore: Center on Families, Communities, Schools and Children's Learning, Johns Hopkins University.

Siu, S. (1994). Taking no chances: A profile of a Chinese-American family's support for school success. *Equity and Choice, 10*(2), 23–32.

Solomon, Z. (1991). California state policy on parent involvement: Initiating a process for state leadership. *Phi Delta Kappan, 72,* 359–362.

Swap, S. (1994). Irish-American identity: Does it still have meaning in supporting children's school success? *Equity and Choice, 10*(2), 33–41.

Swap, S. M., & Krasnow, J. (1992). *A saga of Irish-American achievement: Constructing a positive identity* (Center Rep. No. 11). Baltimore: Center on Families, Communities, Schools and Children's Learning, Johns Hopkins University.

Wisconsin Department of Public Instruction. (1994, August/September). Sharesheet. *The DPI Family–Community School Partnership Newsletter, 3,* 1–2.

Wynn, J., Costello, J., Halpern, R., & Richman, H. (1994). *Children, families, and communities.* Chicago: University of Chicago, The Chapin Hall Center for Children.

15

New National Directions in Research and Policy

Oliver C. Moles
U.S. Department of Education

It is a great pleasure for me to offer my comments on the chapter by Joyce Epstein and related matters. This is a very substantial chapter, a real tour de force by a preeminent researcher and thinker in the area of school, family, and community partnerships. Joyce Epstein has been working diligently in this area for more than a decade. Her intellectual leadership is apparent in her many articles in scholarly journals as well as the numerous programs she has advised and the many who are using her concepts and findings in their daily work. This is indeed an exciting area for interaction between researchers, policymakers, and practitioners.

I want to comment first on the chapter and then discuss some recent federal education initiatives—new laws and a partnership—which draw on and also demand research. These initiatives are carving out new policy agendas on families and schools, and research is a central part of this picture.

Epstein presents a wealth of information gleaned from her studies, conceptual frameworks, experience, and the work of others. She portrays the development of different forms of parent involvement since the 1960s, how they were tied to changing conditions of family life and education reforms, and the shift from parent involvement to a more inclusive emphasis on school, family, and community partnerships. This new emphasis is reflected in the federally funded research center on this topic, which she co-directs, as well as various other studies. The interest in family–school links has indeed grown in recent years. I too have witnessed the proliferation of sessions at the American Educational Research Association meetings and seen other professional and advocacy organizations placing this issue on their agendas, plus the emergence of a new national Family Involvement Partnership for Learning among many organizations that I discuss shortly.

The public may continue to expect that families should initiate contacts with schools, but more and more educators, researchers, and policymakers recognize that families often cannot do so and agree with Epstein that the question now is how schools can take the initiative and help all families do the kinds of things that will benefit their children.

Epstein sees as the main goal of partnerships "to develop and conduct better communications . . . with more families . . . [in order] to assist more students . . . to succeed in school" (pp. 213–214). To this emphasis on enhanced information sharing, I would add the need for stronger collaborative activities between schools and families. This may be implied in her formulation, but the development and implementation of shared sustained activities bear emphasis as tangible manifestations of continuing partnerships along with enhanced communication.

The perspective of overlapping spheres of influence between schools and families is described briefly and drawn on repeatedly in the chapter. Although Epstein explains this perspective elsewhere, for the present discussion it would help to say more about the kinds of influence of interest and, in addition, whether this perspective is purely descriptive of different conditions between schools and families or whether it also has some ability to generate predictions regarding subsequent or prior actions. What makes the school and family spheres get pushed closer together or farther apart?

Epstein is perhaps best known for her six types of involvement between schools and families. Here they are identified as parenting, communicating, volunteering, learning at home, decision making, and collaborating with community. All of these "fall within the areas of overlap in the spheres of influence" (p. 215), although it is not clear in what sense this occurs. It is important to recognize that this is not a typology of parent roles in education because critical roles such as parents as learners are not included. Instead, in this chapter, she emphasizes the role of schools in communicating with families to help them remain informed, involved, and linked to the community. In earlier writing on the six types, Epstein described parenting as the obligation of families and communicating as the obligation of schools (Epstein, 1988). Because many need assistance in developing their parenting skills and family routines, the new emphasis on school roles in working with families seems quite appropriate. In addition, other of her types, such as parents in decision-making roles, are now becoming obligations too as schools are being required to include parents in planning for school improvements. Thus, the old category of school obligations has become less distinctive.

This chapter also reminds us of Epstein's striking research findings that have challenged common sense understandings of family–school links. A sampling of these follows:

1. Differing views of parents. Teachers are often unaware of parents' hopes and wishes for their children and what parents do with their children. For example,

studies by various researchers show that most parents want to know how to help their own children at home (Moles, 1993). This leads to her plea for measuring both teachers' and parents' views so as to identify gaps in knowledge of each other.

2. Students and partnerships. Rather than students wanting to minimize parents' involvement in their education, students want their families to be informed partners with their school and available as resources for information and assistance. They also want an active part in parent–teacher conferences and school committees.

3. Teacher and family practices. What teachers do to involve parents is at least as important as family background variables for influencing family practices of involvement in children's education, and these family practices are also at least as important for influencing children's education as family background variables such as race, ethnicity, social class, marital status, or mother's working outside the home.

4. Teacher practices as stereotypes. Teachers who often involve parents rate single and married parents and those with more and less formal education as more similar in help given their children at home. Those who less often involve parents rate single parents and those with less education as less helpful.

The five topics Epstein selects for her look ahead represent key areas for further study and connections with policy and practice—issues such as the management of transitions across grades, school level, or teachers. At such points, students often lose ground. Epstein poses a number of questions for research into each of the key areas including the development of effective summer learning programs to sustain academic progress. Especially interesting in the area of transitions is her finding that when parents continue to be involved from middle school to high school, they and school staffs have better relationships, and student attitudes, attendance, and grades also are better. She notes the sore need for more studies at the high school level. I would add that the need for conceptualizing school–family relationships and parent influences among older students is equally important to advance our knowledge of the processes involved.

On the key topic of communities, Epstein notes that studies are currently exploring strengths of parents and communities and organizations. She lists areas of family strengths including their values and aspirations, participation in children's schooling, and supports in extended families and religious groups. My own recent review of studies revealed several near-universal strengths of families that pertain directly to their children's education (Moles, 1993):

1. Parents are the first and foremost teachers of their children.
2. Families have vast opportunities to influence children by instruction and by example.
3. All parents want their children to do well in school and have good futures.

4. Parents want to work with the schools to aid in their children's education.

Family strengths is one key concept in a set of workshop materials our office sponsored for training school staffs to build school–family partnerships for student learning (Moles & D'Angelo, 1993).

Turning to methodological considerations, there is indeed a need for better designed studies covering a wider range of topics in the area of family–school linkages. Epstein notes the importance of more representative sampling, of controlling for extraneous variables to rule out competing explanations, and of longitudinal studies to determine long-term effects as well as to get a better fix on short-term ones. Hardly any existing studies look at long-term effects, yet this is what makes the difference in education. Her call for multiple methods and multiple measures is a refreshing reminder that different methodological approaches can yield important and complementary insights. Multiple measures instead of the common single indicators can help to reduce measurement error. I would add the need to evaluate programs and practices of schools to foster partnerships with families.

NEW FEDERAL LAWS

The U.S. Department of Education has several family initiatives that involve the interplay of research and policy. The Goals 2000: Educate America Act, signed into law in March 1994, sets new standards for student, family, and school performance. One part of this law is a new National Education Goal on parent participation. It reads: "Every school will promote partnerships that will increase parental involvement and participation in promoting the social, emotional, and academic growth of children" (p. 11). Progress toward this goal will now be tracked by studies as is being done for the other goals (National Education Goals Panel, 1994).

One objective under this goal calls on schools to help parents strengthen home learning activities and to involve them in school decision making. The reference to home learning activities clearly builds on a long line of research showing the benefits of school interventions to assist families, including low-income and minority families (Epstein, 1991; Leler, 1983; Tangri & Moles, 1987; Walberg, 1984). The decision-making aspect builds on democratic ideals of participation by all affected parties and long-standing research showing that real influence in planning contributes to commitment and improved organizational performance (Mohrman, Lawler, & Mohrman, 1992).

Parents must also be involved in planning state and district school improvement programs that seek federal support under Goals 2000, probably for similar reasons. Finally, this law authorizes federally funded parent information and resource centers in the states to serve parents of children from birth through high school and parent educators. Along with other activities, the centers will be required to promote programs for preschool children such as the Home Instructional Program for Preschool Youngsters (HIPPY) and the Missouri Parents as Teachers. Both have been evaluated in detail and do show promising results (Baker & Piotrkowski, 1993; Fruchter, Galletta, & White, 1992; Pfannenstiel, Lambson, & Yarnell, 1991).

A second recent federal law is the Improving America's Schools Act of 1994. This comprehensive statute reauthorizes the program of aid to low-income and low-achieving students, first created under the Elementary and Secondary Education Act of 1965, which is now again called Title 1, and a number of other federal education programs including Even Start and bilingual education. These latter programs require family education and parent outreach and training to facilitate the educational achievement of affected children.

Title 1 requires consultation with parents in developing and reviewing local school improvement plans and an annual meeting to explain the program to parents. A new feature of Title 1 is that 1% of local program funds must be set aside for parent involvement activities in school districts that receive $500,000 or more. Required activities include helping parents to monitor their child's progress and to work with educators to improve the student's school performance. But significantly, teachers and other school staffs are also to be educated in the value of parent contributions and how to reach out to and work with them as equal partners. Roles for community-based organizations and businesses in parent involvement activities are also to be developed.

One other new Title 1 requirement is a school–parent compact that outlines how parents, the entire school staff, and students will share responsibility for higher student achievement. The form of the compact is to be determined by the school and parents. As schools develop compacts, research will be important to trace effects on the behavior of the signers. However, it seems likely that compacts will need to be coupled with follow-on activities to produce real change, and such activities deserve special attention. Thus, these new laws invite research and evaluation studies on a number of fronts to explore the implications and effects of their various parent-related provisions.

THE FAMILY INVOLVEMENT PARTNERSHIP

Another example of research and policy links has occurred recently on the national scene. The U.S. Department of Education has entered into an ambitious national Family Involvement Partnership for Learning with over 100 national organizations including the 50-member National Coalition for Parent Involvement in Education. This Partnership aims to increase family involvement in children's education and to encourage schools, businesses, and communities to support families more fully. The Partnership momentum began with the concerns of

Secretary of Education, Richard W. Riley, expressed in his February 1994 State of American Education speech. In this speech, he argued that children and youth need more support and guidance from their families, friends, and the community and that families and schools need to be reconnected to strengthen each other's efforts.

From this beginning, Department of Education officials and senior staff have met with over 125 organizations in education, business, community service, religion, civil rights, and local government. Strategic planning is under way with many of these organizations on how to increase awareness and a sense of shared responsibility and action to promote learning and development of children and youth. This will obviously represent a long-term commitment. The Secretary inaugurated the Partnership with a speech on September 7, 1994. It is designed to advance the new National Education Goal on parent participation by doing the following things:

bringing together organizations and individuals working in this field;

encouraging schools, businesses and communities to establish a supportive environment for family involvement;

conducting and sponsoring research showing the relationship between effective school practices and family involvement in learning;

identifying and publicizing outstanding examples of family involvement around the nation;

providing useful information to parents; and

setting an example by encouraging federal employees to participate in their children's learning (U.S. Department of Education, 1994a).

The Department decided at an early point to issue a white paper giving the rationale for the Partnership in terms of therelated research, program evaluations, and best practices. Fortunately, there is a strong research base, and the participating organizations provided new evaluative data on some of their programs. Members of the Department's Planning and Evaluation Service (PES) and I wrote the paper. Alan Ginsburg, the director, and other PES staff have a long interest in parent involvement and have analyzed large data sets and written for scholarly journals in this area.

The white paper, called "Strong Families, Strong Schools" (U.S. Department of Education, 1994b), points to 30 years of research showing that family involvement is a critical link to high quality education. It notes that what the family does is more important to student success than parent income or education, a point made also in Epstein's work. Critical factors include reading with children, limiting television viewing, monitoring out-of-school activities, setting high expectations, and offering support and encouragement for achievement. "Strong Families, Strong Schools" cites surveys of parents, teachers, and students themselves all indicating that parents are not devoting enough time to children's education and then discusses some of the reasons: employment demands on parents, uncertainty about what to do, cultural barriers, and lack of a supportive community environment.

Besides things parents can do at home and with the school, the larger part of "Strong Families, Strong Schools" discusses how other institutions can support families directly and also provide services such as mentoring and after-school programs to help when parents cannot do so. These sections are on:

1. school–family partnership practices of schools
2. community activities connecting families and schools
3. family-friendly business practices
4. state policies and activities connecting families and schools
5. what federal programs are doing to support families

The white paper concludes that the task of connecting families and schools is formidable but also attainable. It will require "a shift in public attitudes regarding the importance of learning, a willingness of educators to fundamentally rethink the role of parents and school–family relationships, and the cooperation of the entire community" (U.S. Department of Education, 1994b, p. 44).

The Family Involvement Partnership is an instructive example of the convergence of public policy and social research. It began with Secretary Riley's experience as governor of South Carolina in building support among diverse constituencies for education reforms and the parallel track of extensive research on parent involvement in education in recent decades, of which Joyce Epstein's work is a prime example. The white paper review of research provides a strong rationale for the Department's initiative to build a national partnership and the conviction that a new federal program is not enough—that many independent institutions, organizations, and individuals must work together. Moreover, it points to many programs and practices that hold promise for improving family–school connections.

Would the Partnership have proceeded without a strong research base? Perhaps so, given the urgency of the situation and the experience of Secretary Riley. But the white paper adds legitimacy to the effort, and more importantly, it points to some actions that can make a bigger difference than others. It helps us focus our energies on alterable practices rather than despair over fixed conditions that may be less important than was thought.

A set of resource papers is also being developed to guide Partnership efforts. Some are based on inquiries regarding ongoing activities across the country. These will identify family-friendly practices in business, specific programs on school–family relationships, and the work of various current partners. Finally, research is planned to track progress of the Partnership and help make adjustments to improve its work. Thus, the Family Involvement Partnership is a vital contemporary example of the ways in which research and policy can inform and support each other.

REFERENCES

Baker, A. J. L., & Piotrkowski, C. S. (1993). The effects of participation in HIPPY on children's classroom adaptation: Teacher ratings. *NCJW Center for the Child Report.* New York: National Council of Jewish Women.

Epstein, J. L. (1988). How do we improve programs for parent involvement? *Educational Horizons, 66*(2), 58–59.

Epstein, J. L. (1991). Effects on student achievement of teacher practices of parent involvement. In S. Silvern (Ed.), *Advances in reading/language research, Vol. 5. Literacy through family, community, and school interaction.* Greenwich, CT: JAI.

Fruchter, N., Galletta, A., & White, J L. (1992). *New directions in parent involvement.* New York: Academy for Educational Development.

Leler, H. (1983). Parent education and involvement in relation to the schools and to parents of school-aged children. In R. Haskins & D. Adams (Eds.), *Parent education and public policy* (pp. 141–180). Norwood, NJ: Ablex.

Mohrman, S. A., Lawler, E. E., and Mohrman, A. M. (1992). Applying employee involvement in schools. *Educational Evaluation and Policy Analysis, 14*(4), 347–360.

Moles, O. C. (1993). Collaboration between schools and disadvantaged parents: Obstacles and openings. In N. Chavkin (Ed.), *Families and schools in a pluralistic society* (pp. 21–49). Albany: State University of New York Press.

Moles, O. C., & D'Angelo, D. (1993). *Building school–family partnerships for learning: Workshops for urban educators.* Washington, DC: U.S. Department of Education, Office of Educational Research and Improvement.

National Education Goals Panel. (1994). *The National Education Goals report: Building a nation of learners 1994.* Washington, DC: Author.

Pfannenstiel, J., Lambson, T., & Yarnell, V. (1991). *Second wave study of the Parents as Teachers program.* St. Louis: Parents as Teachers National Center.

Tangri, S. S., & Moles, O. (1987). Parents and the community. In V. Richardson-Koehler (Ed.), *Educator's handbook* (pp. 519–550). New York: Longman.

U.S. Department of Education. (1994a). *Riley calls for greater family involvement to increase learning; announces nationwide partnership.* (Press release) September 7.

U.S. Department of Education. (1994b). *Strong families, strong schools.* Washington, DC: Author.

Walberg, H. J. (1984). Families as partners in educational productivity. *Phi Delta Kappan, 65,* 397–400.

16

Research and Practical Application for School, Family, and Community Partnerships

Gary M. Lloyd
Utah Center for Families in Education

Over the past decade, much research and practical application on parent, school, and community relationships has taken place. We are still on the threshold of becoming a real family of learners who are willing to take a risk to assist the one person who is, after all, the single most important individual we can focus on—the student.

Judy Carter (1994), executive director of the Family Resource Coalition, stated, "If as research and common sense indicate, the family is the most important and effective resource available to any individual child, then, we must make this resource the cornerstone of strategies to improve children's well-being" (p. 6).

The wave of extreme individualism, with its emphasis on self-indulgence, primarily created during the 1960s and 1970s, began to undermine family and community values in the United States. Prior to this time, values had been taught in the home, and then reinforced in the school and the community. The traditional family, as we once knew it, is eroding at an alarming rate. It is clear in the mid-1990s that the moral decline is reaching epidemic proportions, especially in certain large cities across the nation.

Hansen and Ginsburg (1985, cited in U.S. Department of Education, 1994) said, "Values instilled by parents—honesty, belief in the work ethic, responsibility for one's actions, and religious principles—are twice as important for school achievement as family economic or educational background" (p. 10).

The family develops a unique culture of its own, which in turn impacts the school and the larger community. Ramsey (1992), from the Parent Knowledge

Network, indicated that "Culture helps members deal with their daily lives by indicating what is important and how to achieve it. Family culture then, presents a 'road map' that influences the development and achievement of individual members and the group as a whole" (p. 24).

If we simply try to encourage parents to get involved with their children in school without first strengthening their own family culture, parents will become frustrated. Parents want the best for their children but often do not have the tools needed to create a successful family learning culture. Some children grow up in increasingly difficult family conditions. Many parents have not had successful models or training that would enable them to provide the nurturing, structure, and security needed to protect their children and prepare them to become successful and good citizens. I share the belief that every child in the United States should have the opportunity to develop to his or her full potential. This cannot happen without the shared responsibility of parents, other family members, community, institutions, employers, government at the federal, state, and local levels, and the media.

The Utah Center for Families in Education has struggled with these concerns, but is building positive partner relationships with individuals and agencies including the state director of human services, the director of the Governor's Office of Child Care, and with the Governor's Initiative on Families and the Utah Coalition on Families. The community at large, including the federal Headstart Program, businesses, and churches have also helped find ways to strengthen Utah families. A key priority of this coalition is to provide the care and support children need to enter school ready to learn, and to provide adolescents and adults with the social, educational, and financial opportunities for success throughout their lives.

UTAH CENTER FOR FAMILIES IN EDUCATION

On April 1, 1990, the Utah State Office of Education opened the Utah Center for Families in Education with the Utah PTA as a cosponsor. The center is funded by the Utah State Board of Education through requests from the Utah State Legislature.

The combination of the state Office of Education and the state PTA has been a formidable team in communicating and inservicing educators and parents about their roles in providing an academic future for children.

The twofold mission of the Utah Center for Families in Education is as follows:

1. It provides parents with the opportunity to create "responsible family learning cultures that prepare their children for success as life-long students, citizens, parents, consumers, and workers in our global society."
2. It provides opportunities for parents, schools, and communities to become involved more fully in coordinating and communicating with each other.

In 1994, the director of the Utah Center for Families in Education requested a meeting with key Utah educators, state and federal agencies, and private providers to determine if the education system was providing adequate services for parents and their children from birth to kindergarten. The clear message from these meetings was that the state education system needed to address early childhood education, beyond the area of the at-risk student, including coordinating more closely with other organizations and agencies.

A statement from the National Commission on Children (1991), *Beyond Rhetoric*, helped focus the discussions on early childhood education.

Parents are responsible for guiding their children's social and intellectual development, for ensuring that their children enter school ready to learn, and for monitoring and encouraging their academic progress. Parents should view themselves as partners with schools in the education process, reading to young children, monitoring homework, and creating home environments that encourage learning" (p. 211).

The center places particular priority on the Goals 2000: Educate America Act. This education reform bill, which was signed into law March 31, 1994, provides resources to states and communities "to develop comprehensive education reforms." Goals 2000 emphasizes the following goals:

1. All children in America will be ready to learn (as they enter school).
2. Every school will promote partnerships that will increase parental involvement and participation in promoting the social, emotional, and academic growth of children.

ORGANIZATIONAL STRUCTURE

The director of the center is hired by the Utah State Office of Education and reports to the associate superintendent of public instruction. A central steering committee, made up of three representatives each from the Office of Education and Utah PTA, provides direction and support to the center administrator. A full-time secretary and three part-time staff members assist with the activities of the center.

The center has a 33-member advisory council made up of outstanding leaders from across the state. The council includes leadership of all major educational organizations, legislators, businessmen, church administrators, parents, and teachers, along with the state director of human services, state director of the Governor's Office of Child Care, and the dean of the College of Education at Weber State University (Epstein, 1992).

The center has eight committees. The committees and their functions are as follows:

1. Public Service—handle publicity and media relations;
2. Materials Development—produce brochures, calendars, and center materials;

3. Model School Programs—identify model parent–school programs in and out of state;
4. Business and Community Advocacy—develop partnerships;
5. Teacher Education—liaise with Utah's six teacher-training institutions to develop training materials for potential teachers;
6. Inservice—provide training for parents and educators, including the Student Education Plan (SEP);
7. Evaluation—evaluate pilot schools and center activities; and
8. Early Childhood Development—coordinate with Utah state agencies and local school districts, individual schools, and private providers.

Each of these committees is chaired by a volunteer from the community, and co-chaired by a representative of the Utah PTA.

The center provides the following services:

1. Annual conference for Utah parents, families, and members of the community.
2. Annual Parent–Child Activity calendar (60,000).
3. Quarterly newsletter for parents and educators.
4. EDInfo Hotline, a 24-hour computer service with recorded messages concerning educational, social, and health issues.[1]
5. Parent–educator library with materials, books, software, and so on that are mostly free to the public.
6. Inservice support and funding to 12 pilot schools participating in a 5-year study to evaluate selected practices relating to parent, school, and community relationships.
7. Nine-hour inservice training program for Utah parents relating to basic family values, character education, and ways to reinforce learning at home, so children become proficient in school subjects.
8. Speakers for educational, parent, and community groups concerning the importance of the partnership of parent, school, and community, and to explain the availability of the Family Education Plan (FEP) training and other services of the center.
9. Coordination with agencies, organizations, and school districts relating to parents with children from birth through Grade 12.

---

[1]In 1994, the service was expanded to include messages from eight additional agencies, including the governor's office. The system has three regular lines and one 800 line for parents to call and listen or request information. (Over 40,000 calls have come from parents requesting information, or to just listen to timely messages, since the service opened in 1992).

10. Committee on teacher education, with representatives from each teacher education program in Utah, is currently developing a 10-hour unit of instruction that will provide potential teachers with skills on how to involve families at school and at home (see Epstein, chap. 14, this volume).

UTAH'S PILOT SCHOOL PROGRAM FOR FAMILIES, SCHOOLS, AND COMMUNITIES

Soon after the opening of the Utah Center in 1990, 12 pilot schools (8 elementary, 2 middle, and 2 high schools) were selected to became part of a 5-year study on family–school–community involvement.

At both the elementary and secondary levels, schools from rural and metropolitan areas were selected to participate in the study. Care was taken to assure as much diversity as possible in areas relating to parent education, income, and ethnic background.

Each of the schools received funding from the center and paid matching amounts from their own school or district.

Most schools were involved in the pilot study for 4 years at the completion of the school year in June 1995. The model framework used in each of the 12 pilot schools was developed by Epstein (Epstein & Connors, 1992).

The Epstein model of six types of involvement with school, family, and community include:

1. Basic obligations of families.
2. Basic obligations of schools.
3. Involvement at school by parents and other volunteers.
4. Involvement in learning activities at home.
5. Involvement in decision making, governance, and advocacy, by parents.
6. Collaboration and exchanges with community organizations.

Each school participating in the model has initiated a seven-committee structure, each chaired by a teacher and a parent, who, by assignment, interact with families, schools, and the community to assure that the "overlapping spheres of influence" (Epstein, 1994) can be realized. Each of the seven committees at each school receive inservice training quarterly from the center. The principals meet quarterly with the center to review successes and to offer recommendations for improvement.

Dr. Lloyd McCleary, an international evaluation expert, employed by the University of Utah, has completed the first of three evaluations of the 12 pilot schools conducted over the 5-year period of the study. A sampling of students was tested, and a sampling of teachers and parents was questioned to determine how and if the model provides additional support to students, and if students are excelling academically because of the model practices being used at the pilot schools.

Encouraging news came from the carefully controlled pilot schools report (McCleary, in press), and results indicated that students have improved their academic performance by as much as 20% in the majority of the participating pilot schools. This evaluation completed by the University of Utah confirms findings from studies already undertaken by many researchers that parental involvement improves student learning (Epstein, 1992; Henderson & Berla, 1994; Keith & Keith, 1993; Stevenson & Baker, 1987).

Three additional practices were added to the Epstein model by the center for the purpose of reaching some of the goals established by the Utah State Office of Education. They are discussed here.

Pre-Kindergarten Contracts

Kindergarten teachers are given extended contracts to visit the homes of children who will enter kindergarten the following school year. The teacher visits the family several months before the beginning of the coming school year, and explains what the parents and child can expect the next fall. A picture of the family, in their own environment, is taken by the teacher to place in a file that will be reviewed when the child enters kindergarten. Before their child begins school, the parents are invited to visit the school at least twice to meet the principal and teachers, and to visit the classroom to watch the teacher in action. Two positive experiences occur in this practice. First, the teacher gets to know the family and their environment. Second, the parents become acquainted with the school environment long before they take their child to school for the first time. Teachers and parents in the pilot schools have indicated extremely positive experiences as they have taken part in this family–school coordination practice.

Parent–Teacher Hotline

At the school level, administrators and teachers have centered their vision of what schools and teachers can provide to parents. Middle and high school studies have lagged behind research done at the elementary level but are now focusing on the effectiveness of two-way communication between parents and schools (Rutherford, Billing, & Kettering, 1993). To address this need, each of the 12 pilot schools purchased a computer system (from funds supplied by the center) to provide a direct communication link for parents and teachers. Teachers record their daily homework assignments on the system, and parents can call in after 4 p.m. each day, and for a period of 24 hours after a given assignment has been placed on the computer system, to find out what homework assignments have been given to their children. The system works well for both elementary and secondary school programs. Parents may also speak with the teacher about specific needs relating to their children by dialing a number assigned to that family for the child or children who attend that particular school.

Student Education Plan

In what Utah has chosen to call the Student Education Plan (SEP) for elementary schools and the Student Education Occupation Plan (SEOP) for secondary students, teachers, parents, and the student at the elementary school and teachers, counselors, parents, and the student at the secondary school meet for 20 minutes quarterly. The student's long- and short-range goals are reviewed, and each of the three or four in attendance sign a commitment that they will accept responsibility to assist in the furthering of the student's goals. In the large majority of pilot schools, between 95% and 100% of the parents attend, and after the SEP/SEOP meeting, leave supportive and interested in public education, and—even more important—they improve relationships with their children. This program is in contrast to the traditional approach, usually called "Parent–Teacher Conference," which is often a negative experience. By the time the parent spends 30 minutes or more waiting to see a teacher and then, more frequently than not, is given 5 minutes to hear about their child's problems/strengths, the time element alone has defeated the relationship, and the positive celebration of the child is forgotten. This system, currently used in the large majority of U.S. schools, is sending a negative message to parents. It really says, "We tolerate you," not "We *need* you."

With all of the success of the parent–school interaction, the SEP/SEOP is not completely without problems. At the elementary school level, teachers have raised some concerns about where they can find time to prepare for these conferences (Utah has the highest student–teacher ratio in the nation). State funds allow for three parent–teacher conferences per year. However, some leeway is given as to how each administration may best use those funds.

At the secondary level, where counselors and teachers are involved in the SEOP conferences, administrations are, through innovative funding sources, finding ways to solve coordination and teacher/counselor load problems and, more importantly, support student needs for effective SEOPs.

UTAH NATIONAL DEMONSTRATION PROJECT

At a statewide press conference in November 1992, the president of the Parent Knowledge Network and the Director of the Utah Center for Families in Education announced the selection of Utah as the first of two national demonstration sites. The Parent Knowledge Network, a 26-year-old private, not-for-profit corporation based in Washington, DC, focuses on parent inservice training, particularly on the "Family Education Plan" training project. Co-chairing their National Council are Dr. T. H. Bell, former U.S. secretary of education, and Pat Henry, immediate past-president of the National PTA. The project's other sponsors in Utah include the Utah governor's office, Utah PTA, the Utah Education Association, Chapter I, The Utah Partnership for Education and Economic Development, 100 participating demonstration school principals, public officials, and leading Utah-based corporations.

The Family Education Plan training program for parents is broken into three 3-hour training sessions with the following components included:

1. Basic needs that include training in communication, becoming responsible learners, physical survival, love and belonging, safety, and self-esteem.
2. Character education providing all family members with additional skill development in areas of citizenship, respect, justice/fairness, responsibility, and trustworthiness.
3. Academic skill development in areas of art, humanities, English, history, math, science, reading, writing, and physical education.

The program clearly illustrates that as parents become informed about their role in the education of children and work to provide a strong environment within the home, they are positioned to interact more effectively with classroom teachers, and the school as a whole. After each training session, parents are given training exercise material to take home and work through with the full family for a period of 2 weeks before returning for the next training.

The project demonstration program has been implemented in three phases:

Phase 1: Following 4 months of community coalition building with educational and other community leaders, and state, regional, and local chapters of PTA, 50 schools were selected as demonstration sites. Between January and April 1993, 160 parents participated in three 3-hour small group workshop training sessions, plus an additional 20 hours of supervised application exercises within their own families.

Phase 2: From April through December 1993, an additional 300 parents requested and received the FEP training.

Phase 3: In January 1994, all daily newspapers in Utah, at their own expense, ran an eight-page insert entitled, "Education: Parental Guidance Required." The insert provided positive material for families to further their commitment to strong family values, to improve communication within the home, and to develop self-esteem. The insert was distributed to more than 750,000 families. Immediately following the newspaper insert, Utah's two television public broadcasting stations ran two 1-hour weekly TV specials, simultaneously, during prime time. The focus of the TV broadcasts was to help Utah families improve the "learning cultures" in their homes and to inform them how they can participate more effectively with their children in the education system. More than 700 families called in during the 2-week period after the program was aired, requesting involvement in the FEP and asking to receive more information about the Utah Center for Families in Education. The TV productions were developed by the Utah Center for Families in Education.

As of late 1994, more than 1,800 parents from 370 schools had received the 9-hour training. Because of the unusual demand by parents for training in the FEP, it was necessary to expand the training staff. Because of limited funds, parent volunteers were sought, who would be willing to participate in a 30-hour training course to prepare them to teach the FEP program. Twenty volunteers, including some current or former teachers, completed the master trainer program, and with the expanded training staff, 4,000 additional parents were expected to receive the FEP training by July 1, 1995.

TODAY AND THE FUTURE

In the mid-1990s, there were 42 million students in 83,500 public elementary and secondary schools in the United States. As worthy as GOALS 2000 is, these children cannot wait until the year 2000 for schools and parents to connect.

No one strategy will effectively bring parent–school partnerships into being. Multiple strategies that include a willingness to take a risk by all the players— parents, schools, and the community—will provide the opportunity to witness the increasing success of the children in our society.

Utah is making progress in reaching and improving the lives of its children and families through dedicated parents, schools, and the community.

REFERENCES

Carter, J. L. (1994). Moving from principles to practice. *Equity & Choice, 10*(3), 4–9.

Epstein, J. L. (1992). Paths to partnership: What we can learn from federal, state, district, and school initiatives. *Phi Delta Kappan, 72*(5), 344–349.

Epstein, J. L. (1994, November). *Perspectives and previews on research and policy for school, family, and community partnerships.* Paper presented at the Pennsylvania State University national symposium, "Family–School Links: How Do They Affect Educational Outcomes?"

Epstein, J. L., & Connors, L. J. (1992). School and family partnerships in middle grades and high schools. *NAASP Practitioner, 18*(4), 1–8.

Henderson, A. T., & Berla, N. (1994). *A new generation of evidence: The family is critical to student achievement.* Washington, DC: National Committee for Citizens in Education.

Keith, T. Z., & Keith, P. B. (1993). Does parental involvement affect eighth-grade student achievement? Structural analysis of national data. *School Psychology Review, 22*(3), 474–496.

McCleary, L. (in press). *Utah Center for Families in Education pilot schools evaluation report.* Salt Lake City, UT: Utah State Office of Education.

National Commission on Children, Final Report. (1991). *Beyond Rhetoric: A new American agenda for children and families.* Washington, DC: Author.

Ramsey, D. (1992). Parental leadership in developing responsible family learning cultures. *Parents as educators* (Training Manual for Parent Volunteers). Arlington, VA: Knowledge Network for all Americans.

Rutherford, B., Billing, S. H., & Kettering, J. F., (1993). *Evaluating education reform: Parent and community involvement in the middle grades.* Denver, CO: RMC Research Corporation.

Stevenson, D. L., & Baker, D. P. (1987). The family–school relationship and the child's school performance. *Child Development, 58,* 1348–1357.

U.S. Department of Education. (1994). *Strong families, strong schools: Building community partnerships for learning.* Washington, DC: Author.

17

▼▼▼▼▼▼▼

Family Diversity, Intellectual Inequality, and Academic Achievement Among American Children

Daniel T. Lichter
Pennsylvania State University

Elementary and secondary schools in the United States today face the daunting task of preparing *all* children—the next generation of workers—for an increasingly competitive national and global economy. Unfortunately, it is still fashionable today to blame schools for the perceived failures of U.S. education. In my estimation, the main problems are not bad teachers, inadequate facilities, or watered-down curriculums. Nor is the problem a lack of parental involvement in partnerships with schools and teachers. The main challenge facing schools today is the changing family. If schools have failed, it is largely because they have been unable to keep pace with the profound demographic changes in the family.

To be sure, both families and schools are vitally important to the cognitive development and academic achievement of children. Joyce Epstein (this volume, chap. 14) argues that the main task facing schools today is one of being proactive, that is, of building school, family, and community partnerships. Schools must help parents be better parents. They must communicate more effectively with parents about student progress. They must solicit help from parents in promoting school programs. They must engage parents in learning activities with their children at home. They must involve parents in school decision making. And they must integrate families and communities. These six tasks—these overlapping spheres of influence for schools, communities, and families—are vital to student academic success. Simply, school must reach out to families and communities, encourage their involvement, and acknowledge that we share a collective responsibility our children's well-being.

The payoffs in academic performance seem clear: Parental involvement benefits children in school. Zill and Nord (1994), for example, showed that the children (Grades 6–12) of parents who fail to attend school activities (e.g., PTA meetings) or who do little school volunteer work are nearly twice as likely as children of highly involved parents to be in the bottom half of their class and over twice as likely to have repeated a grade or to have been suspended from school. The consensus among educators is that getting parents invested in the educational process is a worthwhile goal.

My question is not whether such school–family partnerships work—they clearly do—but whether they adequately respond to the rising share of children at risk. How do they benefit the growing share of poor children, immigrant children, children in lone-parent families, and children having babies? Epstein does not speak directly to this issue. Instead, she raises a more general question: "What do we need to know and do to help all children succeed in school?" (p. 213). She eschews a family-deficit model.

My concern resides with disadvantaged children and with the question of whether partnerships exacerbate *between-* and *within*-school inequalities in academic performance. This is an old issue (e.g., Jencks et al., 1972). What may be new in this debate is whether academic inequality should now be viewed as politically acceptable or unacceptable—and this is ultimately a value judgment. My objective here is, first, to discuss the challenges of building school–family partnerships in the context of the changing demography of the family. I then address the question of how partnerships may promote academic inequality rather than equality—in contrast to the past policies that seemed most concerned with "leveling" differences. And, finally, I conclude with some explicit questions about the goals of family–school–community partnerships in light of existing group inequalities in innate ability or intellectual resources. Should the goal be to benefit at-risk children the most, thus leveling differences among groups? Or should the goal be for all children to realize their fullest intellectual potential (whatever that is), rather than for all groups of children to realize the same academic goals (as measured by standardized achievement tests, grades, or drop-out behavior)?

PARTNERSHIPS AND DEMOGRAPHIC CHANGE

In view of rapid changes in the family, it is hardly surprising that schools often fall short of their objectives. What is surprising is that they have accomplished as much as they have. School dropout rates have declined, SAT scores have inched upwards in recent years, and standardized achievement tests have stopped their long-term decline (U.S. Department of Education, 1991). This has taken place in concert with growing family diversity and economic inequality:

• The proportion of children living in single-parent families increased from 17% to 24% between 1980 and 1990 (Hogan & Lichter 1995). Roughly 40%–50%

of children will spend some time in a single-parent family before age 18. Children growing up in single-parent families, on average, have higher drop-out rates and score lower on academic achievement tests (Lichter, Eggebeen, & Cornwell, 1993; McLanahan & Sandefur, 1994).

• Nearly one half of all marriages involve a partner marrying for the second or more time. Today, 15% of all children live with a biological parent and a stepparent, stepsibling, or halfsibling (U.S. Bureau of the Census, 1994). Children living in blended families have lower academic achievement then other children (Amato & Keith, 1991). There is little evidence that children benefit academically from remarriage, despite improvements in their economic status.

• The retreat from marriage has coincided with the rise in nonmarital cohabitation (Bumpass & Sweet, 1989). In 1990, 3.5% of all children lived with a parent and cohabiting partner and nearly 1 in 7 children who lived with a single parent also co-resided with their parent's unmarried partner (Manning & Lichter, 1994). Thomson, Hanson, and McLanahan (1994) showed that children living in households headed by cohabiting couples have lower well-being—including dropping out of school—than children in virtually any other living arrangement.

• The poverty rate among children was higher in 1992 than any year since the 1983 recession, and the number of poor children exceeded that of any year since the early 1960s (Lichter & Eggebeen, 1994). Low socioeconomic status is strongly associated with poor academic achievement (McLanahan & Sandefur, 1994).

• Income inequality increased during the 1980s in the United States. The proportions of children in the both the highest and lowest family income quintile increased, whereas the median income-to-poverty ratios diverged. The poorest children became poorer while the richest children became richer (Lichter & Eggebeen, 1993). The implication is that inequality in family income will fuel inequality in educational outcomes.

• Poverty is increasingly concentrated spatially (and, by extension, so are poorly funded schools). Economically disadvantaged children are thus increasingly segregated with other "distressed" children in poor neighborhoods (O'Hare, 1994). Disadvantaged children perform better academically in schools populated mostly by middle-class than by poor children.

• An increasing share of children are foreign born or have foreign-born parents. These children are at risk. About 16% speak only English in the home, average number of siblings is larger than for natives (2.7 vs. 2.4), and poverty rates are higher (21.8% vs. 16.5%; Jensen & Chitose, 1994).

• Until this past year, fertility rates among unmarried teens have increased over the past 7 years (Ventura, Martin, & Taffel, 1994). Between 1980 and 1991, the rate of unmarried childbearing increased from 29.4 to 44.8 births per 1,000 unmarried teen women, an upswing of 52%. Teenage pregnancy and childbearing is associated with school drop-out behavior and low academic achievement.

• The proportion of employed married women with school-age children increased from 61.7% to 73.6% between 1980 and 1990 (U.S. Department of Education, 1991). Increased maternal employment presumably diminishes the time available for monitoring children's progress in school (e.g., homework) and their behavior outside of school (Coleman, 1988).

Many of these changes have preyed disproportionately on minority children (e.g., female headship among Black families). From a strictly demographic standpoint, the potentially deleterious effects associated with these changes have been offset by positive trends in fertility and education among parents. Low rates of fertility, for example, mean that average family sizes are much lower than a generation ago (Eggebeen, 1992); family size is negatively associated with academic achievement (Blake, 1989). Moreover, delayed childbearing implies that a larger share of children are now receiving parenting from mature parents with more secure jobs and incomes. Finally, the educational levels of parents have increased substantially since 1970 (Hogan & Lichter, 1995). These changes in fertility patterns and parental education presumably mean that parental attention is less diluted than in the past and of higher quality.

On balance, changes in the family are clearly working against the best laid plans of schools and communities, especially if reducing inequality in academic achievement is a goal. What is remarkable is that schools have done as well as they have *overall* in the context in increasing family diversity.

FAMILY–SCHOOL PARTNERSHIPS AND AT-RISK CHILDREN

Can family–school partnerships respond effectively to the aforementioned demographic changes and the growing diversity of at-risk children? Among other things, the answer depends on (a) *which* kinds of schools have the "climate," leadership, or resources necessary to encourage partnerships with parents and communities and (b) *which* parents participate in the activities of schools and are involved in their children's educational progress.

On both counts, the evidence seems fairly clear: The most economically disadvantaged schools and families. Zill and Nord (1994) showed, for example, that parental involvement in school activities is much higher in private than in public schools. In private schools, only 16% of parents show no involvement, compared with 45% of parents in public schools. Parental involvement also is lowest among the least educated, among mother-only families, and among racial and ethnic minorities. The implication is clear: A disproportionately small share of at-risk schools and children will potentially benefit from school–parent partnership programs.

The problem from a programmatic standpoint is that within- and between-school inequalities can only be reduced if at-risk schools and families either *differentially* participate or *differentially* benefit from such programs. For the reasons discussed later, this is unlikely on both counts. The implication then is that family–school partnerships will promote intellectual and academic inequality rather than level differences.

For example, between-school inequality in educational outcomes will be increased by low rates of parental involvement in resource-poor relative to resource-rich schools. The ability of school districts to initiate new partnership programs depends on their level of economic and human resources. Consider the goal of promoting good parenting skills. Epstein (this volume, chap. 14) suggests that workshops can be conducted. But this requires resources that many poor schools simply do not have. The result is that between-school differences will be exacerbated as resource-rich schools increasingly distance themselves from resource-poor schools on various student outcomes (e.g., dropouts, standardized achievement scores).

Between-school inequality also will be increased by the lower effectiveness of such programs in resource-poor schools. Indeed, the lower participation in partnerships programs by poor schools will exacerbate cognitive and academic inequality *unless the effects of partnerships, once initiated, differentially benefit at-risk schools.* In other words, between-school inequality could be lowered if the family-school programs were more effective or successful in at-risk schools than in other schools. But this seems unlikely. Such evidence for at-risk schools is limited, whereas between-school differences in levels of funding, the quantity and quality of faculty, and other resources means that partnership programs would most likely differentially benefit the students of economically advantaged schools (e.g., middle-class suburban schools).

It is also worth asking whether partnerships may promote within-school differences in academic achievement. The lower parental involvement of at-risk children, such as those in single-parent homes, means that these programs are most likely to reinforce the existing relative disadvantages of these children. To do otherwise, partnership programs must either (a) elicit greater relative involvement of the parents of at-risk children and/or (b) show stronger beneficial effects for at-risk than other children.

Eliciting relative greater involvement among the parents of disadvantaged children (e.g., poor or those living in single-parent homes) compared to affluent parents seems difficult on the face of it. Parental involvement and the acquisition of knowledge of their child's progress and school activities incurs expenses (e.g., childcare, transportation, telephones, membership dues) that are simply beyond the means of some low-income families. Poorly educated and single parents also are less likely to be involved in their children's learning. They also may be less equipped for volunteer work (e.g., language problems) or they may lack the time or resources necessary for involvement. Given current socioeconomic differentials in parental involvement, partnership programs may well exacerbate rather than narrow existing cognitive and academic achievement inequalities among children.

At the same time, the educational and cognitive benefits associated with parental involvement apparently manifest themselves equally between at-risk and other children. Zill and Nord (1994), for example, reported that "higher levels of [parental] involvement were associated with better student outcomes in disrupted as well as intact families" (p. 52). But parental involvement did not on average "make-up" for negative effects on children associated with living in mother-only and mother–step-parent families. The benefits of involvement must differentially benefit the disadvantaged for academic inequality within schools to be reduced. And there is little evidence of this.

The implication is that building effective partnerships will be more difficult in resource-poor school districts. If reducing inequality in academic performance is the goal, it will require reaching out especially to the children in single-parent families, poor families, and disadvantaged minority and immigrant groups (Epstein, 1990). Between- and within-school inequality will grow without differential participation and/or differential benefits among at-risk children.

ASSUMPTIONS ABOUT EQUALITY OF EDUCATIONAL OUTCOMES

As in most recent studies, Epstein's implicit assumption seems to be that schools can make-up for the deficits in socially or educationally disadvantaged families. Simply, reducing group differences in academic achievement (say, between children in single-parent families and those in intact families) is both a desirable goal and one that can be achieved if schools do the right things for at-risk children. But I have already argued that partnership programs will likely create greater—not less—cognitive and academic inequality, although they may well raise the achievement levels of all groups. Moreover, it is debateable whether equality can be achieved or whether it is even an appropriate or realistic goal.

In the past, Head Start, Title 1, and other compensatory educational programs have been directed at high-risk groups. And one result has been the steady improvement in standardized academic achievement tests among some disadvantaged groups (e.g., Blacks and other minorities). The problem is that these gains occurred at the same time that scores for the highest achievers in the United States have stagnated, if not declined (Zill, 1993). As a result, the report, *A Nation At Risk*, emphasized the need to improve all schools so that all or most students benefit (National Commission on Excellence in Education, 1983). The concern was that schools had watered-down their curriculums and that textbooks had been dumbed-down. The debate now seems to be whether resources and attention have been directed at low achievers at the expense of high achievers.

Indeed, the leveling of differences may have had a social cost. The question today is whether schools—those with the right programs—can produce levels of academic achievement among socially and economically disadvantaged students that are comparable to those of advantaged students. This is the implied assumption of most studies on educational outcomes, that is, if families or schools functioned better, then group differences would be reduced. The recent monograph by McLanahan and Sandefur (1994) is a case in point. They suggest that roughly one half of the difference in school drop-out rates between children in single-parent and married-couple families is attributable to income differences. The rest of the difference presumably resides largely in parenting practices or in the ability of parents to choose better neighborhoods (with better schools).

The problem with such analyses is that children in single and married-couple families may bring different intellectual resources or innate abilities to the school. The recent book on intelligence and social status by Herrnstein and Murray (1994) has been controversial. But their analysis has potentially serious implications for whether educational reform—including school–family partnerships—can meet the implied goal of parity in educational outcomes. For example, they showed, for White women, high correlations between measured IQ and nonmarital childbearing and between IQ and divorce. Among the brightest women, only 2% were unmarried mothers, compared with 32% among the "very dull." The very brightest women had a 9% chance of divorce within 5 years, compared with a 21% change among the those with the lowest IQ. These patterns persisted even when income was controlled.

If 40%–70% of IQ is heritable, then there is little reason to expect that we can explain away family structure (e.g., female-headed families) effects on children with conventional explanations like low income, inept parenting, or inadequate schools. Most studies, including the one by McLanahan and Sandefur (1994), fail to control for parental intelligence in their models. Is the effect of poverty, for example, due to the inability of single parents to provide for the educational needs of their children (e.g., choosing good neighborhoods and schools) or are the effects of poverty and family structure confounded by intelligence? Unfortunately, this is an empirical question ignored by Epstein and others interested in school and family effects.

Zill (1994) observed that the weakest "adjusted" relationship (i.e., adjusted for income and education) of family structure is with standardized test scores that are heavily reflective of innate talent. But this may simply mean that we are indirectly controlling for intelligence (which is related to parental income and education). Zill (1994), in fact, said that "one could argue that by controlling for income we are really controlling for the mother's competence" (p. 20). Is competence another word for intelligence?

The lack of attention to IQ or the innate component of IQ may also explain why children living with stepfamilies or with a cohabiting couple do not perform as well academically like those living with both biological parents. Controlling for family income per se may matter little here (even though family income presumably is augmented by the nonbiological parent). If one accepts Herrnstein and Murray's (1994) analyses, these children on average have lower intellectual resources. This also implies that the apparent unstated goal of achieving between-group parity in educational outcomes is not likely to be achieved with partnership programs.

CONCLUSION

Epstein (this volume, chapter 14) provides a useful overview of the increasing academic productivity (i.e., groups gains in achievement) associated with the growth of school, family, and community partnerships. I have argued instead that recent family demographic trends and the building of family–school–community partnerships may perpetuate or even exacerbate inequality in academic achievement between schools and among children. This is likely, not only because of group differences in program participation and in their sensitivity to school effects, but also because of variability in aptitude or innate ability. Intellectual inequality is a fact of life and should be incorporated into conceptual and statistical models of school and family effects.

My point is not to reinforce stereotypes regarding group differences in ability or to lower our expectations about student performance for some groups. Nor is my point is to endorse Herrnstein and Murray's policy implications, which seem to be benign neglect of the "intellectual underclass." Mine is a call to Epstein and other education researchers to be explicit about the equality goals of educational reform or the effective schools movement. Simply, should the emphasis be placed mostly on academic productivity—for all groups—or on reducing academic inequality across diverse population groups?

REFERENCES

Amato, P. R., & Keith, B. (1991). Parental divorce and the well-being of children: A meta-analysis. *Psychological Bulletin, 110*, 26–46.

Blake, J. (1989). *Family size and achievement.* Berkeley, CA: University of California Press.

Bumpass, L. L., & Sweet, J. A. (1989). National estimates of cohabitation. *Demography, 26*, 615–626.

Coleman, J. S. (1988). Social capital in the creation of human capital. *American Journal of Sociology, 94* (Suppl.), 95–120.

Eggebeen, D. J. (1992). Changes in sibling configurations for American preschool children. *Social Biology, 39*, 27–44.

Epstein, J. (1990). Single parents and the schools: Effects of marital status on parent and teacher interactions. In M. T. Hallinan, D. M. Klein, & J. Glass (Eds.), *Change in societal institutions* (91–121). New York: Plenum.

Herrnstein, R. J., & Murray, C. (1994). *The bell curve.* New York: The Free Press.

Hogan, D. P., & Lichter, D. T. (1995). Children and youth: Living arrangements and welfare. In R. Farley (Ed.), *Social diversity in the United States* (pp. 93–139). New York: Russell Sage Foundation.

Jencks, C., Smith, M., Ackland, H., Bane, M. J., Cohen, D., Gintis, H., Heyns, B., & Michelson, S. (1972). *Inequality: A reassessment of the effect of family and schooling in America*. New York: Harper and Row.

Jensen, L., & Chitose, Y. (1994). Today's second generation: Evidence from the 1990 U.S. census. *International Migration Review, 28*, 714–736.

Lichter, D. T., & Eggebeen, D. J. (1993). Rich kids, poor kids: Changing income inequality among American children. *Social Forces, 71*, 761–780.

Lichter, D. T., & Eggebeen, D. J. (1994). The effect of parental employment on child poverty. *Journal of Marriage and the Family, 56*, 633–645.

Lichter, D. T., Eggebeen, D. J., & Cornwell, G. T. (1993). Harvesting human capital: Family structure and education among rural youth. *Rural Sociology, 58*, 53–75.

Manning, W. D., & Lichter, D. T. (1994). *Cohabitation and children's economic well-being* (PRI Working Paper No. 94-25). University Park: Pennsylvania State University, Population Research Institute.

McLanahan, S. S., & Sandefur, G. (1994). *Growing up with a single parent*. Cambridge, MA: Harvard University Press.

National Commission on Excellence in Education. (1983). *A nation at risk*. Washington, DC: U.S. Government Printing Office.

O'Hare, W. P. (1994, September). 3.9 million U.S. children in distressed neighborhoods. *Population Today, 22*, 4–5.

Thomson, E., Hanson, T. L., & McLanahan, S. S. (1994). Family structure and child well-being: Economic resources vs. parental behaviors. *Social Forces, 73*, 221–242.

U.S. Bureau of the Census. (1994). *The diverse living arrangements of children: Summer 1991*. (Current Population Reports, Series P-70-38). Washington, DC: U.S. Government Printing Office.

U.S. Department of Education. (1991). *Youth indicators 1991*. Washington, DC: U.S. Government Printing Office.

Ventura, S. J., Martin J. A., & Taffel, S. M. (1994, October 25). Advance report of final natality statistics, 1992. *Monthly Vital Statistics Report, 43*. Hyattsville, MD: National Center for Health Statistics.

Zill, N. (1993). The changing realities of family life. *The Aspen Institute Quarterly, 5*, 27–51.

Zill, N. (1994). *Family change and student achievement: What we have learned, what it means for schools*. Paper presented at the National Symposium on Family–School Links: How Do They Affect Educational Outcomes? University Park, PA.

Zill, N., & Nord, C. W. (1994). *Running in place: How American families are faring in a changing economy and an individualistic society*. Washington, DC: Child Trends.

18

Family–School Links: An Overview

Karen L. Bierman
Pennsylvania State University

The basic premise that positive linkages between families and schools can promote children's abilities to adapt positively to school and to achieve is well supported. As the two primary contexts for child development and socialization, the nature of family and school influences on the child's developmental trajectory are each important in their own right. In addition, however, a number of models suggest that the quality of the communication and relationship between parents and teachers and between communities and schools may be critical determinants of children's educational life course.

Although the over-riding importance of linkages between families and schools is a shared feature of the models described in this volume, investigators differ in terms of the particular factors they identify as critical to the development of family–school networks to support children's school adaptation. Much like the fable of the blind men and the elephant, the various researchers have different perspectives on the particular characteristics of families and schools that play a central role in promoting school adjustment. The authors differ also in terms of their corresponding recommendations for social policy changes and intervention efforts.

In the following overview, some of the various models of family–school linkages are reviewed. Then, the issues raised concerning social policy and intervention directions are reviewed, along with the implications for future research.

MODELS OF FAMILY–SCHOOL LINKAGES

Several models have been suggested to characterize the ways in which home and school socialization practices may affect the trajectories of children's academic development. Some models focus primarily on the role that parents play in helping their children become ready for and responsive to the behavioral, social, and academic demands of schools. Others focus primarily on the ways in which school practices may affect child adjustment and achievement, as well as the influence school practices may have on the extent to which positive parental involvement and support is attained. Finally, some models address the ways in which various child characteristics may increase or decrease the likelihood of positive family–school bonds and school success. Of course, these models are not mutually exclusive, and many are multifaceted. In the following discussion, family, school, and child influences are discussed separately; then, the ways in which these factors may interact to affect children's adaptation to and achievement in school are considered.

Models Focused on Parent or Family Effects

In the model proposed by Eccles and Harold (this volume, chap. 1), parents directly influence their children's achievement at school by providing academic support (e.g., exposure to intellectually stimulating experiences, direct instruction, monitoring, and help with homework) and by participating and communicating with the school (e.g., volunteering at the school, supporting school activities, maintaining communications with the teacher by attending school conferences and requesting information, and participating in school governance). These parental behaviors may increase the child's positive attitudes about school and the child's academic attainments. Other characteristics of parents and families are important as predictors of these direct parent support behaviors and may also have more distal influences on child educational outcomes. For example, parental beliefs, both generally about the role that parents should play with regard to their child's schoolwork and specifically about a particular child, are included in the model. Even more distally, certain characteristics of the parents and family, including demographic characteristics, parent education and income level, marital and employment status, and general psychological well-being may all affect the quality of parental beliefs about the school and the child and the parent's behavior. These factors may affect the extent to which parents have the time, energy, motivation, and resources to engage in various kinds of helping behavior with the child's schoolwork and in various sorts of direct involvement at school.

In the model presented by Alexander and Entwisle (chap. 5), parent and family contributions to children's school achievement are also highlighted. Pointing to longitudinal data, these investigators emphasize the extent to which family socioeconomic status (SES) is correlated with child academic achievement. Not only do they report data showing that children from lower SES families are at a grave disadvantage compared to children from higher SES families at school entry, they note that the gap between high and low SES groups becomes more marked over time, as differences in educational attainments widen in achievement scores, academic course levels, graduation rates, and college entrance. By examining the growth curves of children from high and low SES families during winter versus summer seasons, Alexander and Entwisle conclude that the disadvantage of the latter group stems primarily from lags in development that occur when school is not in session. Hence, they suggest that it is the extent to which the family has the resources, motivation, and capability to provide enrichment experiences outside of the school setting to support children's intellectual development that accounts for a substantial amount of the social class differences observed in the academic attainments of children.

A third model emphasizing family influences on children's school adjustment has been presented by Zill (chap. 10). In Zill's model, however, the nature of the family influence is somewhat different from that postulated by the others. Zill focuses primarily on the ways in which family structure may affect child school adaptation. Noting that, even when parent education and race are controlled, children coming from single-parent families or stepfamilies are more likely than children from intact two-parent families to experience school-based problems, Zill focuses on the extent to which family interactions may affect a child's social, emotional, and behavioral response to school demands. Zill argues that, relative to indices of school achievement such as test scores and, to some extent, grades that may be heavily influenced by a child's innate talents, school behavior problems may be more highly affected by family interaction patterns and by marital discord, divorce, and remarriage. He suggests that some of the factors that may predispose some individuals to have marital difficulties (e.g., youth, lower education levels, lower earnings, minority ethnic backgrounds) may be linked to disadvantages for their children, particularly lower levels of financial resources. However, he argues that low income per se may be less important to child achievement than some of the parental characteristics that may be associated with low income—such as the mother's employability and earning power, her own academic skills and attainments. Even more important may be the quality of parenting that the child receives and the relationships that are established and maintained between the various parenting figures and the child, including communication patterns, warmth and positive involvement, close monitoring, and consistent, nonpunitive discipline strategies.

Hence there are several ways to think about family contributions to children's school adaptation. The models focus on direct effects on the child's academic attainment (such as the extent to which parents provide help with school work and expose their children to intellectually stimulating experiences), and they include parallel effects of parent involvement in the schools (such as the extent to which parents volunteer and support the school and communicate actively with the teacher). Indirect effects of parents on child school adjustment are also noted, particularly in terms of the ways in which the quality of the relationships formed between parents and children in the home (e.g., the degree of positive involvement and monitoring and the type and consistency of discipline used) prepare the child for the behavioral and social demands of the school situation. Distal influences affecting parent behavior are noted (such as income, race, family structure) and the proximal influences of parent characteristics (such as their attitudes, competencies, psychological status) that may affect parental behaviors toward their child and toward the school are also identified. In contrast to the models focused on parental influences on child school adjustment, other models emphasize the ways in which school characteristics and teacher attitudes and behaviors may influence both parental involvement and child school adaptation.

Models Focused on Teacher/School Effects

In the Eccles and Harold chapter, teacher attitudes toward parental involvement and the extent of and nature of teacher and school communications with parents play an important role in determining how welcome parents feel and how well informed parents are to contribute to decisions regarding their child's academic course. They point out that middle schools, being larger and characterized by more diversified teacher–child assignments, discourage parent involvement. Specific teacher practices, such as scheduling conferences with parents and giving feedback about the child's progress, requesting that parents help with particular projects, providing parents with suggestions for how to help their child, and encouraging and providing opportunities for parental involvement may all be important predictors of parental involvement and support of their child's school attainment.

Dornbusch (chap. 2) emphasizes the extent to which structural aspects of the school and community may affect parent–school linkages. In particular, he argues that as students are assigned to multiple teachers for various classes in middle schools and high schools and as teachers are responsible for teaching large numbers of students in staggered classes, close teacher–student relationships are unlikely to develop. Teachers don't get to know their students well and may find it impractical and unappealing to encourage active involvement and pursue communication with all of the families of their many students. Hence, the focus of teacher time tends to go to those students achieving at the very top of the curve and to those students who are "bottoming out" and requiring extensive management or remedial services. In addition, he argues that the common use of tracking by ability level may lead to the premature limiting of academic options for students of the middle group, whose parents may often be unaware of the academic limits effectively placed on their children by the tracking procedures.

Hence, teacher and school effects may also be direct (as in the extent to which teacher attitudes and practices invite and make possible informed parental involvement in the child's schooling) and indirect (as in the extent to which tracking practices may limit child opportunities).

In addition, characteristics of the broader community may affect both parent and teacher attitudes and behaviors, affecting the likelihood of positive parent–teacher communication and collaboration. Eccles and Harold focus on the ways in which living in a dangerous or resource-poor neighborhood may create additional stressors for parents, decreasing the time, energy, and resources they have available for parenting. Sandy Dornbusch notes that the social networks that parents are part of, which may be influenced by their linguistic and ethnic backgrounds, may also influence their attitudes and beliefs about appropriate behaviors with regard to relating to schools. Elaborating on this theme, Lareau (chap. 4) suggests that there are social class differences in how parents think about the process of education. Whereas middle- and upper-class parents are more likely to think of the educational process as one that should be mutually encouraged by parents and teachers, parents in lower-class families are more likely to view education as the teacher's job. They may be less likely to see themselves as equal partners in the educational process and more likely to perceive the teacher as the expert who is in charge of making education related choices. In addition, the parenting strategies selected by middle-class parents living in safe neighborhoods may support codes of social behavior that are more similar to those expected by teachers at school than the parenting strategies selected by poor families living in dangerous areas. In the latter case, parents may feel that it is important to teach their children to be self-protective and to defend themselves as needed to avoid being victimized. This orientation may be viewed by teachers as parents condoning or even encouraging aggressive behavior, which is unacceptable in school settings. Hence, the extent to which the community pressures and social networks supporting the belief systems and behaviors of the parents match the expectations of teachers and schools may also be an important predictor of positive parent–teacher collaboration.

Models Focused on Child Effects

Child characteristics have also been identified as factors that may influence the quality of family and school linkages. Eccles and Harold note that the child's age influences parental involvement at school, which declines rather dramatically as children move into secondary school. In addition, they suggest that parental involvement may vary as a function of the child's experience at school. For example, parents may become more involved when teachers request their support for the child who is struggling academically or behaviorally.

Lichter (chapter 17) points out that a child's academic attainment may be more influenced by that child's innate ability than by the way that parents and teachers relate to each other or even by the specific behaviors engaged in by parents and teachers. However, the extent to which the child's skills may serve as a moderator, influencing the impact of parent and teacher interactions on children's school attainment, remains unclear. That is, rather than viewing the contributions of family–school linkages to children's school adaptation as a single model of influence, it may be more appropriate to think of multiple models of influence that vary depending on the subgroup of children described by the model and the particular school outcome of focus.

Integrated Models

Returning to the analogy of the blind men exploring the elephant, it is unlikely that any one of the models described can alone explain the influence that parents, schools, and parent–school linkages have on the educational experiences of children. Instead, multiple influences are likely to operate. In addition, differentiated models may be useful to describe particular outcomes. For example, Eccles and Harold point out that the factors that predict how involved parents may become in helping their child with schoolwork at home may differ from those that predict which parents will become involved at the school. As another example, Cook (chap. 6) notes that the role of parental involvment may vary with development, with parents more able to contribute to and affect the developmental trajectories of their children during the early than the later school years.

In contrasting the models of influence suggested by Alexander and Entwisle versus Zill, the first model emphasizes primarily the degree to which parents provide academic support and intellectual stimulation, whereas the latter model emphasizes the role of nonpunitive discipline practices and positive communication patterns. Although seemingly inconsistent, the differences in these models reflect the different school outcomes addressed. Whereas parental support for the child's academic work may be a more important predictor of academic success at school, the more general aspects of the parent–child relationships may be more important predictors of social-emotional and behavioral readiness for school. As research moves forward in the study of family–school linkages and their impact on child school adaptation, these sorts of differentiations and complexities require further consideration and exploration. Rather than choosing among the models, our goal should be to examine the transactions and explore the variations. Understanding the complexities of the causal models may be particularly important as these models become the basis for guiding social policy and preventative interventions.

IMPLICATIONS FOR INTERVENTION
AND SOCIAL POLICY

A number of intervention strategies have been suggested reflecting the range of models of family–school links. A number of the intervention recommendations made in this volume are designed to enable schools to create and encourage more support from parents and communities. In addition, some researchers suggest compensatory models of intervention—that is, strategies that schools could implement to compensate for or remediate deficits in the parental and community support available to some children. The suggestions made for intervention design and social policy change raise a number of issues and highlight the need for systematic intervention research in the future. In the next sections, some of the intervention strategies suggested are reviewed, followed by a discussion of the implications these suggestions have for future research directions.

Suggested Intervention Strategies

Reflecting models focused on the direct influence of parental support for children's academic work at home and the direct effects of active parental involvement at school, a number of intervention strategies were suggested to target these areas. Epstein (chap. 14) identifies a variety of such programs that target school practices with the following goals:

1. to increase the opportunities and encouragement parents receive to serve as volunteers and audiences at their children's schools,
2. to increase the extent to which families work with their children in learning activities at home,
3. to increase the inclusion of parents in decision making at school including school governance, and
4. to increase the extent of collaboration between schools and the community at large.

In her recommendations, as well as those made by Eccles and Harold, the importance of schools reaching out with information for parents and invitations to respond is emphasized. For example, Eccles and Harold encourage teachers to communicate more effectively with parents, giving them individualized information about their child's progress so that the parents are better able to monitor their child's social-emotional and academic development and providing parents with information about the curricular choices available to their child. Both also suggest that schools may need to provide clearer guidelines for parents, explaining how to monitor homework, helping parents to understand the school's expectations for their children, and creating new opportunities for positive parental involvement.

Other researchers are less optimistic about the extent to which the provision of information and opportunities for parents would be useful to the children most disadvantaged in their school attainment. For example, Lareau suggests that, in planning interventions, it is critical to keep in mind the skills and orientation toward education that many parents from lower socioeconomic backgrounds may have. Given the past educational experiences and the level of attainment of many of these parents, they may be deficient in the skills needed to help their children. In addition, Lareau suggests that these parents may be more bonded to kinship than to community social networks and may view contacts with "outside" institutions, such as schools, as foreign and potentially unfriendly. Hence, even when schools attempt to open their doors to parents, these parents may not feel comfortable responding, nor may they view it as their responsibility to participate. Hence, other models of intervention suggested attempt to compensate for low parent involvement, based on the assumption that a number of parents (particularly of low-achieving youngsters) may not be ready for or responsive to demands for increased involvement with their children's schools.

Alternative models focus on programs that schools could initiate to compensate for low levels of parent involvement, including additional child-focused services or programs to help remediate parenting deficits and strengthen parental abilities to support their children's development. For example, Alexander and Entwisle suggest that it may be useful for children from low SES homes to have a longer school year, an extended school day, or an earlier start in school. Other researchers, particularly Epstein, suggest that schools could sponsor parent skill training programs that might assist families with parenting and child rearing skills, provide support to families, and help parents to understand child and adolescent development, thus fostering their ability to establish home conditions to support learning at each age and grade level. Lareau emphasizes the importance of setting realistic goals in working with parents, avoiding the pitfalls of expecting too much or making an overwhelming number of requests. She also advocates the search for supplementary support systems, such as the identification of designated homework monitors within the broader community or kinship network. Importantly, she suggests that interventions for low SES families may be more effective if they could be organized around the kinship networks that often provide support for these parents, rather than being organized around schools and grades that may cut across kinship networks.

A few models suggest that interventions should focus more broadly on structural aspects of school organization—the goals of the school, the climate of the classroom, and the degree of clear communication and shared expectations among faculty and between teachers and parents. For example, Goldenberg and Alexander and Entwisle focus on the importance of gaining consensus among faculty and parents for a set of goals that include: (a) high and clear expectations for *all students'* performance; (b) an orderly, disciplined environment; and (c) a sense of community, so that the order and discipline are achieved consensually rather than imposed. They suggest that intervention strategies might need to focus on developing the dedication and motivation of the administrative and teaching staff so they see themselves as united in this general set of goals. In addition, several researchers focus on the need to increase the flexibility of early tracking procedures, providing early remedial help without pigeon-holing children into rigid tracks. That is, a call is made for limited grouping and frequent reassignments that might allow children to receive the level of support they need without shortchanging them in terms of their educational opportunities.

FUTURE DIRECTIONS IN INTERVENTION
RESEARCH

The various models of intervention and social policy change highlight the need for careful intervention research in the next decade. Although it is tempting to move directly from models based on population sampling and large-scale regressions to large-scale intervention efforts, the research includes caveats and restrictions that suggest that the movement from basic research to applied programming must be done with care. Attention to causal mechanisms, to the possibilty of different models operating for different groups, and to developmental differences all warrant more attention in the planning of intervention efforts. In addition, research oriented toward better understanding the process of change is needed to guide future intervention efforts. These issues are discussed further in the next sections.

Searching for Causal Mechanisms

In order to design intervention programs that lead to improvements in child school adaptation, it is important to understand the mechanisms or processes that link parent/family involvement to child outcomes. Although data demonstrate that parent involvement in school is a correlate of children's school adaptation, the causal role of various parent or school attitudes or behaviors to specific child outcomes has not been well elucidated. When the various research data are considered, it becomes clear that parent–school linkages is a multifaceted construct. In addition, there is a range of ways to conceptualize the child outcomes of school adaptation, from positive child attitudes and behavior at school to attendance to test score achievement and grades. In designing an intervention, it would be important to have a clear causal model linking the target of the intervention to a specific child outcome or set of outcomes. For example, some aspects of parent involvement (such as helping with and monitoring homework) might be expected to foster increases in homework compliance more than other aspects of parent involvement (such as participating in PTA governance). However, indirect models could also be postulated. For example, it may be that increasing parental participation in school governance does have a distal effect on the child's homework compliance, if such parental participation leads to a positive shift in parental attitudes toward the school and parental agreement with school policies that, in turn, may affect the consistency with which the parent monitors the child's homework.

The issue is complicated in that the correlate nature of positive parental involvement in regression studies does not necessarily convey causal status. For example, it may be that parent involvement is a marker of other core characteristics of family interaction patterns and parenting characteristics and that it is important to address these "deeper" family structures. For example, if some parent–child relationships are characterized by conflict and punitive punishment, an intervention that increases teacher-initiated requests for parents to monitor homework may lead to increased conflict and tension at home. Similarly, a program that simply makes available to parents more detailed information about their children's curriculum choices and progress without any guidance concerning how best to understand and use this information could backfire in situations in which parents lack skills. Parents may increase punitive punishments in reaction to "bad news" from school or may make choices that do not adequately take into account their child's academic needs.

In addition, it is quite possible that the role played by positive parental involvement in children's school adaptation is different for families of different ethnic or social class groups or for children at different levels of academic functioning. Many of the studies done to examine the effects of social class or ethnic status on parent involvement and child educational attainment involve group comparisons. Investigators may be drawn to the conclusion that if lower SES parents simply acted more like White middle-class parents, their children would be better off. This conclusion belies the complexity of the factors that contribute to parenting children in disadvantaged circumstances as well as differences in values and belief systems that reflect different socializing systems. Perhaps a more useful research orientation from the perspective of planning interventions would be one that utilizes a within-group comparison, for example, identifying the differences in attitudes and behaviors of parents who share a particular social group status (e.g., lower SES or ethnic group membership) and have children who are or are not doing well in school.

Developmental Issues

In addition to potential differences among various social groups, it is probable that the role played by various forms of parent involvement in school changes as a function of the child's developmental level. As Epstein points out, patterns of parent–teacher partnership change across the grades, along with the developmental challenges facing students and parents. Optimal intervention goals and structures may vary depending on both short-term developmental changes, such as the time of academic year in which the program is implemented (e.g., summer, winter, or fall) or more global developmental changes, such as the level of the child's school and the timing of major school transitions.

One reoccurring issue involves the optimal point for intervention. Several investigators point to the increasing spread between high and low achievers over time and argue for early intervention. Early intervention is appealing in many ways, as it is often linked with an "innoculation" model. For example, the guiding hope of early preschool programs was that by intervening before formal school started, poor children could be innoculated or protected from the academic disadvantages that were associated with their economic backgrounds. Although these early intervention models did prove effective in many ways, the idea that a one-time innoculation could adequately compensate for the disadvantages associated with poverty was not confirmed. Unfortunately, the disadvantages appear to be continuous, leading many prevention researchers to move to more of a "dental" model of preventive intervention, which involves longer-term and sustained efforts at protective intervention (analogous to fluoride in the water during the formative years, along with regular check-ups and periodic remediation as needed). In addition to the theoretical implications for intervention models of the movement from an innoculation to a dental model of prevention services, the issue of early versus later intervention involves some methodological complications. That is, early intervention requires the early identification of at-risk children or families. The earlier the point of screening, the greater the likelihood of prediction errors. Hence, methodologically, the challenge is to find a developmental period at which a screening method attains a reasonable degree of predictive validity, while at the same time the developmental system still offers enough fluidity to make remedial intervention promising. Basic research is needed to address issues in the screening of children and families for intervention and to answer questions about the relative efficacy of various screening measures and methods as well as the optimal time period for risk screening and prediction. Given the complications associated with selecting a method for screening high-risk candidates for intervention, some of the investigators suggest that more general interventions be pursued focused at the community or school level rather than selected individuals. The issue of who to target in an intervention and what level of intervention to design are thus raised as additional important questions for future research.

Selected Targets and Levels of Intervention

Implicit in the issue of selecting targets and levels of intervention is the assumption that no intervention can meet all goals. Although it is tempting to assume that an intervention addressing the general public will meet the needs of all individuals comprising that general public equally well, it is probably a mistaken assumption. Hence, inevitably, prevention researchers need to be clear about the particular target group as well as the target goals they are setting as they go about the business of designing inteι ventions.

Investigators suggest different strategies for selecting groups most likely to benefit from an intervention. For example, Dornbusch suggests that the children in the top 10% and those in the bottom 40% appear to be very stable in their school achievement over time. He suggests that the variety of factors contributing to the optimal versus difficult progressions of children in these two groups argue against the need (in the upper group's case) or the likely responsivity (in the lower group's case) to intervention. However, he argues that the middle group might be ideal candidates for intervention, as their developmental course does not appear to be highly determined from an early time period, and they may therefore be quite responsive to intervention efforts. In contrast, other investigators such as Alexander and Entwisle focus primarily on children at the bottom in terms of their economic disadvantage and corresponding school difficulties. Rather than choosing among these options, the issue for intervention researchers to grapple with is the possibility that different prevention models may be needed depending on which of these groups (or others) are targeted for change.

In addition, it may be particularly important for investigators to be wary of group status as a marker of a deficit, rather than selecting target groups on the basis of a proximal measure of the deficit targeted in intervention. For example, based on regression studies, a model targeting low SES families might assume that these families engage in inadequate communication with teachers and provide inadequate monitoring and help with children's homework. Although these deficits might be true of many low SES families, they may not characterize other low SES families very well. One might assume that an intervention focusing specifically on increasing parent communication with teachers and help with homework would help only those low SES families who engaged in low levels of these behaviors prior to the intervention. The point is that not all members of a particular group share the characteristics that define the mean level of the group. If a skill-training intervention is implemented, a screening based on the skill (or behavior or attitude) targeted in the intervention may be warranted, rather than relying on the assumption that multiple members of the particular group will benefit from the same intervention.

Just as different intervention foci may be relevant for different subgroups, different levels of intervention may be appropriate for different goals. Some researchers suggest that interventions addressed at the entire school or community might be most effective, as they might meet the needs of the greatest number of children. This type of intervention, labeled *universal* in the recent report on intervention research commissioned by the Institute of Medicine (IOM, Mrazek & Haggerty, 1994) is one viable strategy for prevention. This sort of intervention may be most effective for those individuals in the middle in terms of their risk status. Such interventions are rarely intensive enough to meet the multiple needs of the most high-risk group but may be particularly appropriate for less intensive, large-scale intervention efforts. Other levels of intervention identified in the IOM report include *selective* interventions (e.g., those tailored to meet the specific needs of a group at risk for a particular set of difficulties, such as low SES or single-parent families in the case of school adjustment) and *indicated* interventions (e.g., those designed to address the needs of children and families who have already experienced dysfunction, such as those who have already experienced significant school adjustment difficulties). Rather than choosing between the options of these various levels of intervention, it is important to recognize the unique purposes and advantages of each level. These levels of intervention need not be viewed as mutually exclusive, but rather as complementary. For example, a universal intervention involving increased information and opportunities for parents might be paired with a more intensive support program for parents with special needs served collaterally via a selective or indicated intervention. For example, in one program focused on reducing conduct problems at school, a classroom curriculum (universal level) is paired with more intensive parent-training and child social-skill training services for identified high-risk children (Conduct Problems Prevention Research Group, 1992).

Understanding the Change Process

One of the questions raised is: What changes can be made to strengthen family–school links? A second question raised is: How can these changes be accomplished? To answer this second question, our current research efforts must expand beyond simple program evaluation (e.g., "Did the program work?") and begin to address questions concerning the mechanisms and nature of the changes wrought through various aspects of the intervention. Issues in implementation need to be studied, to determine the most effective strategies for carrying out particular intervention ideas and to document the extent to which planned intervention components were implemented. Research questions on intervention effectiveness need to include an examination of the types of family, community, school, or child characteristics that predict the effectiveness of particular kinds of interventions. Causal models concerning the postulated effects of various intervention components warrant study, by examining the extent to which changes in proximal goals (such as parent or teacher behaviors) are related to longer term distal goals (such as child achievement scores). Only by designing and analyzing intervention research trials in systematic ways can we better develop a prevention science that will ultimately allow us to understand change processes more fully and develop effective and replicable interventions. In this volume, a variety of models are described, illustrating the complexity of the issues involved in understanding how family–school linkages may promote children's school attainment and providing a solid basis for further research in this important area.

REFERENCES

Conduct Problems Prevention Research Group. (1992). A developmental and clinical model for the prevention of conduct disorders: The FAST Track Program. *Development and Psychopathology, 4* 509–528.

Mrazek, P. J., & Haggerty, R. J. (Eds.). (1994). *Reducing risks for mental disorders: Frontiers for preventive intervention research.* Washington, DC: National Academy Press.

Author Index

289

Subject Index